Money, Power, and Influence
in Eighteenth-Century Lithuania

Money, Power, and Influence in Eighteenth-Century Lithuania

THE JEWS
ON THE RADZIWIŁŁ ESTATES

Adam Teller

STANFORD UNIVERSITY PRESS
STANFORD, CALIFORNIA

Stanford University Press
Stanford, California

An earlier version of this work was published in Hebrew under the title *Kesef, koaḥ, ve-haspa'ah: Ha-yehudim be-'aḥuzot bet Radzivil be-Lita' ba-me'ah ha-shemonah-'esreh* [Money, Power, and Influence: The Jews on the Radziwiłł Estates in Lithuania in the Eighteenth Century]. ©2005, Merkaz Zalman Shazar le-Toledot Yisrael, Jerusalem.

Printed in the United States of America on acid-free, archival-quality paper

Library of Congress Cataloging-in-Publication Data

Names: Teller, A., author.
Title: Money, power, and influence in eighteenth-century Lithuania : the Jews
    on the Radziwiłł estates / Adam Teller.
Other titles: Kesef, koaḥ, ve-hashpa'ah. English
Description: Stanford, California : Stanford University Press, 2016. | "An
    earlier version of this work was published in Hebrew under the title
    Kesef, koaḥ, ve-hashpa'ah." | Includes bibliographical references and
    index. | Description based on print version record and CIP data provided
    by publisher; resource not viewed.
Identifiers: LCCN 2016021293 (print) | LCCN 2016020113 (ebook) | ISBN
    9780804799874 () | ISBN 9780804798440 | ISBN 9780804798440q(cloth :qalk.
    paper)
Subjects: LCSH: Radziwill family. | Jews--Lithuania--History--18th century. |
    Jews--Lithuania--Economic conditions--18th century. |
    Latifundio--Lithuania--History--18th century. | Lithuania--Ethnic
    relations--History--18th century. | Lithuania (Grand Duchy)--History--18th
    century.
Classification: LCC DS135.L5 (print) | LCC DS135.L5 T4513 2016 (ebook) | DDC
    305.892/404793--dc23
LC record available at https://lccn.loc.gov/2016021293

Cover illustration: Jean-Pierre Norblin, *Chartier Juif*, 1817. Wikimedia Commons
Cover design: Rob Ehle
Typeset by Bruce Lundquist in 11/14 Adobe Garamond Pro

To my Parents,
Neville and Sheila Teller,
With Love, Affection, and Thanks

Contents

Preface

In the decade that has passed since my study of the Jews on the Radziwiłł estates was published in Hebrew in Jerusalem in 2005, a great deal has changed in the field of Jewish history, particularly in the English-speaking world—so much, in fact, that I became convinced that a revised English-language version of my book, updated to take the new trends into account, would have something fresh to contribute.*

The most significant of the changes is the reintroduction of economic history into the mainstream of Jewish historical research. This is in no small measure a reaction to the dominance in recent decades of the "cultural turn," which has focused attention on representation (in particular, self-representation) and identity in the Jewish historical experience. While in no way negating the value of this approach, a group of scholars has come to feel that a grounding in the concrete realities of Jewish life is also of great importance for historical analysis. From there to the study of the economic activity that was a constitutive factor of Jewish society in every time and place has been but a small step.

I have witnessed this development with a great deal of satisfaction since this is the approach adopted by my own study. In it, I try to assess how the economic roles Jews played on noble-owned estates in the eighteenth-century Polish-Lithuanian Commonwealth led to their deep penetration of both the estate economy and the society around them. I go on to show how this development had a transformative effect on Eastern European Jews, reconstituting them as a group wielding significant economic power that could be leveraged into a much stronger position in society. Finally, I argue that, beyond shaping the internal relations of Jewish society, the phenomena

---

* The original study was Adam Teller, *Kesef, ko'ah ve-hashpa'ah: Ha-yehudim be-'ahuzot bet Radzivil be-Lita' ba-me'ah ha-shemonah-'esreh* (Jerusalem: Merkaz Zalman Shazar le-Toledot Yisrael, 2005).

discussed in the book had far-reaching implications for the history of Poland-Lithuania as a whole.

At the time I wrote the original study I felt somewhat isolated academically, rather like a voice in the wilderness. Very few scholars appreciated my claims that economic activity was a transformative force that empowered rather than marginalized Jews, that it was a crucial element in the growth of their communities rather than just a cause of hatred and violence, and that the development of the societies surrounding them cannot be understood without taking it into account. Today that is no longer the case. New publications in the field of Jewish economic history appear every year. Conferences, research groups, and academic discussions are now more common, and scholarly dialog flourishes. I have been privileged to take part in some of this activity.

Though the immediate audience for this work is the scholarly community of Jewish historians (by which I mean historians of the Jewish past), I trust that the book will have a great deal to say to other groups, too. Since the original Hebrew study was inaccessible to this broader audience, the publication of a revised version in English seemed to me all the more important. Knowing that the book, in its updated form, is open not just to Jewish historians but to economic historians and scholars of Polish history, too, gives me a great deal of satisfaction.

Economic historians will find here a new analysis of the late feudal economy in Poland-Lithuania that emphasizes not questions of production, as so many have done before, but the role of the markets in the agricultural economy. The focus on Jews is crucial for this analysis, because they not only dominated these markets but also helped shape them.

Important on its own terms, this analysis also has something to contribute to the extensive discussions on the rise of capitalism. It can do so by providing valuable comparative perspectives drawn, paradoxically enough, from an examination of a road not taken. The late feudal economy proved not to be viable in a Europe undergoing the beginnings of capitalist development. The story of the Polish-Lithuanian economy and its Jews, for all their efflorescence during the eighteenth century, is ultimately one of failure and as such is highly instructive.

Another audience for this study is the historians of Poland. Since the fall of communism—and even a little before that—Polish historiography has begun to acknowledge that Jews formed a part of Polish society from at least the High Middle Ages. Much of the scholarship treats them as a separate, largely self-contained element within Polish society and focuses on the relations that developed between the Christian majority and the Jews who lived in their midst. It has proved a highly fruitful perspective, enriching both Polish and Jewish historiography.

I here propose a different approach. Rather than viewing Jews as a distinct group that lived on its own terms and maintained a set of relations with the society around it, this study treats them as an integral part of eighteenth-century Poland-Lithuania. Thus, it shows that the Jews were defined not so much by their religious or cultural distinctiveness as by the ways in which they participated in economy and society. The Jews emerge from the analysis transformed from objects of Polish-Jewish relations into subjects of Polish history itself.

Such a point of departure raises the intriguing question of how the presence, activity, and socioeconomic relations of Jews in Poland-Lithuania influenced the society around them. As will become clear from this study, the Jews were by no means an isolated and marginal group in the Commonwealth. The roles they played in the economy were of fundamental importance in shaping not only the magnate families they served but the very development of the state.

In writing, revising, and then rewriting a book that makes such bold claims, I have benefitted from the help and advice of very many people. Foremost among these was my teacher, mentor, and eventually dear friend, the late Prof. Jacob Goldberg of the Hebrew University in Jerusalem. It was he who first introduced me to the issue of economic history, taught me the research skills I needed to pursue it, and encouraged me to learn the most up-to-date methodologies from specialists in the field. My intellectual and professional debt to him is enormous. Though he passed away a few years ago now, I continue to miss him.

Another senior colleague and now friend whose scholarship has deeply influenced me and whose support I have enjoyed for many years is Prof. Gershon Hundert of McGill University in Montréal. His work, which seamlessly integrates economic perspectives into a cultural history of Polish-Lithuanian Jewry, first opened my eyes to the broader perspectives that the study of economic history can bring. Prof. Israel Bartal of the Hebrew University has not only been a teacher, mentor, and friend, but has written a number of quite inspirational studies, providing newer and ever richer perspectives on the history of the Jews in Eastern Europe. Prof. Steve Zipperstein of Stanford

University has supported both myself and this project staunchly for many years. It was he who encouraged me to embark on the translation and revision of the Hebrew monograph and his enthusiasm has played a very important role in getting the final version written and into print. I have benefitted from his generous help and advice on occasions too numerous to mention.

I owe a particular debt to Prof. Moshe Rosman of Bar-Ilan University in Ramat Gan. His 1990 study, *The Lords' Jews: Magnate-Jewish Relations in the Polish Lithuanian Commonwealth during the Eighteenth Century*, opened the field of magnate-Jewish relations to detailed research. Though my study differs from his in approach, methodology, and conclusions, his work provided me with a crucial comparative perspective. Moreover, as I was doing the research for this book, I became aware that without his groundbreaking efforts I would have found it considerably more difficult to reach the conclusions I did.

The sources for the study were found largely in the Archiwum Główne Akt Dawnych in Warsaw, the Natsyial'ny histarychny arkhiŭ Belarusi in Minsk, the Central Archives for the History of the Jewish People in Jerusalem, and the National Library of Israel. The staffs of all these institutes were extremely friendly and helpful to me. My thanks to them all.

There have been numerous others who have helped me in many and varied ways, often much more than they know. They include: Alina Cała, Elisheva Carlebach, Glenn Dynner, David Engel, David Frick, Michał Galas, Judith Kalik, Jonathan Karp, Adam Kaźmierczyk, Ewa Lechniak, Maud Mandel, the late Czesław Miłosz, the late Mordechai Nadav, Sylvia Noll, Derek Penslar, Antony Polonsky, David Ruderman, Thomas Saffley, Shaul Stampfer, Magda Teter, Francesca Trivellato, Hanna Węgrzynek, Marcin Wodziński, Hanna Zaremska, Teresa Zielińska, and Natan Zussman. Thank you all.

The research and publication of this study in its various forms was supported by Yad Hanadiv, the Memorial Foundation for Jewish Culture, the Planning and Budget Committee of the Council for Higher Education of Israel, the Center for the History and Culture of Polish Jews and the Mandel Institute for Jewish Studies, both at the Hebrew University of Jerusalem, the Gotteiner Institute for the History of the Bund and the Jewish Labor Movement and the Department of Jewish History at the University of Haifa, the Lucius N. Littauer Foundation in New York City, the Koret Foundation in San Francisco, and finally the Dean of Faculty and the Program in Judaic Studies at Brown University. I am very grateful.

I also wish to thank the staff of Stanford University Press.

I have enjoyed the support of my family throughout. My parents supported me financially and emotionally in difficult times, as did my brothers. I want to mention two particular debts of gratitude: one to my father, who has unselfishly put his considerable literary talents at my disposal by reading, critiquing, and editing almost every word I have ever written in English; the other, to my brother Richard, who has always been willing to give an extra helping hand in times of special need.

My three daughters, Osnat, Shira, and Na'ama, grew up as I was writing the original study. Their love and enthusiasm was always a beacon of light for me, pulling me back from the eighteenth century to the twentieth and twenty-first to help me remain sane and keep a smile in my eyes. My fourth daughter, Inbal, grew up during the revisions. Her very special brand of love has taught me a huge amount about fatherhood, and that is a treasure I shall always prize.

Above and beyond all these, I owe my life and my happiness to my soul mate, Rachel Rojanski. I remain constantly amazed at my good fortune in finding her and at the joy of sharing all my experiences, intellectual and mundane, with her. Words simply cannot express my love.

Brookline, Massachusetts
March 2016

Note on Place Names and Transliteration

The historical geography of those regions of East-Central Europe discussed in this book is very complex. The borders between states and regions were fluid and changed on a regular basis, a phenomenon not restricted to the distant past but of crucial importance in the twentieth century, too. The boundaries between the different ethnic and cultural groups that inhabited the area were also highly porous, which meant that different populations might be living in the same space at the same time. This situation was further complicated by the existence in the region of a number of extra-territorial groups, such as Jews, for whom the very concept of geographical borders between them and the peoples among whom they lived was largely irrelevant.

One of the concrete expressions of this complexity is the issue of place names. Each of the different groups in a given region or town would have its own name for it. In some cases, these might have been very similar, in others quite different. This leaves the author of a study such as this in a bind when it comes to choosing one form over another. Worse, the act of simply making a choice can be fraught with difficulties, because in the age of nationalism, the name used for a place can have political overtones. Various solutions to this conundrum have been suggested over the years, none of them entirely satisfactory.

The decision here has been to reproduce place names as they appear in the sources used to write the book. This means that the vast majority are given in their Polish forms. The contemporary names together with the state in which they can currently be found appear in parenthesis after the first mention of each place.* For ease of reference, the same information appears

* I should like to thank Charles Trumbull for his indefatigable research in tracking down these names.

after the name of each place in the index, too. Well-known English versions of place names, such as Warsaw and Königsberg, have been used in only the most commonly used cases.

Unless otherwise stated, the name Lithuania refers in this study to the Grand Duchy of Lithuania in its eighteenth-century borders.

The notes and bibliography adopt a simplified system of transliteration from Hebrew that should make the meaning of the words clear to a Hebrew speaker. English translations of all non-English-language titles are given in the bibliography for the convenience of those who do not speak the source languages.

Money, Power, and Influence
in Eighteenth-Century Lithuania

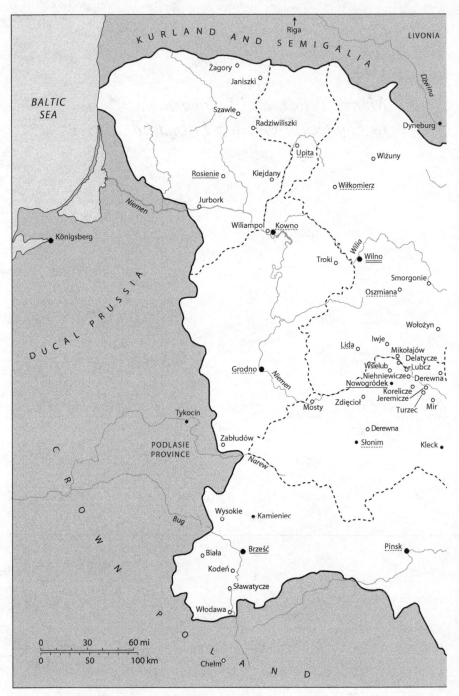

The Grand Duchy of Lithuania in the Eighteenth Century

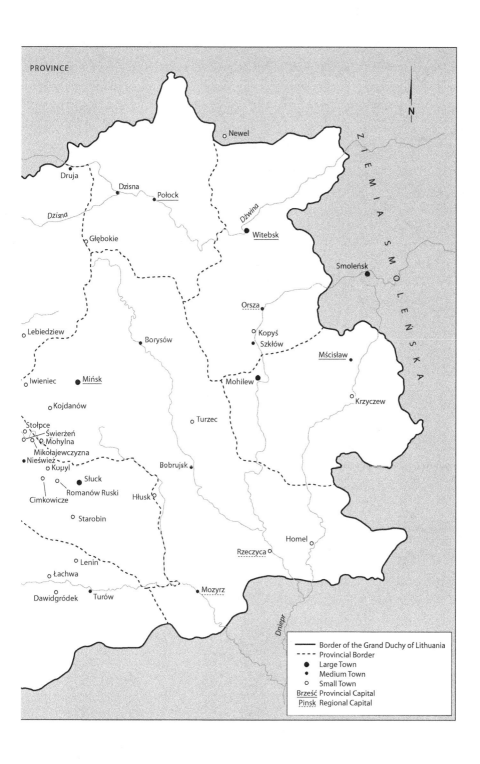

PROVINCE

Newel

Druja

Dzisna

Połock

Dźwina

Dzisna

Głębokie

Witebsk

Z I E M I A   S M O L E Ń S K A

Smoleńsk

Lebiedziew

Borysów

Orsza

Kopyś

Szkłów

Mścisław

Iwieniec

Mińsk

Mohilew

Krzyczew

Kojdanów

Turzec

Stołpce
Świerżeń
Mohylna
Mikołajewczyzna
Nieśwież
Kopyl

Bobrujsk

Słuck

Romanów Ruski

Cimkowicze

Hłusk

Starobin

Homel

Lenin

Rzeczyca

Łachwa

Dawidgródek

Turów

Mozyrz

Dniepr

⬤	Border of the Grand Duchy of Lithuania
---	Provincial Border
●	Large Town
•	Medium Town
○	Small Town
Brześć	Provincial Capital
Pinsk	Regional Capital

N

Introduction

The General Issues: Jewish Economic History

The aim of this book is to examine the economic choices made by Jews in the eighteenth-century Polish-Lithuanian Commonwealth, to see how they were translated into action, and to explore the economic, social, and cultural effects that these choices had on both their own and non-Jewish society.

The setting was chosen because Poland-Lithuania was at that time home to the largest Jewish population in the world. Beyond that, the state's devolved power structure had, since the late fifteenth century, seen extensive rights ceded to the *szlachta* (the Polish term for the nobility) at the expense of the king. This development opened up significant economic opportunities for the Jews, who actively positioned themselves to serve the needs of the burgeoning *szlachta*.[1] As that nobility—and particularly its upper stratum, the magnates—flourished, so too did the Jews.[2] They made intensive use of the economic possibilities on the seigneurial estates that allowed them to overcome the competition of their non-Jewish neighbors and greatly enrich themselves and their society. In fact, during the eighteenth century Jews effectively ran a number of key sectors in the economy—an accomplishment that gave them considerable (if unofficial) standing in estate life. Poland-Lithuania is, therefore, an ideal setting in which to examine not just the ways in which Jews in the pre-modern world went about making a living, but also how they were able to leverage their economic activity into positions of power and influence.

Jewish economic history is today a newly developing area of research.[3] Before the mid-twentieth century the field had flourished among the Jews of Eastern Europe, who were influenced by socialist, even Marxist, approaches.

This meant that their interest was engaged by the activity of the Jewish masses and their struggle against exploitation. In the West the field, such as it was, was deeply influenced by Werner Sombart's book *The Jews and Modern Capitalism*, which saw in the Jews the progenitors of capitalism.[4] Following the Holocaust and the destruction of Polish Jewry, research on Jewish economic history languished, kept alive, barely, by a handful of survivors in the People's Republic of Poland who wrote in the state-imposed Marxist vein. It was not until the turn of the twenty-first century that the field began to revive. Recent research, carried out in a world of American-led globalization, has been dominated by questions of economic modernization as well as the accommodation of Jews to the capitalist system, particularly in the United States.[5]

This study is a conscious attempt to break that mold. For the vast majority of their history Jews lived and worked in socioeconomic settings that were neither capitalist nor in transition to capitalism. If the study of Jewish history has among its goals the search for commonalities (and variations) in Jewish experience in different times and places, then a more-or-less exclusive focus on a single phenomenon, even one as important as capitalism, is not helpful. To be able to generalize or even theorize about Jewish economic activity, we must have studies from a range of contexts on which to draw. Examining the Jews' role in what is often termed "a late feudal economy," such as that in the Polish-Lithuanian Commonwealth, is to see how Jews fared in a system that had little or nothing to do with capitalism.[6]

Of course, the study of Jewish economic life can tell us a great deal more than just how Jews managed under one economic regime or another. It is an important tool for examining the relations that developed between Jews and the rest of society. Most economic activity engages the individual in a broad network that extends well beyond his or her immediate surroundings. The line extending from owner of the means of production to producer, to distributor (and those servicing the market), and thence to consumer, is often very long. It crosses and re-crosses seemingly impenetrable barriers of class, ethnicity, religion, and gender (not to mention physical segregation where that existed) in the most natural way, connecting its constituent parts in a mutually beneficial relationship—irrespective of whether the benefits are equally shared. In this sense, the study of Jewish economic history is a way to understand one of the most important mechanisms of social integration that functioned wherever Jews lived—even in societies where their integration was frowned upon. This is particularly clear in the Polish-Lithuanian setting, where the Jews were at the same time a despised religious minority and key players in the economy with a social standing that few could afford to ignore.[7]

This situation has important implications for the kinds of questions that are asked in this study. Issues of exploitation, so dear to the hearts of previous generations of scholars of Jewish economic history, are not emphasized. "Exploitation" suggests that there was a permanent and irrevocable imbalance of powers between economic actors, with one benefitting at the other's expense. Such a black and white view misses the ambiguities of the Jews' economic relationships. In the terms of this study, there was indeed an imbalance of power between the Jews and the magnates, as there was in all feudal relationships. But Jews also benefitted from their dealings with their lords, both financially and in terms of social standing vis-à-vis other groups in society. It was a tradeoff—an apt term for an economic choice. So the discussion here revolves around choices: in particular, the economic choices made by Jews and by magnates as both searched to secure and improve their income and the social benefits it brought. Also examined are the implications of those choices for each group and the economy as a whole.

Though at first sight it might seem presumptuous for a book on Jewish economic history to claim to shed light on the entire economy of the country in which they lived, this is not the case. Even an economic niche almost exclusively occupied by Jews, such as the leasing of the alcohol monopoly on the noble estates of Poland-Lithuania, has no significance unless it functions within a broader economic context—in this case, that of the late feudal economy.[8] Over the course of the study then it will become clear that the Jewish economic activity under examination was structured and shaped by the economic system within which it functioned.

On the other hand, since the Jews acted as part of a large network of economic actors most of whom were not Jewish, the ways in which they managed their economic lives affected broad strata of society. To put this in terms of a popular (though problematic) economic theory, if the Jews formed a "middleman minority" in Poland-Lithuania, they could only have done so in the framework of an economic system composed largely of non-Jews, who were directly affected by the Jews' success or failure in their economic activity.[9] This is thus a book that is as much about the history of Poland-Lithuania as it is about that of the Jews.

The key issue is the nature of the economic niche that the Jews inhabited. Since the sale of alcohol played a crucial role in the Polish-Lithuanian economy, particularly under the tutelage of the magnates, the Jews' choice to enter and eventually control this niche gave them an economic importance that extended well beyond Jewish society. It also gave them an almost unprecedented standing in the broader social order. Widely recognized as agents, both official and unofficial, of the magnates, they enjoyed significant "second-hand" power: all groups in society understood that the Jews were the recipients of magnate support and so had to be treated with respect, even though as Jews they were often looked down upon and even hated. Jews did sometimes suffer attacks and persecution, but on the whole they were not only protected but could also, on economic issues at least, exert their own influence on their non-Jewish neighbors.[10] Jewish economic agency brought with it a significant degree of social empowerment.

It is of course impossible to generalize about these issues without first examining them in a concrete context—in our case the Jews' economic functions on one specific magnate estate (or to be more accurate, conglomeration of estates) in the eighteenth-century Polish-Lithuanian Commonwealth. The *latifundium* in question was situated in the Grand Duchy of Lithuania (today's Belarus and Lithuania) and belonged the noble and mighty Radziwiłł family.[11]

The Specific Issues: The Jews on Magnate Estates in the Polish-Lithuanian Commonwealth

To make a close analysis of the implications of the Jews' economic life on the magnate estates, we first need to understand what brought them there. It was only in the early modern period that Jews in the Polish-Lithuanian Commonwealth moved in large numbers from the royal cities to those owned by the nobility.[12] In the Middle Ages the Jews in Poland, as in the rest of Europe, regarded the king, not the nobility, as their main protector. In previous centuries Jews had come to Poland as part of a broad wave of migrants from the German lands, in response to the efforts of the Polish crown to promote settlement and develop urban markets. Jewish settlement was relatively small and mostly concentrated in the royal cities. The Jews received from the king protection and rights in the form of "general privileges" (charters granted to the Jews as a group which defined their rights and duties in the state), but faced tough resistance from non-Jewish towns-people when they attempted to integrate into the urban economy.[13]

Only with the weakening of royal authority in Poland and Lithuania in the sixteenth century, especially following a law of 1539 that removed Jews living on noble estates from the king's jurisdiction, did Jews began to look to the *szlachta* for effective protection and guarantees of their rights.[14] At the same time, the nobility, the rising power in the state, began to take advantage of the Jews' economic talents, first to undercut the urban monopoly of trade in the royal towns that was not in their favor, and then to help develop the markets and economic functioning of their estates. This was of enormous importance to the nobles because it was their estates that provided their income and the basis of their social status. Any means of enhancing their revenues was thus pursued with vigor.

An economic tradeoff between nobles and Jews resulted. Jewish merchants and businessmen served the economic needs of the nobility, and the nobility gave the Jews protection against their competitors and enemies. As a result, more and more Jews left the royal towns to settle on the noble estates.

Their numbers grew further following the Union of Poland and Lithuania, concluded in Lublin in 1569. According to the unification agreement, extensive areas of Ukraine, which was exceptionally fertile agricultural land, were transferred from Lithuanian rule to Polish. On the Polish king's orders they were soon distributed to his counselors, magnate families, and other prominent nobles, who set about developing them. They colonized the region and invited in large numbers of settlers, including Jews, tempting them with various tax breaks and other incentives.[15]

This proved a highly successful strategy. Agricultural productivity grew rapidly, as did Polish grain exports to Central and Western Europe, and the estate owners profited handsomely. Jews, originally brought to the towns to enliven the urban markets, then moved into estate management by taking estates on leasehold (called *arenda* in Polish). They also contributed to the estate economy by managing the manufacture and sale of alcohol—a key growth sector. They did this by leasing the income from the estate owners' monopoly on the alcohol business (*prawo propinacyjne*). As a result, the economic ties between Jews and magnates grew ever stronger.[16]

Though the violent Khmelnytsky Uprising of 1648 put an end to this period of development (which had already been slowing for several decades), many Jews continued to seek preferential terms of settlement by moving to magnate estates—especially in the economically lagging eastern regions of Poland and the Grand Duchy of Lithuania. This second wave of settlement began in the second half of the seventeenth century and lasted until late in the eighteenth.[17]

The export market for Polish grain collapsed following the end of the Thirty Years War, so the magnate estate owners began to exploit the home market much more intensively in order to extract the revenues they needed. Alcohol sales were key to this process and grew dramatically during the eighteenth century.

The Jews' activity as merchants, leaseholders of entire estates or of monopoly rights on estates, and in a few cases even as salaried managers, expanded, further deepening their integration into the estate economy. Their roles in the markets for commodities and particularly alcohol became highly significant. As a result, Jews also became an integral part of the estates' social structures—a situation that, as we will see in the course of this study, was reflected in the development of Jewish society itself.

These complex processes seem to have reached their apogee in the eighteenth century, as the magnate class grew ever stronger socially, economically, and politically. Since the magnates appreciated the ways in which Jewish businessmen helped improve their revenues, they made their estates particularly comfortable for Jewish life. A vibrant Jewish society developed.

It is this interplay of the ways in which Jewish economic activity contributed to the development of the magnate estates and the importance of life on the estates for the development of Jewish society that is examined here. To do this, some effort is devoted to understanding the nature of the magnate estate, its internal workings, and the relations between the various groups that lived on it. Still, the main questions that the study asks focus on the Jews: In which ways did Jewish economic actors contribute to estate profitability? How did their activity answer the needs of the magnate estate owners? To what extent was it undertaken in response to the nobles' conscious policy decisions in estate management? How did conditions on the estates influence both the relationships between Jews and other groups living there and the development of Jewish society itself?

Such questions necessitate a rethinking of how the East-Central European magnate estate should be studied. Until now, largely under the influence of Marxist approaches, the major focus of research has been on production, emphasizing issues of peasant labor and its administration by estate own-ers.[18] Since Jews did not work the land and were rarely engaged in organiz-ing the means of production, their significance in that kind of research was marginal at best. This study follows a different approach, one already current in research, arguing that a latifundium such as that of the Radziwiłłs was essentially an economic enterprise run by its owner with the highest degree of efficiency he could manage.[19] Doing this brings the Jews center stage be-cause the roles they played in the estate economy were crucial in improving its profitability.

The goal of the magnate estate owners in managing their lands was to ensure a level of income stable and high enough to finance all their many needs. In the Commonwealth, like most of pre-modern Europe, the nobil-ity was the major political group in society, and political activity involved significant financial outlay. The higher the status, the greater the activity and so the expense.[20] Beyond this, magnate status was demonstrated by stylish and opulent living. The great families spared no expense in copying the lifestyle of the French and Central European courts, which also involved considerable expenditure.[21] Finally, estate management itself, especially the development and upkeep of infrastructure, was an expensive business. Since the estates were the major source of the nobles' income, their financial man-agement in all aspects needed to be taken very seriously. This meant not just production but distribution and sale too.

Thus, the second thread of this study is the socioeconomic complex of the latifundium. Running a latifundium was not something that any in-dividual could undertake independently. It involved the establishment of an entire administration. The magnates might sit in their chancelleries and direct matters from on high, but running the different sectors of the indi-vidual estates on a daily basis fell to the administrators on the ground. For this reason, the questions posed here cannot be answered just by examin-ing the direct relationships between estate owners and Jews. Though these could have significant implications for all sides, such relationships were rare. In most cases the magnates had no idea precisely who it was that was bringing them their incomes. The benefits that Jews brought to magnates came not directly, but through their activity within the estate economy and estate society.[22]

In the same way, magnates as individuals had little interest in or impact on the development of Jewish life. They viewed Jews as one of the groups living on their lands. Each group had its own characteristics and functioned within the broad policy of estate administration. The processes of change undergone by Jewish society can thus only be understood in the context of the estates' complex social structure.

The huge Radziwiłł latifundium, which was one of the largest, most complex and successful sets of estates in eighteenth-century Poland-Lithuania, makes an excellent case study for examining the Jews' roles in the estate economy and society.[23] Beyond this, its very complexity adds a further dimension to the study. Since the estates had been in the family for generations, they were divided and re-divided among the heirs, sometimes passing from one branch of the family to another and sometimes even leaving the family's control as dowries given to daughters. The latifundium thus had multiple owners. During the seventy-five-year period of our study, the Radziwiłł estates were managed by five different members of the family over three generations. This gives a comparative perspective to this study permitting the examination of both continuities and differences in the management strategies of different individuals in different places and times. As a result, the problems involved in generalizing about Jewish experience on magnate estates on the basis of a single case study are, to some extent at least, alleviated.

The focus on the Radziwiłł estates in Lithuania also makes this something of a regional study that can deepen our understanding of the evolution of Jewish society in a relatively understudied part of the Polish-Lithuanian Commonwealth.[24] Even though the Union of Lublin combined Lithuania and Poland into a single state, the merger was not total. It is no wonder, then, that Jewish society in the Grand Duchy of Lithuania developed somewhat differently from that in Crown Poland. This was largely because the two states had slightly different social structures and legal traditions, and the Lithuanian economy was less developed. In addition, large-scale Jewish settlement on the magnate estates of eastern Poland, especially Ukraine, began after 1569 and lasted until 1648, while the corresponding process in Lithuania was slower and accelerated only after the wars of the mid-seventeenth century.[25]

Though the research here is not primarily regional in nature, it does shed some light on the specifics of Jewish life in the Grand Duchy during the eighteenth century and so adds to our understanding of the diversity of experience in Eastern Europe in the early modern period.[26]

The Radziwiłł Family and Its Latifundium

The study covers the period from 1689 to 1764, from a time at which the Radziwiłł family's fortunes were at a low ebb to a moment at which it was possibly the most powerful dynasty in the Polish-Lithuanian Commonwealth.[27] Though clearly a period of intensive development for the family and its estates, these seventy-five years were not marked by any drastic changes in their history. Even the transfers of lands from generation to generation and from owner to owner seem to have happened without serious upheaval. It is thus an excellent period for examining continuity and change in estate administration and the ways in which these affected the economic roles of the Jews. Before we do this, however, we need first to say a few words about the history of the family and its estates before 1689.

In the sixteenth century the Radziwiłłs were one of the leading noble dynasties in the Grand Duchy of Lithuania. Their status improved dramatically in 1547, when Barbara Radziwiłł married Zygmunt August, the heir to the throne, a development that extended their influence into Poland. The family's powerful position continued into the late sixteenth and early seventeenth centuries, particularly in the colorful figure of Mikołaj Krzysztof Radziwiłł. Baptized a Calvinist, he converted to Roman Catholicism, made a pilgrimage to the Holy Land, and wrote an account of the experience. A staunch monarchist, he held many high positions in Polish-Lithuanian society as well as donating much time, effort, and money to religious and cultural causes.[28] He substantially enlarged his estates around the town of Nieśwież (Nesvizh, Belarus) and earned great prestige for his family.[29] Following his death in 1616, however, the family's status began to decline and continued to do so during the wars of the mid-seventeenth century.[30]

At that time Janusz and Bogusław Radziwiłł were the leading figures in the family. Janusz played an active role in the Commonwealth's military operations against Bohdan Khmelnytsky's Cossack rebellion. When, at the end of that conflict, Russian forces invaded Lithuania from the east, Radziwiłł decided to conclude a separate Lithuanian treaty with the Swedish king, then attacking Poland from the north. These separatist ambitions were supported by his cousin Bogusław, who also decided to throw in his lot with the king of Sweden. This proved an expensive blunder. Within five years the Swedish forces had been repelled and the Radziwiłł cousins were condemned as traitors to the Polish crown. In retribution the king confiscated many of the family estates.[31]

For most of the later seventeenth century the Radziwiłł family's political status remained in the doldrums.[32] Bogusław maintained connections with the Holy Roman Empire, marrying off his daughter Ludwika Karolina first to Louis of Brandenburg, and then, after Louis's death, to Charles Philip, Count of Palatinate-Neuburg and future elector Palatine. Her dowry, particularly for her second marriage, comprised a number of major Lithuanian properties (which later became known as the Neuburg estates). The income they brought the family was thus lost,[33] yet another blow to the status of the Radziwiłłs at home. It took decades to recover.

That process really began in 1689, when at the age of twenty Karol Stanisław Radziwiłł inherited the family estates, which were mired in debt.[34] A popular figure among the Lithuanian nobility, Karol Stanisław was a nephew of King Jan III. After the king's death Radziwiłł supported the candidacy of Augustus, Elector of Saxony, a prescient choice. Once Augustus was elected king, Karol Stanisław became a favorite and was even named grand chancellor of Lithuania. Not a particularly hardworking character, he did his best to reinstate the family fortunes, though his efforts were hampered by the enormous destruction wrought by the Great Northern War of 1702–1720. Still, when he died in 1719, he did leave his wife and son a latifundium in better shape than when he received it.

The rise of Karol Stanisław thus launched a new era for the Radziwiłłs and their estates. He had also inherited the bulk of the family's property in Lithuania and so became the central figure in the large and widespread family.[35] For the next seventy-five years he, his wife Anna (née Sanguszko), their two sons Michał Kazimierz and Hieronim Florian, and their grandson Karol Stanisław, the son of Michał Kazimierz, made up the dominant branch of the dynasty.

After his father's death, Michał Kazimierz inherited the majority of the estates; only a relatively small number were left to Karol's wife Anna. She was a smart and hardworking woman who administered her lands with some efficiency—so much so that she was able to teach Michał the intricacies of estate management when he was still a young man. Anna devoted much time and effort to increasing her revenues and making innovations in the running of her estates, including the establishment of glass and textile manufactories.[36]

She was also instrumental in bringing back the lands that had been lost in the marriage of Ludwika Karolina, which she did by arranging a union between her younger son, Hieronim Florian, and the princess of Sulzbach, Elizabeth Wittelsbach, who had inherited them. Under an agreement drawn up before their marriage (which never took place), the Neuburg estates were restored to Anna's control.[37] In exchange the Radziwiłłs agreed to pay millions of złoty to the elector Palatine, plus two million to the Sapieha family (another magnate dynasty) so that they would relinquish their claim to the property.[38] When Hieronim Florian turned twenty-one, Anna transferred to him most of the estates that she had administered until then.[39]

Michał Kazimierz Radziwiłł, the eldest son, was a somewhat colorless character, probably best known to posterity through his nickname "Rybeńko," roughly translated as "Honey," a term of endearment he used in everyday speech. He had an extremely successful career administering his estates. Not only did he increase the revenue they brought in, he also substantially added to their number, boosting his income still further and making the family a dominant force in the Polish-Lithuanian Commonwealth during the reign of Augustus III (1734–1763).

His marriage to Franciszka Urszula Wiśniowiecka also advanced his fortunes. The only daughter of Janusz Wiśniowiecki, she was a highly educated and cultured figure, more so than her husband. She was a talented writer of drama and helped establish a theater in Nieśwież, the Radziwiłł family seat.[40] On the death of her father in 1741 Franciszka Urszula inherited extensive estates in southeastern Poland that became part of the family latifundium.[41] Michał Kazimierz also acquired other estates in the region, especially Żółkiew (Zhovka, Ukraine), which he purchased from the Sobieski family in 1740. His political advancement continued until in 1744 he was named to the highest office in the Grand Duchy of Lithuania, the *województwo* of Wilno (Vilnius, Lithuania). One of the perks of holding such a position was for him to take over the running of crown lands and adding them to his latifundium.[42]

Michał Kazimierz's brother Hieronim Florian was a totally different type.[43] He showed little enthusiasm for either public affairs or the administration of his estates. His main interest in life was his private army, and particularly the officer training school that he founded in Słuck (Slutsk, Belarus). A man of sadistic inclinations, he caused a great deal of grief and suffering not only to his family—especially his wife—but also to anyone who came into contact with him.[44] In his early years he succeeded in making his estates more profitable, thanks mainly to his employment of Shmuel Ickowicz, a highly talented Jewish businessman and entrepreneur, who acted as his agent. After Ickowicz was arrested in 1745, revenues began to decline.[45] Quite unexpectedly they received a significant boost when Marcin Mikołaj Radziwiłł, Hieronim Florian's cousin, was declared insane and locked away.[46] This meant that Marcin's estates and their incomes fell into the hands of his cousin, who managed them until his death in 1760. At that point, all of Hieronim Florian's estates, including those of Marcin Mikołaj, passed to his brother, Michał Kazimierz.

Michał Kazimierz himself died just two years later, leaving one of the largest latifundia in the country to his son Karol Stanisław. These estates, which included more than two thousand cities, towns, and villages, had a total value estimated at 150 million–180 million złoty.[47] They brought in some 1.3 million thaler a year in revenues.[48]

Research on the family's latifundium in the eighteenth century has shown that because the revenues it brought were the source of the family's wealth, the family's rise in Polish-Lithuanian society should be understood in the context of its success in enlarging its landholdings.[49] This raises another question, very pertinent here: Did the ways in which the Jews helped increase revenues from the latifundium also play a role in boosting this family's power and status in Polish-Lithuanian society and making it one of the two leading dynasties in the Commonwealth?

Karol Stanisław Radziwiłł was only twenty-eight years old when his father died. Known as "Panie Kochanku" ("My Dear Sir"), which was how he addressed his friends and acquaintances, he was a disreputable character, notorious among the *szlachta* for being a drunkard and a wastrel, totally lacking in self-control.[50] When in 1764 King Stanisław August was elected to the throne with Russian backing, the young Radziwiłł took up arms and barricaded himself and his troops in his palace at Biała Podlaska. After the new king's supporters declared him an enemy of the state, he waged an armed struggle against the Russian forces that had invaded Lithuania.[51] He was defeated and many of his estates were expropriated to be given to his main rival, Michał Czartoryski, and his supporters. Karol Stanisław himself fled the country and went into exile for a number of years.[52]

This marked a major break in the history and administration of the estates, many of which were not restored to the family for a decade or more.

The year 1764 then is a natural endpoint for this study. It was also a year of significance for both Poland-Lithuania and its Jewish population as a whole, marking the beginning of reforms undertaken by King Stanisław August Poniatowski, as a part of which the Jewish parliament, known as the Council of Four Lands, was abolished.[53] In fact, the seventy-five-year period studied here corresponds more or less to the years of the Saxon Wettin dynasty in the Polish-Lithuanian Commonwealth (1697–1763), when the power of the magnates was at its height.

APPROACHING THE SUBJECT

The Sources

The main source for this study is the Radziwiłł family archive, which contains documentation shedding light on the family's life as well as the day-to-day administration of its estates. In more than four hundred years of political, social, and economic activity, the Radziwiłłs amassed a vast collection of papers that they preserved in their personal archive, primarily as an aid to managing the family's affairs, but also to create a historical record, and so a priceless sociocultural pedigree. A huge number of these documents are now held in the Central Archives of Historical Records in Warsaw.[54] Others are scattered among numerous archives in Eastern Europe with the most important collection being in the National Archive of the Republic of Belarus in Minsk.[55] It is a truly enormous archive: the part held in Warsaw takes up 250 meters of shelf space, while that in Minsk holds some 25,000 files.

The Radziwiłł papers contain records of purchases, inheritance, sales, and leases of the estates in the latifundium; documents on the political activity of family members; correspondence; and personal documentation (for example diaries).[56] In addition there are documents on the running of the estate, such as administrative instructions, reports from clerks, requests from subjects, contracts, and bills.[57] Records of the Jews' activity in the estate economy are found here and for the eighteenth century they are extremely extensive.[58]

In contrast to the vast amount of documentation to be found in the Radziwiłł family archives, the records that have survived from the archives of Jewish communities on the Radziwiłł estates in Lithuania are extremely limited. Only one Jewish community record book (Hebrew *pinkas*, plural *pinkassim*) from the Radziwiłł estates in Lithuania in the period in question exists, that of Zabłudów.[59] There are, however, several *pinkassim* from places near the Radziwiłł estates in Lithuania (for example, Boćki, Horki, Włodawa, and Tykocin), that provide important comparative material.[60] The record book of the Council of the Land of Lithuania also sheds light on the activity of the Jews and Jewish communities on the Radziwiłł estates and in Lithuania in general.[61] Another sort of record book used here is that of the burial society of the Słuck Jewish community.[62]

The great imbalance between sources of Polish and Jewish provenance provides a serious challenge to a study focusing on economic choices made by Jews. Though the existing documentation gives excellent detail on the running of the estate economy and the ways in which Jews acted within it, it says much less about their motivations. The problem is not as great as it might seem, though, for some of the documentation in the archive is correspondence between Jews and the Radziwiłłs or their administration. In addition, many of the reports written by administrators shed light on the Jews' actions. "The Jewish voice" can thus be heard even in documents of non-Jewish provenance.

More importantly, the estate records, by helping us grasp the economic system within which the Jews acted, do allow for an understanding of motivation. Economic agency is never wielded in a vacuum. The choices any individual makes are to a very great extent determined by their context. While personal, social, cultural, or religious factors may come into play, the basic parameters for these decisions are a function of the possibilities that the wider economic context allows. In short, by analyzing the economic system within which the Jews acted, we can understand why they made the choices they did. The gaps that remain can be covered through the use of either archival sources of Jewish provenance from other settings or literary sources written by Jewish estate residents.

Of those, memoirs of Jews who lived on the estates, such as Solomon Maimon, a philosopher born and raised on the Radziwiłł latifundium, can be extremely revealing.[63] Rabbinic literature, especially responsa and homiletic works, is also useful for understanding the religious, and even cultural, background for Jewish life on the estates from the point of view of the rabbinic leadership.[64] Two of the leading Polish-Lithuanian rabbis of the period started their careers on the Radziwiłł estates: Rabbi Ezekiel Landau (later chief rabbi of Prague and author of the famous collection of responsa, *Noda'*

Bi-Yehudah) and Rabbi Ḥaim Ha-kohen Rapoport (who led the rabbinical side in a disputation with the Frankists in Lwów [L'viv, Ukraine] in 1759).[65] Since religious and cultural values clearly spread well beyond the boundaries of any single latifundium, however, there is no need to focus exclusively on their works.

Historiographical Underpinnings

The conceptual basis for this study is derived in no small measure from developments in the field of economic history pioneered by scholars trained in economics rather than in history. "New institutional economics (NIE)" started as a revolt of economists against the level of abstraction utilized by economic theorists in creating the models they use to predict economic activity. The NIE school under the tutelage of Oliver Williamson, among others, argued that the assumptions of neoclassical economics, such as individuals having perfect knowledge of the state of the market, or complete freedom to act in their economic best interest (as laid down by the neoclassicists), were totally unrealistic. To create a credible model of economic activity that would truly explain why people acted as they did, it was necessary to develop a model that would be able to take into account the limitations and uncertainties that daily life imposes on everyone.[66]

Various economic thinkers took up the challenge and developed a theory constructed around the concept of economic institutions. Though this was by no means a new idea in the 1980s and 1990s when NIE became influential, these new institutional economists broadened it significantly. Ronald Coase laid special emphasis on "the institutions of a country: its legal system, its political system, its social system, its educational system, its culture, and so on." He continued, "In effect, it is the institutions that govern the performance of an economy, and it is this that gives the 'new institutional economics' its importance."[67]

Douglass North, another leading proponent of NIE, though one who specialized in historical research, fleshed out this definition in the introduction to his book *Understanding the Process of Economic Change*:

> Economics is a theory of choice—so far so good. But the discipline neglects to explore the context within which choice occurs. We choose among alternatives that are themselves constructions of the human mind. Therefore how the mind works and understands the environment is the foundation of this study.

But what is the environment? The human environment is a human construct
of rules, norms, conventions, and ways of doing things that define the framework of human interaction. . . . The new institutional economics . . . focuses
on . . . the institutions (political, economic, and social) that they [i.e. humans]
create to shape that environment.[68]

For Avner Greif, a prominent NIE historian, North's definition is problematic on two counts. First, it does not explain why individuals are prepared to accept these institutions and to go along with their prescriptions.
Greiff argues that it is crucial to integrate into any theory of institutions the
cultural, religious, and even psychological motivations that bring members
of any society to accept its economic institutions and follow their rules. Second, according to him, North's formulation fails to deal with the issues of
causality and function: "A major fault line in institutional analysis separates
those who adopt an *agency perspective* of institutions from those who adopt
a *structural perspective*. According to the former, individuals shape institutions to achieve their goals; according to the latter institutions transcend individual actors . . . and shape their interests and behavior." Greif emphasizes
that this is a false dichotomy and suggests that both perspectives need to be
taken into account.[69]

The NIE's approach is extremely powerful for the economic historian
trained in history. The focus on institutions, whether as organizations or
cultural attitudes towards economic activity, allows the historian to keep his
or her eye on the specifics of the historical situation. And, of course, questions of social structure and cultural development are now bread and butter
for most historians. This study too follows the NIE, paying special heed
to Greif's call for the integration of the structural and agency perspectives:
On the one hand, it analyzes the magnate estate and its functioning from
an institutional perspective, showing how its economic structures shaped
the choices Jews took about how to improve their income; on the other, it
shows how by pressing willing Jewish businessmen into service the magnate
estate owners were able, at least to a certain extent, to remold the estate
economy in order to respond to changing conditions. This allows for a degree of dynamism in the discussions and helps explain further the processes
of economic empowerment enjoyed by the Jews over the eighteenth century.

The study departs from Greif and most of the other new institutional
economic historians in that it is unwilling to use its specific analysis in order
to create a prescriptive model.[70] The analysis here is meant to explain a par-

ticular historical situation rather than human economic behavior in general. There is also no attempt to explain the rise of capitalism—a goal of most NIE historians, even Greif in his study of medieval trade networks.[71] To the extent that this work does present the reader with a model, it is one that shows how a particular magnate latifundium functioned in the eighteenth century. When generalizations are drawn, they are done only by means of comparison with other studies that treat different estates that functioned in the same broad geographic and chronological context.[72]

Particularly important for making such generalizations is the classic study by Witold Kula, *An Economic Theory of the Feudal System: Towards a Model of the Polish Economy 1500–1800*, originally published in Polish in 1962. In this work, Kula attempted to create a general model of the Polish economy in the early modern period. His starting point was Marxist—the feudal system as precursor to capitalism—but he restricted his focus to conditions in Poland before the advent of capitalism, thereby avoiding a teleological approach. Eschewing views of feudalism as a largely political-legal, social, or cultural phenomenon, he treated it as a set of economic relations, predominantly between the noble estate owners and their peasants.[73] Concentrating on feudalism in this way led him to a close examination of conditions on the noble estates—particularly as regards production and control of the means of production. His interest in the market was limited to the question of the relations between production and price, and among his most startling findings was that increases in grain prices could depress rather than stimulate production.

Another of the main thrusts of Kula's analysis was his insistence that this was a rational economic system, even though its rationality was quite different from that of capitalism. Kula showed that some parts of the estate economy, including natural resources and labor, had a value that could not be measured in monetary terms, since there was no market on which they could be sold. Exploiting them in the feudal system in the same way as in a capitalist environment where everything has a monetary value would have been quite illogical. In turn, this meant that the accounting system of the day could really only deal with goods that could be sold on the market and so have a monetary value. This affected not only how profitability was measured, but also the ways economic actors viewed the choices they could make. By their own lights, they were acting rationally; it was just that the nature of that rationality was determined by their historical situation.[74]

Kula's study, therefore, is extremely important for its description and analysis of the economic structures of the estate system examined here. It also helps lay bare some of the cultural views, such as the importance of mercantile activity, the value of labor, and the meaning of value itself, that underlay it. On the other hand, Kula's limited interest in the workings of the market in the system, as well as the limitations imposed on him by the conditions in the People's Republic of Poland, meant that he could not really investigate those aspects of the economy in which Jews were active and so assess their roles.[75] That is, of course, the goal of this study.

I did not write it in a historiographical vacuum. Scholarship such as that of Jacob Goldberg and Gershon Hundert, who examined the Jews' economic roles on the magnate estates, was extremely helpful.[76] In particular Hundert's study of the private town of Opatów in eighteenth-century Poland was enlightening in its attribution of the landlord's support for Jewish economic activity to a desire to improve economic conditions in the town and its discussion of the importance of the Jews for the urban economy.[77]

The only comprehensive examination of the history of the Jews in a particular latifundium is that by Murray Jay Rosman.[78] His book focuses on the economic relations between the Sieniawski family—and then the Czartoryskis—and the Jews who lived on their estates in the late seventeenth and early eighteenth centuries. In this pathbreaking study that provided much of the conceptual groundwork on which my book is based, Rosman took a stand against the prevailing opinion, of Jewish and Polish historians alike, that relations between the Jews and the magnates were based on rank exploitation. He argued that the Jews' economic interests were consistent with the economic goals of the Sieniawski and Czartoryski families, particularly in commerce and leasing, and that this prompted the magnates to support the Jews and their economic activity.[79]

In fact Rosman took his argument a step further, claiming that magnates and Jews had "common interests." He described their relationship as "a marriage of convenience," emphasizing that "marriages of convenience are still marriages."[80] For him it was the direct relationship of magnate and Jew that was the key to understanding developments on the estates.

In working on the Radziwiłł materials, I found this idea somewhat problematic. In the hierarchical relations of the feudal estates I was studying, the only interest that counted was the noble owner's. All that was left for his subjects was to answer his needs as best they could. The magnate was not, therefore, "wedded" to his Jewish subjects any more than to other groups on his estates. He pressed them all into his service, each in its own way. Since it was only to the extent that the Jews were able to provide him with added incomes that they could derive maximum benefit from their economic activity, they did what they could to meet his demands. These should then be seen less as "common interests" and more as Jews finding new and more effective ways of serving their lords.[81]

For the most part this was not personal service. Only a very few extremely wealthy and prominent Jews worked directly for the magnate. The vast majority lived their lives and earned their livings without any direct dealings with their lord at all. Contact with the estate administration was almost exclusively with administrators and officials, many of whom were not too concerned about what their master saw as his best interests as far as Jews were concerned.[82] In fact, most Jewish economic actors did not serve the estate administration directly at all; they just got on with making their daily bread. Doing that brought them into much greater contact with the other populations who lived on the estates: peasants, townspeople, the local nobility, and the clergy. As a result, the Jews should be viewed not as simply providing economic services to the magnate in person but rather as part of a broad estate economy, put in place to serve the lord's needs, and encompassing all the different groups of his subjects.[83]

The Eastern European historiography of the magnate estates is not helpful in understanding how that system worked. Studies have dealt mostly with the peasants and the estate administration, almost totally ignoring other groups, especially the Jews. Soviet Belorusian historiography is particularly frustrating in that regard, though Polish-language scholarship is only a little better.[84] While there are studies of many different estates and their economic activity, issues such as exchange, sale, and marketing—not to mention the Jews—are given short shrift.

Janina Bergerówna's 1936 book about the Kock estate in eastern Poland under the management of Princess Anna Jabłonowska in the late eighteenth century is a welcome exception. Though she did not deal with the Grand Duchy of Lithuania, Bergerówna made a conscious effort to examine the interactions of the different groups on the estate. Jews were treated in just a few pages, but they did at least appear as major players.

A more recent study to examine the place of the Jews in estate society is that of Adam Kaźmierczyk, which is a monograph entirely devoted to the juridical integration of the Jews into the estate system from the sixteenth through the eighteenth centuries.[85] This work has special importance here because it examines the different jurisdictions on the noble estates where trials concerning Jews could be heard. Since the legal system was one of the major institutions regulating economic life on the estates, Kaźmierczyk's study makes a crucial contribution to understanding how life on a latifundium shaped the development of Jewish society.

In all, though the existing historiography sheds light on some of the economic institutions of the magnate latifundium, it leaves in the dark much of the processes of exchange and sale that allowed the magnate to turn the agricultural product of his estates into cash income. This is strange, because without those processes the estates would have been worse than useless to their owners, whose main interest was in increasing cash revenues. Of course it was precisely into the sectors of exchange and sale that Jewish businessmen moved en masse in order to help boost their masters' (and their own) incomes. It is that move and those processes, then, that will form the focus of this study, which aims to provide a new model for understanding the functioning of the magnate latifundium by placing at its center the economic institutions that controlled the marketing process and the Jews who used them.

The book opens with a discussion of the demographic background, asking how many Jews settled on the Radziwiłł estates in this period and why they did so. It then looks at the town as the major setting for Jewish life, examining it as an economic institution to see what roles it and the Jewish community played in improving estate revenues.

The analysis then moves on to examine those economic institutions on the latifundium whose role was to create cash revenue from agricultural production. Chapter Three explains the different strategies of revenue generation used by the Radziwiłłs, thus mapping out the major economic institutions on their estates. Using this as a guide, the following chapters examine the ways in which the Jews functioned within them.

The first of these deals with the extremely lucrative field of estate leasing, whose riskiness dissuaded many Jews from engaging in it. The discussion revolves around two Jewish brothers who leased almost the whole of Hieronim Florian Radziwiłł's estates in the early 1740s. The next chapter looks at the popular business of leasing the incomes from alcohol manufacture and sale. It asks both why the estate administration preferred Jewish leaseholders and why Jewish businessmen flocked to this sector. The last chapter examines the roles Jews played in trade, noting that while they were active in some commodities they were much less so in others. Again it asks why the administration steered Jewish merchants into the fields it did and why the Jews were so enthusiastic in answering its call.

The conclusion addresses three questions that run like a thread through the whole book. First, what can the experience of the Jews on the Radziwiłł estates teach us about the nature of Jewish economic agency in a non-capitalist setting? Second, what forms did Jewish economic empowerment take in this period and how did they affect the development of Jewish society? And third, what were the consequences of the Jews' economic activity not only for the Radziwiłł family, but for the Poland-Lithuania as a whole. It will become clear that the Jews' economic activity was by no means a marginal, or even sectorial, phenomenon, as most previous studies have assumed. It was, rather, a factor of major importance in the history not only of Eastern European Jews, but of the Polish-Lithuanian Commonwealth itself during the eighteenth century.

ONE

Jewish Settlement on the Estates

Before we can come to any understanding of how important the Jews' economic activities were for the Radziwiłłs and their estates, we need some idea of just how many Jews lived there. This is not a simple task because the basic sources from the period are fragmentary and raise a number of highly complex issues of interpretation. All we know for certain is that the number of Jews on the estates grew substantially over the course of the eighteenth century. This is far from enough. We really need to quantify the absolute numbers of Jews on the estates and then calculate their rate of growth. It is only once we have done that, that we can begin to work out the reasons for the increase.

Even this, however, is not the end of the story. To understand how the population growth came about, we must establish first whether it was caused by factors specific to the situation of the Jews on the Radziwiłł estates or whether it formed part of broader trends, common either to all the inhabitants of the estates (Jewish and non-Jewish) or to Polish-Lithuanian Jews as a whole.

Next, the factors at work just on the Radziwiłł estates have to be identified and assessed. Since the evidence strongly suggests that the Jewish population there increased largely as a result of the family actively encouraging Jewish settlement on its lands, we need to understand why it did so. So the question then becomes one of the benefits that the growth of the Jewish population brought to the family and its estates.

The discussion here answers these questions first by assessing the extent of Jewish settlement on the Radziwiłł estates in Lithuania at three different times. It starts at the turn of the seventeenth century and then looks at both the beginning and the end of the period under discussion (1689–1764). Next it examines the nature and causes of the Radziwiłłs' settlement policy, pointing out some of the financial benefits it brought. Finally, it weighs up the significance of general demographic factors in order to determine just how successful was the family's policy of bringing Jews to the estates.

EARLY SETTLEMENT

Jews had lived on Radziwiłł estates since the sixteenth century, but it was only in the eighteenth century that Jewish population growth really began to take off. A look back at early stages of Jewish settlement will help explain this.

The first source referring to Jews living on Radziwiłł lands is from the mid-sixteenth century. In 1529 the Jewish community of Kleck was included in a list of those paying a special tax imposed on Lithuanian Jewry by King Zygmunt I.[1] So when the city became Radziwiłł property in 1551, it already had a Jewish community.[2]

Jews seem to have come to the town of Nieśwież, the Radziwiłłs' family seat in the Grand Duchy of Lithuania, a little later, in the second half of the century. The earliest documentation is a 1589 privilege granted to the local Jewish community at the request of its representative, Joseph ben Isaac, by Mikołaj Krzysztof ("the Orphan") Radziwiłł, lord of the town.[3] In the charter Radziwiłł permitted the Jews to settle there and enjoy the tax exemption that King Stefan Batory had granted its other inhabitants. The privilege permitted Jews to purchase houses on only a single street that had gates at each end.[4] Some Jews were allowed to rent houses and apartments outside the Jewish street, while those living in the market square on the basis of personal privileges could remain there until they sold their homes to Christians. Radziwiłł also allowed the Jews of Nieśwież to build a synagogue and ritual bath and to purchase a plot of land outside the city for a cemetery. The final clause of the privilege gave the *kahal* (the governing body of the local Jewish community) the right to admit new members to the community and expel existing ones if the need arose.[5]

The third Jewish community on Radziwiłł lands seems to have been established in Słuck, near Nieśwież. In 1601, Janusz Radziwiłł granted the Jews of the town a privilege that was based on a previous charter, so presumably this community too had been founded in the second half of the sixteenth century.[6] By 1623, Jews occupied sixteen houses on a single street that could be roped off at both ends.[7]

Next to be settled seems to have been the town of Birże (Biržai, Lithuania). Documents from the early seventeenth century indicate that there was a Jewish community there too, since in 1609 Krzysztof II Radziwiłł issued an order formalizing the status of the Jews in the town. Based on the context and the names of the Jews in the documents, Bardach has argued that this was actually a Karaite community that flourished until the mid-seventeenth century. According to him, there was no community of rabbanite Jews in Birże until the 1660s.[8]

The Radziwiłłs' attitude towards Jewish settlement in this period can be seen in an order given by Aleksander Ludwik Radziwiłł in 1621 to the Jews in another of their early settlements, Biała Podlaska. There they were allowed to own thirty houses, for each of which they had to pay only a low annual fee to the town council.[9] Were they to purchase any more houses, they would have to pay the council the full amount of tax for each and do compulsory service for the lord of the town just as a Christian householder did. This ruling was a kind of balancing act. Radziwiłł wanted to bring Jews to town, and so gave them a tax break. On the other hand, he needed to put a limit on this Jewish settlement, presumably in the face of opposition from the town council, which stood to lose income from the houses these Jews occupied (as well as suffering business losses as a result of increased Jewish competition).[10] The net result was probably positive for Jews considering settling in Biała, though there were certainly tensions involved in doing so. The late sixteenth and early seventeenth centuries were not, then, a period of untrammeled encouragement for Jewish settlement.

The situation began to change following the wars of the mid-seventeenth century. Between 1648 and 1654, Bohdan Khmelnytsky's Cossack forces ravaged much of Belarus, reaching as far as Słuck, though the Jews there managed to flee and save themselves.[11] In the ensuing war between Russia and Poland that began in 1654, Belarus was the major theater of battle, and destruction was immense.[12] After the fighting formally came to an end in 1667, the Radziwiłł estates—at least those that remained to the family— began slowly to recover.

This was not a process that happened naturally but was the result of a deliberate policy.[13] The first order of business was to encourage the repopulation, and then the continued growth of the villages and towns, many of whose inhabitants had either died or fled during the wars. Jews played a not insignificant role in this process, at least as far as the towns were concerned. In the 1660s the first rabbanite Jews settled in Birże, and by 1695 they owned fifty-three houses in the town.[14] In 1661 there were eighty-six Jewish families living in Słuck and another twelve in the new town (that is, the suburbs).[15] Twenty-two years later, 150 Jewish families were living in Słuck and another 15 in the new town.[16]

Even more significantly, the proportion of Jews in the total population of Słuck also grew, from 10.1 percent in 1661 to 13.5 percent in 1683. This meant that the Jews' population growth outstripped that of the non-Jews. Bearing in mind that the town council consistently opposed Jewish settlement, we can infer that the rapid expansion of the Jewish population was due to a policy adopted by the Radziwiłłs themselves. Nor was this policy limited to the Jews of Słuck; it extended across the latifundium, continuing and even gathering momentum in the eighteenth century.[17] As a result the Jewish population of the estates grew dramatically.

DEMOGRAPHIC GROWTH IN THE EIGHTEENTH CENTURY

In an ideal world we could examine the size and nature of population growth by comparing a census of the Jews on the Radziwiłł estates from the beginning of the period with one from the end. No general census of the estates was ever made, however. The first sources of this sort that can be usefully mined for data concerning Jews on the estates are the censuses of all Polish-Lithuanian Jewry taken in 1764–65 and 1775. However, the lack of a similar census from an earlier period means that is impossible to assess the growth rate of the Jewish population.

There is another problem here too: the size of the Radziwiłł latifundium was never stable. Estates were added or lost over the years (for example, as dowries for daughters). In fact, by the early 1760s Karol Stanisław adminis-tered a latifundium that was at least three times as large as his grandfather's had been.[18] A simple comparison of the number of Jews on the estates at two different dates would not yield very valuable results.

The solution is to use as a basis for comparison partial details drawn from the local censuses and inventories[19] that the Radziwiłłs made from time to time. Creating from these sources series of data dealing with places that re-mained part of the latifundium over the whole period gives at least a sense of the demographic trends among the Jewish population. Since these sources always included both Jews and non-Jews, they are also useful for identify-ing changes specific to the Jewish population. To round out the picture, the general census of Jews in 1764–65 gives a snapshot of the size and structure of Jewish settlement on the estates at the end of the period discussed here.

The Beginning of the Period: The Late Seventeenth Century

Suitable data are available for the Jewish population of nine Lithuanian towns owned by the Radziwiłłs in the late seventeenth century (Table 1.1).

The figures in the table are based on inventories showing the taxes owed to the Radziwiłłs. The major tax in the towns was the *czynsz*, assessed on each chimney. Most houses had just one chimney, so the number listed for Jewish and for non-Jewish householders can be used to give a sense of the relative size of each population.[20] The figures cannot be taken entirely at face value because Jews in the towns generally lived in more crowded conditions than their non-Jewish neighbors. As a result, the average number of Jews per house was probably larger than the average number of Christians.[21] We can therefore assume that the proportion of Jews in the towns was in fact larger than the percentage of houses owned by Jews shown in the table.[22]

Calculating the actual number of people is difficult unless we have some idea of the average number of people in each house. Several attempts have been made to come up with such averages for various periods (presumably, the average changed as conditions changed), but the results vary widely and

Table 1.1. Jewish Urban Settlement in the Late Seventeenth Century by Chimney

Town	Year	Total Chimneys	Chimneys in Houses Owned by Jews	% Chimneys Owned by Jews
Biała Podlaska	1702	269	61	23
Delatycze	1680	103	1	1
Kojdanów	1695	206	22	11
Korelicze	1672	83	1	1
Krzyczew	1694	367	27	7
Łachwa	1691	174	11	6
Mir	1681	314	1	—
Nieśwież	1696	—*	56	—
Nowy Świerżeń	1681	78	2	2
Total		1594	182	8%**

SOURCES: AR XXV, 123; AR XXV, 681; AR XXV, 698; AR XXV, 1706; AR XXV, 1797; AR XXV, 1928; AR XXV, 2168/1; AR XXV, 2444; and AR XXV, 2670/1.
*Data missing
**Not taking into account the incomplete data from Nieśwież

are not helpful.[23] Given the sketchy source base, coming up with even an estimate of the total number of Jews in the towns on the estates is simply impossible.[24]

So what can we learn from these data? Even in the late seventeenth century Jewish settlement in the estate towns was relatively sparse. In the nine towns for which we have details Jews owned only 182 houses. In most cases the number of Jewish-owned properties formed less than 10 percent of the total. There were only two places where Jews owned a greater proportion than that: Biała, 23 percent and Kojdanów (Dzyarzhynsk, Belarus), 11 percent. On average, Jews owned just 8 percent of the dwellings in the towns surveyed here. Clearly widespread Jewish settlement had not yet begun. Though the Radziwiłłs had been encouraging some Jewish settlement in the second half of the seventeenth century, they seem to have kept it within bounds.

The End of the Period: The 1760s

By the later eighteenth century the picture had changed dramatically. To see this we need to compare the figures from the late seventeenth century with corresponding data from the 1760s. Doing this involves going back to the nine localities for which we have data from the earlier period (in Table 1.1) and examining the Jewish population of those same localities in the 1760s, or as close to them as the sources allow (Table 1.2).

Table 1.2. Jewish Urban Settlement in the 1760s* by Chimney

Town	Year	Total Chimneys	Chimneys in Houses Owned by Jews	% Chimneys Owned by Jews
Biała Podlaska	1740	290	108	37
Delatycze	1761	68	10	15
Kojdanów	1792	221	79	36
Korelicze	1762	147	38	26
Krzyczew	1747	342	65	19
Łachwa	1764	188	22	12
Mir	1757	351	110	31
Nieśwież**	1733	524	77	15
Nowy Świerżeń	1754	160	44	27
Total		2291	553	34%

SOURCES: AR XXV, 127, AR XXV, 703, AR XXV, 1709, AR XXV, 1789, AR XXV, 1936, AR XXV, 2172, AR XXV, 2173, AR XXV, 2457/1, AR XXV, 2458, and AR XXV, 2624.
* In cases in which there is no inventory from the 1760s, the one chronologically closest is used.
** These figures are an estimate based on the conflation of two separate sources.

The most striking detail in Table 1.2 is perhaps the growth in the number of Jewish-owned houses: in the nine towns, Jews now owned 553 properties—an increase of 204 percent. This could be seen most impressively in Mir, where Jews owned only one house in 1681 but 110 in 1757.

Even more significant was the growth in the proportion of Jewish-owned properties: while the number of Jewish-owned houses in these towns rose by 204 percent, the total housing stock grew by only 45 percent. As a result, the Jews in these nine towns, who had owned only 8 percent of the houses in the late seventeenth century, now accounted for no less than 24 percent. In none of the places did the Jews own less than 10 percent of the houses. In fact in three of them, Biała, Mir, and Kojdanów, Jewish-owned properties accounted for more than 30 percent of the total. So, if we take into account the fact that conditions in houses owned by Jews were relatively crowded compared to those owned by non-Jews, we can conclude that Jews made up between a third and a half of the total urban population on the Radziwiłł estates in the 1760s.[25]

The reasons for this sharp growth in the size of the Jewish population on the estates are to be sought in the encouragement of Jewish settlement by the Radziwiłł family and in the rapid natural increase of Polish-Lithuanian Jewry in this period. Another factor was the effect of war on the Jewish population. Eighteenth-century Lithuania suffered much death and destruction from military actions, most significantly during the Great Northern War (1702–1720). To assess the importance of the war, its differing impact on the Jewish and non-Jewish populations of the estates must now be considered.

THE IMPACT OF THE GREAT NORTHERN WAR

The 1702 entry of the Polish-Lithuanian Commonwealth into the Great Northern War, fought principally between the Tsardom of Russia and the Swedish Empire, proved a fateful moment in its history.[26] The Commonwealth quickly became the main battleground and endured prolonged destruction and depopulation, at a time when it had not yet completely recovered from the horrors of the mid-seventeenth century wars. Lithuania experienced the worst of the conflict because Russian and Swedish forces crossed it time after time, plundering as they went, even when they did not fight any real battles.[27] The Radziwiłł estates suffered along with the rest. The towns of Nowy Świerżeń (Novy Sverzhan', Belarus) and Nieśwież, including the family's palace there, were razed by Swedish troops in the spring of 1706,[28] and Krzyczew (Krychaw, Belarus), where Karol Stanisław Radziwiłł was *starosta*, was sacked by the Russians in 1708.[29] Jews were frequently targeted not only by the troops but also by the local townspeople, who regarded them as dangerous economic rivals as well as a hostile religious element.[30] The estates, like the country as a whole, also suffered from all the side effects of early modern war including depopulation from flight, famine, and disease.[31]

Urban populations were also hit hard. At war's end the towns had to be repopulated and Jewish settlement was again encouraged. Though the reasons for this policy were never made explicit, it may have had to do with one of the economic limitations imposed on the Jews in Poland-Lithuania. Unlike the Christian townspeople, Jews were not allowed to own agricultural land, which was an important way for those living in towns to augment their incomes. During times of upheaval, many non-Jewish townspeople survived by giving up their urban occupation and turning to agriculture to support themselves. Jews, on the other hand, had no choice but to continue with trade and crafts, becoming in effect the main group keeping the towns alive and functioning. In these conditions, encouraging Jews to settle in towns was a logical choice, though one which could have significant consequences for urban development.

To demonstrate these, Table 1.3 shows some of the changes in the population structure of four towns between the turn of the century and the 1720s.

The table shows a clear trend. Although the total number of houses dropped in the war years, the number that belonged to Jews actually grew.

Table 1.3. The Influence of the Northern War on the Urban Population

Town	Year	Total Chimneys	Chimneys in Houses Owned by Jews	% Chimneys Owned by Jews
Biała Podlaska	1702	269	61	23
	1725	252	77	30
Łachwa	1691	174	11	6
	1727	144	20	14
Mir	1712	382	8	2
	1721	262	63	24
Krzyczew	1694	367	27	7
	1727	284	30	11

SOURCES: AR XXV, 123; AR XXV, 126; AR XXV, 1928; AR XXV, 1932; AR XXV, 2168/7; AR XXV, 2170; AR XXV, 2447; AR XXV, 2448.

This is best seen in Mir, where the total housing stock dropped from 382 to 262 (down more than 30 percent), while the number of Jewish-owned houses rose from 8 to 63 (up more than 750 percent). This did not happen just in the Radziwiłł towns; the same thing can be seen on the Neuburg estates, which were no longer under the family's control. In Słuck, for example, the total number of houses dropped from 1,353 in 1683 to 787 in 1712, while the number of Jewish-owned properties rose from 171 to 200; in Kopyś the total number of houses dropped from 336 to 183 between 1694 and 1713, while the number owned by Jews grew from 12 to 17.[32]

One of the factors at work here was probably the ability of the Jews to recover from the disaster and rebuild their lives more quickly than non-Jews.[33] This allowed them to penetrate urban life much more deeply than had previously been possible, which could be seen in both their buying up houses in the town and their increasing dominance of urban trade. Jews taking possession of vacant houses continued on the Radziwiłł estates throughout the first half of the eighteenth century, as can be seen in this excerpt from a 1753 letter by one of Michał Kazimierz Radziwiłł's administrators:

> Several Christian heads of household in the cities lack the means to repair their homes, build new [houses], or build on empty lots. The Jews undertake to repair [old houses] and put up new houses, but . . . they insist on maintaining possession of the buildings until the Christian owner pays the construction expenses.[34]

A new dynamic seems to have been created. Their situation during and after the war helped the Jews strengthen their position in the towns and may even have attenuated the opposition of non-Jewish townspeople to their presence there. Beyond this, the more the Jews penetrated urban life, the bigger their contribution to the lord's revenues, and the more reason there was for him to support their settlement.[35] So, far from proving a hindrance to the growth in the number of Jews on the estates, the Great Northern War, and more particularly the period of reconstruction that followed the fighting, may well actually have created conditions that encouraged it.[36]

Before we can look deeper into the causes of this growth, however, it is important to have a sense of the total number of Jews on the estates at the end of the period as well as the patterns of Jewish settlement that had developed.

POPULATION AND SETTLEMENT PATTERNS
IN 1764

To get a clear picture of Jewish settlement on the Radziwiłł estates in Lithuania by 1764, the two censuses mentioned above are the best sources. Like
all demographic materials from they period, they present those who use
them with significant problems, some intrinsic to the sources themselves,
others a result of historical circumstance.

The 1764–65 census, the most comprehensive and detailed listing of
Eastern European Jews until the last years of the nineteenth century, was
destroyed in the bombing of Warsaw during World War II. Fortunately
Raphael Mahler made a comprehensive study of the census (at least as
related to Poland) in the 1930s and published his findings in 1958. Thus,
though the original source no longer exists, we do have an excellent sense of
what it contained. Mahler did not include data from Lithuania in his study,
but this gap can be filled by the 1775 census of Lithuanian Jewry, which
has survived. It was based on the findings of the 1764–65 tally but updated
somewhat, making it extremely valuable for our purposes.[37]

Nonetheless, the materials cannot be taken at face value. The terms of the
1764–65 census stated that all Jews of both sexes in the Polish-Lithuanian
Commonwealth over the age of one year were to be counted. This means
that the numbers must be adjusted to include babies. In addition, many
Jews avoided being counted apparently in order to reduce the tax burden on
the Jewish communities (the determination of which was the whole point
of the census). After some complex calculations to determine both how
many children under the age of one there might have been and the extent
of Jews' evading the census takers, Mahler concluded that the figures as they
appear in the census should be increased by about 25 percent to reach the
true numbers.[38] Since the 1775 data are based on the census of 1764–65, they
should probably be adjusted similarly.

The census results regarding Jewish communities on the Radziwiłł estates
in Lithuania in 1775 are shown in Table 1.4.

This is not the whole story however. The family owned *jurydyki* (enclaves in royal towns that legally formed part of its holdings) in Wilno,
Kowno (Kaunas, Lithuania), Grodno (Hrodna, Belarus), Nowogródek
(Navahrudak, Belarus), and Kamieniec (Kamenets, Belarus). Jews resident
in these places were also Radziwiłł subjects and so need to be included in

Table 1.4. The Jewish Population of the Radziwiłł Estates in 1775*

Town	Number of Jews	Total Following Mahler's Adjustment
1. Słuck	1,577	1,971
2. Nieśwież	1,097	1,371
3. Birże	1,040	1,300
4. Żagory (Nowy)	840	1,050
5. Zabłudów	831	1,039
6. Głębokie	755	944
7. Szawle	687	859
8. Kleck	651	814
9. Smorgonie	649	811
10. Kiejdany	634	793
11. Mir	607	759
12. Pompiany	583	729
13. Kojdanów	561	701
14. Kodeń	435	544
15. Krzyczew	424	530
16. Kopyś	410	512
17. Dawidgródek	408	510
18. Czymkowicze	351	439
19. Newel	338	423
20. Korelicze	336	420
21. Żagory (Stary)	313	391
22. Dzięcioła	296	370
23. Sławatycze	267	334
24. Kopyl	258	322
25. Niechniewicze	188	235
26. Wiżuny	180	225
27. Łachwa	157	196
28. Nowy Świerżeń	132	165
29. Orłowo	132	165
30. Siebież	113	141
31. Lebiedziew	121	151
32. Delatycze	50	62
Total	15,421	19,276

SOURCES: Lietuvos TSR Centrinis Valstybės Istorijos Archyvas, Vilnius, SA, b. 3739; Alexandrov, "Di Yidishe bafelkerung," 31–83; Korobkov, "Statistika," 541–62; and Korobkov, "Perepis," 164–77.
* Unlike the inventories, the census data do not refer just to the urban population. All leaseholders in the villages, along with their families and households, are included in the figures for the community nearest their place of residence.

this count. Though there is no way to assess how many Jews lived in the five *jurydyki*, an estimation of a thousand or so does not seem unlikely. This would mean that that the Jewish population of the estates at the time was slightly more than 20,000. The Jewish population of Lithuania as a whole in that period is estimated at 200,000, so about 10 percent of the entire Jewish population of the Grand Duchy of Lithuania lived on the Radziwiłł estates at the end of our period.[39]

We should now examine the patterns of Jewish settlement on the estates because they are an important indicator of the ways in which Jews integrated into the estate society and economy. Most striking is the fact that they tended to live in small communities. After adjusting the figures, we see that only five of the thirty-two communities on the list had a Jewish population of over 1,000; almost half the communities had fewer than 500.[40] The average size of the Jewish communities on the estates was just 482.

Even this does not give a picture of the true size of these Jewish centers, however. Among the members of these communities were counted those who leased taverns in nearby villages and small towns where there was no community. These Jews did not live in town or participate in community life on a daily basis, only visiting to do business or receive religious services. According to the figures that we have, up to 30 percent of the Jewish population lived in the villages, making the picture one of really quite small communities.[41]

Typically, these communities were found in small towns scattered across the rural heartlands of the estates, leaving the Jews well placed to play key roles in the estates' agricultural economy.[42] It was to a large extent in doing this that they brought the Radziwiłłs the revenues they needed, convincing them that the encouragement of Jewish settlement was indeed worthwhile. So to understand why the Jewish population grew as rapidly as it did, we must now turn to the family's policy on bringing Jews to live on their estates.

THE RADZIWIŁŁS' SETTLEMENT POLICY

One of the first signs of the Radziwiłłs family's desire to attract Jewish settlers at the turn of the eighteenth century is a privilege granted in 1701 to the small town of Nowy Świerżeń by Karol Stanisław Radziwiłł. He was engaged in revitalizing the family fortunes and so needed to improve estate revenues. As part of this effort, he urgently needed to repopulate his cities and towns, which he did by offering settlers various incentives, including a ten-year tax exemption: "[To] everyone—people of all religions—who want to settle down and build a proper home on these empty lots, I grant an exemption for ten years from the date [of promulgation] of this order of mine. During this time they will have no obligations to my court for these lands and fields and will not pay any property taxes."[43] This policy of granting a tax exemption to new settlers was not unique to the Radziwiłłs; it was an accepted means of encouraging settlement.[44] In this case it was significant in that it more-or-less openly included Jews.

The policy of encouraging Jewish settlement continued throughout the period under discussion. A very clear expression of it can be seen in mid-century in Michał Kazimierz Radziwiłł's management of the *ekonomia* of Szawle (Šiauliai, Lithuania).[45] This royal estate, which came into Radziwiłł's hands in the early 1740s, included five towns—Szawle, Janiszki (Joniškis, Lithuania), Radziwiliszki, (Radviliškis, Lithuania) Żagory (Žagarė, Lithuania), and Gruździe (Gruzdžiai, Lithuania)—and 336 villages of various sizes.[46] When he took possession of the estate, it was run-down and not very profitable, so one of his first steps was to issue detailed instructions to his administrators on how to improve infrastructure and increase profitability.[47]

A key issue was Jewish settlement. The Jews had been expelled from the *ekonomia* in 1731 on the orders of Antoni Apriasz, the general commissar.[48] Although the non-Jewish townspeople had agreed to take upon themselves payment of the Jews' *czynsz*, estate revenues, especially from commerce and *propinacja* leases, had fallen dramatically.[49] Radziwiłł addressed this problem in the third point of his instructions: "The court [i.e., the administration] should make an effort [to establish] leases wherever possible in order to enrich [our] treasury, and when it is impossible [to do this under present conditions, it should be done] by bringing in the Jews."[50]

Actively attracting Jews in order to improve revenues seems to have been a very successful policy. First, the Jewish population grew rapidly. In 1756 there were only sixteen Jewish-owned houses in Szawle, whereas the 1775 census recorded 687 Jews in the community.[51] But much more importantly for the Radziwiłłs, their annual revenues from the *ekonomia* jumped from around 28,000 złoty in the early 1740s to almost 290,000 złoty some twenty years later.[52] More than a quarter of this growth came from Jews; the lease on *propinacja* and related incomes, which had brought in 600 złoty in the early 1740s (when there were no Jews on the *ekonomia*), was worth more than 67,000 złoty in the early 1760s, when the leases were almost exclusively held by Jews.[53] Renewed Jewish settlement had clearly brought much greater incomes.

For their part, Jews seem to have understood the situation on the estates, and sometimes even petitioned the Radziwiłłs for permission to settle on family land.[54] When the Jews of Kowno were expelled by the town council in 1753, they appealed to one of Michał Kazimierz Radziwiłł's local administrators, asking that that the family establish an enclave (*jurydyka*) in the town so that they could remain there. Radziwiłł agreed. He knew full well that the *jurydyka* (where, since it was not under municipal jurisdiction, the expulsion order had no effect) would become a center of commercial activity in Kowno and would both enrich him and make him a highly influential figure in what was an important royal town in Lithuania. Construction of homes in the Wiliampol (Vilijampolė, Lithuania) enclave began in a matter of months,[55] and soon afterwards representatives of the local Jews traveled to the family palace in Biała to thank their new lord.[56] What made this case unique was not the Radziwiłłs' support for Jews who wanted to settle in their *jurydyka* nor even the establishment of such an enclave in order to attract Jews, but the fact that the initiative came from the Jews themselves.[57] The family's policy of encouraging Jewish settlement was clearly received very favorably by those at whom it was aimed.

Another aspect of the family's drive to increase the settlement of their towns was to make living conditions there as attractive as possible. The Radziwiłłs focused their efforts on two major issues, the organization of urban life and the maintenance of urban infrastructure, especially houses.[58] Each town had its own institutions, generally a municipal council and courts, which the family largely respected, although their autonomy tended to be limited in practice, with the family or its officials able to intervene at will.[59] To encourage Jews to settle, they were permitted to set up parallel institutions of their own, principally a *kahal* and a rabbinical court.[60]

The Radziwiłłs seem to have recognized further that untrammeled tensions between non-Jewish and Jewish townspeople would tend to discourage Jews from settling. In response they freed the Jews from the jurisdiction of the municipal institutions by requiring all lawsuits between Jews and non-Jews to be adjudicated by their own (i.e., Radziwiłł) courts and not those run by the town council.[61] Making Jews and non-Jews separate but parallel groups in town, a policy standard throughout Poland-Lithuania at the time, seems to have been the sine qua non for increased Jewish settlement and was adopted by the Radziwiłłs as well as by almost every other estate owner in the Commonwealth.

The family also took pains to ensure that Jewish life on its estates had a sound legal basis. When new Jewish communities were founded, as in Człuchów in the 1720s and Żagory in the 1750s, the family issued special regulations governing the legal status and living conditions of the Jewish newcomers.[62] In the case of Jewish communities that had previously been issued foundational privileges, the Radziwiłłs gave the documents further validity, either by issuing official confirmations or by having them copied into the local inventory for future reference.[63] Building a synagogue, another crucial means of ensuring Jewish settlement in a town, required a license from the local bishop, who was not always cooperative. The lord would intervene if necessary to make sure that the local Jewish community received the necessary approval from the clerical authorities.[64]

Improving the housing stock was another fundamental aspect of the family's settlement policy. They often issued proclamations to their towns stressing the importance of restoring houses destroyed by war or fire and replacing "shacks" (Polish, chałupy—generally small, poorly built wooden structures) with brick buildings.[65] These instructions applied to all urban residents irrespective of religion, but the Jews did not really need to be told. Improving their housing conditions was an important aspect of their urban culture, and they greatly preferred proper houses to shacks. For instance, of the 200 properties owned by the Jews of Słuck in 1712, only 36 (18 percent) were shacks; in contrast, among the non-Jews, shacks accounted for 76 percent of residential buildings (448 shacks and 139 houses).[66] In Krzyczew the Jews owned 49 of the 84 houses in the town (58 percent) but only 16 of the 182 shacks (9 percent).[67] As we have seen, rebuilding houses was an important way for Jews to improve their standing in town, which certainly goes a long way toward explaining these figures.[68] Another explanation can probably be found in the Radziwiłł's policy of encouraging Jewish settlement by allowing Jews to live in the better-developed, central parts of its towns rather than in the underdeveloped suburbs, where shacks abounded.[69]

To make Jewish life in their towns easier, the Radziwiłłs often adapted the Jews' feudal obligations in order to take into account needs that were different from those of their non-Jewish neighbors. A crucial issue was an exemption from corvée labor. This exemption was standard on the estates and included a release for Jews not only from agricultural work but also from the hated duty of delivering mail.[70] In exchange the Jews often paid the family a higher *czynsz* than the Christian townspeople. In Mir, for example, Christians were taxed at four and a half złoty per lot in the market square and three per regular lot in the town. About the Jews Radziwiłł declared, "The Jews who are exempt from delivering mail and from corvée labor [pay] . . . twelve złoty per lot in the market square and eight złoty per regular lot."[71] In Nowy Świerżeń, the differences were even greater: one and a half złoty in the market square and one złoty elsewhere in the town for Christians, compared with eight złoty in both the market square and the rest of the town for the Jews. The reason for the difference was the same, an exemption from delivering letters and doing corvée labor.[72] In Biała, Christians paid one złoty per lot, while the Jews paid one and a third; in addition, Jews were required to pay one red złoty (worth eighteen regular złoty) per house in the market square.[73] In Lebiedziew the payment that the Jews made in exchange for their exemption from corvée labor was not included in the *czynsz* but was collected separately.[74]

These high taxes should not be regarded as a form of anti-Jewish discrimination or extortion. They were levied in exchange for release from labor duties. In fact, Jews may well have derived additional benefit from them because they gave the Radziwiłłs added incentive, in the form of much greater tax revenue, to encourage Jewish settlement.[75]

The Jews' obligations to the towns where they lived, such as nighttime guard duty to protect against fire and theft, participation in urban defense, and repairing infrastructure, were not automatically commuted. Unless the *kahal* reached a separate agreement with the municipal council regarding the substitution of a monetary payment for these duties, the Jews were required to fulfill these obligations and did so in many places.[76]

The Radziwiłł's settlement policy also had some more problematic aspects for their Jewish subjects. Mobility became an issue. The flip side of bringing more Jews to settle the estates was ensuring that those who were already there did not leave. Like many other magnate families, the Radziwiłłs frequently instructed their administrators to stop Jews moving to other towns, especially outside the estate; they were also required to make every effort to bring back any who did try to leave.[77] On the other hand, there were almost no restrictions on non-Jewish townspeople moving from place to place,[78] which was perhaps a sign that Jewish presence in the towns was more important to their lords than that of their non-Jewish neighbors.[79] That said, there are no signs that the Jews on the estates found these restrictions excessively burdensome.

Just how successful was the Radziwiłłs' policy on Jewish settlement? To answer this we need to determine the Jews' role in the overall process of estate settlement. Returning to the data from nine towns on the estate presented in Tables 1.1 and 1.2, we see that from the start of the eighteenth century until the 1760s, these towns grew by a total of 697 houses, 371 of which were Jewish-owned. Though they made up at most about a quarter of the urban population, Jews accounted for more than half of its total growth in the period examined here. This is a reliable measure of the Radziwiłłs' success in encouraging, not to say preferring, Jewish settlement in the towns on their Lithuanian estates.

It might be argued that the growth in the Jewish population was caused by natural increase or some other factor external to the estates rather than by the family's settlement policy. One way of assessing the relative importance of natural increase and settlement is to compare Jewish population growth in the Radziwiłłs' towns with that in similar localities not administered by the family. The natural increase of the Jewish population was more or less uniform across Lithuania, so its effects would have been comparable in both types of town. Any differences in the growth of the Jewish population must have been the result of settlement policy alone.

A comparison of this kind can be made of the rate of Jewish settlement on the Radziwiłł estates with that on the neighboring Neuburg estates, which had been transferred to German princes in the late seventeenth century and were restored to the Radziwiłłs only in 1731. Because the administrative methods of the foreign princes and their local agents were not based on the Radziwiłłs' kind of deliberate and relatively efficient economic policy, juxtaposing the data from the two types of town gives a clear indication of the impact of the family's settlement policy.[80]

Data are available for Jewish settlement in eight towns on the Neuburg estates in the late seventeenth century and in the 1760s. During the period under discussion, the number of Jewish-owned houses in these towns rose from 280 to 569, i.e., a growth of 100 percent. This is considerably less than the rate of growth on the Radziwiłł estates. In the nine Radziwiłł towns examined above, the number of properties owned by Jews grew by 204 percent. Clearly the Jewish population on the Radziwiłł estates had grown much more rapidly than that on the Neuburg estates. This is conclusive evidence that natural increase was not the major factor; it was the family's settlement policy that played the key role in encouraging such substantial, sustained Jewish population growth.[81]

As a final point here, it is worth noting that the dramatic increase in the number of Jews on the Radziwiłł estates in the first half of the eighteenth century coincided with an equally dramatic growth in the family's status and power in the Commonwealth. The Radziwiłłs' rise to the first rank of the magnates was the result of the ever greater sums of money they were able to spend on improving their social and political standing. They had the resources to do so because they had made their estates much more profitable. Since they had invited Jewish settlement for the significant economic benefits it brought them, the Radziwiłłs' policy towards the Jews should thus be seen as contributing to their rise to power.

The nature and significance of this contribution will become clearer in the various chapters of this study as we examine the roles played by Jews in the estate economy and the ways they helped the Radziwiłł revenues grow.

Jews and Jewish Communities in the Urban Economy

The Jews on the Radziwiłł latifundium, and throughout the Polish-Lithuanian Commonwealth, lived mainly in towns, where they were encouraged to settle in order to fill a range of functions in the economy. The development of Jewish life there needs then to be understood in the context of the urban economy as a whole. It is crucial to identify how the Jews fitted into the towns' economic life, what their roles were in wealth creation, and the ways in which they contributed to the family's revenues.[1]

This contribution was both direct and indirect. Most directly, the Radziwiłłs regarded Jews as moneyed individuals who could be taxed, both individually and through the Jewish communities to which they belonged.[2] Since these bodies were the legal representatives of all the Jews in a particular town and its surroundings, they too had important economic functions to play, particularly in the collection of taxes.[3] This turned them into seemingly bottomless sources of income for the estate administration, which could impose on the communities a whole range of levies, old and new, as a way of further increasing its revenues from Jews.

On the indirect level, what attracted the Radziwiłłs was not so much the Jews' capital as their economic activity, especially in trade. Its value for them was twofold: first, it generated significant revenues in the form of customs charges,[4] and second, it created more wealth for the Radziwiłłs to tax.

Thus it was that the Jews' economic dynamism not only led to their being encouraged to settle on the Radziwiłł lands but also allowed them to entrench themselves in their economy. They soon become an integral part of estate society, too, and so subject to the needs and orders of the administration. The way they lived could not but be affected. So if we want to understand the full implications of Jewish settlement on the estates, we also need to examine the ways it caused Jewish society to change and develop.

The discussion that follows begins by showing how the Jews' economic activity in the Radziwiłł towns fitted into the estate economy. It then looks at the ways urban Jews contributed to estate incomes by analyzing both the direct levies and the indirect taxation they paid. Finally, it examines the Jewish communities not only as subjects of taxation but also as part of the administrative system of the Radziwiłł latifundium in Lithuania, showing how these roles helped shape Jewish society in new ways during the eighteenth century.

JEWS IN THE URBAN ECONOMY

Jews lived in various types of settlement. Some made their lives in the major urban centers such as Słuck, but the vast majority lived in smaller towns (known by Jews as *shtetlach*).[5] There were also groups of Jews living in the Radziwiłłs' *jurydyki* and in the Jewish communities in those royal towns where the *starosta* was a Radziwiłł. Unfortunately, the surviving sources are too fragmentary to allow a comprehensive comparison of the Jews' economic roles in all of these places.

It is possible, however, to compare the situation in what were the two most common forms of Jewish settlement on the estates - the larger and the smaller town.[6] The first will be represented here by Słuck, the second by the nearby small town of Kopyl. There is an inventory of these towns from 1750 that provides remarkably full details of both the Christian and Jewish populations[7] and so allows us to reconstruct the occupational profiles of the two groups and see how they fitted into the urban economy where they lived.[8]

Słuck

Słuck was one of the biggest towns in what is today Belarus, and its market served the entire region.[9] Its large population and commercial activity led to a degree of occupational specialization not found in the smaller towns; a large number of craftsmen lived and worked there, offering an impressive range of services.[10] In addition, the Radziwiłłs had a palace in Słuck; Hieronim Florian Radziwiłł held court there on a permanent basis and used the town to garrison his private army. This gave a huge boost to urban consumption and ensured that there was always an extremely diverse selection of merchandise on the local market.[11]

In 1750, Słuck had a total population of 4,888, of whom 1,593 (33 percent) were Jews. There were 1,287 heads of household, 367 (31 percent) of

whom were Jewish.[12] Economic activity was divided into five main categories: trade, crafts, *propinacja* (the income from the town owner's monopoly
on the production and sale of alcohol), services,[13] and agriculture.[14] The
indigent and beggars were also counted: there were 65 of these, of whom
18 (28 percent) were Jews. Although *propinacja* was both a craft (alcohol
production) and a branch of trade (alcohol sales), Radziwiłł, like all town-
owners, treated it as a single category, leasing out his rights to the income it
generated to a third party, usually a Jewish businessman.

Table 2.1 shows the occupational distribution in Słuck in 1750.

These data do not take into account the fact that many Jews had more
than one occupation. Craftsmen often did some selling on the side and
merchants included alcohol among the other things they traded. There is
no way to estimate how many Jews did more than one job and what impact
this might have had on the urban economy. Nonetheless, it would seem reasonable to assume that this phenomenon was widespread enough to affect
all the occupational categories and so does not fundamentally change the
picture obtained from the data on primary occupations.

Jews were particularly prominent in trade and *propinacja*, in both cases
making up more than 75 percent of all those working in those fields. Trade
was not seen as a single category. The inventory distinguishes a number of
different types of Jewish merchant, with most designated as either a tradesman (*handlujący*) or a stall owner (*kramarz*). The practical difference between the two is not clear.[15]

In addition, a fairly large number of Jews worked as brokers (*meklerzy*),
bringing customers to merchants and receiving a percentage for each sale
they arranged.[16] The majority of Christian merchants were peddlers, of
whom twenty-seven—63 percent of the total—were female (*przekupki*).[17]
The others, fourteen in all, enjoyed the title of merchant (*kupiec*), presumably because they were richer and had a higher status. Apparently, then, in

Table 2.1. Occupational Distribution of Household Heads in Słuck, 1750

Group	Trade	Crafts	Propinacja	Services	Agriculture	Indigent	Total
Jews	141	92	58	88	—	18	397
Non-Jews	41	617	16	155	14	47	890
Total	182	709	74	243	14	65	1,287
% Jews	77%	13%	78%	36%	—	28%	31%

SOURCE: AR XXV, 3837

Christian society trade was not a popular profession. In fact, it was mostly single women, presumably widows, who made their living from it, perhaps because they had no other source of income. In contrast, more than a third of the Jews worked in commerce, accounting for the vast majority of the town's tradesmen.[18]

Jews also dominated the production and sale of alcoholic beverages. Having Jews sell agricultural produce in the form of alcohol solved a major marketing problem for the estate owners, and made this a highly significant sector of the economy. Of the Jews working in *propinacja*, more than 90 percent were liquor sellers or concession holders who sold alcohol. Only two of the sixteen Christians in *propinacja* worked in sales; the rest were engaged in production. These numbers reflect the overall division of economic activity in the town: most skilled craftsmen were Christians, most merchants Jews.

As the predominant tradesmen and liquor sellers, Jews played a crucial role in sustaining and developing the estate's network of markets.[19] Raw materials from the estates, mostly agricultural produce of various types, were typically sold to Jewish merchants who traded them on. In addition, goods and materials from outside the estates would be brought in by Jewish businessmen for sale locally. It was, therefore, the Jewish merchants who had the key function of providing market access for all estate inhabitants.

The Jews' role in *propinacja* only added to their importance because the grain grown on the estate was sold mostly in the form of alcohol. In fact, the *propinacja* market helped the estate owner increase his revenues from his subjects still further. When peasants came into town to sell their surplus produce, they would normally spent at least some of their takings at the tavern. This money too became part of the income from *propinacja* and, as such, went straight into the lord's pocket.[20] So, when it came to the sale of agricultural produce, the Jewish merchants were key figures; and since the income they created formed the basis of estate revenues, they had special importance for the magnate and his administration.

In the service professions in Słuck, Jews stood out as teachers. Twenty-two—one quarter—of all the Jews in these occupations were teachers. Nine of the town's twenty-five teamsters were Jews. The one physician and all six barber-surgeons in Słuck were also members of the Jewish community.[21]

Of the Christians in town forty-three served as soldiers in the Radziwiłłs' private army.[22] Only Christians worked in agriculture because Jews were prevented from receiving agricultural land as part of their urban rights.[23] The small number of Christian farmers in the inventory suggests that for most townspeople agriculture was just a secondary occupation, a way to supplement their income from traditional urban occupations.[24]

Ninety-two Jews—almost a quarter of the heads of household—were craftsmen, accounting for 13 percent of all the craftsmen in the town.[25] The distribution of Jewish and non-Jewish craftsmen is shown in Table 2.2.

The largest concentration of Jewish craftsmen was in those occupations that served the Jewish community's religious needs—particularly as regards *kashrut* and *sha'atnez* (the laws on slaughter and the ritual purity of food, and the prohibition on combining wool and linen in a single garment). More than half of the Jewish craftsmen were thus tailors, bakers, and ritual slaughterers.[26] Beyond this, Jews tended to choose occupations in which Christians either did not work at all (silversmiths and haberdashers) or were relatively few (printers, glaziers, and engravers). The Jewish candlemaker and painter were the only Jewish craftsmen to work in fields with a large number of Christians.[27]

Table 2.2. Jewish Craftsmen in Słuck by Profession, 1750

Craft	Jews	Non-Jews	Total
Tailor	21	25	46
Baker	20	22	42
Butcher	13	11	24
Haberdasher	11	—	11
Silversmith	8	—	8
Glazier	5	1	6
Bristlemaker	3	—	3
Engraver	2	1	3
Bronzesmith	2	4	6
Painter	1	13	14
Candlemaker	1	11	12
Gunpowder Manufacturer	1	—	1
Printer	1	1	2
Bookbinder	1	—	1
Total	92	89	181

SOURCE: AR XXV, 3837

Jews who had to work in a particular trade (for religious reasons, for example) were usually admitted to the local non-Jewish guild for a special fee and so did not form a separate organization.[28] This arrangement did not always reduce the tensions between Christian and Jewish craftsmen. The Christian butchers in Słuck complained again and again about the large number of Jewish competitors they faced, asking that a quota be imposed on them.[29] In other cases Jews and Christians did manage to coexist. In 1770 "the entire guild of tailors, Christians and Jews," made a joint appeal to the estate management to receive payment for work they had done for the Radziwiłł private army.[30] The only evidence hinting at the possible existence of a Jewish guild in Słuck is an undated complaint, perhaps from earlier in the century, in which two Christian haberdashers alleged that their Jewish competitors had interfered with their work and even tried to force them out of town. Though the document does not explicitly mention a specifically Jewish body, such organized activity against competitors was typical of guilds.[31]

Kopyl

Kopyl was a small town of just 189 houses in 1750. Its total population was 1,086, which included 353 Jews (33 percent). Its size and location approximately midway between Słuck and Nieśwież made Kopyl a local center in a heavily agricultural region. It is reasonable to assume that its economic structure was typical for the smaller towns on the Radziwiłł estates in Lithuania.

There were 367 heads of household in Kopyl, of whom 90 (25 percent) were Jews. Their occupational distribution is shown in Table 2.3.

The data present a similar pattern to Słuck. In fact, here, the Jews' dominance of commerce was absolute; there was not even one non-Jewish mer-

Table 2.3. Occupational Distribution of Household Heads in Kopyl, 1750

Group	Trade	Crafts	Propinacja	Services	Agriculture	Indigent	Total
Jews	28	16	23	17	—	6	90
Non-Jews*	—	227	7	16	1	10	277
Total	28	243	30	33	1	16	367
% Jews	100%	7%	77%	52%	—	38%	25%

SOURCES: AR XXV, 3837; AR XXV, 3838.
* The occupations of 16 Christians are not listed.

chant in the town. In the field of *propinacja*, too, none of the Christians worked in sales; they were all in production. The proportion of Jews in the services was higher than in Słuck, presumably because there were no soldiers in Kopyl.[32] Among the indigent the percentage of Jews was higher, which might reflect the limited range of economic options open to poor Jews in small towns as compared to poor Christians, who could always find work as agricultural day laborers.[33] Jews made up a smaller proportion of the crafts-men than in Słuck (7 percent in Kopyl vs. 13 percent in Słuck), perhaps because their control of commerce made trade more attractive for them.

The distribution of Kopyl's Jewish craftsmen by occupation is shown in Table 2.4

Though Kopyl's small size meant that the range of crafts was more lim-ited than in Słuck, there was still a consistent division of labor between Jews and Christians. In fact, in some of the crafts at which the Jews worked, including some of the occupations that they had to follow for religious rea-sons, there was no competition with Christians at all. It was only in tailor-ing that Jews formed a tiny minority. Ninety percent of Christian craftsmen in Kopyl worked in textile-related trades (weavers, spinners, and tailors) while only two Jews did, and that was clearly so that they could provide clothes without fear of *sha'atnez*. It would seem that the small-town setting made it much easier for Jewish and Christian craftsmen to keep their oc-cupations separate.

The most significant difference between the occupational patterns of the Jews in Kopyl and Słuck was in the field of *propinacja*. Alcohol sales pro-vided a living for 15 percent of Jewish household heads in Słuck but 26 per-cent in Kopyl, suggesting that it was a more important source of income

Table 2.4. Jewish Craftsmen in Kopyl by Profession

Craft	Jews	Non-Jews	Total
Butcher	6	—	6
Silversmith	4	—	4
Baker	2	—	2
Tailor	2	98	100
Glazier	1	1	2
Furrier	1	—	1
Total	16	99	115

SOURCE: AR XXV, 3837

for Jews in the smaller towns. The fact that a quarter of the Jews of Kopyl made their living from *propinacja*, a key component of estate revenues, suggests that their involvement in this field was an important incentive for the Radziwiłłs to have them settle in their smaller towns.[34]

To summarize: in the urban economy of the Radziwiłłs' estates, Jews dominated commerce, with a only relatively small percentage working in crafts. While some Jews worked in those crafts in which there was a religious need for them, others chose branches in which competition with the non-Jews would be limited. The less-developed economies of the small towns, where there were fewer craftsmen, allowed for an almost complete separation between Jews and non-Jews. The small number of Jewish craftsmen in general indicates their low status among Lithuanian Jewry at the time and perhaps also the magnates' disdain for this kind of occupation.[35]

More significant was that most of Słuck's merchants, especially at the middle and lower levels, and all of those in Kopyl were Jews.[36] They clearly formed the backbone of the local market, which both served (and so connected) all the economic actors on the estate, and linked town to countryside.[37] One market particularly dominated by Jews was that in agricultural produce sold in the form of alcohol—by means of *propinacja*, a monopoly of fundamental significance for the estate owner's income.[38] The Jews' success in creating wealth from these markets made them key players not only in the urban economy but also in the estate economy as a whole and was undoubtedly one of the reasons that prompted the Radziwiłłs to bring them to their towns in the first place.

Once settled there, the Jews formed a tax base that the Radziwiłł family had an interest in exploiting. It is to how it did so that we will now turn.

DIRECT TAXATION

The most common levy on the Radziwiłł estates in the eighteenth century was the *czynsz*, a municipal property tax assessed on each house. It was collected from Jews by the *kahal*, the Jewish community council—and at a rate higher than for non-Jewish townspeople.[39] This is often interpreted as exploitation by the estate owners, though that was not always the case: Jews could be assessed at a higher rate for a number of reasons: first, because, as we have seen, they were exempt from some labor obligations and second because non-Jewish townspeople already paid higher taxes in the form of an additional *czynsz* on the agricultural lands they received from the town. In fact, when these other payments are taken into account, it becomes clear that direct revenues from the Jews in the towns were proportionately less than those from the rest of the population (Table 2.5).[40]

In 1729, Jews owned 30 percent of all the houses in Biała, but the income they brought the Radziwiłłs in direct taxation amounted to only 24 percent of the total from the town. In Mir in 1750 the discrepancy was even greater: Jews owned 31 percent of all the houses but paid only 23 percent of the total income from direct taxation.

Of course, this was not the whole picture. There was a range of other direct taxes aimed at increasing revenue from Jews that estate owners could impose. Because the majority of merchants were Jewish, it was they who paid most of the levies on market stalls (in Mir this fee was included in the *czynsz* but elsewhere was often assessed separately). Jewish craftsmen, especially kosher butchers, paid license fees to the estate administration that were sometimes more than double those paid by their non-Jewish counterparts.[41] Finally, if the need arose, the Radziwiłłs could impose on the Jews special payments without warning or explanation.[42] Karol Stanisław Radziwiłł ("Panie Kochanku") imposed such a levy on the Jews in all his communities in Lithuania and Poland in May 1764, ordering them to pay the huge sum of 138,500 złoty within three weeks.[43] No explanation was given, but apparently it was in connection with his military preparations following the royal election of that year.[44]

Table 2.5. Jewish Participation in Estate Income from Towns

	Biala (1729)	Mir (1750)
Total Income from *Czynsz*	983 zł., 20 gr.	2,195 zł.
Czynsz from Jews' Houses	235 zł.	460 zł., 18 gr.
Czynsz from Christians' Houses	135 zł., 20 gr.	692 zł., 1gr.
Czynsz from Agricultural Land	613 zł.	1,002 zł., 11 gr.
Other Payments*	—	40 zł.
Czynsz Paid by Jews as a Proportion of Total Income	24%	23%
Houses Owned by Jews as a Proportion of all Houses in Town	30%	31%

SOURCES: AR XXV, 125; AR XXV, 2457/1.
* This was a fee collected from market stalls and is therefore considered in the calculation here as part of the taxes paid by Jews.

INCOME FROM THE COMMUNITIES

Aside from individual Jews, the Jewish communities—those institutions that represented all the Jews in a town and its surroundings—were also a crucial source of income. These were legally recognized bodies with rights and obligations defined in special community privileges. Like the town councils, to which they were very similar, the Jewish communities were autonomous bodies charged with the administration of local society, in this case Jewish.[45] In practice, however, the financial needs of the estate owners often led them to limit the autonomy of the communities and make the *kehillot* and the town councils subject to their orders.[46] When it came to money, the community budgets, which were often quite large, were a tempting target for an estate owner in need of extra income. The Radziwiłłs were no exception.

One strategy they adopted was to force a community to exchange money at a rate more favorable than they could find in the market.[47] Another was to make the communities buy goods or agricultural products such as salt, glass, field crops, mead, and even vegetables and small animals from their farms (*folwarki*) at price they set themselves.[48] These were not always higher than the going rates, but gave the Radziwiłłs an easy market for theirs goods and left the Jews with the problems and costs of doing the selling. When the urban market was in a slump, these forced sales effectively transferred the losses onto the local community.[49]

In those situations, the communities could find themselves stuck with goods that were hard to sell. Their solution was to divide them among the community members, so that everyone would have to bear a part of the loss. Sometimes a larger community would compel dependent smaller communities to buy some of the goods at high prices. This can be seen in a complaint by the small community in Nowy Świerżeń against the major Nieśwież *kahal*: "This *kahal*, in accordance with the will and instruction of His Highness the Gracious Lord, distributed grain to the Jews [here], but forced them [to buy it] not at the marked price of eight złoty—but for nine złoty."[50]

Yet another source of income for the estate owner was the license fee paid by the Jewish communities when they appointed rabbis. In exchange for this payment the rabbi received from the magnate a letter of appointment spelling out his powers and some of his rights in the community, usually for a period of three years.[51] The sums charged for these licenses could be extremely high: Starobin (a small community near Słuck with thirty-four Jewish homes) paid 400 złoty in 1760; Kopyl and Nowy Świerżeń paid 50 czerwony złoty (900 złoty); and Nieśwież paid 300 czerwony złoty (5,400 złoty).[52] In 1760 the Słuck community appointed a rabbi for life, rather than for a limited period as was the usual practice; they paid Radziwiłł 1,000 czerwony złoty (18,000 złoty) for the license.[53]

The Radziwiłłs, keen to maximize their income, kept a close eye on rabbinical affairs in their communities, and when a rabbinate fell vacant they urged the *kahal* to appoint a new candidate as quickly as possible.[54] The Jews on the other hand were not always in a rush to pay the fee and appoint a new rabbi. When they acted in this way, they received warnings from the estate administration and even punishments for non-compliance.[55] In order to cover the costs of the license fees the Jewish communities either demanded sizable sums of money from successful applicants or left them to pay for it themselves.[56]

These different levies were undoubtedly a burden on the communities, but did have a positive side. Since the Radziwiłłs were interested in keeping their Jewish communities wealthy in order to go on extracting money from them, they also had a stake in protecting them in difficult times. For example, when the peasants' uprising in eastern Belarus was put down in 1744, Hieronim Florian Radziwiłł ordered all those involved in destroying synagogues to compensate the local Jewish communities so the rebuilding costs would not bankrupt them.[57]

In another instance, the Jews of Słuck requested and received from Radziwiłł the right to representation on the town committee that determined excise taxes to ensure that they would not be overcharged.[58] In cases where Jewish communities had difficulty paying their poll tax assessments to the state, the Radziwiłłs, like other magnate families, would intervene with the treasury on their behalf.[59] Finally, a community that fell into debt and could not meet its obligations to the estate administration could appeal directly to Radziwiłł for help, which was often forthcoming.[60]

COMMUNITY BUDGETS

The interest that the Radziwiłł administration showed in the communities' economic activity is best demonstrated through the ways it dealt with their budgets. Jewish communities had to present their accounts for review once or even twice a year.[61] After the administration's audit, any community leader who had spent money in a way that appeared unjustified had to pay it back.[62] The Radziwiłł administration even took an interest in the ways payments were made from the community chest (the funds were generally kept in a locked box in the *kahal* office). In Słuck for instance it issued regulations stating who was responsible for taking money out of the chest and under what circumstances it could be opened.[63]

The estate owners were also concerned that the communities' revenues, especially from the *kropka* (a value-added tax on the sale of meat and other transactions), remain high, and so issued orders that all community taxes were be paid on time and in full.[64] Of course the goal was not simply to strengthen the kahal, but to ensure that it would be able to continue contributing to the family's revenues. Thus when the administration felt that it could make a greater profit by taking the *kropka* from the *kahal* and transferring it to the general *arendarze* or other Jewish businessmen who worked directly for them, it did not hesitate to do so.[65]

A particular problem for the economic health of Jewish communities throughout the Polish-Lithuanian Commonwealth was their heavy debt burden. How it had developed is not entirely clear. Before 1648, many communities took loans from nobles and other wealthy individuals for investment purposes. Later in the seventeenth century, however, the nature of the loans changed, and they seem often to have been taken to finance capital projects, such as building synagogues. The loans were known as *widerkaf,* standing loans on which a low rate of simple interest was charged and for which a piece of communal real estate (often the synagogue) was put up as security.[66]

With such cheap loans available, it was not surprising that communities began to take on more and more debt until they had difficulty making even the annual interest payments. In 1732–33, for example, the Słuck community's debts totaled 174,600 złoty, on which the annual payments were 17,500 złoty[67]—this at a time when the community's entire annual income was only 26,000 złoty.[68] The solution seemed obvious: that same year, the community took out yet another loan in order to balance its budget![69] Other reasons for taking out loans might include the need to pay the poll tax when money was short or unforeseen expenses such as bailing out *arendarze* who had been jailed for nonpayment of debts (which the communities called, "redemption of captives").[70]

The *widerkaf* loans were the most widespread form of connection between Jews and the Roman Catholic Church in Poland-Lithuania. Some loans were taken directly by the communities from church institutions, which, despite all the theological objections to doing business with Jews, seem to have viewed the Jewish bodies as a solid investment opportunity. Others developed indirectly. Many nobles, including the Radziwiłłs, gave money to monks and nuns to pray for their souls after death in the belief that doing so would assure them a place in Heaven.[71] Instead of handing over the money directly to the monasteries or convents, however, they gave it to the Jewish communities as a *widerkaf*, stipulating that the annual interest be paid directly to the church.[72] Upon a noble's death, the capital would often also be transferred to the church institutions, further increasing the communities' debt to them. Thus by the mid-eighteenth century there were strong economic ties between the Jewish communities and the Roman Catholic Church, a situation that often provided the communities added protection since their ecclesiastical creditors were unwilling to harm their profitability.

As the debt burden increased, the communities' freedom to take on these loans became more limited. The Radziwiłłs did not want their Jewish communities to spiral into debt and default on their obligations and so insisted that they stop taking out loans without express permission to do so. Nonetheless the family did remain willing to help its communities if they ran into serious problems making their annual payments.[73]

THE COMMUNITIES' ROLES
IN ESTATE ADMINISTRATION

Participating in estate administration was something quite new for the communities in the eighteenth century. Although they had always been responsible to the non-Jewish authorities for collecting taxes from the Jews, little else had been demanded of them. Now the importance of the Jews in the estate economy meant that the Radziwiłłs, like the other magnate families, were interested in supervising the Jews' economic activity as closely as they could. The *kahal* was their most efficient tool.

There was no evading orders given to a community council by the estate owner or his administration. Sometimes these could be quite invasive: The Radziwiłłs or their administrators might even intervene directly in community elections to put their own (Jewish) candidates on community councils.[74] For the most part however, their instructions were administrative in nature. For example, when Michał Kazimierz Radziwiłł wanted to limit the sale of poisons in his towns, he told the Jewish communities of Nieśwież and Mir to appoint one merchant who would have the sole right to deal in these substances.[75]

In another case Ludwik Szylling, Hieronim Florian Radziwiłł's administrator, ordered the Słuck community council to ensure that the claims for compensation submitted by Jewish merchants whose goods had been damaged in the fire of 1745 were honest. The results of this action were revealing. Szylling and his noble lord were surprised by the number of merchants who took back their claims under pressure from the *kahal*—a clear sign that the community council was representing the interests of the estate administration above those of the Jewish merchants.[76] In a few cases Radziwiłł even ordered the local *kahal* to arrest a Jew who owed him money and to confiscate the prisoner's property. Here, the community council was clearly torn between its desire to protect its people and its need to obey its lord. Realizing this, Radziwiłł added a direct threat to the members of the *kahal* if they did not comply, a reminder that their first duty was to him.[77]

The rabbi too had administrative tasks to fulfill for the estate management. As Radziwiłł saw it, the rabbi's main function was as judge and head of the rabbinic court. This is emphasized in the letters of appointment and licenses (*konsensy*) given to rabbis taking up their posts.[78] In practice, this meant that the estate owner could take advantage of the rabbi's authority for his own administrative ends. When Radziwiłł wanted to verify the accounts of one of his *arendarze*, he might order him to deliver his books to the rabbi for examination.[79] Similarly, when Radziwiłł suspected an *arendarz* of bribery and counterfeiting, he could order the rabbi to choose another judge and investigate the matter together.[80]

Such commissions of inquiry were not unusual on the Radziwiłł estates. Often a Jew, usually an *arendarz*, would be accused of irregularities, and the estate owner would then appoint a commission comprising the local rabbi plus three to five other Jews to investigate.[81] These commissions were authorized to summon non-Jewish witnesses and even to interrogate them as suspects if need be.[82]

On the Radziwiłł estates, as elsewhere in Poland-Lithuania, each Jewish community was held collectively responsible for the actions of any one of its members. As a result, the crimes and misdemeanors of any individual Jew could be visited on any other, or, more commonly, on the community as a whole. In many cases the *kahal* had to sign a bond of surety for the economic activity of wealthy merchants or *arendarze* in their community. On other occasions the *kahal* was made responsible not only for choosing the *arendarz*, who would lease estate monopolies, but also for paying his dues should he default on them.[83] It was therefore imperative for the *kahal* to supervise Jewish economic activity as rigorously as it could.

This was by no means easy. Many wealthy Jews were unwilling to cooperate and found backing in the estate administration itself. Those subjects whom Radziwiłł felt were directly serving his economic (and other) needs enjoyed a special status, and so were released from the community's jurisdiction: the general *arendarze*, for example, were placed under the sole protection of the Radziwiłł court.[84] Others who served the family in various ways, such as a doctor or skilled craftsman, also received special status as "servant of the court" (*serwitor*) and could be granted extra-ordinary privileges, such as an exemption from community taxes.[85] For example, Michał Kazimierz Radziwiłł employed Hirsz ben Leyb (known as Hirsz Leybowicz), a coppersmith and engraver. Hirsz made engravings from portraits in the Radziwiłł family gallery and was involved in the publication of a book of these pictures.[86] Radziwiłł exempted him from having to purchase salt from the Nieśwież *kahal*, an obligation incumbent on all members of the community.[87]

The policy of removing prominent individuals from the jurisdiction of the Jewish community did not mean that the Radziwiłłs were trying to abolish the institutions of Jewish autonomy as Rosman claims the Sieniawskis and Czartoryskis were.[88] All the documentation suggests that the Radziwiłłs were actually trying to support the communities and integrate them into the administrative system of the estate, with the aim of controlling the Jewish population.[89] Although this integration was only partial and obtained mainly in the economic realm, it did significantly change the communities' authority over Jewish society. As long as the Jewish bodies served the estate administration, the Radziwiłłs supported them. However, as soon as they clashed with the lord's interests, even when they were only fulfilling roles traditional to Jewish communities, they lost their independence of action and ability to control the Jews under their purview.

Not unsurprisingly, this process caused significant tensions within Jewish society. A powerful new grouping of Jews developed whose strength was based on its connections with the estate owner. When the interests of these "new men" clashed with those of the community, it was they who enjoyed the magnate's protection, and the *kahal* had to acquiesce.[90] Many of them also tried to build a power base within the community, but the old leadership did not give in easily.[91]

Tensions were particularly high when it came to the rabbinate. Because of the high prices charged for rabbinical licenses, it was usually only wealthier Jews who could afford them.[92] The rabbinical elite opposed the granting of positions to rich men's sons just on the basis of the support they enjoyed from the noble lord, but were powerless to prevent it.[93] Thus, Jewish life on the estates experienced the creation of a new elite, whose power was derived not from scholarship and family lineage, nor even from a combination of rabbinic scholarship, lineage, and wealth, but solely from their financial status and connections with non-Jewish society.

CONCLUSION

Living on the Radziwiłł latifundia in the eighteenth century helped the Jews reach a prominence in trade almost unparalleled in Jewish history. This could not but have a significant effect not only on their economic life, but on their social structures, too.

The Jews' new economic status found expression in a clear occupational division that developed between them and their neighbors.[94] Whereas most non-Jews in the towns were craftsmen, most Jews worked in commerce and so dominated the local markets. The most prominent sector of Jewish trade, the sale of alcohol, was of particular economic importance because it strengthened the market for grain on the estate, allowing the magnate to sell the produce of his *folwark*s and to absorb any cash income his subjects made.[95] Here too there was a clear division, with the Jews working primarily in sales and the Christians in production. Among the craftsmen in the towns, the number of Jews was not particularly high, and occupational division developed in this sector too, with Jews preferring crafts in which they would not have to compete with their neighbors.

As a result, the Jews became major wealth creators for the towns, which further buttressed their position in urban society in both economic and demographic terms. This situation benefited the estate owners in three ways: it created a strong base for direct taxation; it increased indirect revenues through duties on commercial activity; and it boosted his income from grain sales (in the form of alcohol).

The Radziwiłłs collected various dues from their Jewish subjects: the income from direct *czynsz* payments made by Jews was not particularly large, but they also paid other taxes, both individually and as communities. These made up a much more substantial contribution.

Beyond that, the Jewish communities acted as administrators for the estate owners, overseeing Jewish economic activity and to an extent directing it too. It was therefore in the Radziwiłłs' best interest to support the Jewish bodies, though they had no hesitation in limiting their independence if they felt it necessary. While using the communities to keep most of the Jews in line, the magnate was willing to exempt from their jurisdiction those who played a major role in the estate economy. The result was the growth of a group of powerful Jews whose social status was based not on the traditional values of Torah study and family lineage, but on economic success and connections at court.

These developments were not accidental. They were the result of the Radziwiłłs' management policies in the eighteenth century, as a part of which Jews were given significant, not to say crucial, roles in the estate economy. Exactly what those policies were, and how they affected the Jews economically, socially, and culturally, will become clear in the chapters to come.

THREE

The Economic Institutions of the Estates

In administering their estates the Radziwiłłs had two largely interconnected goals: maximizing their income and improving their standing in Polish-Lithuanian society. Once achieved, these put them in a position to amass great political power and influence in the affairs of the Commonwealth. In the eighteenth century the family was involved in a bitter political struggle over the character of the state with their main rivals, the Czartoryski dynasty (known as "the Familia").[1] To realize their political ambitions the Radziwiłłs needed support from the mass of the nobility, and so spent huge sums of money not only on pursuing an ostentatious lifestyle, but also on giving these lesser nobles financial incentives to enter their service.[2] The money they used came to a great extent from their estates, their main source of income. It was therefore no coincidence that the meteoric rise in the family's political fortunes during the eighteenth century coincided with a dramatic increase in the revenues from their estates.

The Jews were key players in improving estate profitability for the Radziwiłłs, as for all the magnate estate owners, so any discussion of their roles in this process must begin with how the family derived its incomes. To do so, this chapter examines the economic institutions of the estates, that is, the various frameworks for economic activity, the administrative arrangements that dictated its character, and the rules governing its conduct.[3]

EXTRACTING REVENUES FROM THE MAGNATES' ESTATES

The Radziwiłł latifundium, a complex of estates in different parts of the Commonwealth, included *folwarks* (magnate-owned farms where peasants performed corvée labor) and peasant farms, as well as the villages, towns, and cities; infrastructure (roads, bridges, mills, etc.); and the estates' natural resources.[4] All these legally belonged to the Radziwiłłs and formed the basis for their income. Managing such a wide-ranging enterprise for profit was a complex business, for which the magnate estate owners developed a number of strategies. The four most common were direct management by the family, mortgaging land, leasing out estates, and leasing out monopoly rights derived from estates. The Jews' main involvement was in the last two, though all four will be discussed here.

Direct Management

When the Radziwiłłs decided to manage one of their estates directly, their first step was to deploy a staff of administrators to do the daily work. There was a clear hierarchy to the management structure. At the bottom of the pecking order was the overseer of an individual *folwark* (*podstarości*)[5]; higher was the local estate manager (*ekonom*), and at the apex of the pyramid was the person responsible for all the estates in an entire region (the *gubernator*). These officials were responsible for the smooth running of the estate economy in all its aspects. This involved organizing corvée labor by peasants, seeing that the produce got sold, collecting fees from peasants and other subjects (in money or in kind), and maintaining law and order, particularly in economic matters. Each one of these officials had a number of junior administrators under his control, each of whom was responsible for running a particular sector of the economy or a specific economic activity (perhaps the best known of these was the *pisarz prowentowy*, who managed the *folwark* accounts).[6]

The most senior administrators remained in direct contact with the Radziwiłłs, giving them the information they needed to set economic policy and implementing those policies once they were set. Since these were the only administrators with whom the family corresponded on a regular basis, the archival record contains a great deal of documentation about them, their economic roles, and their management activity. They were personally appointed by the family, and were given excellent salaries in addition to generous amounts of agricultural produce (known as *ordynaria* a form of payment in kind, common in estate administration for centuries).[7] Upon appointment a senior administrator would receive detailed instructions from his noble lord. His task was to comply with them, report back to Radziwiłł with information on the daily running of the estate, and consult with him whenever any non-routine problem arose.[8] In principle Jews could hold these positions, but in practice rarely did.[9]

The benefits of this method of management were clear. The Radziwiłłs received a steady flow of information from their estates that enabled them to determine policy and respond to changes on the ground. Costs were low because cash salaries were supplemented by payments in kind, which spared the family the trouble and risk of marketing the produce in question.[10] Maintaining direct contact had the advantage of keeping senior administrators on their toes and providing them with motivation to work efficiently.[11] There was a political bonus too: by handing out these jobs, which carried with them the *de facto* status of estate owner, the Radziwiłłs were effectively buying the support and loyalty of those middling and lower nobles who took them.[12]

There was also a significant downside. The huge extent of the estates made their direct managment a difficult and time-consuming business. The Radziwiłłs had active social and political lives to lead, yet were forced to spend a large portion of each year away from the Commonwealth's major centers visiting as many of their lands as possible, meeting with their administrators, and seeing for themselves what was going on. Regular contact with the more remote regions of the latifundium was even harder to maintain and had to be conducted by correspondence alone, which was much less efficient.

For these reasons the Radziwiłłs, like other magnate families and much of the upper nobility, would sometimes prefer to derive revenue from their estates in other ways. The most common was leasing, the partial transfer of ownership rights to land or of rights derived from ownership. First, however, we need to consider another, older method of raising money from land, the mortgage.[13]

Mortgage (Zastaw)

The *zastaw* was not strictly speaking a form of estate management but a means of raising money on the land. The creditor received the estate as a "pledge" (the primary meaning of the word *zastaw*) against the loan of an amount of money. De facto ownership rights to the property were transferred to him and he received his interest on the loan in the form of the revenues he derived from the estate. Customarily the mortgage holder would enjoy those rights only for the period stipulated in the contract, but if the loan was not repaid on time, the land would remain with him until it was paid in full. If the borrower defaulted, the land could remain in the creditor's possession permanently.[14]

Thus, unlike a modern mortgage on a house in which the borrower retains possession of the property and can lose it only in the case of default, the *zastaw* was similar to a sale because the borrower essentially lost all his rights to this property until it was bought back through repayment of the debt.

The *zastaw* had a relatively long history in Poland, where it was known from as early as the thirteenth century. It continued in use until at least the end of the early modern period, though it was often displaced by different forms of lease that developed in the sixteenth and seventeenth centuries. The Radziwiłłs made frequent use of mortgages in the eighteenth century, so at any given time various of their estates were not under their direct control.[15]

It is not always clear what motivated the family to mortgage its lands in this way. Sometimes it required a large sum of money urgently, and the *zastaw* was the best way of raising quick revenue.[16] It is also possible that mortgaging an estate was done for political purposes, such as cementing an alliance with a local noble family. The advantages of the zastaw were therefore threefold: it brought immediate income; it absolved the family of having to manage the estate; and it served to build up a bloc of political supporters.

The zastaw was not used extensively for a number of reasons. First, there was a risk that it might not be possible to repay the loan on schedule, which meant that the creditor would take permanent possession of the estate.[17] Second, during the period of the mortgage, the family lost all control over the lands. The mortgage holder had total freedom of action in managing them: He could appoint his own people to administrative positions and demand from his subjects taxes and levies at levels higher than sound management would dictate.[18] The political aspect could also be problematic. The Radziwiłłs wanted the local nobility to be dependent on them, or at least to support them politically. Mortgaging an estate could have the opposite effect however. Having taken the mortgage, the Radziwiłłs found themselves indebted to a lesser nobleman who now controlled a sizeable estate and so owed them nothing by way of support.[19] Little wonder, then, that the *zastaw* proved a much less popular option than the lease.

Leasing Estates (Dzierżawa)

Dzierżawa, the leasing of entire estates, grew out of the *zastaw* mortgage system during the sixteenth century, developing a number of characteristics all its own.[20] Though the leaseholder (*dzierżawca*) managed the estate exactly as if he were a mortgage holder, formal rights of ownership remained with the lessor (in our case, the Radziwiłłs).[21] Second, while the leaseholder had rights to all the revenues from the estate during the period of the contract, when the lease expired, the property automatically reverted to its original owner. The estate lease seems to have been particularly popular during the sixteenth and first half of the seventeenth century, especially in the period of the colonization of Ukraine, since it was an excellent way of developing new lands.

The reason for this lay in the structure of the lease itself. The initial payment that the leaseholder made on signing the contract for the lease was not returned to him as a lump sum when it expired, as was the case with a mortgage. Instead, the leaseholder made back his money incrementally over the life of the contract from the revenues that the estate brought in.

The price of the leasehold was fixed on the basis of an inventory, specially drawn up before the lease was signed. It formed a record of all the property on the estate, the inhabitants, and the payments they were supposed to make in cash and in kind. From it were calculated the revenues that the estate was supposed to bring in and these were stipulated in the contract. Any income that the leaseholder made beyond the amounts stated in the contract remained with him as his profit on the deal.[22] This arrangement was thought to give the leaseholder every incentive to make the working of the estate more efficient in order to increase its revenues and so his profits.[23]

By the eighteenth century the flaws in this reasoning had become clear. Rather than leading to greater efficiency and profitability, the estate leases had encouraged overexploitation by leaseholders, who did whatever they could to maximize their short-term profit, often at the expense of long-term development.[24] To avoid this problem, estate leases in the eighteenth century stipulated explicitly that any income beyond the amount given in the inventory belonged not to the leaseholder but to the owner.[25] This change removed the profit motive from the leaseholds, making them a form of fixed income. The leaseholder became less an independent economic agent and more an administrator, working on behalf of the owner often with quite limited freedom of action. In return for the decrease in profitability, the owner was more willing than he had been previously to bear any losses that might accrue.[26]

Another way of limiting overexploitation by leaseholders was to set up commissions at the termination of each lease to examine the state of the property. These also heard subjects' complaints against the leaseholder, from whom (theoretically, at least) the owner could demand compensation for any unreasonable damage.[27]

The upshot of this development was that the estate leases as they developed on the Radziwiłł estates in the eighteenth century gave the family an estate administrator at almost no cost. It received its income according to the schedule fixed in the contract, without having to raise a finger and without the risk that the ownership of the lands might be lost. In fact, even when leased, an estate remained part of the family's latifundium, so a certain degree of continuity in its administration was possible.[28]

From a political standpoint too this kind of lease had advantages. It allowed the Radziwiłłs to give their supporters if not the economic freedom, at least the social status of an estate owner, and this without any expenditure on their part. The leaseholders liked the system because it gave them a fixed income but more importantly because it allowed them to live the life of a wealthy landed nobleman.

The problem was that this kind of contract turned estate leasing into a noneconomic system. It provided no incentive for the leaseholders to increase estate revenues because what they wanted was improved social status. So, instead of being a tool for making properties more profitable, the estate leases only perpetuated the economic status quo. Even when a contract contained clauses that encouraged the leaseholder to rebuild and improve an estate, he had no motivation to do so because the contract fixed his income in advance.

This was a clear expression of the tension between the family's desire to make its estates more profitable and its exploitation of the leaseholders for political rather than economic ends.[29] Further, leaseholders were chosen not necessarily for their economic talents but because they were supporters (or potential supporters) of the Radziwiłłs and their political goals.[30] There was thus no guarantee that they were even capable of administering an estate efficiently.

So it was that in the eighteenth century estate leases, such as those used by the Radziwiłłs, were no longer very helpful for the family in achieving one of the most important goals in managing its estates—maximizing income.[31] For that it had to turn to leases of its monopoly rights.

Leasing Monopoly Rights

In early modern Polish-Lithuanian society ownership of landed estates brought significant rights. Legally most of the inhabitants—peasants, townspeople, and Jews—belonged to the estate on which they lived and could not move away. As the result of an almost century-long process, by the mid-sixteenth century the owner (as feudal lord) was the sole source of jurisdiction for them.[32] He also enjoyed various economic prerogatives: Peasants were required to perform corvée labor on their noble lord's *folwarks* and pay him taxes in cash and agricultural produce;[33] merchants who passed through his estates had to pay various tolls and customs duties; and he held certain monopolies, notably those on the sale of alcohol and the milling of grain, anywhere on his lands.[34] The income from all this became an important engine for economic growth during the eighteenth century.

The Monopoly on Alcohol (*Propinacja*)

The most profitable monopoly seems to have been that on the production and sale of alcoholic beverages (called in Polish *prawo propinacyjne* or *propinacja* for short). This meant that all those living on landed estates could buy only alcohol produced and sold under license of the estate owner, and that the income from these alcohol sales belonged solely to him too.[35]

The history of *propinacja* stretched back to the period of the German colonization of Poland in the Middle Ages. At that time the exclusive right to sell alcoholic beverages in a village was often granted to the village head (*sołtys*) or to tavern keepers with special privileges. The right was sometimes vested in the tavern itself.

Things began to change during the sixteenth century when estate owners started taking the taverns away from the village heads and innkeepers and leasing them out for themselves.[36] There was economic logic behind this policy. The fees paid for the tavern rights had remained at levels sometimes fixed in medieval times. With rising inflation during the sixteenth century their value decreased significantly. At the same time the price of grain increased, and since the sale of beer and vodka provided a market for grain that could not be exported, estate owners sought to exploit their *propinacja* monopoly to increase revenues.[37] Removing the holders of medieval rights and replacing them with leaseholders who had to pay higher fees to renew their leases allowed the estate owners to benefit from the rising prices.

The income from leasing the *propinacja* monopoly dramatically increased in importance in the eighteenth century. The wars that had swept across Poland-Lithuania in the mid-seventeenth century had not only destroyed much of its agricultural infrastructure but also made exporting produce much more difficult. In addition, grain prices on the international market had fallen due to the political and economic stabilization in Central and Western Europe following the 1648 Peace of Westphalia and the subsequent rise in agricultural productivity there.[38] Perhaps as a result of these two factors, a gap opened between the prices for unprocessed grain, which fell because it had no market, and prices of grain processed into alcohol, which rose because its market grew with the population. It thus became much more profitable for estate owners such as the Radziwiłłs to sell an ever greater proportion of the grain grown on their estates in the form of alcohol. The *propinacja* monopoly gave them a captive market for it—their own subjects.[39]

The Monopoly on Milling

The estate owner's monopoly on milling was also related to the need to market his agricultural produce. In Poland, as in many other countries, the peasants in each village who wanted their grain milled into flour had to take it to the local mill, which belonged to the estate owner. The payment for this service was made in the form of flour, sometimes as much as a third of the amount milled. This accrued to the estate owner because he held the monopoly on milling. However, accumulating huge amounts of flour was not his priority; what he wanted was cash. By leasing his monopoly on milling (invested in the mill, which was the object of the lease), he could receive his income in the form of cash. Collecting the flour and selling it became the job of the leaseholder. An added benefit of this monopoly was that it drew on the grain grown by the peasants on their own farms, further increasing the estate owner's income at the expense of his subjects.[40]

Customs and Duties on Trade

The particular value of customs and duties for a magnate estate owner was the increase in income it brought from the independent agricultural activities of his peasants. They had to pay customs not only on the sale of the grain from their farms, but also on any purchases they made with the cash income they received for it. The customs and duties also formed an additional tax on tradesmen and merchants in the estate towns and had the added benefit of deriving income from merchants outside the estate who came to do business. These were therefore another important means of enhancing incomes at a time when estate leases did not do so.

The estate owners seem to have identified these three sources of income as important tools of economic development in the eighteenth century, since they often chose to lease them together in a single contract.[41] They overwhelmingly chose to give the leases to Jewish businessmen, a clear sign

THE ECONOMIC INSTITUTIONS OF THE ESTATES   69

that they viewed them as the economic actors on their estates best able to maximize their revenues.[42]

This was achieved by putting up the prices paid for the leases as much and as frequently as possible.[43] The Radziwiłłs, like the other estate owners, did this by encouraging competition among potential leaseholders, that is, Jewish businessmen. Of course, the price raises were limited by the need to ensure that the lease remained profitable, but so lucrative was this sector in the eighteenth century that they could be increased on an almost continuous basis.

Leasing out their rights freed the Radziwiłłs from the burden of running taverns, mills, and customs collection points as well as the problems of devising and supervising the various revenue collection mechanisms. All these became the responsibility of the leaseholder, who knew that the more efficient he was the greater his profits would be. He had considerable freedom because the Radziwiłłs had no special arrangement for supervising their leaseholders.

Included in the leases were lists of penalties for contract violations, which suggests that some leaseholders may have been collecting more than they should have in order to line their own pockets. Cutting alcohol with water was a common complaint. On the other hand, these "violations" actually made the lease more profitable, which meant that the family would be able to put up the price of the lease to include the extra incomes. Not infrequently the Radziwiłł administrators seem to have preferred collecting the extra income to supporting their subjects' complainants against the leaseholders.[44]

There could be tensions nonetheless. Jewish leaseholders tended to be overseen by Radziwiłł administrators or noble estate leaseholders for whom the economic functioning of the leases was not of paramount significance. In addition, noneconomic factors such as religious antipathy towards Jews could sometimes take on significance in the day-to-day running of their businesses. Though the Jewish leaseholders could usually count on the family's support if things got out of hand, they often had to deal with hostile local administrators in their day-to-day affairs.[45]

The benefits of this system, though significant in the short run, did not bode well for the long term. The Radziwiłłs liked it because it was extremely efficient at channeling a range of estate incomes into their hands. Their peasants were not only a captive market for the *folwark* produce sold as alcohol, but they bought it with the income that they had earned from working their own farms. The monopoly on milling similarly forced the peasants to pay with their own grain. In addition, all sales on the local market were charged customs and duties by the family who further increased its income at the expense of its subjects. However, this kind of streamlined marketing, where most income from the agricultural produce of the estate found its way into the family's pockets, had a fatal flaw. It made both increased agricultural productivity and the development of larger markets much less worthwhile, thus hindering the long-term economic development of the estates.

Even though the Radziwiłłs were interested in attracting the business of merchants from outside the estates so that they could tax it, local markets were sluggish because the peasants and townspeople had less money to spend and were encouraged to part with what they had in the taverns. As a result, as the eighteenth century progressed, local markets failed to grow and the family's policy of commercial development began to stall.[46] These problems became acute at the end of the century, but for the period under discussion here the estates seemed to be a huge resource that could be squeezed ever tighter for bigger and bigger revenues.

CONCLUSIONS

The four methods of estate administration described here were never mutually exclusive. The Radziwiłłs used them all to manage their huge latifundium. Some parts of it they managed through their own administrative organization, others they mortgaged off to create short-term income, while yet other estates were given to lesser noblemen as leases.[47] The leasing of incomes from monopoly rights, particularly *propinacja*, was done across the whole latifundium. On the mortgaged estates these leases brought no revenue since the family had relinquished control of the land. On the estates that had been leased out, revenues from the monopoly leases formed part of the incomes of the noble leaseholders with the Radziwiłłs benefitting only indirectly. Nonetheless, so important was the revenue from the monopoly leases that even when the family did lease out an estate to a lesser nobleman, it was careful to keep for itself the right to appoint the Jewish leaseholders and set the terms of their contracts.[48]

This was the complex administrative system that made up what we are calling here the economic institutions of the estates. The ways in which the

Radziwiłłs managed to control the whole system determined their success in converting the natural resources of their lands, as well as the legal rights they derived from them, into financial income and political power. Jews played a number of key roles in this process, and it is those that form the focus of the next two chapters.

FOUR

Jews as Estate Leaseholders

The Rise and Fall of the Ickowicz Brothers

It was a feature of the estate economy in the eighteenth century that Jewish businessmen mostly preferred leasing monopoly rights to leasing estates.[1] This had not been the case a century earlier. Among the reasons for the shift was the hostility aroused by the fact that Jews who leased estates became de facto estate owners, and assumed a status similar to that of a noble. While Jews might have found this attractive, it was bitterly resented by much of Christian society, particularly peasants, and had been one cause of the horrendous violence of the 1648 Khmelnytsky Uprising. In the wake of all that death and destruction, Polish-Lithuanian Jewish businessmen seem to have concluded that other, safer ways to make a living had to be found.

In addition, the years after the uprising saw the upper and middle nobility begin to lease estates themselves at the encouragement of the magnate owners. As we have seen, this served both parties well. The magnates increased their influence over the noble lessees, while the noblemen could live in a dignified manner in return for supporting their patron. Jews who tried to engage in this kind of leasing thus found themselves in competition with the nobility and the object of hostility, often voiced in the anti-Jewish legislation of the *sejmiki*, the local noble councils.[2]

If the factors pushing the Jews away from estate leases were largely a function of their relations with non-Jewish society, those pushing them into monopoly leases were almost entirely economic in nature. Since the magnates were now using estate leases more as a political than an economic tool, they turned to monopoly leases as the most effective way of maximizing their income. As a result, they steered the Jews, whom they seem to have seen as the most effective economic actors among their subjects, into monopoly leasing.

Though most Jewish businessmen simply went along with this, there were a dauntless few who decided to brave the problems and restrictions and take on estate leases. Presumably they felt that their dynamic brand of estate management might yield greater profits as well as an improved social status and were willing to take the risks involved.[3] This was certainly true on the Radziwiłł estates, where in one case two Jews who leased entire estates became not only incredibly wealthy but even confidantes of the family.

These were the Ickowicz brothers, who came to control almost all of Hieronim Florian Radziwiłł's latifundium before their careers ended in ignominy, exile, prison, and death. Their careers were, then, not only different from those of noble leaseholders but highly unusual in Jewish society, which makes their story extremely instructive as to both the possibilities and dangers involved in estate leasing during the eighteenth century.[4]

ON THE RISE, 1726–1738

Getting Started

The brothers, whose full Hebrew names were Shmuel and Yosef-Gedaliah bnei [i.e., sons of] Yitzḥak Segal, were known to the Radziwiłł family as Szmojło and Gdal Ickowicz.[5] When they signed their names in Hebrew, they noted that they came "from the Holy Community of Olik," which was the Jews' name for the town of Ołyka in Volhynia—a town owned by the Radziwiłłs and the site of one of their largest palaces.[6] Their father, Yitzḥak, seems to have lived in the town and made his living as a leaseholder. According to some reports he was an extremely unsavory character, hated by his community, which accused him of overcharging for alcohol not to mention sorcery and even murder.[7] Perhaps this is why, in 1720, he accepted Anna Radziwiłł's invitation to move to distant Biała on the Lithuanian border to begin leasing there.[8]

Yitzḥak's move prompted the first mention of his two sons in the sources. Once Yitzḥak had left, the administrator of the Ołyka estate wrote a letter to his lady, discussing the candidates to take Ickowicz's place as the local leaseholder. Among them were Yitzḥak's sons, whom the letter described as "engaged in trade and not suitable."[9] This inscrutable comment is probably a sign that the administrator had something against them rather than evidence that they did not have the qualifications to take over the lease from their father.

In fact it was only a few years later, in 1726, that the brothers signed a lease with Anna Radziwiłł for the entire Duchy of Mir. This was their first foray into estate leasing, though they were clearly already very wealthy: their annual payments on the lease amounted to the huge sum of 77,000 złoty.[10] At around this time they also left Ołyka to join their father in Biała, which was where Anna Radziwiłł kept her main residence.[11]

Anna's decision to lease Mir to the brothers was part of her effort to develop the estates devastated in the Great Northern War that she had inherited from her husband.[12] The brothers were presumably recommended to her by their father, who had originally come to Biała as a leaseholder but soon became her agent. The lease she gave them was quite generous and did not limit their income to the amounts registered in the inventory.[13] The brothers' motivation for taking the lease can be seen in a special clause added to the contract that allowed them to cut timber in the estate forests so they could build rafts and ship merchandise down the Niemen (Neman) river to Königsberg in East Prussia. They thus acquired relatively easy and cheap access to the lucrative international Baltic market.[14]

As leaseholders of Mir the brothers' status rose rapidly. They were in constant contact with noblemen, both as part of their management of the estate and in their other business dealings[15] and were often addressed (particularly by people on the estates, though not the Radziwiłłs themselves) with titles reserved for the nobility.[16] Jews being treated, and acting like noble estate-owners, caused resentment, especially among peasants, so Anna Radziwiłł intervened. Her directives to the new leaseholders included the following unambiguous warning, "I strictly instruct the leaseholders that no Jew must raise his hand against a Christian."[17]

The issue was the use not just of physical violence but of judicial violence too, as Anna Radziwiłł made clear in her instructions to Szmojło when he leased the Duchy of Biała in 1736: the Jewish leaseholder could not serve as judge in any case involving a non-Jew; instead, Radziwiłł, as lady of the estate, would make a special payment to a local *folwark* manager for him to sit in judgment.[18]

Within a very short time business began to flourish. As well as running the Duchy of Mir, the Ickowicz brothers became deeply involved in international trade - and on an impressive scale. Their business network not only covered much of Poland-Lithuania, but stretched as far as Königsberg in the north,[19] Moscow in the east,[20] and the German principalities of Brandenburg and Saxony in the west.[21] They traded in a broad range of commodities, including grain, hemp in its various forms, beer and other alcoholic beverages, fabrics of all types, leather and leather goods, potash, wine, salt, iron, coffee, and tobacco.[22] It did not take long for them to become principal suppliers to the Radziwiłł court, using their wide range of business contacts to bring in everyday goods and luxury items (including on one occasion diamonds).[23]

The secret of the brothers' success seems to have been their ability to combine estate leasing with large-scale trade. Having leveraged their lease of the Mir estate to break into the Baltic markets, they then used the profits from their trade as leverage to lease more estates from the Radziwiłłs. In 1729, they leased the *starostwo* of Krzyczew in eastern Belarus, and in subsequent years took other leases, including Birże, Biała, and eventually Słuck.[24] By 1733 their lease payments to Anna Radziwiłł totaled 370,000 złoty and grew still greater over the next few years (see Table 4.1).[25]

These were huge sums. By way of comparison, the poll tax paid by the entire Jewish population of Poland in those years came to less than 230,000 złoty.[26] What stands out from the data in Table 4.1 is that the lease payments grew from year to year. Only 1735 saw a decrease, which was probably due to the havoc wrought by the Russian army as it crossed Belarus during the war of succession following the death of August II.[27] The reasons for the growth that followed that bad year are hard to determine. There was no consistency in the way the amounts were calculated, so we simply cannot tell whether it was related to rises in the amounts paid for individual leases, to the brothers taking new leases, or to inflationary pressures. It was presumably some combination of all three. Whatever the reason, the amount grew by some 75 percent in just five years.

Table 4.1. The Value of the Ickowicz Brothers' Leases from the Radziwiłł Family, 1733–1738

Year	Value (in złoty and groszy)
1733	370,000 zł.
1734	394,000 zł.
1735	320,462 zł., 24 gr.
1736	433,021 zł.
1737	526,500 zł.
1738	653,253 zł., 5 gr.

SOURCES: AR XXIII, 91; AR XXIII, 150; and AR X, "Ickowicz."

By 1733 the brothers were firmly entrenched in estate society. They began to invest heavily in real estate, particularly in Słuck, the largest Radziwiłł-owned town in Lithuania.[28] That year for the first time Szmojło Ickowicz and his wife, Henia, bought a house and a plot of land in the town and moved there from Biała. Local tradition connected this move with the visit to the town of Israel Baal Shem Tov (often viewed as the founder of the Hassidic movement). According to legend, Henia invited the Baal Shem Tov there to exorcise demons from their new home, then asked him how long their good fortune would continue. He prophesied that the good times would last twelve years. The prediction came true and the Ickowiczes fell from grace with disastrous consequences in 1745.[29] Despite the Baal Shem Tov's gloomy forecast, Szmojło continued to invest in property in Słuck. By 1737 he had completed no fewer than eighteen real estate deals in the town.[30]

The brothers continued to make the combination of estate leasing and large-scale trade work for them. Their leases in eastern Belarus, particularly Krzyczew, acted as a springboard for them to do business in Rīga, making it their third Baltic outlet after Gdańsk and their favored port, Königsberg.[31] In the East Prussian town, the Ickowiczes traded with major German merchants, most notably the brothers Adolph and Friedrich Saturgus, local agents for the Radziwiłł family.[32] They dealt in futures: each year the Ickowicz brothers undertook to provide a certain quantity of agricultural produce from the estates they leased, while the agents in Königsberg pledged to buy it all at a fixed price.[33] In addition the local merchants gave the leaseholders a line of credit both for their personal needs and for the business they were doing on behalf of the Radziwiłłs.[34]

During the 1730s it became increasingly clear that Szmojło was taking the lead in the brothers' partnership. He not only fronted most of their deals but also formed personal relationships with the Radziwiłłs and the upper echelons of their administration, even receiving a special title in recognition of the economic services he provided. Rather than being called just "leaseholder" (in Polish, *dzierżawca* or *arendarz*), he was addressed as "chief accountant" or "chief cashier" (*kasjer generalny*).[35]

Zielińska argues that this title, evidently created especially for Szmojło, was a version of the more generally used title "chief treasurer" (*podskarbi generalny*) and that the change from "treasurer" to "cashier" reflected Szmojło's inferior status as a Jew.[36] Whether or not this was true, it became Szmojło's official designation and is an accurate reflection of the broad powers he wielded on Anna Radziwiłł's Lithuanian estates.[37] He was her liaison with her administrators and sometimes even acted as her representative, for example during her first attempts to set up manufactories in Lithuania.[38]

The relationship between Anna Radziwiłł and Szmojło grew closer over the years. In his letters to her, Szmojło not only discussed the management of the estates he had leased, but gave her news of interest from the Lithuanian *sejmik*s and noble law courts.[39] In addition he sent her information (or rather rumors) about rival business deals such as when the magnate Sapieha family tried to interfere with the Radziwiłłs' negotiations for the sale of their estate produce in Königsberg. Having identified these "plots," as he called them, Szmojło also took steps on behalf of his mistress to frustrate them.[40]

The duchess's confidence in him grew year by year, and bonds of mutual trust were created. When Szmojło found himself in temporary financial embarrassment that prevented him from making one of his payments on time, he did not hesitate to inform her.[41] In 1738 when she leased him three relatively small estates, she did not even bother to stipulate the payment due, relying on him to submit his accounts honestly and pay her the handsome sum she expected.[42]

The Secret of the Brothers' Success

Szmojło and his brother Gdal did not disappoint Anna Radziwiłł. The kind of hugely increased revenues they brought her can be seen very clearly in the case of Krzyczew, a *starostwo* (royal holding) that had been granted to the family more or less in perpetuity. The brothers first leased the estate in 1729. The revenues it brought the Radziwiłł treasury had been recorded two years earlier as 7,027.5 thalers. They held the lease for some twelve years, a stormy period that included the beginning of the massive Krzyczew peasant uprising that lasted from 1740–1744. In 1747 estate revenues stood at 17,120 thalers.[43] This was a jump of about 150 percent over twenty years, an impressive achievement that might have been even greater had it not been for the peasant rebellion.[44]

Szmojło and Gdal used aggressive management techniques to make the revenues from the estates they leased grow so much. Particularly important was their unwillingness to accept the traditional arrangements, which laid down—or, as the Radziwiłłs saw it, limited—how much different subjects paid the estate treasury. They did everything they could to increase these payments. One way was to resurvey the estates in order to make certain that every square centimeter of Radziwiłł land was fully exploited and that no peasant held any land on which he did not pay dues of one sort or another.[45] When the accepted division of the land between individuals or villages was not to the Radziwiłłs' benefit, the brothers did not hesitate to ride rough-shod over local tradition and change it.[46] They collected all the dues owed by the Radziwiłłs' subjects, Jew and non-Jew alike, down to the last grosz and did away with as many of the customary exemptions and reductions as they could. Those who could not meet their obligations were evicted from their homes and even arrested.[47] Peasants who found themselves in diffi-cult circumstances and submitted petitions asking for special consideration (*supliki*) met with considerably less sympathy from Szmojło and Gdal than they had from the Radziwiłłs themselves.

The brothers' harsh treatment extended even to Christian clergymen, who often took advantage of their status to evade estate restrictions, par-ticularly on the sale of alcohol, and so boost their rather meager incomes. In Słuck for example, Szmojło and Gdal made every effort to stop Orthodox clerics bringing vodka to town.[48] And in Krzyczew they saw to it that the Orthodox clergy were closely supervised to ensure that any alcohol they made was strictly for their own use.[49]

The same invasive treatment was meted out to the Jewish communities on the estates.[50] In 1736 Szmojło visited Biała to reorganize the community's financial affairs and took over the monopoly leases in the town and its sur-rounding districts to increase profitability.[51] That same year he also visited Zabłudów, and there too did his best to reshape the Jews' economic activity in order to boost incomes.[52] For the Ickowiczes, then, economic restructur-ing was the key to success.

As we have seen, it was the brothers' ability to parlay the incomes from the estate leases (in the form of agricultural produce) into trade, and the profits from that trade (in the form of cash) into taking new leases, that helped them to get so rich so quickly.[53] The basis for the trade was not just the grain produced on the *folwark*s but also timber and potash from the forests, which were shipped on the Niemen and Dwina rivers to Königsberg and Rīga respectively.[54] In eastern Belarus, where the *folwark* system was not well developed, the brothers received produce directly from the peasants' farms. The major product there was hemp, which was in great demand in the Baltic ports.[55] This was another market that Szmojło and Gdal tried to monopolize, exploiting their position as leaseholders to force peasants and local merchants to sell their hemp only to them or their agents.[56]

As business expanded, it demanded more and more of the brothers and their families. When Szmojło went on business trips he left Henia, his wife, with full authority to conduct negotiations on his behalf and pay out any money necessary. Anna Radziwiłł was well aware of this arrangement and, on more than one occasion, wrote business letters directly to Henia.[57] The Radziwiłł family archives even hold a letter written by Henia in Polish to Anna Radziwiłł herself.[58] Gdal's wife, Sarah, was also active in the business, deeply involved in negotiations with Jewish merchants from eastern Belarus. Dozens of contracts bearing her signature have survived from the early 1740s.[59] Even Gdal's daughter Deborah was involved in her father's economic activity, maintaining a commercial correspondence from her home in Wołożyn (Valozhyn, Belarus).[60] The women's participation clearly played an important role in the success of what had become a family business.

The Brothers and Estate Society

The brothers' aggressive treatment of the residents of the estate—nobles, peasants, and Jews—may have been a good strategy for increasing the Radziwiłł treasury but it did not make them popular figures. Complaints were heard from all strata of society. The noble Stefan Olędzki complained to the *sejmik* in Starodubów that his mother had been evicted from her home on Szmojło's orders, that peasants and townspeople in Mir who had not complied with Gdal's orders had been beaten, and that the rabbi of Biała, who had delivered a sermon criticizing Szmojło, had been summarily dismissed and replaced by an Ickowicz nominee.[61] Despite Anna Radziwiłł's efforts to limit the brothers' authority over peasants in judicial matters, they had clearly amassed a great deal of power, which they soon turned to economic advantage. They would sometimes pay extremely low prices for the produce that the peasants had to sell them,[62] force those paying debts in cash to accept an unfavorable exchange rate,[63] and rigorously exploit even the most hated forms of corvée labor such as providing transport services.[64] If unpopularity was the price for all the money this brought in, Szmojło and Gdal seem to have had no problem paying it.

On the plus side, estate leasing always offered rich opportunities for patronage, an excellent way of purchasing popularity. Like other leaseholders the Ickowicz brothers found work on the estate for relatives and friends, including jobs that Jews did not usually hold. So in this period Jews sometimes ran *folwark*s, served as *folwark* accountants (*pisarze prowentowe*), or

were employed as agricultural administrators.[65] Ickowicz appointees also occupied positions commonly held by Jews, such as monopoly leaseholders
and trading agents.[66] Unlike noble leaseholders, the brothers expected their
appointees to adopt an aggressive management style and exert ever greater
pressure on estate residents to increase incomes.[67] Outside the administration, the Ickowiczes contracted with an extensive network of Jewish merchants on the estates who purchased agricultural produce and brought it to
the river ports as part of the brothers' export trade.[68]

For the nobles, townsfolk, peasants, and Jews who lived on the Radziwiłł
latifundium, the Ickowicz brothers' activity was not only unheard of but
also hated because it hit their pockets hard and eroded the rights that they
had traditionally enjoyed. The brothers' attitude toward those subject to
their power was similar to that of the nobles, ranging from simple contempt to outright violence. For many of the Christians who had to bear the
brunt of this behavior, the fact those doing it to them were Jews was an almost unbearable humiliation. Nearly all the complaints about the Ickowicz
brothers' conduct made by Radziwiłł subjects emphasized their Jewishness,
as in this complaint filed by a resident of Mir: "I further declare that day in,
day out the *Panowie*[69]—leaseholders—cause problems and beat townsfolk,
subjects, Jews. . . . They have no right to strike Christians with their own
hands, but *Pan* Gdal ignores this and sets Christian and Catholic blood at
naught. With his Jewish hand he has struck more than 20 men, drawing
blood more than once."[70]

The Jewish communities too took a jaundiced view of the Ickowiczes,
probably because they did not come from the communal élite of learning
and wealth but held their vast powers simply on the basis of their ties with
the duchess.[71]

The most vocal example of resistance to the brothers was probably Stefan
Olędzki, whom we met above. In 1738 he took his complaints from the local
sejmik to the *Sejm* in Warsaw, where he complained to the collected nobility
about his family's suffering at the hands of the Radziwiłłs and their Jewish
agents. His refusal to be appeased delayed the *Sejm*'s deliberations for more
than a full day.[72]

Back on the estates the hostile atmosphere reached such a level that, according to the indictment against them, a Jewish-led band of Christian
highwaymen plotted to murder Szmojło when he passed through Biała.
The conspirators were caught, arrested, and tried, so their plan never came

to fruition.[73] This was clearly an extreme case. Resistance to the Ickowicz brothers was usually more restrained, and rarely went further than letters of protest and complaints sent to a generally unsympathetic Anna Radziwiłł.[74]

AT THE TOP OF THE GAME, 1739–1745

The Ickowicz brothers' economic activity reached its height between 1739 and 1745. However, their success was accompanied by greater risks in their dealings with the family. Between 1739 and 1741 an aging Anna Radziwiłł withdrew from management of a large group of estates that included Słuck, Birże, Newel, and the Krzyczew *starostwo*, control of which she handed to her younger son, Hieronim Florian.[75] This transfer of power proved decisive for the brothers, whose meteoric rise had so far been fueled by their close ties with the duchess. They now had to deal with Anna's son, and that was a very different prospect.

Hieronim Florian inherited little of his mother's intelligence, judgment, or administrative skill, but instead showed a rigid and cruel (some would say pathological) temperament and little aptitude for or interest in managing the estates.[76] Although his mother's influence did not vanish overnight, it declined steadily until her death in 1746. As a result, the "chief cashier" and his brother found it increasingly important to stay in the good graces of their volatile new patron.

The late 1730s and early 1740s were an extremely difficult period for the Radziwiłłs in general and for Hieronim Florian in particular. The family was deeply involved in rebuilding their estates after the destruction of the Great Northern War (1700–1721) and the War of the Polish Succession (1733–1735). The War of the Austrian Succession (1740–1748) disrupted the commercial links between the estates (and Poland-Lithuania generally) and the German states of Central Europe.[77] Hieronim Florian himself also faced the problem of keeping up his payments to the king of Prussia and the elector Palatine for the return of the Neuburg estates.[78]

It is hard to be precise about the extent of the brothers' leasing activities in the period of transition between 1739 and 1741. In 1740, Hieronim Florian Radziwiłł leased all his estates to Szmojło Ickowicz for an annual payment of 600,000 złoty.[79] In 1741 both brothers paid Anna Radziwiłł 135,246 złoty and 25⅔ groszy to lease her estates, and Hieronim Florian 551,663 złoty and 15 groszy to lease his.[80] For that year their transactions with this branch of the family came to a total of 686,910 złoty and 10⅔ groszy, an increase of some 5 percent over 1738.[81] To this must be added Szmojło's dealings with Hieronim Florian's cousin, Marcin Mikołaj Radziwiłł, who leased him two of his estates for an annual payment of 130,000 złoty.[82]

Like his mother, Hieronim Florian soon came to rely on the brothers' administrative skills. In a letter to Szmojło dated November 22, 1742, he granted his Jewish agent the exclusive right to collect all the revenues from his estates, oversee their administration, and run the river trade along the Niemen.[83]

International Trade

International trade continued to play a crucial role in the brothers' commercial dealings. They cultivated ties with the Russian court and did business with St. Petersburg,[84] but the German lands, especially Prussia, remained their preferred destination for trade. The extent of the brothers' activities can be seen in a promissory note that Gdal issued to "Ezekiel, son of the late and renowned leader, our master and teacher Benjamin Wolf of the holy congregation of Tarnów," as part of his deal to purchase the rabbinate of Kraków for Szmojło's son-in-law. Gdal pledged that the note could be redeemed "in any place where he may find me and my property, whether in Poland or Lithuania, or in Königsberg or Gdańsk and Breslau and Frankfurt on the Oder."[85] Szmojło's children had commercial ties with Hamburg, and he himself dealt in various items (including precious stones) with Ephraim, Court Jew to the king of Prussia in Berlin.[86]

Since the brothers' economic activities were centered on the Radziwiłł estates in Lithuania, the Baltic ports of Königsberg and Rīga were their most important markets. In addition to grain and hemp, forest products were an important commodity for the brothers, a further sign of the way they integrated estate leaseholding with mercantile activity.

In the early 1740s Szmojło and Gdal held the leases on all of Hieronim Florian's forests in Lithuania, and they traded in forest products on both the home and the international markets, especially Rīga.[87] As far as the return trade from Königsberg was concerned, the brothers bought among other things, salt, fabrics, wine, spices, silver, paper, and rice for resale in Lithuania.[88] In all, Szmojło shipped merchandise worth 171,391 Prussian thalers to Königsberg in 1744.[89] Gdal's accounts alone for 1741 indicate that his business turnover for the year came to 56,590 złoty and 11 groszy,[90] with his shipments of rye and wheat to Königsberg accounting for two-thirds of the volume. Taking into account that these figures do not include all the brothers' dealings with Königsberg and completely omit their trade in Rīga and Gdańsk (not to mention elsewhere outside the Commonwealth), their total volume of trade on all international markets must have come to at least several hundred thousand złoty a year—a vast sum by any standard.[91]

International Connections

As Hieronim Florian came to rely on Szmojło more and more, he began to exploit his Jewish agent's international connections to help in the lengthy and complex process of returning the Neuburg estates to the Radziwiłł family. The final stage of these negotiations with the king of Prussia and the elector Palatine dragged on from the late 1730s to the mid-1740s. The Radziwiłłs had to pay hundreds of thousands of złoty each year to the two German rulers. It was left to Szmojło with his extensive business connections to raise the necessary cash.

While still doing everything he could to increase estate revenues, he also began to search out new sources of credit.[92] In the late 1730s he used his ties with Lipman Levy, Court Jew in St. Petersburg, to obtain a loan of 1,000,000 złoty.[93] In addition, he contacted several of the Königsberg merchants and promised them exclusive rights to some of the produce of his lord's estates in exchange for loans[94] and was also sent by Hieronim Florian to Berlin and Mannheim to raise funds and reach the best possible settlement concerning the payments due.[95]

Ickowicz seems to have done everything that was asked of him, but the deteriorating international situation of those years made his job highly complex.[96] Things got so bad that he spent most of 1743 and 1744 in Königsberg searching for economic solutions, which he did with a great deal of success.[97] To judge from their correspondence, Szmojło's titanic efforts earned him the gratitude and support of the normally aloof and cruel Hieronim Florian.[98]

The brothers' success on all these fronts did not pass unnoticed among the magnates of Poland-Lithuania. In 1739, Szmojło and Gdal signed a three-year contract to lease August Czartoryski's estate of Wołożyn and Stołpce (Stoŭbtsy, Belarus) for an annual payment of 35,000 złoty.[99] The importance of this transaction went far beyond the direct profits it generated. Because Stołpce was located on the Niemen, the town quickly became the brothers' commercial base for the river trade to Königsberg.[100] Szmojło became the Czartoryskis' agent in Lithuania and, among other assignments, supervised the work to enlarge the family palace in Grodno.[101] About two years later the brothers signed a lease with the magnate, Paweł Sanguszko, and took over the administration of the principality of Smolny in eastern Lithuania. This was another sizeable contract, for which they agreed to pay a total of 225,000 złoty over a three-year period.[102]

Soon it was not just magnate families that took an interest in the Ickowiczes but royal houses, too. In 1740, Gdal was granted the status of Court Jew by the king of Prussia and was permitted to settle with his family in Königsberg. Szmojło received the less prestigious status of *Schutzjude* (protected Jew).[103] In 1742, August III Wettin, elector of Saxony and king of Poland, also became interested. What happened next was described in a letter Anna Radziwiłł wrote to Hieronim Florian on February 6, 1742:

> Let me tell you, my son, about a particular matter we learned of when the Jews were with us: now, by the king's pleasure, Count Brühl[104] has summoned Gdal to Saxony. They want to grant him the lease on the royal estates of Kraków (*wielkorządy krakowskie*)[105] and are relying [on the transaction] very much. In fact they were interested in our Szmojło, but he is not leaving us and I do not know if he will allow his brother to take such a large affair upon himself. I will know more about it when he himself comes. [The Jews] themselves knew nothing about the matter. It was only when His Honor Wilczewski arrived here that he told them he had heard from Brühl that they were interested in them as [lessees].[106]

Acquiring the lease on the royal estates of Kraków would have brought the brothers to the very pinnacle of Polish-Lithuanian society and given them a status without peer in the Jewish society of Poland-Lithuania.[107] For reasons that remain unclear, however, the deal was never finalized.

In Estate Society

Despite this, the Ickowicz brothers' position on the Radziwiłł estates and their ties with various magnate families in Lithuania and Poland as well as with the Prussian royal house made them the most influential members of Polish-Lithuanian Jewish society. Their influence extended well beyond the Jewish world and could be felt in non-Jewish society too.

In Jewish Society

Jewish community records are sparse, so it is difficult to determine for certain whether Szmojło and Gdal Ickowicz played official roles or held formal positions in the Jewish institutions of Lithuania. What can be said without hesitation, however, is that there is no surviving evidence that they were members of any *kahal* or of the Council of the Lithuanian Land.[108] This is not to say that they played no part in communal life. We know of at least two cases in which Szmojło interfered in *kahal* affairs to arrange matters to his liking—in Biała in 1736 and in Zabłudów in 1738 (in both cases he had people opposed to him dismissed and replaced with candidates of his choice).[109] In Słuck, too, the community seems to have done his bidding.[110]

Another realm of community life in which the brothers played an active role was the appointment of rabbis, particularly in communities on the lands that they leased. The following is a letter addressed to Gdal that gives a picture how they did so:

> My signature below attests, with the force of one hundred valid and reliable witnesses, that I have pledged myself to the illustrious prince of the Torah. . . . His Excellency our master and teacher Joseph Gedaliah the son of our master and teacher Yitzḥak Ha-levi, that after the aforesaid prince presents me with the writ of appointment to the rabbinate of the holy congregation of Krzyczew and Chocimsk [Hotsimsk, Belarus] with all that pertains to this rabbinate, as it was during the tenure of the illustrious rabbi, the great luminary, our master and teacher Zvi Hirsch Katz, the president of the religious court of the holy congregation of Ołyka (may God protect it), I pledge to remit to the aforesaid prince the sum of 12,000 Polish złoty, the currency employed here in the holy congregation of Słuck (may God protect it). And if by God's will I am also successful in acquiring the rabbinate of the holy congregation of Mścisław (Mstsislaŭ, Belarus), may God protect it, i.e. that my lord father and teacher, the Gaon, may his light burn bright, and my brother the great rabbi Meshulam Zalman are willing to sign over to me the rabbinate of the aforesaid holy congregation, I undertake to give another 400 Polish złoty at the expiration of one year from the day on which I receive the letter of appointment to the rabbinate. . . . Today, Thursday, 26 Adar 5496.[111] Signed, Shimon the son of the Gaon, our master and teacher, Yitzḥak Isaac Ginsburg.[112]

The brothers' immediate interest was obviously financial. Licenses to serve as rabbis did not come cheap, and formed yet another source of income for them. In addition their ability to hand out these prestigious posts was an important source of patronage that further cemented their position as leading figures in Jewish society.[113]

The brothers found rabbinic posts for their immediate family too. In 1743–1744, Gdal purchased the rabbinate of Wilno for Naḥman Katz, the husband of his daughter Deborah.[114] Yitzḥak Yosef Te'omim-Frankel, who was married to Szmojło's daughter Treina, became rabbi of Słuck at a young age, and then in 1743, after vigorous lobbying by his father-in-law, was appointed rabbi of Kraków and its district.[115] Neither of these rabbis actually took up residence, preferring to live elsewhere while enjoying the ample incomes that the posts brought.[116] Nonetheless, Kraków and Wilno were two of the most important Jewish communities in Poland-Lithuania, so the Ickowiczes' ability to acquire the rabbinical posts for their immediate family was a clear sign of their enormous power and influence.

The brothers were also figures of note in German Jewish society, particularly in Prussia. As Court Jew in Königsberg, Gdal obtained permission from the king of Prussia to open a private synagogue (more precisely a chapel) in his house.[117] He also had ties to the rabbi of Dessau in Prussia.[118] Szmojło's son-in-law, who was appointed rabbi of Kraków, preferred to live in Breslau (Wrocław) and ultimately became rabbi there.[119] Szmojło's commercial dealings in Berlin with Ephraim, Court Jew to the king of Prussia, gave him an entrée into that family and he betrothed his daughter to one of Ephraim's sons.[120]

The brothers' standing in Jewish society and their ties with the magnates also allowed them to serve as a bridge between the Jewish and non-Jewish worlds. An entry from the record book (*pinkas*) of the Mścisław community in eastern Belarus notes appreciatively all the efforts that Szmojło, and even more so his wife Henia made to help the Jews who lived on the Radziwiłł estates.[121]

That being so, if a magnate or any other non-Jew wanted to arrange something inside the Jewish community, Szmojło was an excellent agent for getting it done. In 1738 for example, Jan Klemens Branicki, the owner of Białystok and a contender for the Polish crown, asked Szmojło to help the daughter of one of his Jewish merchants, the widow of the rabbi of Slonim, collect a debt of 150 red złoty from a Jew who lived in Kopyl, which was on the Radziwiłł estates.[122] That same year, Barbara Radziwiłł, the wife of Marcin Mikołaj, asked Szmojło to help the widow of the local rabbi extricate her inheritance from her late husband's creditors.[123] In 1740, Anna Radziwiłł ordered Szmojło to send to Biała a Jew who was under suspicion of committing various crimes (the letter does not specify what they were). She added that he could ignore the need to bring the man to trial and work independently of the local *kahal*.[124]

In Non-Jewish Society

The Ickowicz brothers' influence in non-Jewish society derived mainly from their status as estate leaseholders. All those who lived or worked on the estates leased by Szmojło and Gdal had to deal with the brothers and were dependent on their good graces, since they basically represented Radziwiłł interests.[125] In economic affairs, as we have seen, the brothers usually took an aggressive stance, which brought them into conflict with many people, including the local clergy. Even this they took in their stride: In Słuck they acted to prevent the local priests from boosting their income by dealing in alcohol;[126] in Wołożyn they refused to pay the Bernardine monastery the annual stipend laid down in the lease contract;[127] and when the prior of the monastery in Stołpce tried to interfere with the brothers' commercial activities, they asked the lord of the town to replace him![128]

Peasants complained that the brothers ignored their requests for help when they needed it and treated them with great harshness, not only economically but physically too.[129] Even people who lived outside the estates could find themselves suffering at the brothers' hands, especially where the river trade along the Niemen was concerned. This was a very lucrative business in which the brothers wanted as little competition as possible. So, for example, one rainy day in the spring of 1743 they refused to allow a merchant representing Jerzy Fleming, soon to be appointed grand treasurer of Lithuania, to store his carts laden with grain and hemp in their warehouses in Stołpce. Though he offered to pay for the storage, the brothers refused to take in the carts, and the goods were ruined.[130] Fleming was extremely angry and with the help of the Czartoryskis, his political allies, issued a formal complaint. The brothers' initial insouciance shows just how secure they felt and how little they were worried about wielding their power against non-Jews of even the highest rank.

OPPOSITION:
THE PEASANT UPRISING IN KRZYCZEW

As the Ickowicz brothers were reaching the peak of their influence in the early 1740s, opposition to them was growing too. In Jewish society they were called despots and loathed.[131] Jews on the estates could, like the rabbi of Biała, run into trouble with the brothers if they spoke openly, so presumably dissatisfaction was muted.[132] Jews who lived elsewhere were freer to express themselves, in words and in actions. On one occasion Jews from Białynice lay in ambush for Szmojło as he traveled from Kopyś to Słuck, attacked him physically, and made off with several dozen distilling vats.[133] The brothers' involvement in purchasing rabbinic posts for relatives also triggered fierce opposition: in Kraków for example, things got so bad that a fistfight broke out involving Gdal himself (an incident that certainly did not add to his popularity).[134]

Szmojło and Gdal could arouse strong opposition among non-Jews too. In Połock, the *sejmik* issued a ban on leasing estates to Jews with the clear intention of bringing the brothers down.[135] Adolph Saturgus, the merchant from Königsberg, seems thoroughly to have disliked Szmojło. He had no hesitation about confiscating the Jew's property to cover debts, even despite their long years of doing business together; nor did he miss an opportunity to discredit Szmojło in his letters to the Radziwiłłs.[136]

Though open hostility to Szmojło in estate circles does not seem to have been expressed widely in writing, it does seem to have been whispered, even to Hieronim Florian Radziwiłł himself. In his letters to his chief cashier, Radziwiłł would often include assurances that he would not listen to Ickowicz's detractors and would continue to trust him regardless of any accusations.[137]

The most extreme opposition to the régime imposed by Szmojło and Gdal was that of the peasants on the Krzyczew *starostwo*, which the brothers leased. It took the form of a violent uprising that lasted from 1740 to 1744.[138] By looking at this outbreak in some detail, we can get a picture not just of the relations that developed between the brothers and the peasants under their jurisdiction, but also of the dangers that lay in wait for Jews who chose to make their living by leasing estates in the eighteenth century.

Background

The *starostwo* of Krzyczew was located in the eastern part of the Grand Duchy of Lithuania, near the border with Russia, in what today is eastern Belarus. It was situated a long way away from the major centers of the Polish-Lithuanian Commonwealth and was economically underdeveloped.[139] The *starostwo* came into the possession of the Radziwiłł family in the early eighteenth century as a royal grant originally intended to last only the lifetime of its holder. As often happened with this kind of estate however, it remained in Radziwiłł hands for several generations, like a regular part of the family property.[140]

Because Krzyczew was so distant from the Radziwiłłs' other lands in Lithuania, those who administered it on the family's behalf had virtually a free hand to do as they wished. Peasants were treated harshly because the estate administrators' only aim was to maximize revenues and they were not concerned about the long-term consequences of their actions. The Ickowiczes were by no means the first people to run the estate and be hated by the peasants. In a petition submitted in the first quarter of the eighteenth century, before Krzyczew was handed over to Szmojło and Gdal in 1729, the peasants complained bitterly about their treatment.[141] Once the brothers took over, however, their aggressive management techniques only increased the peasants' distress.

Krzyczew was a royal domain, so those who lived there were subjects of the king and not of the *starosta* (i.e., Radziwiłł). Although the estate was managed as if it were part of the Radziwiłł latifundium, its inhabitants had the legal right to invoke the king's protection against harassment and to appeal the *starosta*'s decisions to a special tribunal.[142] This right was rarely invoked, however. To the best of our knowledge, the court did not intervene on behalf of the peasants even when the rebellion broke out. The Radziwiłłs—and the leaseholders who acted in their interests—seem to have been able to block the peasants' access to it.[143] This denial of legal protection further increased the discontent.

The local nobility was hostile to the Radziwiłłs too. Fiercely independent, the nobles resented being dictated to by a distant magnate family, however important it might be. The upper nobility of the region saw themselves as the Radziwiłłs' rivals and hoped to undermine the family's status by fomenting revolt.[144] The middle nobility seem to have aligned themselves with the rebels because they felt victimized by a resurvey of the *starostwo* conducted by Szmojło at his noble lord's behest in the summer of 1740.

Economic Causes

The period of Szmojło and Gdal Ickowicz's control of the *starostwo* was marked by intensive development and new settlement.[145] The 1727 inventory listed dozens of new villages and towns whose residents had been granted a tax exemption lasting fifteen to twenty years.[146] These exemptions notwithstanding, revenues from Krzyczew more than doubled during the period that the district was leased to the brothers, an indication of their success in squeezing all sectors of its population.[147] It was this economic pressure that eventually led the peasants to revolt. We can get some idea of how it worked from a long letter of complaint against Gdal and Szmojło that the people of Krzyczew sent to Radziwiłł at the beginning of the rebellion. The charges were as follows:

1. The peasants were being forced to sell their produce (hemp) to the brothers at excessively low prices.

2. New settlements that had been established on the site of old ones were being taxed according to the previous number of houses, even though there now many fewer.

3. Payments were being calculated at exorbitant exchange rates between the different currencies in use.

4. The payment in kind that those wishing to mill their grain had to make had been increased from 1/10 to 1/7 of the amount of grain to be milled.

5. The leaseholder of the incomes from the mills was making everyone give him a separate amount, thus doubling the price of milling.

6. Duties were being levied on salt purchased for private consumption.

7–8. State taxes were being collected at an excessive rate.

9. The holiday payments to the Jewish leaseholders (*kolendy żydowskie*) had reached excessive proportions.[148]

10–11. When measuring the grain to be paid as taxes, fraudulent weights were being used. In general the prices charged for grain were unfair.

12. The brothers were making life difficult for people who sold wax in those villages where there were beehives.

13. Peasants were being forced to transport merchandise for the brothers in their carts, even to remote destinations, such as Newel and Nowy Świerżeń in Lithuania and St. Petersburg in Russia. This was a new burden which had never been imposed before.

14. Peasants were being forced to sell their lumber to the brothers at unreasonably low prices.

15. Customs exemptions were being given to peasants and townspeople who did service for Jews holding sub-leases from the brothers. This was at the expense of all the others in the village or town.

16. Peasants were being forced to transport merchandise in their carts for these sub-leaseholders.

17–19. The court system was under Jewish control. It had reached the point that a Christian could no longer expect to receive a fair verdict in a suit against a Jew, even in criminal cases (including murder).

In conclusion, the authors of the document estimated that the economic damage done to the residents of the *starostwo* by the brothers amounted to some 65,000 złoty.[149]

Even if the charges made here were exaggerated for effect, they give an excellent indication of how the Ickowicz brothers operated: to maximize revenues they intruded into every aspect of the peasants' economic life, including ones that leaseholders had not touched before. They were not afraid to impose new taxes and labor requirements, to use doctored weights and measures and exorbitant rates of exchange, and even to force the peasants to sell them their produce. It is no surprise that the peasants, deprived of much of their already meager income, became extremely angry.

The situation was exacerbated by the feeling that the brothers were granting preferential status to Jews on the *starostwo*. It was this perception that underlay complaints about Jewish influence over the court system and collusion among sub-leaseholders to collect double fees for milling flour.[150] Christians viewed preferential treatment of Jews as a special humiliation, which they expressed as a fear that the Jews were taking over their lives. In fact what was really happening was only the usual process of the leaseholder exercising the possibilities for patronage that his lease offered him.

The Religious Factor

Religious tensions in eastern Belarus were running high. Although most of the peasants were Orthodox, the ruling nobility was polonized and largely Roman Catholic.[151] The arrival of Jewish settlers complicated matters even further.[152] The Jews were viewed as a destructive element, not only because Jews were seen as the enemies of Christianity, but also because they acted as agents of the hated Catholic rulers. Anti-Semitic discourse and even violence was not uncommon. One of the most extreme cases happened in 1693 in Kopyś, when a blood libel accusation was mounted against the local Jewish community (though it does bear noting that it was finally refuted with the help of a Christian estate official).[153] The hatred continued to rumble even after the brothers no longer wielded power in the region. In 1762, Jerzy Koniski, the Orthodox bishop of Belarus, attacked the Jews in a letter to Michał Kazimierz Radziwiłł about a dispute between a local priest and a *propinacja* leaseholder: "In ancient times the Jews sealed the tortured Lord Jesus Christ in his grave. Now they are torturing his Christian brethren and sealing his church."[154]

When the brothers took over the Krzyczew lease a serious deterioration of religious relations in the *starostwo* ensued. That this was not only between Jews and non-Jews becomes clear from a petition submitted by the Krzyczew *kahal* to Anna Radziwiłł sometime before 1740:

> We, the members of the impoverished *kahal* of Krzyczew, fall at our lady's feet in tears and make this request of her. We, who live under the rule of Her Grace and Highness, thanks to privileges granted [us] by their Highnesses the Enlightened Kings, make accusation against the burghers of Krzyczew, all of whom abuse us with the goal of totally expelling us from the city. They have threatened us with these words, [that] they will rise up against us just like in Ukraine, because they have a pretext to take action against the Catholics and against us poor Jews.[155]

The allusion is to the Khmelnytsky Uprising in Ukraine almost a century earlier, when Cossacks and Ukrainian peasants rebelled against the Catholic rulers and their Jewish agents (many of whom were estate leaseholders). Clearly the violent events of the uprising had remained in the collective memory of the peasants, even in regions quite distant from Ukraine, and their attitude towards Catholics and Jews had not changed much in the interim.[156]

The leader of the Krzyczew uprising, one Woszko Woszczyło, went so far as to compare himself to Khmelnytsky in a proclamation he sent to Radziwiłł shortly before the end of the uprising in 1744. It began, "[I] Woszko Woszczyło, grandson of Bohdan Khmelnytsky, leader and commander in chief of the armies that gathered to uproot the Jewish people and to defend Christianity."[157] Woszczyło went on to emphasize that the rebellion was aimed not at the nobility but only the Jews, an attempt (and a rather feeble one at that) to deflect Hieronim Florian Radziwiłł's rage at what the rebels had done.[158]

The local Jews also explained the outbreak of the rebellion in religious terms. A document composed by the Jews of Mścisław after its suppression, reads, "[It happened] because the nations of the world [i.e., the non-Jews] were envious that the verse had been fulfilled, 'Yet, even then, when they are in the land of their enemies, I will not reject them'[159] . . . and that, Thank God, the brothers, the high lord and prince, our teacher and master Shmuel [Szmojło] and his brother the prince our teacher and master Gedaliah achieved greatness and honor. [It was from envy that the non-Jews] sought to destroy the people of the aforesaid lords."[160] There was no hint here of any economic resentment or anger at ill treatment. The sole motive for the peasants' uprising, according to the Jews of Mścisław, was their envy of the Jewish leaseholders who had attained high office—a status the community clearly viewed as a sign of divine favor for the Jewish people as a whole.

Surviving the Uprising

The Krzyczew peasant revolt broke out in 1740 and led to brutal attacks on Jews in the *starostwo*. It was the Ickowicz brothers who seemed to be the main target of the peasants' hatred, and initially at least the Radziwiłłs took the charges against them seriously. Just before the violence began Anna Radziwiłł wrote to Gdal and warned him that he would pay the price if the complaints of the people of Krzyczew turned out to be justified.[161] Once the rebellion broke out, however, attitudes began to change. Reports suggested that the causes of the rebellion were much more complex. In a letter written during the rebellion Anna told her son, "You can understand . . . that this uprising is not provoked by any damage [caused to the peasants] . . . but by the incitement of the nobility."[162]

The marauding peasants sacked the town of Krzyczew twice and caused enormous damage and loss of life. The Jewish community was forced to flee with only the clothes on their backs. The rebels also attacked the Belarusian towns of Orsza (Orsha) and Szkłów (Shkloŭ) as well as the Mohilew (Mahilioŭ) *ekonomia*, and even threatened to turn on Wilno. Though there are no figures as to how many Jews and non-Jews were killed in the uprising, many communities suffered horribly.[163] It took nearly four years for Hieronim Florian to end the uprising, which he did with his usual cruelty, noting proudly in his diary that he had had thousands of rebels executed. He also brought Woszczyzło and his confederates to Słuck for public execution.[164] When peace finally came, the Jews in particular gave a huge sigh of relief. An entry in the record book of the Mścisław community proclaimed the establishment of a "Little Purim" festival to celebrate its deliverance from the ravages of the uprising.[165]

By that time the Radziwiłł family had made up its mind about the relative importance of the different factors that had sparked the uprising, and no longer put the management style of the Ickowiczes high on the list. Not only were the brothers not punished but Hieronim Florian continued to employ them, use their services, and treat them as he had always done. Nevertheless, prudence did demand that when Szmojło and Gdal's lease of Krzyczew expired in 1741, it was not renewed but given to a Christian nobleman.[166]

When things had quieted down, Hieronim Florian Radziwiłł visited the *starostwo*, apparently accompanied by his adviser and confidante, Szmojło. While in Krzyczew, Radziwiłł issued a series of instructions to start the process of rebuilding the shattered local economy. Issues concerning the Jews were quite prominent. Many Jews seem to have made a living (or supplemented their income) by borrowing from the nobility to lend to the peasants. It was therefore necessary to settle the peasants' debts to their creditors so that the Jews could pay off their own debts to the nobility. Since this would take some time, the nobles were instructed not to pressure the Jews for immediate repayment.

Another crucial issue was reviving trade. To this end Radziwiłł tried to shield the Jews and the townspeople from taxes and levies that had been imposed by the *starostwo* administrators. He also gave instructions to repair and renovate the *starostwo* infrastructure—taverns, mills, dams, and breweries—as a means of increasing lease revenues. Perhaps at Szmojło's suggestion, Hieronim Florian ordered that the Jews receive financial compensation for the three synagogues in the *starostwo* that had been plundered during the uprising.[167]

It took a relatively long time for the Jews to recover. In 1745 the Jews of Krzyczew again petitioned Radziwiłł for help. He agreed and instructed the acting governor accordingly.[168] This did not help much, and even years later the situation of the Krzyczew Jews did not show significant improvement, particularly as regards their relations with their non-Jewish neighbors. In 1753, Michał Karpatowicz, the governor of the *starostwo*, stripped Jews of their leases and evicted them from their houses overlooking the Krzyczew central market square.[169]

The Ickowicz brothers on the other hand survived the dislocations without much damage. Nonetheless the uprising must have been a shock to them. In many respects, the problems that estate leasing by Jews had caused in mid-seventeenth-century Ukraine seemed to have repeated themselves. Jews took estate leases because they knew that with energetic management they could increase revenues for their lord and turn a pretty profit for themselves. However, their aggressive and invasive policies ratcheted up tensions among the local population. When these combined with the religious resentment felt by Christians at being ruled over by Jews the situation soon became explosive.

The Jewish leaseholders knew that even when things turned bad they could expect the support of their noble lords. Still, this was not always total protection, particularly when the nobleman was as fickle as Hieronim Florian. In the case of the Krzyczew uprising, he stood firm with his Jewish agents and helped them overcome the danger. Nonetheless, the precariousness of their situation must have been brought home to them. Certainly Gdal Ickowicz seems to have understood this, because after 1740 he retired from all of his business dealings with the Radziwiłł family.[170] He established his family's residence at the Czartoryski court in Wołożyn, while he himself spent much of his time in Königsberg and Rīga dealing with his commercial affairs.[171] From that time on Szmojło managed all the affairs with Hieronim Florian on his own.

SZMOJŁO AND HIS MASTER, 1740–1745

In the immediate wake of the uprising, relations between Szmojło and Hieronim Florian grew closer, particularly since Szmojło was busy raising money to redeem the Neuburg estates. Their correspondence, though largely devoted to matters of business, also reflected a feeling of shared destiny. Both men felt isolated and exposed in a hostile world. Szmojło complained about the unpleasant rumors being spread about him in the Radziwiłł court and the various intrigues he was being drawn into, while Hieronim Florian vented his paranoia and inability to trust anyone.[172] In late 1743 he offered Szmojło an armed escort as protection against his enemies.[173] Radziwiłł's mental problems clouded his relations with his own family too. He accused his brother Michał Kazimierz of speaking ill of him in public.[174] With family interactions so strained, Szmojło soon became a kind of go-between for Hieronim Florian with his mother and brother.[175]

During these years Szmojło developed closer ties with other members of the Radziwiłł family. Marcin Mikołaj, from whom he leased several estates, referred to him in his letters as his "beloved leaseholder."[176] Szmojło provided services, mostly loans and purchases, to Marcin's wife, Barbara, to Michał Kazimierz and his wife Franciszka Urszula, to Jerzy Radziwiłł, the *wojewoda* of Nowogródek (Navahrudak, Belarus), and to Udalryk Krzysztof Radziwiłł.[177] They all addressed him with respect as "panie Szmojło" and wrote to him with the courtesy appropriate for a senior and honored retainer. Relations were not always good however. When Szmojło proved unable to satisfy the family's demands he was severely taken to task, even by Anna Radziwiłł, who was usually quick to defend him.[178] On at least one occasion Michał Kazimierz complained that he had tried to cheat him in a request for credit.[179]

On the whole, however, relations seem to have been respectful if not precisely cordial. When Szmojło was making efforts to obtain the rabbinate of Kraków for his son-in-law, the Radziwiłł family gave him its help and support.[180] On another occasion they stood by his side and gave him every assistance to have his daughter released from prison (see below); once she had been freed, they even hosted father and daughter in one of their Lithuanian palaces.[181]

For all his previous successes, Szmojło found himself in economic difficulties in the 1740s. In 1742, Szmojło and Gdal had extended their lease of Wołożyn and Stołpce from August Czartoryski for another year, but when the contract finally expired, they were hard-pressed to pay him what they owed.[182] The next year Szmojło found himself in trouble with the magnate Pawel Sanguszko too because he had failed to make his payments for the lease of the latter's Smolny estate in Lithuania.[183] In response, Sanguszko, who also owned the town of Tarnów in Little Poland, had Szmojło's daughter thrown into prison.[184] As we have seen, Szmojło asked the Radziwiłłs for help in getting her released. They wrote to the upper echelons of Polish society, finally turning to Heinrich Count von Brühl, chief minister to the king.[185] With such backing, Szmojło's daughter was soon free and reunited with her father.

This gives yet more proof of the precarious position Jewish leaseholders found themselves in when they achieved high status in non-Jewish society. Because their standing depended entirely on the economic services they gave their lords, any financial difficulties they might find themselves in could have grave consequences for themselves and their families. This was in sharp contrast to noble leaseholders, who faced few consequences if they mismanaged the running of their estates.[186]

Szmojło's financial difficulties can probably be traced to the disruption of international trade caused by the War of the Austrian Succession. The Krzyczew peasant uprising greatly affected Szmojło's hemp supply and led to a general downturn in the estate economy. Hieronim Florian was affected no less than his agent. He desperately needed funds to redeem the Neuburg estates, but his sources of credit outside the country were drying up owing to the unsettled international situation, while his estates were producing less income than before.[187]

These financial pressures seem to have exacerbated his mental instability and may also have affected his relations with Szmojło. Although Radziwiłł continued to depend on his chief cashier and treated him with warmth and respect, he forbad Szmojło to take his family with him on his many trips to Königsberg. More than once he turned down Szmojło's entreaties to be allowed to do so, though he did promise his full protection for the family left behind in Słuck.[188] It is not clear whether Szmojło's requests were innocent or formed part of a plan to flee the country - and his increasingly unstable patron. Whatever the case, he continued to work conscientiously for Radziwiłł and there is no evidence that he ever tried to slip away. Hieronim Florian's motives are also hard to discern. He continued to treat Szmojło as he had always done, and there is nothing in their correspondence to suggest he was displeased with his chief cashier.

DOWNFALL

The crisis came in the spring of 1745. On April 11, a fire broke out in Słuck and destroyed much of the town.[189] Having to rebuild the most important urban center on his estate while he was still struggling with the destruction in the Krzyczew uprising, hit Hieronim Florian's revenues extremely hard. The problems could barely have come at a worse time since he needed to raise a small fortune to make the final payment for the Neuburg estates. In desperation he turned to his mother, suggesting that they put up the Zabłudów estate as security in order to raise the money. Anna Radziwiłł, who had retained Zabłudów for her own personal use, refused.[190] Hieronim Florian appealed to his mother again in late June, pointing out just how tenuous his economic position was: he was committed to pay 700,000 złoty for the Neuburg estates while his revenues barely reached 500,000 złoty.[191]

It was a bad year for Szmojło too, and he could not collect all the money he was owed. Still, for the first few months of the year he and Radziwiłł remained on good terms, exchanging letters as usual. As late as June 29, 1745, he received a routine business letter from his patron. Then Radziwiłł's mood darkened. Within a week he had Szmojło arrested, accusing him of fraud to the tune of 6,125,236 złoty.[192] Szmojło's imprisonment came only a few days after Hieronim Florian's second unsuccessful appeal to his mother, so Radziwiłł's real motive was almost certainly to confiscate his agent's assets and use them to pay off his obligations.[193] Of course, it is not impossible that Szmojło had exploited his status to take money he had no right to; he may even have cheated his patron from time to time. Still it is hard to believe that he had embezzled such a huge sum.

Hieronim Florians's cruel rage soon made the truth irrelevant. On July 15 Szmojło signed a confession "of his own free will" in which he surrendered the whole amount given in the indictment.[194] Even before this, Radziwiłł had instructed the officials on his Lithuanian estates to arrest the brothers' relatives and friends and confiscate their property. He also ordered that all of Szmojło's papers be packed up and sent to him in Słuck.[195] By the time Szmojło signed his confession no fewer than fifty-eight Jews were under arrest in Słuck.

Radziwiłł made promises both in a letter and a proclamation to the Jews of Krzyczew that he would cause no harm to the Jews he had arrested, only to those who were, in his words, guilty.[196] The number of Jews he imprisoned continued to rise, eventually reaching ninety-seven. Heading the list were Szmojło's wife, Henia, and his father, Yitzhak. Szmojło and Gdal's names however did not appear.[197]

Gdal was safely ensconced in Königsberg, where he enjoyed the protection of the king of Prussia. Later he moved to Berlin and in 1749 was betrothed to the daughter of the rabbi of Dessau.[198] Szmojło continued to languish in the fortress of Słuck even after he had signed away all his property. It seem likely that he was kept in solitary confinement, which would explain why he was not mentioned among the detainees.

Under pressure to make the Neuburg payment, Radziwiłł began selling off Ickowicz property without delay. As the tangible assets began to be realized, he decided to extend his reach, even demanding the return of money that Szmojło had spent while in his service. For example, Szmojło had expended large sums to purchase the rabbinates of Wilno and Kraków for his sons-in-law. Radziwiłł seems to have written to the communities in question demanding the money be returned. He even sent his agent to Kraków where he had the rabbi's horses confiscated and his scribe arrested.[199] In short order both men lost their rabbinical posts. The fate of Naḥman Katz in Wilno is unknown. Yitzhak Yosef Te'omim-Frankel, having lost the Kraków rabbinate, made Breslau his permanent home, eventually becoming chief rabbi of Silesia.[200]

Hieronim Florian was not satisfied with confiscating Szmojło's property in Lithuania. On the basis of his agent's signed confession, he also laid claim to all of Szmojło's holdings in Prussia - most notably a tannery he owned there.[201] Radziwiłł then contacted Ephraim, the Court Jew in Berlin, demanding the return of the dowry Szmojło had paid to have his daughter betrothed to Ephraim's son (though the wedding does not seem to have taken place).

This was a step too far. Ephraim, enjoying the support of the Prussian king, would not be bullied. He refused to comply and countercharged that Radziwiłł's claims against Szmojło were illegal. The issue soon became tied up in litigation. Ephraim obtained a lien against Radziwiłł's goods and chattels in Königsberg, which paralyzed trade between his Lithuanian estates and the Baltic port. Litigation dragged on for six years and caused the magnate huge losses. In 1751 the two sides reached a compromise under which the Jews were released from prison and at least some of their property was returned to them.[202]

The usually very helpful Radziwiłł family archives hold no information about the fates of Szmojło and Henia, and it is left to the Jewish sources to fill the gap. The following entry appeared in the record book of the Słuck burial society for 1747: "On Monday, 6 Tevet,[203] the illustrious chief, our master and teacher Shmuel son of Yitzhak Segal passed away. He was buried on Thursday, 9 Tevet, because he lay in the fortress from Monday until Thursday. He rests next to Rabbi Naphtali Hertz Haran . . . in the first row."[204] Szmojło (Shmuel) had spent almost a year and a half in prison before he died. He was not the only victim of the affair to die in the Słuck fortress. The burial society record book mentions ten other men and women who died in prison, "among those held by the lord's court." These included Szmojło's father, Yitzhak, who died in the month of Sivan 1747.[205]

Henia was eventually released and prospered, marrying Yisrael, the rabbi of Kamieniec (Kamianets-Podilskyi, Ukraine), who went on to serve as trustee of the Council of the Four Lands.[206] However, she soon found herself in the eye of another storm—the clash between Rabbi Jacob Emden and Rabbi Jonathan Eybeschütz. In the early 1750s she wanted to marry off her daughter to Eybeschütz's son, which infuriated the Emden camp. The Rabbi of Biała interceded and went so far as to have Henia's son-in-law, by then Rabbi of Breslau, persuade her to call off the match. These efforts were successful and the marriage never took place.[207]

The arrest of Szmojło, his relatives, and friends also attracted attention outside Poland-Lithuania. Radziwiłł found himself under pressure to release his former agent not only from Ephraim in Berlin but also from Lipman Levy, the former Russian Court Jew, who had taken up residence in Vienna. In a letter dated September 1, 1745, Lipman advised Radziwiłł not to listen to Szmojło's enemies, emphasizing that Szmojło had rendered faithful service to his lord for many years and respectfully asking him to show mercy.[208]

From his safe haven in Prussia, Gdal also wrote to Radziwiłł, begging him to show mercy to the women and children in custody, since they were innocent of any wrongdoing.[209] Appeals of this sort, however, did not impress Hieronim Florian. He did finally release the surviving prisoners, but only because he needed to put an end to the biting economic sanctions that Ephraim had imposed on him in Königsberg.[210]

CONCLUSIONS

Thus ended one of the most glittering careers pursued by any Polish-Lithuanian Jew in the eighteenth century. In the fifty years that remained in the life of the Polish-Lithuanian Commonwealth, it would be matched by only one other, Shmuel Zbytkower, who achieved similar wealth and status in non-Jewish society in the last decades of the eighteenth century.[211]

The careers of Szmojło and Gdal had much in common with those of the Court Jews in Central Europe, at least in terms of their economic activity and the social status it brought them. Perhaps the major difference was that the Court Jews functioned in an absolutist setting, where the rights of the different groups in society were being systematically eroded in favor of the monarch, while the brothers functioned on a magnate latifundium that was still essentially feudal in nature. The Radziwiłłs were not interested in creating a new kind of relationship with their subjects nor in restructuring estate society. Their goal was simply to increase their revenues. If in doing that they had to deepen their control over their estates and their subjects they would do so, but it was never an end in itself.

Like the Court Jews, Szmojło and Gdal helped their Radziwiłł lords and ladies maximize the family's incomes. Unlike them, however, they never received from their patrons legal recognition in the form of a personal privilege granting them a special legal status. Their position was determined solely by the economic services they provided. Once they could no longer deliver them, not only were their positions taken away from them, their very lives were placed in danger.[212]

Still, it was by exploiting the possibilities offered by the feudal economic structures of Poland-Lithuania that the brothers were able to build their fortunes. In this they were very different from noblemen who leased estates. The latter saw these leases mainly in sociopolitical terms—a means of improving their social status. The Ickowiczes viewed them in exclusively economic terms—as a means of enriching both their masters and themselves.

So while the noble estate leaseholders were invested in the status quo, the brothers were interested in change. They adopted highly aggressive management policies and squeezed their subjects' feudal obligations, in labor, in goods, and in cash. Nothing was sacred. Customary arrangements and traditional ways were arbitrarily discarded in the search for enhanced incomes. The peasants were not the only group to be targeted: townspeople, the local nobility, and even the clergy all felt the pinch.[213]

The road to real wealth for the brothers lay in understanding the workings of the economic system. Since the Radziwiłłs needed money to run the estates and maintain their social status, marketing agricultural produce was crucial. In its basic structure, however, the estate economy was geared to production: the peasants' main feudal obligation was met through labor on the *folwark* and it was in return for that that they received their own small farms. This meant that the key to successful management as far as the family was concerned was turning the agricultural production from both its own and the peasants' farms into cash income.

Szmojło and Gdal Ickowicz excelled in marketing. Certainly, the competition they faced was weak. The Polish nobility, who did most of the estate leasing, looked down on trade and largely refused to sully their hands with it.[214] On the other hand, Polish-Lithuanian Jews were primarily merchants, so working with the markets was second nature to the brothers. Though a great deal of their effort was devoted to the home market, particularly in using networks of Jewish leaseholders of monopoly rights to market grain as alcohol, the big money was to be made on the international markets, especially Königsberg. The very earliest leases that the Ickowiczes took from the Radziwiłłs granted them access to the Baltic ports. They then used their mercantile profits to expand their leasing activities, and their income from the estates (largely in agricultural produce) to expand their mercantile profits.

This was a winning combination that made Szmojło and Gdal very wealthy very quickly. The Radziwiłłs, most prominently Anna and Hieronim Florian, recognized the brothers' success and tried to harness it to their other economic needs: supplying both estate and court and, crucially, finding sources of credit to help redeem the Neuburg estates. As they grew closer to the Radziwiłłs, the Ickowicz brothers acquired a social standing second to none. Whether as a result of their formal status as estate leaseholders or because of their informal status as confidantes of the Radziwiłł family, the Jewish brothers were treated with enormous respect, on a par with that enjoyed by the gentry. They also wielded a great deal of power. Within the Jewish community, too, the Ickowiczes became prominent and powerful, purchasing leadership positions for their family, dispensing patronage at will, and interfering in communal administration when it suited them.

There was a price to be paid for this success and it came in the form of isolation. The brothers were too rich and powerful to participate in Jewish communal and other organizations. Though they were respected for their achievements, they were not liked by their fellow Jews, with whom they now had little in common socially and economically.[215] In non-Jewish society, their situation was, if anything, worse. The nobility resented the brothers for usurping the leaseholds they wanted and could not stand the idea of Jews wielding power that they felt was rightly theirs. And when the other estate residents felt their usual sources of income under attack from Jewish leaseholders—even though they were acting on behalf of the Radziwiłłs themselves—anger and frustration rose to such a level that it could soon boil over into violence.

As long as the brothers retained the Radziwiłłs' support, the hatred and opposition meant little, even when it led to rebellion such as that in Krzyczew. In a strange way, the brothers' social isolation even found an echo in their master, Hieronim Florian's feelings of paranoia; this seems to have tightened the bond between him and Szmojło. Gdal, on the other hand, understood his tenuous position following the peasant uprising and withdrew from cooperating with the Radziwiłłs. Sadly we will never know whether this was because he grew afraid of Hieronim Florian's psychopathic tendencies or because he grasped the dangers inherent in large-scale estate leasing undertaken by Jews.

He would have been right on both counts. The moment Szmojło could not answer his master's economic needs he fell from grace and found himself exposed to Radziwiłł's vicious temper. Worse than that, he brought down nearly a hundred members of his family, friends, and business colleagues, who were all thrown in jail. Eleven, including Szmojło himself, did not survive the ordeal.

This was surely an enormous price to pay even for twenty years of resounding success. It certainly seems to have deterred other Jews from following in their footsteps. Only one other Jew is known to have leased an estate from the Radziwiłł family in Lithuania in the first six decades of the eighteenth century. This was Zalman ben Yitzhak, who leased the *starostwo* of Kamieniec Litowski from Michał Kazimierz for just two years between 1745 and 1747.[216] Clearly, the game was simply not worth the candle.

Nonetheless, the Jews on the estates do seem to have understood the underpinnings of the brothers' success. The best way to serve their lord as well as to make money for themselves was to operate in the market sector. If they wanted the benefits that directly serving the Radziwiłłs could bring, they needed to help the estate administration market agricultural produce and because the home market was crucial, this meant selling grain to peasants in the form of alcohol.

Leasing monopoly rights, the mainstay of Poland-Lithuania's feudal economy, was the key. Leaseholders essentially became economic agents for the Radziwiłłs which gave them with all the support that such a status implied without bringing them into positions of power over the non-Jewish population. It was an exercise in risk management. Of course, rights leaseholders, who could control only one sector of the estate economy, would never be able to provide the Radziwiłłs with all the services that the Ickowiczes had done, nor could they ever become their lords' agents or confidantes. As far as they were concerned, though, this was probably all to the good.

So Jews did not lease estates. Nor did they hold clerical or administrative positions on the latifundium, except for the years when Szmojło and Gdal managed it. This tells us something about how posts were filled on the Radziwiłł family estates, and in particular that economic logic played no part in the matter. Administrative posts were granted in order to reward intimates or attract potential supporters. Jews could not be Radziwiłł intimates nor provide political support, so there was no reason for them to receive such positions on the estates.[217] Only when a Jewish businessman attained a position in which he was responsible for hiring could he give jobs to family members and friends. It was little surprise then that when Szmojło Ickowicz fell from grace, his friends and associates also lost their jobs in estate administration.

The noneconomic logic that underlay the Radziwiłłs' administrative appointments meant that they had little need to lease estates out to Jews. Estate leases were used for sociopolitical ends, even if this undercut their importance for the family's revenues. As a counterbalance the Radziwiłłs, like many magnate estate-owners, began to exploit leases on monopoly rights much more intensively. This led them to grant these leases to Jews, who used their business and administrative skills to increase their profitability.

A new kind of equilibrium developed. The Radziwiłłs wanted to get the Jews out of the largely non-economic estate leases and into the profitable monopoly leases, while the Jews wanted to avoid the risks involved in estate leasing and preferred the safer monopoly leases. The logic and implications of this development form the subject of the next chapter.

Arendarze

Jewish Lessees of Monopoly Rights

On the Radziwiłł latifundium, estate leases and monopoly leases formed two separate, though not unrelated, sources of income. They were related because the monopolies derived from the estate and so, when it was given on lease, were transferred from owner to leaseholder (often known as a *dzierżawca*). The revenues they brought formed an integral part of estate income, and had certainly been taken into account when the price of the estate lease had originally been set. Thus, the *dzierżawca* was, in principle at least, entitled to lease out any or all monopoly rights on his estate. In reality, however, Radziwiłł very often reserved the right to determine the fees charged for monopoly leases (each of which was called in Polish an *arenda*), even on estates he had leased out in their entirety.[1] This allowed him to ensure that the revenues from the *arenda* remained as high as possible.

The family and its administrators saw their monopolies as a sales outlet, whose purpose was to turn the surplus agricultural produce of the estate into revenue. This can be seen in a set of orders issued by Michał Kazimierz Radziwiłł to his administrators on the Słuck estate in 1760. One began, "As for the crops, on which the entire economy [of the estate] depends."[2] Another, dealing with monopoly leases, opens: "The inns on which . . . the greatest part of the lord's [Radziwiłł's] revenues [depends]."[3] So, while the Radziwiłłs believed that the basis for all the economic activity on the estate was agricultural, they understood that their revenue in the form of money was dependent on the monopoly leases. The importance the Radziwiłł administration attributed to this income can also be seen in the fact that they did not exempt those who came to live on the estates from monopoly payments as part of their general policy of tax breaks to encourage settlement.[4] Regulations for the establishment of new Jewish communities also contained detailed references to the management of these leases because they would be held mostly by local Jews.[5]

The importance of revenues from monopoly leases for the reconstruction of the Radziwiłł estates in the eighteenth century becomes quite clear in Michał Kazimierz Radziwiłł's strategy for increasing profitability on the royal estate (*ekonomia*) of Szawle, which he took over in the early 1740s.[6] Improving alcohol sales played a key role. Among the orders he issued to his administrators were instructions to build taverns in all parts of the estate and expropriate those built illegally; to ban peasants from producing alcohol in their homes except for holidays and family festivals; to prohibit Jews from importing alcohol from outside the estate; to institute the organized leasing of monopolies and, when necessary, to transfer them to Jews, who were to be allowed to return to the estate for this purpose (they had been expelled about a decade earlier). He also ordered his administrators to ensure that all the taxes and customs owed to him were collected and to maintain the infrastructure of roads and bridges.[7]

This policy seems to have been highly successful, since Radziwiłł's annual income from Szawle leapt from around 28,000 złoty in the early 1740s to 290,000 złoty about twenty years later, an increase of over 1,000 percent.[8] The importance of the monopoly leases in this growth is evident from the enormous jump in their price, from some 600 złoty in the early 1740s (when there were no Jews on the estate) to more than 67,000 złoty in the early 1760s—an increase of about 11,000 percent. Income from the *arenda* as a share of total estate income also jumped in those two decades, from 2 percent to 23 percent, an increase of 1,050 percent.[9]

These and corresponding figures from fourteen other estates in Lithuania belonging to the Radziwiłł family indicate the growing importance of the income from monopoly leases. Table 5.1 shows total income from each estate and *arenda* income both in cash and as a share of total income. Data are given for each estate for two years, one towards the beginning of the period discussed here and the other towards the end. After the figures for the second year, the growth in the proportion of *arenda* incomes as part of general incomes is also given.

The data are taken from inventories compiled by the Radziwiłł administration, usually before a particular estate was leased out.[10] Before drawing any conclusions it is worth remembering the random nature of these sources. Since we do not have a full data series it is hard to know whether a

Table 5.1. *Arenda* Income as a Share of Total Estate Income

Estate	Year	Total Income*	Income from Arenda	% of Total	% Growth
Birże	1731	8,202	1,610	20	—
	1764	33,995	12,460	37	85
Dawidgródek	1693	14,359	10,000	70	—
	1760	36,609*	19,500*	53	–24
Głębokie	1702	7,017	3,000	43	—
	1761	37,360	15,100	40	–7
Delatycze	1680	8,695	667	8	—
	1757	7,695	1,456	19	137.5
Dubińka	1735	6,000	480	8	—
	1760	6,588	1,048	16	100
Kojdanów	1695	11,657	4,500	39	—
	1792	78,017	37,551	48	23
Kopyś	1694	32,647	5,770	18	—
	1755	48,872**	22,568**	46	156
Korelicze	1672	7,415	800	11	—
	1762	46,381	17,000	37	236
Łachwa	1691	3,981	800	20	—
	1742	16,631	8,500	51	155
Mir	1681	12,223	6,000	49	—
	1757	72,311	38,276	53	8
Newel	1712	26,512	4,965	19	—
	1761	177,504	60,128	34	79
Radziwiliszki	1694	1,345	200	15	—
	1755	3,629	880	24	60
Romanów Ruski	1699	21,922	5,000	23	—
	1755	19,640**	7,294**	37	61
Siebież	1694	4,940	800	16	—
	1762	52,375	12,800	24	50
Szawle	1742	28,304	639	2	—
	1764	291,980	67,103	23	1,050

SOURCES: AR XXV, 236, 243, 677, 681, 698, 702, 923, 925, 1044, 1047, 1076, 1709, 1775, 1789, 1797, 1811, 2168, 2172, 2444, 2458, 2614, 2619, 3506, 3511, 3552, 3686, 4169, and 4172.
* All prices are in Polish złoty (rounded to the nearest whole) unless otherwise stated.
** These prices are given in tynfs, each tynf being worth one złoty and eight groszy.

particular figure is representative or reflects a blip in prices due to war, fire, etc. Nonetheless, despite all the caveats, we do see fairly consistent increases.

On average, *arenda* income made up some 24 percent of total estate income at the beginning of the period and 36 percent at the end. At the beginning of the period revenues from the *arenda* were less than 20 percent of total income on ten estates while at its end this was true of only two. By the end of the period *arenda* income was more than 30 percent of the total on ten estates, compared with just four at the beginning.[11]

In order to understand the nature of this growth, we should look at it in more detail. Before we draw any conclusions, however, we should examine the two cases, Dawidgródek and Głębokie, where the share of *arenda* income within total income dropped. The decrease in Głębokie was marginal (3 points, from 43 percent to 40 percent). The drop in Dawidgródek, on the other hand, was larger (from 70 percent to 53 percent). This was apparently due to the unusually low income from the estate's agricultural activity in the first year (1693), which resulted in the share of *arenda* income rising to an atypical 70 percent. Three years later the estate's agricultural revenues returned to usual levels, so the percentage of *arenda* income fell back to 56 percent, where it more or less remained throughout the eighteenth century.[12]

Leaving aside these two exceptional cases, the figures from the other estates seem to indicate that growth was significant. The increases in the share of *arenda* income ranged from 8 percent (the Mir estate) to 1,050 percent (the Szawle *ekonomia*), with an average of 170 percent. The case of Szawle is especially striking. The huge increase is explained by the fact that at the beginning of the period, *arenda* income was an unusually small part of total income (2 percent), so even a small increase would result in a change of hundreds of percent.[13] If we ignore this case as exceptional too, we are left with twelve estates where the increase ranged from 8 percent to 236 percent and the average increase was 96 percent. This meant that the importance of the *arenda*s in the Radziwiłł's income from their estates nearly doubled over the course of the eighteenth century.

Was this the result of a deliberate policy by the Radziwiłł family to exploit their *arenda*s more heavily? No written instructions to this effect have survived, but some light can be shed by comparing the situation on the estates that remained in the Radziwiłłs' possession throughout the eighteenth century with that on the Neuburg estates, which had passed out of the family's control when they were given to Ludwika Karolina Radziwiłł as a dowry on her marriage in 1687 to Prince Karl Filip of Pfalz-Neuburg.[14] Twelve of the estates in Table 5.1 can be divided into two groups: estates that the family retained (Delatycze [Dzialiatsichy, Belarus], Kojdanów, Korelicze [Karelichy, Belarus], Łachwa [Lakhva, Belarus], and Mir) and the Neuburg estates (Birże, Głębokie, Kopyś, Newel,

Radziwiliszki, Romanów Ruski, and Siebież).[15] The average increase in the share of *arenda* income on the five estates managed by the Radziwiłłs was 112 percent, whereas on the seven Neuburg estates it was only 69 percent. This would seem to indicate that in the eighteenth century the Radziwiłłs consistently exploited their *arenda*s more than other estate owners, perhaps a sign that they viewed the monopoly leases as an important means of increasing their income and pursued a deliberate policy of exploiting them to that end.[16]

IMPROVING EFFICIENCY: THE GENERAL *ARENDA*

One of the most important ways of increasing revenues from the monopoly leases was to invest in infrastructure, especially building and maintaining taverns, mills, bridges, roads, and fish ponds. As we have seen, this was Michał Kazimierz Radziwiłł's policy when he came to reorganize the Szawle *ekonomia*,[17] and the inventories from many other estates show that he adopted the same strategy there. For example, the Kopyś estate had seven active mills and three taverns in 1684.[18] About ninety years later there were fourteen mills and no fewer than thirty-nine taverns.[19] Similarly, on the Newel estate in 1712 there were six mills and six taverns, whereas in 1764 there were seven mills and forty-eight taverns.[20] In both cases the main growth was in taverns; the number of mills rose more moderately.[21]

Investing in infrastructure was not the only way in which the Radziwiłłs sought to increase their *arenda* income. In the early eighteenth century the system by which the leases were granted was reorganized. Previously, individual taverns had generally been leased out separately as had been the monopolies on milling, the collection of taxes at markets, and the receipt of bridge tolls. In the late seventeenth century and the first half of the eighteenth century the Radziwiłłs instituted on each of their estates what contemporary sources called a "general *arenda*" (*arenda jeneralna*), a comprehensive three-year lease that included all of the rights that had previously been leased out separately.[22]

The contract for one of the last general *arenda*s instituted on the Radziwiłł latifundium makes the logic of the system clear. When Hieronim Florian Radziwiłł died in 1760, his brother Michał Kazimierz Radziwiłł inherited all his estates, including Słuck and Kopyl, the two most important ones. As had been his policy for forty years, Michał Kazimierz instituted a series of general *arenda*s on his newly acquired lands. In the Kopyl contract he gave his reasons for doing so:

> In order to ensure the better management, economic oversight, and stable administration of the extensive estates in my principality of Słuck, I have decided to divide the estates in my principality of Słuck into three parts. . . . [They] will be run by three managers, each responsible for a different part and [all] subject to a general administrator. That being so, I have also decided to change the secondary *arenda*s, which each *arendarz* [lease holder] has, until now, received on the basis of personal contracts, into a general *arenda*, and to appoint, for all [three parts of] the estate, general *arendarze*, from whom the secondary *arendarze* will receive their contracts, and to whom [the secondary *arendarze*] will be subordinate.[23]

The establishment of the general *arenda* was thus part of a large-scale attempt to make estates more profitable by improving the efficiency of their organization, management, and administration. Like other magnates who established a general *arenda*, Michał Kazimierz Radziwiłł not only adapted the leases to the new structure of the estate, but also appointed special general *arendarze* to run them. These men were charged with issuing individual leases to the secondary *arendarze* (mostly tavern keepers) and were responsible for the efficient running of the *arenda* as well as the collection of payments.

Quite remarkable in Radziwiłł's statement is the clear parallel he drew between the organization of the general *arenda* and that of the estate as a whole. Each of the three parts of the estate was given a manager responsible mainly for its agricultural activity. Alongside him was appointed a general *arendarz* responsible for management of all monopoly leasing issues. In both cases Radziwiłł had simplified management by delegating authority to high level administrators, who were to handle the day-to-day running of the estate and its revenues. This parallel between the managers and the general *arendarze* suggests that the function of the general *arendarze* was not just centralized revenue collection; they were also, in one way or another, becoming part of the estate administration. The importance that Radziwiłł attributed to their function was expressed in the fact that the general *arendarze*, unlike the three managers, answered only to him and not to any other officials.

Słuck and Kopyl were among the last of the Radziwiłł estates in the Grand Duchy of Lithuania to see the establishment of a general *arenda*. After Michał Kazimierz's death about a year later, his son Karol Stanisław managed the estates for another two years. Once Stanisław August Poniatowski was crowned king of Poland in 1764, political and military activity took up all Karol Stanisław's time, leaving none for estate management. In fact, the young Radziwiłł was soon sent into exile and his estates confiscated. Orderly recordkeeping resumed only in the late 1770s.[24] In the interim, estates were increasingly left without a general *arendarz* and the secondary *arendarze* began again to receive their leases directly from the estate administration. It is hard to say whether this reflected the chaos of the 1760s and '70s, or an advance toward more centralized management in which the role of the middleman was being eliminated. The disappearance of the general *arenda* system on other estates in Poland and Lithuania makes the second possibility more likely.[25]

The Structure of the General Arenda

The general *arenda* encompassed many monopoly rights (or, more precisely, many sources of income from such rights) that the *arendarz* began to manage when he signed the lease. Not every right appeared in every lease, whose contents often depended on local conditions. Nonetheless, there were three broad categories of income which appeared in all the contracts.[26] One was from the monopoly on the sale of alcoholic beverages, particularly beer (*arenda piwna*), mead (*arenda miodowa*), and vodka (*arenda gorzalczana*). Some leases provided the exclusive right to sell alcohol in a particular place (*arenda szynkowna*).[27]

The second category of income included in the general *arenda*s was the revenues from mills.[28] The lease specified which mills the general *arendarz* was leasing and what payments he was to receive from them. These were generally given in the form of a part of the grain milled. The usual arrangement was for the *arendarz* to take two-thirds of the payment and the miller one-third.

The third category of income that the general *arendarz* leased consisted of customs and duties charged on commercial activity on the estate. This was a complicated system so it is hard to understand the precise nature of each individual tax. Luckily many lease contracts included a schedule of customs and duties that can be used as a guide.

A typical schedule accompanied the contract for the general *arenda* of Nowy Świerżeń.[29] It included the following customs and duties: *kapszczyzna* (a fee for the manufacture and sale of alcohol not covered elsewhere in the contract); *wagowe* (a duty imposed when goods to be sold were weighed on the town scales; it was charged by weight and was generally paid by both the seller and the buyer; the types of merchandise to which it applied included tobacco, perfume, anise, wax, iron and steel, leather, and cotton); *pleczkowe* (a tax on the sale of livestock);[30] *sosowe* (a tax on salt and salted products, especially various kinds of salt fish);[31] *jarmarkowe* (a fee charged during the annual fair on, among other things, hemp and hops); *targowe* (a tax on goods sold at the weekly market such as salt, fish, fruit and vegetables, horses, and oxen);[32] *mostowe* (a toll collected from merchants crossing the bridge across the Niemen River to do business in the town; it was charged according to the number of horses pulling a wagon). One other fee, the *brzegowe* (riverbank duty), was unique to port towns. It seems to have been a tax on local merchants who traded in goods to and from Königsberg by renting space in the rafts plying the river. The goods taxed included hemp, wheat, salt fish, white tar, and millet.[33]

Assessing the relative importance of these three main sources of income is no easy task because the relevant documentation has not survived. In letters to his noble lord, the general *arendarz* usually referred to his revenue as a single unit, although in his own business dealings he had to distinguish between the different types of income because he leased them out separately to secondary *arendarze*. One indication of the relationship between the three areas of activity is the particular interest shown by the magnate in the taverns on his estates—building, maintaining, and renovating them. This is presumably a sign of the special importance he attributed to the income from *propinacja*.

The smaller increase in the number of mills might suggest that mill revenues were less important.[34] Nonetheless, the administration took steps to ensure that mill revenues did not decrease. Special orders were issued forbidding the milling of grain in mills off the estate or using hand-operated mills at home.[35] This policy was similar to the ban on locals buying alcoholic beverages off the estate or producing it themselves (except for family celebrations). The estate owner does seem then to have viewed these two sources of income as linked.

It is even harder to assess the relative importance in the overall income from the *arenda* of the various customs and duties. This because no record of the actual takings of an *arendarz* has survived. There are, however, many indications that both the magnate and the *arendarze* regarded these revenues as very important too.

The way in which the different elements of the *arenda* were connected may be seen in a petition sent from Romanów Ruski, near Kopyś, to Hieronim Florian Radziwiłł in 1755. The local *arendarze* asked him for redress because the Orthodox church had been closed following a dispute in the town. They claimed to have suffered losses not only because all baptisms, marriages, and funerals were being conducted elsewhere, but because the major fairs and markets had been canceled.

The *arendarze* were thus hit twice: first by losing the revenue from customs and duties on trade, and second, perhaps more importantly, by losing the income from selling liquor to churchgoers as well as to visiting merchants and their customers. They also complained that they had previously received substantial income from merchants coming from outside the estate, especially in the form of bridge tolls, but because outsiders were not being allowed into Romanów, these incomes had disappeared too.[36] All this amounted to a serious loss of revenue, one that the petitioners felt their noble lord would take seriously. The complaint also shows that the finances of the *arendarze* were to one degree or another dependent on the religious life of the Christian populations on the estate.

The Radziwiłłs, for their part, needed to make sure that the markets and fairs on their estates continued to run in good order, and inserted clauses in many leases to that effect. In order to protect local sales on the Jampol estate in southeastern Poland (now Ukraine), they even forbad the townspeople and peasants there to sell their goods at other fairs.[37] Again, clearly, the income from customs and duties on mercantile activity was a very significant source of income, though it is impossible to assess its importance relative to the monopolies on alcohol sales and milling.[38]

CHOOSING AN *ARENDARZ*: THE *AUKCJA*

The importance of monopoly leases can also be seen in the administration's attitude towards the *arendarze*, the ways they chose them, and the process of signing leases with them. Their objective was clear: What they needed was an *arendarz* who would offer the highest price for the lease and could be trusted to comply with its terms.

A clause in almost every contract (not only on the Radziwiłł estates) stated that any *arendarz* who did not want to renew his lease after three years had to give the estate owner at least three months' notice. This implies that, all things being equal, the estate owner preferred to renew leases with the same *arendarze*. Moreover, there do not seem to have been cases on the Radziwiłł estates in Lithuania in which an estate owner forced an *arendarz* to lease an *arenda* against his will.[39] The general *arendarz* was almost always a person familiar both with local conditions and with the people with whom he would be working. Since, the estate owner himself was not involved with the day-to-day running of each estate, he had his administrators choose a suitable *arendarz*, but insisted that those chosen be sent to him to sign the lease in person.[40]

Keeping control of the monopoly lease had great economic significance for the Radziwiłłs, particularly when the estate in question was being leased out to a noble *dzierżawca*. Because the latter's incomes from the estate were fixed in the inventory drawn up before the lease went into effect, he was not supposed to demand from the general *arendarz* more than was specified there. As the man in control, however, he was often in a situation to pressure the *arendarz* (as well as other subjects) to pay more than was specified. By signing the *arenda* contract himself, Radziwiłł not only prevented the *dzierżawca* from overcharging, but actually helped the general *arendarz* maintain the profitability of his *arenda* so he could be asked to pay a higher price when the time came to sign the next contract.

Moreover, if the administration managed to find a candidate who offered to pay more for the general *arenda* than was stipulated in the estate lease (that is to pay an *aukcja* [plural, *aukcje*] in the language of the contracts), the extra money went straight into the Radziwiłł treasury rather than to that of the *dzierżawca*.[41] This allowed the Radziwiłłs to increase their revenues from estates even after they had leased them out in full.

These *aukcje* appeared very frequently in Michał Kazimierz Radziwiłł's instructions on granting monopoly leases in the 1750s and early 1760s. It was his policy to try to put up the prices for the general *arenda* on each of his estates almost every year, even though the leases were for a three-year term. This meant that *aukcje* became very common. This can be seen in the data from the twenty-three estates belonging to Michał Kazimierz for which a series of *arenda* contracts has survived.[42] About half of them explicitly mentioned an *aukcja*;[43] in some 40 percent, the price of the *arenda* remained stable; and only 9 percent mentioned a drop in the price.[44] The average increase was about 16 percent, and the 8 price drops averaged 22 percent (Table 5.2).

Table 5.2. Changes in *Arenda* Prices

Price Change (in %)	1–10	11–20	21–30	31–40	41–50	51+
Increases	22	7	3	—	3	1
Decreases	3	2	—	1	1	1

SOURCE: AR XXIX, 5–11, *passim.*

The majority of *aukcje* (almost two-thirds) were no more than 10 percent, an affordable amount for most *arendarze*. At times, however, price increases were much greater. On the estate at Nieśwież the price rose steeply between 1755 and 1758. Initially the *arenda* cost 36,533 złoty and 10 groszy; in 1756 an *aukcja* of 2,666 złoty and 20 groszy was paid; in 1757 three *aukcje* were paid, totaling 4,066 and 20 groszy; and in the third year, another *aukcja* of 2,666 złoty and 20 groszy was offered. After just three years, then, the cost of the *arenda* had gone up to 45,933 złoty and 10 groszy, an increase of more than 25 percent![45] This was not an isolated case (Table 5.3).

The pressure to obtain annual increases in *arenda* fees led to intense competition between Jews interested in taking the leases. The administration was aware of this, and though it seems to have preferred retaining *arendarze* who made their payments, it did not hesitate to encourage competition in order to push up prices. Almost all the leases signed by the Radziwiłłs stated that they were valid for three years, but in the 1750s new contracts were signed after just two years, one year, or even more frequently.[46] For

Table 5.3. Changes in the Price of General *Arenda*s in the 1750s

Estate	Year	Arenda *Price*	Year	Arenda *Price*	No. Years	Change
Jampol	1752	24,700 złoty	1762	28,033 złoty	11	13%
Jaryczew	1744	8,000 złoty	1754	8,000 złoty	11	—
Kopyś	1749	39,705 tynf	1760	27,515 tynf	12	–30%
Łachwa	1746	9,000 złoty	1760	16,333 złoty	15	81%
Nieśwież	1747	28,333 złoty	1762	74,800 złoty	16	164%
Pomarzany	1748	13,500 złoty	1759	13,500 złoty	12	—
Rochmanów	1748	45,900 złoty	1762	25,300 złoty	15	–45%
Romanów	1750	983 taler bity	1760	1,467 taler bity	11	49%
Świerżeń	1746	8,500 złoty	1760	11,366 złoty	15	34%
Szawle	1755	34,817 tynf	1764	51,811 tynf	10	49%
Żółkiew	1747	44,333 złoty	1759	56,052 złoty	13	26%

SOURCE: AR XXIX, 5–11, *passim.*

example Michał Kazimierz Radziwiłł signed three-year leases for the Kopyś estate in 1752, 1753, 1754, 1756, 1758, and 1760[47] and for the Łachwa estate in 1752, 1753, 1754, 1757, 1758, and 1760.[48] In the case of the general *arenda* of the Kamieniec Litewski *starostwo*, Radziwiłł signed no fewer than three leases in a single day: on June 5, 1750, he signed a three-year contract with two *arendarze*, Avraham and Pinḥas, for an annual sum of 15,666 złoty and 20 groszy; he next signed a new contract for the same lease with Berek son of Shlomo for the price of 18,154 złoty and 6 groszy a year; and then finally, on the same day, he signed a third lease, back with Avraham and Pinḥas, for 19,000 złoty a year.[49]

This intense competition between *arendarze* was probably due to the fact that the prices of the *arenda*s were decreasing in real terms (that is, they were not keeping up with inflation), so they were became more and more worthwhile for the Jewish leaseholders. The result was an extremely volatile market that sometimes spiraled out of control. At times, offers of *aukcje* were even accompanied by bribes to the officials selecting the *arendarze*.[50] The more entrepreneurial candidates tried to avoid that problem by approaching Radziwiłł directly.[51] Some *arendarze* offered price increases that they could not actually afford in the hope of covering their expenses by increasing the tariffs they charged once they had taken the lease.[52] The only security a sitting *arendarz* might enjoy was that the administration generally preferred to continue employing the incumbent, provided he could match any *aukcja* offered by a competitor.[53] In at least one case an *arendarz* tried to protect himself by promising in advance to match any *aukcja* that might be offered for his *arenda*.[54]

Attempts to Restrict Competition

Jewish society had a legal mechanism for preventing competition among Jews, called possessor's rights (*dinei ḥazakah* in Hebrew). This was based on a legal principle that gave any Jew who had been in possession of a property for three years exclusive rights over it. Possessors' rights were widely used in medieval and early modern Jewish society, where they were expanded into the realm of business, giving merchants or craftsmen a monopoly over their share of the market once they had held it for three years.[55] When the *arenda* became common among the Jews of the Polish-Lithuanian Commonwealth, the principle of possessors' rights was further expanded to cover this branch of the economy too. In the sixteenth and early seventeenth century Polish-Lithuanian Jews understood possessor's rights over an *arenda* to be a right that an individual had to buy from his predecessor in order to be able to take over the lease. Their economic significance was such that the Jewish lay leadership took over the responsibility for them, removing them from the jurisdiction of the rabbinical courts.[56]

In the second half of the seventeenth century and in the eighteenth century, the way possessors' rights were granted in the Jewish communities and regional councils of Poland-Lithuania changed significantly. The *kahal* (the Jewish community council) claimed not only jurisdiction over possessors' rights cases between *arendarze* but also the authority to grant these rights to a candidate of its choice in the first place.[57] Just as they charged a fee for the right to live in the community, the community councils began charging fees for the right to take over a local *arenda*.[58] Some communities took this a stage further and sold the possessors' rights in perpetuity to the *arendarz*, who could then resell them when he gave up the lease.[59] As a result some communities continued leasing out possessors' rights to local *arenda*s, while others had lost their prerogative to this by selling them to the *arendarze* themselves.

The importance of possessor's rights in the *arenda* market lay in the fact that an incumbent leaseholder, in principle at least, had acquired exclusive rights to that *arenda*. Jewish law, if obeyed, would have prevented competitors from offering an *aukcja* without the consent of the original *arendarz*. This should have forestalled competition and allowed Jewish society to keep down the costs of taking an *arenda*.

The magnates were strongly, not to say violently, opposed to the imposition of possessors' rights. They clearly understood that open competition would lead to higher prices for the *arenda*s and were willing to support individuals who broke with the community on this issue.[60] Michał Kazimierz Radziwiłł, for example, banned the imposition of possessors' rights in all his estates. He took the matter so seriously that when in 1751 he learned that the Jewish community of Szawle was charging for possessors' rights over a local *arenda*, he fined the community 200 red złoty (worth 1,600 złoty) and ordered that the *arendarz* who held the rights be given fifty lashes at each of the four corners of the market square.[61]

On the other hand, when the Radziwiłł administration had difficulty finding someone to take a given *arenda*, or when a particular *arendarz* had to terminate his lease, it did not hesitate to order the local community to find a suitable candidate.[62] The administration also held the local community responsible for the *arendarz*'s finances, insisting that it sign a bond to that effect; if the leaseholder could not meet his obligations, the community would be forced to manage the *arenda* in his place.[63] Presumably many communities found this provision threatening and made every effort to ensure that the prospective *arendarz* would be able live up to his commitments. From here to imposing possessors' rights as a kind of license to hold the *arenda* was but a small step.

THE *ARENDARZE* IN THE ECONOMIC LIFE OF THE ESTATES

Payment Orders

The *arendarze* were important to the estate administration not just because of the income they brought. The ways in which the leaseholder paid his *arenda* fees also played an important role in the economic life of the estate.

Leases specified a number of dates during the year (usually two or four) on which the *arendarze* were to make payments. In practice, although the money was owed to the estate owner, most of it was not paid directly to him, but on his instructions to a third party. This was done by means of a payment order, known at the time as an *asygnacja*, which functioned more or less like a modern-day check: instead of paying his bills in cash, Radziwiłł wrote a payment order in the name of the merchant or tradesman and gave it to him. The order specified which *arendarz* was to cash it, and the beneficiary would take it to him to receive his money.

This method of payment, which seems to have developed in the eighteenth century, was especially common on noble estates and in the state treasury (although the treasury did not issue payment orders drawing specifically on *arendarze*). The *asygnacja* became popular with estate owners because it freed them from having to maintain a complex collection mechanism for their numerous *arendarze*, who worked on various estates often far distant one from another.

It was also convenient for the general *arendarze*, because it meant that they did not have to raise large sums of cash on the dates stated in the lease. In fact this system turned the *arendarz* from a lender into a borrower. In the sixteenth century the *arendarz* had had to pay the full *arenda* fee upon signing the contract, that is, before he had received any revenue from the estate.

This meant that he was effectively lending money to the estate owner. In the eighteenth century the *arendarz* signed his contract and began collecting the proceeds before he had to make any payment.

The general *arendarz* kept the payment orders (which when signed by the beneficiary served as receipts), and both he and the magnate reviewed them when the accounts were settled. These accounts, known as *klarygacje*, were drawn up on each of the payment dates stated in the lease. If the estate owner had not spent the full amount, the *arendarz* had to pay him the balance; if he had withdrawn more than the *arendarz* owed him, the difference would be taken out of the next installment of the *arenda* fee.[64]

The result was that the Jewish general *arendarz* became a sort of treasury official for the Radziwiłł administration responsible for making payments on its behalf.[65] In addition to one-time payments to merchants and tradesmen, Radziwiłł instructed his *arendarze* to pay salaries to groups and individuals on the estate: the general *arendarz* in Korelicze was instructed to pay the salaries of all skilled craftsmen in the Radziwiłłs' factory in Nowogródek;[66] the general *arendarz* in Biała paid salaries to a number of people, including agricultural labourers;[67] the general *arendarz* in Świerżeń paid salaries to the captains of the Radziwiłł rafts who sailed to Königsberg with his merchandise.

It was not only the poor and humble estate employees who received their salary from the general *arenda*rze, others of a higher status in the Radziwiłł's service did so too: an officer in their private army,[68] a doctor,[69] and an archivist,[70] were among those who were paid by the *arendarz*. The magnate even had his Jewish *arendarze* make payments to Christian clergymen: various priests and clerics received at least part of their income from their patron this way.[71] The system thus forced the general *arendarze* to be in contact with people of different types and classes on the estate, and perhaps even to develop economic ties with them.

Others besides Jews made payments on the Radziwiłł's behalf. Any administrator who collected money from the estates might be called upon to execute a payment order.[72] The majority of them, however, were given to Jewish *arendarze*, who formed the mainstay of the system. This role as unofficial estate treasury officials presumably gave the general *arendarze* not only a position of authority in the running of the estate but also an improved standing in the social hierarchy, where they were perceived as Radziwiłł's representatives on the ground.

Other Roles

The *arendarze* also served the Radziwiłł family as agents and suppliers of merchandise (*faktorzy*). The family was interested in exploiting the mercantile skills of the *arendarze*, who often had a great deal of experience in the markets both on the estates and elsewhere. Among the merchandise they supplied to the court were wines, salt, salt fish, meat, wax, and furs.[73] One of the most active suppliers of this kind was one Joshua ben Michael (Howsiej Michajłowicz), who for many years held the general *arenda* for Nowy Świerżeń, the Radziwiłłs' chief port on the Niemen River, and was deeply involved in trade with Königsberg.[74] Michał Kazimierz Radziwiłł ordered merchandise from him for more than a quarter of a century (1736–1762). Joshua frequently sent barrels of French wine and large quantities of salt and salt fish to the Nieśwież palace.[75] Over the years Radziwiłł seems to have come to know Joshua personally and even addressed letters to him by name, rather than simply calling him "the Świerżeń *arendarz*," as he did with other such suppliers.[76]

The goods that the *arendarze* supplied did not just provision the Radziwiłł court but also helped ensure the smooth functioning of the estate as a whole. Joshua supplied iron for repairing mills and tar for sealing the rafts that plied the river trade with Königsberg.[77] The general *arendarz* from Nieśwież supplied meat to feed workers in the town of Diampol (Belarus),[78] and the general *arendarz* of Żółkiew was instructed to send a craftsman in Stanisławów (Ivano-Frankivs'k, Ukraine) tools and raw materials for the boys from the estate who had been apprenticed to him.[79] The *arendarze* of Urzecz supplied goods and materials to the local mirror factory.[80] *Arendarze* also provided quantities of alcohol, especially vodka and beer: Joshua was instructed to supply drinks to a battalion of soldiers in Nieśwież during the funeral of an officer, and on Radziwiłł's instructions the *arendarz* of Biała sent 22 red złoty worth of wine to the nobles who had convened for the *sejmik* at Brześć (Brest, Belarus).[81]

The Radziwiłłs also gave the general *arendarze* the responsibility of collecting the state tax on the sale of alcoholic beverages (*czopowa*). They were a natural choice for this task since much of their work involved collecting fees from the taverns on the estate. The general *arendarz* knew the region and the people, and he was best qualified to decide how to divide up the tax among the taverns on the estate. *Czopowa* was typically charged as a global sum, so precise calculations of who had sold what were not necessary. The cost of the lease did not usually include the *czopowa* that the *arendarz* had to collect; it was generally mentioned in the lease in a separate clause together with a warning that the tax had to be collected and handed over to the authorities on time.[82]

Rural Arendarze

The system of general *arendas* was based on giving the general *arendarz* responsibility for all the *arendas* on a given estate. These were usually divided into two major groups, the town *arendas* (leases on taverns and mills in town and the collection of customs and duties from business in the town market) and the village *arendas* (leases of rural inns and mills as well as tolls collected on roads and bridges outside the towns). The general *arendarz* did not usually run all these *arendas* himself; instead, he subleased them to secondary *arendarze*, who were almost always Jews. They were usually poorer businessmen who could not afford the price of a general *arenda* and in the vast majority of cases simply ran a single tavern. Their economic ties were therefore not with the magnate himself but with the general *arendarz* which meant that their economic situation and social status were usually far inferior to his.[83]

The best-known description of a secondary *arenda* was written by Solomon Maimon, who was born and raised on one of the Radziwiłłs' estates near the town of Nieśwież. The account tells of his grandfather, an *arendarz* in a village called Żukowy Borek (Zhukaŭ Barok, Belarus):

> [B]esides a few peasants' plots, there was a water-mill, a small harbour, and a warehouse for the use of the vessels that come from Königsberg, in Prussia. All this, along with a bridge behind the village, and on the other side a drawbridge on the river Niemen, belonged to the lease.[84] . . . This lease, on account of the warehouse and the great traffic, was very lucrative. With sufficient industry and economical skill . . . my grandfather should have been able, not only to support his family, but even to gather wealth. . . . His beehives were sufficient for the brewing of mead. . . . The Jews in this neighborhood are continually moving about from place to place; and as there was a great traffic at our village, they were frequently passing through it, and of course they had always to stop at my grandfather's inn. Every Jewish traveler was met at the door with a glass of spirits. . . . He then had to wash his hands, and seat himself at the table, which remained constantly covered.[85]

Maimon mentions all the different areas of activity of the *arendarz*: manufacturing and selling alcohol, managing the revenue of the local mill, and collecting various commercial duties (the bridge toll and a fee for the storage of goods en route to Königsberg). He goes on to give a bleak description of the administration of the lease, discussing at length the difficulty his family had in getting the Radziwiłłs to protect them from their corrupt administrators as well as the low status of the *arendarz*, who was vulnerable to the fury of every passing nobleman. The description is characteristic of the plight of a secondary *arendarz*, although conditions in Żukowy Borek do seem to have been particularly bad.[86]

The lease seems to have been unusual in other ways too. Maimon himself says it was different from a regular rural *arenda* and notes that his grandfather appointed secondary *arendarze* (mostly family members) for the taverns in the surrounding villages.[87] As far as the Radziwiłłs were concerned, the Żukowy Borek *arenda* formed part of the general *arenda* of Mir,[88] but since it covered an area near the river port on the Niemen, it was a little more important than other *arenda*s and had a number of taverns attached to it. This meant that Solomon Maimon's grandfather could act as a low-level general *arendarz* (although he was answerable to the general *arendarz* of Mir rather than to the Radziwiłłs themselves). This was quite unusual; most rural *arenda*s included just one inn, where the Jewish *arendarz* lived with his family and servants.[89]

The main job of the rural *arendarz* was to act as tavern keeper, supplying beer and vodka to the residents of his village as well as of neighboring villages that had no tavern. This was an extremely important task for the administration because it created a market for the agricultural produce of the estate, especially that of the lord's farm, the *folwark*.[90] Since the peasants had to buy their drinks in the local tavern, much of the cash income they earned by selling their own surplus produce ended up in Radziwiłł's pocket. The monopoly that forced the peasants to process their grain at the local mill for a fee paid to the *arendarz* also increased the magnate's income at the peasants' expense.

In addition to their economic function in bringing income to the estate owner, the rural *arendarze* played a significant role in the day-to-day life of the estate. The village inn was not just a place for selling alcohol to locals; it was a sort of village shop, where peasants could buy goods they needed without having to go to town.[91] Full lists of all the goods for sale in village taverns have not survived, but in the tavern in Kłonówna (near Biała) one could buy candles, salt fish, rice, sugar, paper, lemons, and coffee in addition to homegrown agricultural produce.[92] Some secondary *arendarze* were not satisfied simply with buying and selling at the tavern, but went traveling through nearby villages, buying produce from the peasants and selling them goods from town.[93]

Another service that rural *arendarze* provided was a source of credit. The leaseholder lent money against pledges so that peasants whose crops did not provide the surplus necessary to cover all their needs, could borrow enough to buy tools and goods they could not supply themselves.[94] These activities of the rural *arendarz* can thus be seen as a kind of economic service connecting the village and the urban market. This suited the administration that wanted control over the peasants' economic activity as part of its policy of increasing revenue from all sectors of the estate.[95] The rural *arendarz's* involvement boosted the profitability of the *arenda* and so raised its price, which meant that the Radziwiłł treasury would effectively be collecting more money from the peasants.[96]

Sometimes peasants were forced to buy commodities exclusively from the *arendarz* and sell their produce only to him, a policy that could lead to price gouging.[97] More often however, the administration preferred that they go to the urban markets. It was harder to supervise economic activity in the villages than in the towns, where the *arendarz* typically ran a well-organized tax collection mechanism. In many cases trade in the villages was actually banned.[98]

The *arendarz's* commercial activity thus served as a tool that the magnate could exploit to make best use of the peasants' commercial activity for his own ends. In fact, the benefits it brought were not merely economic. The tavern was the social center of the village, a meeting point, and a place to spend one's leisure time. It might also provide lodging for merchants and other travelers.[99] Because the Jewish *arendarz* was involved in all the tavern's activity, he found himself on the one hand a central figure in village life but on the other, as a Jew, an outsider.[100] This kind of alienated integration made the *arendarz* an important source of information for Radziwiłł about everything that happened in and around the village.[101] The *arendarz* would report to the estate administration about anything unusual, such as, in one case at least, the presence of a dwarf in the village. Then, if necessary, Radziwiłł could be contacted for instructions on what to do.[102]

Urban Arendarze: *The Case of Słuck*

The structure of an urban *arenda* differed from that of a rural *arenda* in a number of ways.[103] First, the *propinacja* lease was managed differently. In most cities and towns on the Radziwiłł estates the townspeople were not forced to buy alcohol only in the lord's tavern; they were free to drink at whichever taverns they wished and even sell alcohol if they wanted to. The *arenda* income came from a sales tax paid by all sellers of alcohol.[104] These vendors were apparently considered to be operating with a license from the *arendarz*, so the tax they paid was called just that, *licenty* (licenses). In addition the *arendarz* generally ran his own tavern, where lower-priced drinks were sold on which no add-on license fee was paid.[105]

Few records exist of the daily running of the urban taverns, perhaps because they were part of the general *arenda*, whose papers were kept by the *arendarz* rather than by Radziwiłł himself and so are not preserved in the family archive. In Słuck however, the urban tavern was run separately from the general *arenda*, and the Radziwiłł administration supervised its activities as closely as possible. Thus the family archive contains detailed data on its operation.

Słuck was the biggest town on all the Radziwiłł estates in Lithuania in the mid-eighteenth century, with a population of around 5,000, including some 1,500 Jews.[106] It was also a commercial center and the nearest town to the main residence of Hieronim Florian Radziwiłł. Accordingly the figures from Słuck should not be regarded as typical of those from medium-sized or small towns on the estates.

Particularly informative is the tavern contract of 1753, whose most significant feature was that it did not specify a total amount due from the *arendarz*, Mordechai ben Ya'akov, as most ordinary leases did. Instead it committed him to sell at a fixed price the large quantities of plain vodka supplied him by the estate administration. His profit was to come from reducing the size of the drinks he sold at the given price "This Mordechai [the tavern keeper] . . . may serve smaller portions, that is, according to the older custom, so that from every *miednica* that he serves in the tavern he will have a profit of two tynf."[107] This was standard practice at the time and not considered cheating. Other ways of boosting profits however, such as watering down the vodka, or selling liquor purchased for private use, were considered fraudulent, and the *arendarz* was forbidden to engage in them.

Mordechai was to pay the salary of his tavern servant, but the estate administration was to furnish a still, utensils, and anise (to flavor the vodka). Finer liquor (flavored with cinnamon, oranges, lemons, caraway, or sugar) could be sold by the *arendarz* at a price he set himself. In order to maintain the tavern's monopoly, Mordechai undertook to prevent anyone else from importing vodka into the city without paying a tax, and to prohibit other taverns in town from watering down their liquor. These clauses also ensured that his tavern would be able to charge the lowest prices in town.[108]

The lease stipulated that the tavern should stock various kinds of wine, including Hungarian and French wines (from Champagne and Burgundy), muscatel, and wine from the Rhineland. The tavern was required to sell English and local beer as well as mead, and was to serve coffee, tea, and cocoa. Even though he was contractually obliged to sell all these beverages, Mordechai received no discount on the duty levied on them.

The need to supply so many expensive imported drinks was explained in another clause of the contract. Radziwiłł pledged that another building would be built, purchased, or rented in the Słuck central market square where all these beverages would be sold, and various games, such as billiards, could be played. The plan seems to have been for Radziwiłł to set up an exclusive club for himself and his aristocratic friends. He went on to order that service there be provided by a man of German origin (i.e., not a Jew).[109]

The contract required Mordechai to submit monthly accounts to the supervisor of the Radziwiłłs' treasury in Słuck and to the officer in charge of the private Radziwiłł army. These were to state how much liquor had been sold, how much money the Słuck treasury was owed, and the amount of the *arendarz's* profits.[110] The contract recognized that the tavern would not be Mordechai's sole source of income and permitted him to trade freely in fabric, leather, hemp, salt, and other goods. It also gave him protection from anyone who might try to interfere with his commercial activity but stated that the tavern keeper would not be exempt from the commercial duties levied in Słuck.

Though we have no more details of how Mordechai ben Ya'akov ran his business, the tavern accounts from three years previously have been preserved and give a detailed picture of its finances in 1750. Every week to ten days during the first half of the year (January 1–July 1)[111] slightly more than 108 *miednica* (approximately 3,700 liters) of plain vodka were provided to the tavern by the estate administration, with an extra 18 *miednica* (612 liters) on

St. George's Day.[112] Altogether 2,100 *miednica* (71,500 liters) were received in the first six months of the year. Spring was the slow season for the tavern, so presumably even more liquor was supplied in the second half of the year. Assuming that most of the liquor supplied was actually sold, annual sales must have been around 4,200 *miednica* (143,000 liters) of vodka.

The records of daily sales in the Słuck tavern during 1750[113] show that the income from plain vodka (the only item from which the estate received any revenue) for the year as a whole was slightly more than 67,000 złoty. The average daily income reached almost 185 złoty.[114] It is also possible to track seasonal changes in the tavern's monthly activity (Table 5.4). The tavern was busiest in June, July, and August, when grain was in abundance. Activity then declined and reached a low point before the first harvest of the year. Spring was a time of scarcity in the peasants' lives and was known in Polish as *przednówek*. The seasonal breakdown can be seen clearly in Table 5.5, which shows average daily income by season: spring: March–May; summer: June–August; fall: September–November; and winter: December–February. (For the sake of completeness, January and February 1750 have been considered together with December 1750 as if they were one season.)

Table 5.4. Monthly Income and Average Daily Income by Month*

Month	Total Income	Average Daily Take
January	5,628	182
February	4,874	174
March	4,708	152
April	4,806	160
May	5,468	176
June	6,005	200
July	6,090	196
August	6,342	205
September	5,816	194
October	5,527	178
November	5,884	196
December	5,885	190
Total	67,033	183

SOURCE: NARBM 694, opis 2, teka 7421.
* All prices are in złoty, rounded to the nearest complete one.

Table 5.5. Average Daily Income by Season*

Season	Average Daily Take
Spring	163
Summer	200
Autumn	189
Winter	182

SOURCE: NARBM, 694, opis 2, teka 7421.
* All prices are in złoty, rounded to the nearest complete one.

We can also see the weekly volume of activity in the tavern. Table 5.6 shows that the busiest day was Sunday when the Christians did not work, but came to town to go to church, which provided an excellent opportunity for stopping off at the tavern. Proceeds from the sale of vodka were the lowest on Saturday, presumably because the Jewish innkeeper observed the Sabbath.

Although the contract does not specify special arrangements for collecting payments on the Sabbath, rabbinical sources describe solutions that enabled Jewish tavern keepers to observe the Sabbath while suffering as little loss of income as possible. According to Yehuda Leib Puhovitzer, a Lithuanian rabbi in the second half of the seventeenth century, the owner of an urban inn had to remove the sign from the taproom and refuse to serve drinks until the end of the Sabbath. But he added a qualification: "If people come to buy from them [i.e. the tavern keepers] on the Sabbath, it is absolutely prohibited, even if they want to drink in his tavern—the penalty is a huge fine that they cannot afford. But they can make an exception for the

Table 5.6. Average Daily Income by Day of the Week*

Day	Total Takings	Average Daily Takings
Sunday	12,322	237
Monday	11,000	212
Tuesday	9,283	179
Wednesday	10,621	204
Thursday	9,267	175
Friday	10,918	210
Saturday	3,622	70
Total	67,033	183

SOURCE: NARBM 694, opis 2, teka 7421.
* All prices are in złoty rounded to the nearest complete one.

actual servants of the noble lord—though not for *komorniks*,[115] and all the more so not for other locals, including townspeople—and for high-ranking priests."[116] In other words the locals could not be served alcohol at all, but people in the service of the noble lord of the city should be served as should priests "for the sake of peace," as the rabbi explained. Of course, no payment could be accepted for the drinks on the Sabbath; they were provided on credit. If this procedure was applied in Słuck, the decrease in revenues on Saturdays was caused by the restrictions on the clientele.

There was no similar decrease in sales that year during the Jewish festivals (Passover, April 21–22 and 27–28; Shavuot, June 9–10; Sukkot and Simhat Torah, October 15–16 and 22–23) or the High Holidays (Rosh Hashanah, October 1–2, and Yom Kippur, October 10). On those thirteen days the tavern's daily revenues averaged 161 Polish złoty—slightly less than the annual average but still much more than on Saturdays. It is hard to imagine that a Jew would insist on a commercial arrangement for the Sabbath that involved great loss but would not apply it on the high holidays and festivals. Unfortunately, without additional documentation it is hard to determine the reason for this discrepancy.

The estate owner's revenues from the taverns were not limited to income from the sale of alcohol. There were other ways in which the urban *arendarze* boosted estate revenues as can be seen in a lease signed by Hieronim Florian Radziwiłł for various economic rights in the city of Słuck in 1753.[117] The one-year contract that Radziwiłł signed with five Jews from the town included fees for the licenses as well as for the revenues from the Słuck travelers' inn[118] and three mills in the area. The price agreed upon for this comprehensive lease was 64,000 złoty. Thus we have here an *arenda* lease, as opposed to the contract to manage a tavern given to Mordechai ben Ya'akov. The types of income detailed in this contract were more varied: in addition to the "licence" payments for alcohol sold outside the lord's tavern,[119] the *arendarze* received payments in the form of grain from the mills, and in cash from collecting the various customs and duties imposed by the administration on commerce in the town.[120]

As we have seen, customs and duties charged on business activities formed a significant source of income for the estate. Attracting outside merchants to the urban markets on the estate was therefore a major economic goal because it broadened the tax base. Administrators devoted a great deal of attention to improving the markets and fairs in their towns,[121] and they often tried to stop merchants from doing business in the villages in order to steer most of the commerce to the urban market.[122] Subjects were ordered to go only to the local fairs on the estate[123] and local administrators were told to do whatever they could to attract merchants from outside (while at the same time exerting great efforts to prevent them "smuggling" goods into the estate so as to evade paying the tax on them).[124] In its efforts to attract new merchants, the administration also strictly forbad the *arendarze* from collecting higher duties than specified in their leases.

In appointing the general *arendarze* to collect the commercial taxes, the magnate was giving them an important role in managing estate incomes. Every merchant, Jewish or not, who came to do business in one of the towns on the estate had to come before the *arendarz* or one of his men and pay the duty on his goods. This meant that the *arendarz* was acting as an agent of the estate administration and so in return could enjoy the status of being a representative of his noble lord.

THE SOCIAL STATUS OF THE *ARENDARZE*

The importance the Radziwiłłs attached to the general *arendarze*, their roles, and the revenues that they brought was expressed in the way the contracts were signed. Almost every contract for a general *arenda* stipulated that it had to be signed by the magnate himself and not by one of the family's administrators.[125] This arrangement not only gave the estate owner direct control over the content of the contract but also created a direct relationship between him and the general *arendarz*, putting the Jew, by virtue of his function, in the front line of estate administration. In his announcements to estate society, Radziwiłł often drew a clear distinction between his *arendarze* and the rest of his Jewish subjects, addressing himself to "the Jewish *arendarze*, the elders of the community, and the entire community."[126]

The general *arendarze* also had a special legal status. Unlike other Jews they could not be tried in the Jewish community court or any other court on the estate except that of the lord.[127] Radziwiłł exempted them from paying duties and other fees on the estate either to the *kahal* or to himself.[128] Sometimes he helped them collect money owed them under their leases; for instance, he would dispatch soldiers from his private army to help with the collection of overdue taxes, a sign of both the *arendarze*'s special status and the importance that the magnate attributed to their economic activity.[129]

Like everyone who served the magnate's interests, the *arendarze* could expect support from their noble lord when problems arose in the course of their work. They appealed to the magnate for help against noblemen, *dzierżawcy* of estates, townspeople, and even priests who objected to their collecting money. The Radziwiłłs' orders included a standard protection clause for the general *arendarze* to ensure that they could maintain a steady income for the estate treasury.[130] Even when as a result of force majeure *arendarze* could not pay their dues, the estate owner would take this into account and might even write off their debts.[131]

Arendarze could also expect other benefits from the Radziwiłłs. It was not uncommon to give rural *arendarze* plots of land where they could grow rye, raise dairy cows, keep bees, and gather fodder to sell to travelers for their horses.[132] They might also receive firewood, grain to make their own beer and vodka, and exemptions from property tax.[133] The Radziwiłłs had good reason to improve the financial status of their *arendarze*: increased profitability both drove up *arenda* prices and intensified competition over the leases.[134]

Arendarze could also receive the right to corvée labor from local peasants, who might be required to work the land given by Radziwiłł to the Jewish leaseholders as part of the lease, help in vodka manufacture, serve as night watchmen for the taverns, and even transport goods at the bidding of the *arendarze*.[135] These obligations, especially the transport of goods even when done directly for the Radziwiłłs, upset the peasants; being forced to do them for a Jewish *arendarz* added a religious basis to their anger and so caused even greater resentment.[136] Whether for religious reasons or out of the more practical concern that peasant disaffection might lead to acts of rebellion, a special clause started to appear in Radziwiłł leases in the 1750s eliminating corvée labor on behalf of Jewish *arendarze*. This change says something about the limits of the special relationship between the Radziwiłłs and their general *arendarze*: Although the latter enjoyed a status close to that of noble administrators on the estates, they were Jews nonetheless and so limits had to be set on the power they could wield over Christians.

The Power and Influence of the General Arendarze

So what degree of power and influence did the *arendarze* actually have on the estates? Their role as treasury officials for the Radziwiłłs, paying money to various people on their noble lord's behalf, did give them some chance to influence and possibly even to put pressure on those who came to them for payment. The availability of soldiers also gave them a certain amount of power, which was particularly helpful when they charged higher fees than permitted by the lease.[137] *Arendarze* did not hesitate to collect tolls even from nobles, who were generally exempt from such payments.[138] Furthermore, when churchmen refused to comply with the liquor monopoly, the *arendarz* was entitled to enter their houses in search of alcohol and in at least one case ordered a church sealed.[139] There were certainly cases of *arendarze* using violence against peasants, townspeople, and even Jews.[140]

The leases often required all subjects on the estate to treat the general *arendarz* with respect on pain of a fine. Mill workers had to be particularly careful because the general *arendarz* was authorized to replace millers at will. The contract for the Nieśwież *arendarz* states bluntly, "if any miller does not obey the *arendarz*, does not respect him, and is not diligent and trustworthy in fulfilling his obligations . . . he shall be expelled and replaced."[141]

One important indication of the standing of the *arendarze* on the estates, and particularly in the towns, was their responsibility for weights and measures. In Polish-Lithuanian society, where many aspects of life, including weights and measures, were determined by local custom, controlling them was a significant source of power. For example, in the royal cities, where the price of grain was fixed by the *wojewoda*, the use of smaller weights was a way of concealing price rises.

The Radziwiłłs enforced uniform measures on their estates, both to ensure that they would not be cheated and to fix in their favor the ratio of the measures used on their estates to those used outside.[142] The *arendarze*, as subjects of their noble lord and active participants in the economic life of his estates, had of course to accept this policy. All *arenda* contracts specified severe punishments for those who watered down vodka or falsified measures when serving drinks (thus effectively putting up prices).[143] Although the price of vodka was not usually specified in the contracts,[144] some did link it to the price of grain on the estate, possibly to prevent the *arendarz* from keeping his prices high during the summer season when the price of grain fell.[145]

The *arendarze* not only had to submit to the estate owner's policy on weights and measures, they had also, like the estate administration as a whole, to enforce it.[146] The general *arendarze*, responsible for collecting the customs and duties on trade, were required to ensure that "stamped" weights, that is, those checked by the estate authorities, were the only ones used to measure goods.[147] In the lease for Nieśwież, for instance, Michał Kazimierz Radziwiłł stated explicitly that it was the *arendarz*'s responsibility to ensure that measures on the estate remained uniform.[148]

One of the most important settings for implementing this policy was the major towns, where the large markets were held. Townspeople often tried to use larger measures when buying grain brought into town so as to pay less for it, then replace them with smaller measures when they sold their own goods in order to keep prices as high as possible. The administration sought to curtail this practice by ensuring that the *wagowe* levy on trade formed part of the general *arenda*.[149] In this way, the Jewish *arendarz* became responsible for the operation of the town scales and especially for the use of weights.[150] Any merchant who wanted to sell goods in the town had to have them weighed on the town scales, where the *arendarz* insisted that they use the lord's stamped weights and then charged them a fee for doing so.[151]

By transferring responsibility for the scales to the *arendarz*, the estate owner benefited in a number of ways: the non-Jewish townspeople could no longer use them to improve their terms of trade;[152] the *arendarz*, himself being Jewish, knew the ways in which the Jewish merchants (generally the majority of those doing business in town) tried to avoid paying the *wagowe* levy and so had a better chance of collecting the full fee; and if the *arendarz* himself manipulated the weights, his increased profit would be translated to a higher price for the *arenda* contract, which meant added income for the magnate.[153] Running the scales also seems to have been another way in which the *arendarz* acquired power and influence. All large transactions went through him and he accumulated knowledge and ties that he could put to good use in his own affairs.[154]

Limits to the Arendarz's Power

As a group the general *arendarze* were self-confident businessmen who succeeded in amassing power and influence on the estate by dint of the magnate's support. There were, however, limits to their authority and sense of security. These were a function of their ability to fulfill their financial obligations to the Radziwiłłs. When a general *arendarz* could not pay what he owed, he had to turn to his noble lord for help.[155] If his difficulties had been caused by events that were not under his control, such as military activity or a fire, the magnate would normally absorb the loss. From an economic standpoint, this was undoubtedly the most sensible policy: the Polish-Lithuanian economy in the eighteenth century could be subject to extreme fluctuations, and if the *arendarz* had to bear the entire risk, no reasonable businessman would ever take on an *arenda*.

Even if the *arendarz's* financial difficulties were caused by his own inefficiency, the administration was sometimes willing to help out in the hope that it would eventually receive at least part of the money that was owed.[156] If all else failed, an *arendarz* might drag out payment of his debt for as long as he could before the lord's patience wore out.[157]

When that eventually happened, the *arendarz* and his family faced the same unpleasant consequences as anyone who owed the magnate money. Initially came threats, at first usually from the lord's administrators,[158] then other forms of pressure. For example in 1747 Michał Kazimierz Radziwiłł ordered the rabbi of Złoczów (Zolochiv, Ukraine) not to officiate at a wedding for the daughter of an *arendarz* who still owed money.[159] In another case the market stall of an *arendarz* who had not paid his debts was confiscated.[160] The standard fate that awaited a general *arendarz* who failed to pay was imprisonment, sometimes even in chains and under heavy guard.[161] The unfortunate man would remain in prison until his family or friends managed to raise the funds necessary to cover his debts.[162] Flight was hardly an option: if the fugitive left his family behind, it would be jailed in his place. And the magnate had no qualms about demanding that the local *kahal* bring back the errant *arendarz* or itself be subject to heavy fines and other penalties.[163]

The plight of the secondary *arendarze* in the villages who ran into financial trouble was different from that of the general *arendarze*. The fact that their ties were not directly with Radziwiłł meant that the village leaseholders were not likely to be accorded as much leeway in dealing with their debts. On the other hand, the limited nature of their lease did not allow them to take on financial obligations on the scale of general *arendarze*, so the punishments they faced for nonpayment were not as severe. In addition, the person meting out the punishment (the general *arendarz*) was Jewish, and although this may not have ensured a great deal of compassion, it did have some effect. General *arendarze* would certainly think twice before consigning fellow Jews to the lord's prison. They would have been further deterred by the knowledge that, in the end, they were likely to find themselves paying to have the debtors released because it was a religious duty for all Jewish communities to give money to have their members freed from imprisonment (called in Hebrew, *pidyon shvuim*). The best solution for the general *arendarze* was to send soldiers to confiscate the property of any secondary *arendarz* who owed them money.[164]

Flight was easier for a rural leaseholder: since he was not a prominent figure in local Jewish society, he could disappear more easily.[165] Still, the Radziwiłłs did all they could to prevent escapes. In such cases their losses were twofold: besides having to do without the services of the local *arendarz*, they stood to lose the equipment for the manufacture of liquor that had been provided together with the *arenda*.[166] On the whole, however, the profitability of the *arenda* market was such that it was quite rare for an *arendarz*, general or secondary, to get into such serious financial difficulties.

Scholarship on Jews on the estates has focused on their relationship with the estate-owners,[167] but the general *arendarze* came into contact with many other types of people, including the local nobility, priests, townspeople, peasants, and, of course, Jews and Jewish communities. An examination of these relationships and contacts will shed more light on the status of the *arendarze* and the roles they played in estate society.

SOCIAL RELATIONS

Relations with the Nobility

The local nobility on the estates did not treat the Jews in the same way the Radziwiłłs did. For them, the *szlachta's* traditional anti-Jewish feelings were not mitigated by the economic benefits that the Jews brought because they did not directly benefit from them.[168] These lesser nobles, whether they were *dzierżawcy* or held high positions in the estate administration, were often more interested in showing off their social status than in making a profit.[169] Indeed, noneconomic considerations sometimes led them to do things that were harmful to the *arendarze*, even ignoring orders to the contrary from the estate owner who wanted to protect his income.[170]

It is in the nature of the sources to emphasize cases of conflict rather than of co-operation, so we can assume that nobles on the estates did, for the most part, work in harmony with the *arendarze*. Still, the hostility that was expressed may have reflected a feeling that the Jews did not deserve their improved status, which contravened the proper social order.[171] These cases of tension are enough to show that there was a limit to the magnate's ability to protect his Jewish *arendarze,* and that the local nobility was powerful enough to make life difficult for them if it wanted to do so.[172]

Relations with the Orthodox Clergy

Relations between the *arendarze* and the Orthodox priests on an estate were determined by both religious antagonism and economic competition. In many cases local priests, who were often quite poor, broke the *arendarz's* monopoly on alcohol by making and selling liquor in town.[173] Radziwiłł sometimes took the priests' plight into consideration and let them make liquor for their personal use, but this was not enough for many priests who continued to sell alcohol to supplement their income.[174] To put an end to this the Radziwiłłs brought suit against these rebellious churchmen in the ecclesiastical courts, though not always successfully.

The Jewish *arendarze,* as we have seen, had means of enforcing their monopolies, including the use of force. On occasion they even deployed soldiers against the priests![175] In Słuck the Orthodox clergy complained that soldiers sent by the *arendarze* had taken action to prevent them from smuggling alcohol into the city.[176] In another case the *arendarz* in a village on the Kopyś estate sent the militia to break into the home of a priest suspected of illegally manufacturing alcohol and convinced the estate manager to issue an order to close the church.[177]

Of course such incidents further intensified religious hostility. A letter from the Orthodox archbishop of Belarus regarding the closure of the church complained, "Once the Jews sealed the tormented Lord Christ in the tomb; now they are tormenting the Christian people of that same [Christ] and have already locked up his house of worship."[178]

These difficult relations were also apparent in cases where churchmen and their supporters attacked *arendarze* and other Jews. Solomon Maimon related in his memoirs how the Orthodox priest in his grandfather's village had him (the grandfather) falsely accused of murdering a Christian child.[179]

Relations with the Non-Jewish Townspeople

The Christian townspeople were the Jews' greatest competitors, particularly in the urban markets. Their ability to stand up to the Jews was severely limited not only by the preponderance of Jewish merchants but by the positions of authority held by the *arendarze*. The townspeople's main weapon against the Jews' dominant status, other than physical violence, was to inveigh against Jews employing Christian servants, a breach of canon law. Enforcing that law would have seriously harmed the Jews' ability to manufacture and sell alcohol and to collect duties because they made extensive use of Christian manpower in these activities.[180] The townspeople's use of religious argumentation gave extra weight to their objections, and in some cases the Radziwiłłs issued orders prohibiting Jews from employing Christian servants.[181] For the most part however, the Jewish *arendarze* continued to use Christian labor and the estate owner continued to protect them from their non-Jewish competitors.[182]

Relations with the Peasants

Peasants who lived in the Radziwiłłs' villages tended to come into contact with the estate administration either on the *folwark* where they did corvée labor or in the tavern. As we have seen, almost all the taverns were run by Jews[183] and formed a focal point for village life. So even if the tavern keeper remained a religious and cultural outsider, he soon became an accepted figure in village society.[184] Of course, the imbalance in power between peasant and *arendarz* (who, as the holder of the *propinacja* monopoly, was acting as agent of the noble lord) was clear to all parties. This situation, which seemed to run counter to the proper order of things in a Christian land, could sometimes cause resentment and dislike of the *arendarze* among the peasants.[185]

The Radziwiłłs bowed to these feelings by abolishing those practices that had led to overt domination of peasants by a Jewish *arendarz*, such as the performance of corvée labor.[186] They also set limits on the amount of credit a tavern keeper could give a peasant to buy drinks. This restriction, common on all the estates, had a sound basis. First, a peasant who got into debt might well run away from the estate and seek refuge elsewhere, thus reducing the available workforce. Second, if the peasant were forced to hand over his property to a Jew, the Christian villagers might see it as a religious slight, which could lead to violence and so ultimately harm estate revenues.[187] Therefore most tavern leases stated that an *arendarz* could extend a rich peasant 8–10 złoty in credit and a poor peasant 4–5 złoty. The *arendarz* had to collect the tavern debts every three months, and if he did not do so the peasant's debt was to be written off.[188]

Despite the Radziwiłł administration's efforts to moderate the power wielded by the Jewish *arendarze*, it was clear to everyone where the authority lay. The *arendarz* sold the peasants their drinks and collected duties from them when they milled their grain and did their commercial transactions. Because he was working on behalf of the estate owner, it was hard for peasants to stand up to him, even if he overstepped the authority granted him in his contract by, for instance, watering down his liquor or demanding excessive duties.[189]

A complaint sent by the peasants from Krzyczew *starostwo* not long before the 1740 uprising expressed their helplessness vis-à-vis the *arendarze*. It concerned the collection of fees for the milling of grain. When the local mill was not operational it was standard practice for the *arendarz* to collect from the peasants a token fee (a "dry measure") before they took their grain to a different mill, where they would have to pay full price for the service. The peasants in Krzyczew claimed angrily that the *arendarze* preferred to mill the grain of strangers who came with large quantities of grain and send the local peasants off to a mill in a different village. In this way, they received double payment: both the usual milling fee and the "dry measure."[190] The peasants were left in the same difficult position as any weak consumer facing a cartel. Their only resort was to petition their noble lord and hope for a sympathetic ear. Unfortunately for them, Radziwiłł, who was concerned to keep *arenda* revenues as high as possible, was not inclined to act on their behalf.[191]

On the whole, however, the secondary *arendarze* do seem to have understood that it was not in their best interests to overexploit the peasants, since they would benefit much more from a quiet village with good social and economic relations. This feeling is well expressed in a complaint made by one of the general *arendarze*, "Because the Korelicze estate has been destroyed, people . . . are not staying at home in the summer and winter and bring no profit to the *arenda*; furthermore, the tavern keepers living in the taverns on the estate cannot sell anything at all."[192] Business was best served by peaceful conditions and a hard-working population with grain to sell and a little money in their pockets. To judge by the relatively small number of complaints by and about rural *arendarze*, it would seem that they knew for the most part how to balance making a profit with preserving the dignity of the peasants.

Relations with the Jewish Communities

The relationship between the *arendarze* and the Jewish communities was characterized by economic conflict. Most *arenda* contracts stipulated that the general *arendarz* be under the direct jurisdiction of Radziwiłł and not the *kahal*. Moreover, the *arendarz* was exempt from all taxes on the estate, including the Jewish communal ones.[193] Clearly the estate owner viewed the *arendarze*, who acted directly in his economic interests, as a separate group within the Jewish population. Documents from the communal record books confirm that Jewish society understood and accepted this situation.[194]

As we have seen, however, if a general *arendarz* could not pay his debts, the community would sometimes be held responsible even though it had not appointed him. As a result, the *kahal* had a definite interest in overseeing the *arendarz*,[195] though the leaseholder was typically powerful enough to free himself from its authority. Some kehillot sought to retain a measure of control by appointing bookkeepers to check the *arendarze*'s accounts. Even this solution was not always acceptable to the leaseholders.[196]

Another source of tension between *kahal* and *arendarz* was the *kropka*, the indirect tax imposed by the community on the sale of meat and other business dealings. This tax was an important source of income for the Jewish communities, and its collection was usually leased out by the *kahal* rather than done directly.[197] The general *arendarze* regarded these leases as an extra source of income, and in many cases asked the estate owner to add them to their *arenda*. When this happened the tax effectively stopped being a source of income for the *kahal* and became instead a source of income for the magnate via the *arendarz*.[198]

The Jewish communities also had complaints about some secondary *arendarze* who sought independence from communal jurisdiction and exemptions from community taxes. At this time, when about a third of the Jews in Poland-Lithuania in general (and even more in regions we are examining here) lived in villages, had the secondary *arendarze* succeeded in evading community taxes, it would have been a severe blow to community budgets.[199] On this issue the magnates seem to have supported the communities, leaving the secondary *arendarze* under communal authority, both in judicial matters and in terms of taxes.[200] Since different communities often demanded jurisdiction and rights of taxation over the same nearby villages, many disputes ensued. At times the arguments were so bitter that the issues were sent for arbitration to the major Jewish councils, the Council of the Four Lands and the Council of the Lithuanian Land.[201]

In the absence of a well-developed tax-collection mechanism, it was hard for the Jewish communities to collect taxes from the village Jews. In 1759 the Zabłudów *kahal* came up with a unique solution. Together with the general *arendarze*, the community leadership drew up a list of sums for the poll tax to be paid by the rural *arendarze*. It then transferred responsibility for collecting the tax to the general *arendarze* and authorized them to use whatever methods they wanted.[202] This is another example of the transfer of some of the *kahal*'s economic powers to the general *arendarze*, though this time with its consent.

In most cases the *kahal* retained its powers and collected the tax owed by rural *arendarze* when they came to town, which was usually when they needed religious services, such as in times of mourning, for family celebrations, or for the Jewish holidays. To ensure that they would be able to collect the tax, Jewish communities sometimes asked the estate owner to issue orders banning rural *arendarze* from going to a different town at holiday times; the estate owner usually agreed to their requests.[203]

A final question here is whether some sort of competition developed within Jewish society between the general *arendarze* and the other wealthy Jews. Examining the names of general *arendarze* on various Radziwiłł estates shows that it was rare for one Jewish businessman to hold a general *arenda* for more than five years. Even if a person did sign leases covering a longer period, the years were usually not consecutive. The *arenda* system clearly did not create a separate social stratum within Jewish society. *Arenda* was merely one form of economic activity for wealthy Jewish businessmen.[204] Having said that, a broad new Jewish social and economic elite was emerging in these years, and though only some members of this elite held *arenda*s at any given time, their power and influence was based on their wealth and ties with the Radziwiłłs and the estate administration.

In their relations with the five populations on the estate discussed here the general *arendarze* proved to be active, self-confident economic actors who did their job with great assertiveness and with the estate owner's support. Although the protection and special status that the magnate gave them were usually enough to enable them to operate undisturbed, economic conflicts of various kinds did develop. These were not only a reaction to the aggressiveness of the *arendarze* but also an expression of opposition to the way the estates were being run. The residents had no practical way to express their opposition to the socioeconomic system, so it was easier and safer to take out anger and frustration on the *arendarze*, who served the lord's economic interests, than on the magnate himself. The tensions between the Christian population and the Jewish *arendarze* thus often hid the deeper significance of the unrest, masking repressed feelings of hostility towards the Radziwiłłs and their economic regime.

CONCLUSIONS

As a result of changing economic conditions in the eighteenth century, the Radziwiłłs and other magnate families decided to exploit the monopolies on their estates more intensively in order to increase their revenues. In a society where alcohol was a major item of consumption, the noble lord's subjects were forced to buy the liquor that he supplied. They had to have their grain ground in his mills and to pay a tax for the privilege. All mercantile activity had to take place in the markets on the estate, where the estate residents were again charged customs and duties. The goal was to ensure that all the agricultural produce of the estate, whether produced on the Radziwiłłs' farms or by the peasants, was marketed on the estate so that profits went into the family treasury.[205]

During this period estates were often leased out in order to create a clientele of nobles who would support the Radziwiłłs in their political ambitions. As a result, the nature of estate leasing changed, becoming less important in economic terms. It was to make up for these lost revenues that the Radziwiłłs intensified the exploitation of the *arenda*s on monopoly rights. They were highly successful; *arenda* income as a percentage of the Radziwiłłs' total income from their estates grew substantially in the first half of the eighteenth century. There were significant profits for the *arendarze* too, as evidenced by the extremely tough competition to secure leases, which could sometimes even spiral out of control.

Since the income from these *arenda*s was based on the monopoly rights of estate owners, the Radziwiłłs and their *arendarze* were concerned to prevent infractions. The magnate was willing to give his *arendarze* any support they needed, up to and including the use of his soldiers to collect unpaid debts. For Jews to have such power at their disposal was extremely uncommon and went against the social order accepted in Christian Europe since the Middle Ages. The religious hostility that this caused was also an expression of a deep-seated opposition to the Radziwiłłs' economic policies—an opposition that was effectively masked by the traditional Christian nature of the complaints.

Certain parallels developed between the leases of estates and those of monopoly rights. On any given estate, all the monopoly rights were leased together as a package called a general *arenda*.[206] The *arendarze* thus worked in parallel with those administering other aspects of estate life (though they never held official positions). The Radziwiłłs also invested money and resources in aspects of infrastructure that were important for helping *arenda* incomes grow, particularly in the construction and upkeep of taverns and mills.

The economic importance of the *arenda*s for estate revenues meant that the general *arendarze* formed a distinct group on the estate; the Radziwiłłs gave them a special legal status and support for their economic activity. These leaseholders came into regular contact with all strata of townspeople and peasants and sometimes had occasion to place fellow Jews in positions of authority vis-à-vis non-Jews in both towns and villages. Since they were representing the Radziwiłłs' economic interests, they were generally treated with respect.

Their social status improved in other ways, too. The general *arendarze* supplied goods to the noble lord's court and to others on the estate. Within the administrative system of the latifundium, they also played crucial roles because it was mainly they who dealt with cash and were active in the markets. The use of payment orders turned *arendarze* into de facto treasury officials. Many people who had business ties with the Radziwiłłs, including even some estate officials, were directed to the *arendarze* to be paid the money they were owed. Though the success of any individual *arendarz* continued only as long as he was able provide the services his master demanded, the success of the *arenda* as an institution greatly reduced the risks of failure.

Thus it was that the *arendarze* became key figures in estate administration and a powerful economic and social force in estate life during the eighteenth century, amassing power and influence to an extent that Jews had rarely seen before.

SIX

Jews and Trade
in the Estate Economy

THE GOALS OF COMMERCE
ON THE MAGNATE LATIFUNDIUM

To run smoothly, the Radziwiłł latifundium needed an effective commercial system, working in three interrelated areas: the first was the distribution and sale of the agricultural produce grown on the estates; the second was supplying the estate administration, the family and its court, and the estate residents; and the third was the creation of wealth as the basis for taxation, direct and indirect. Jewish merchants, with the family's explicit encouragement, were involved in all three. However, before we can begin to assess the significance of their roles, we must first understand how the system worked as a whole.

Distribution and Sale

Throughout most of the Polish-Lithuanian Commonwealth, the sale of the agricultural produce from the *folwarks* accounted for most of the estate owners' income. It was thus in their interest to market it in the most efficient way possible. Following the decline of the international market for Polish-Lithuanian exports in the seventeenth century, the importance of the domestic market for grain grew dramatically, especially in the first half of the eighteenth century. This was not an entirely new development: the local market had always served estate owners whose lands had no convenient access to one of the rivers that formed a major trading artery, even when the Baltic grain trade had been at its height. In the period under discussion here, profits from grain sales could be maximized if it was sold in the form of alcohol, which the magnates organized by leasing out the monopolies they held to produce and sell alcoholic beverages on their lands.[1] Even so, the alcohol business could not absorb all the grain grown on the *folwark*s, so estate owners continued to have much of their produce sold directly on the local market.[2] Further, the magnates did not completely sever their ties with the Baltic markets and continued to sell grain there too, through a network of commercial agents and middlemen.[3]

The situation on the Radziwiłł estates in Lithuania, though similar to this in many ways, had a number of special features caused by the unusual economic structure of the region, particularly eastern Belarus. This was an economically underdeveloped area not deeply penetrated by the feudal system that had spread across the rest of the Commonwealth since the sixteenth century. The network of *folwark*s there was not well developed and peasants did relatively little corvée labor.[4] Instead they paid their dues in produce from their own farms. Once grain from the *folwark*s was set aside to produce alcohol and to pay wages, there was not much left over.[5] In fact hemp and flax, the crops most marketable on the Baltic markets, were not grown on the *folwark*s at all but by the peasants on their farms. The Radziwiłłs, who did the lion's share of the trade from their estates to the Baltic, had to buy them for export. Merchants seeking access to the international markets also bought hemp and flax from peasants, though this activity was frowned upon by the Radziwiłł family and restricted whenever possible.

Supply

There were two main groups of consumers on the latifundium: the Radziwiłł court and administration on the one hand, and everyone else on the other. The peasants and many of the townspeople who had little cash income did their best to satisfy their own needs without recourse to the market. Nonetheless, they did have to buy tools, fabrics, salt, tobacco, and foodstuffs they could not produce themselves, notably salt herring. These were sold on the urban markets by local merchants, who also provided more expensive goods to both the wealthier townspeople and the nobles, including even luxury items such as fine wines, spices, furs, and high-quality fabrics.

The largest consumer by far was the Radziwiłł family itself, which sought to maintain the opulent lifestyle of a magnate court. By living at the highest level of conspicuous consumption they confirmed their status at the very pinnacle of Polish-Lithuanian society and this entailed extensive purchases.[6] They also had to lay their hands on everything necessary to keep the latifundium and its administration running properly. Much of what they needed for this purpose, such as agricultural produce, alcohol, wood, charcoal, and potash, could be supplied by the latifundium itself. The rest, including iron for building and for making stills to produce vodka, cloth for the uniforms of soldiers and servants, paper for recordkeeping, and better quality food and drink for members of the administration, had to be brought from outside.[7]

Supplying these goods and the luxury items for the family posed a problem. The Radziwiłłs, in line with contemporary economic thinking, believed that allowing local merchants to trade outside the estate would deplete the money supply and lead to impoverishment. So with one or two exceptions they restricted their subjects' access to outside markets. Instead they encouraged "foreign" merchants (that is, those from outside the estates) to come and sell their wares at fairs in the Radziwiłł-owned towns.[8]

Two groups of merchants on the Radziwiłł estate were allowed regular access to outside markets, the cattle dealers, who transported animals for sale to Breslau and Gdańsk,[9] and merchants active in the river trade with the Baltic ports, especially Königsberg.[10] In fact, it was the trade with East Prussia, undertaken by both the Radziwiłłs and private merchants, that provided one of the major sources for the commodities needed by the estates.

Generating Revenues

The Radziwiłłs encouraged mercantile activity because they wanted to tax the wealth it created. Trade enriched towns and merchants, yielding higher levels of income from direct taxation. In addition, growth in the volume of trade allowed for greater indirect taxation (in the form of charges made on each business transaction). For this reason, the family channeled its subjects into local markets where it could tax their commercial activity. Goods from outside the estates had to be bought from "foreign" merchants on the home market, where these transactions too could be taxed.[11]

Restricting local merchants to trading on estate markets was thus a highly effective way of increasing indirect tax revenues because it allowed the Radziwiłłs to charge all transactions involving both estate products and goods brought from outside. This policy was strictly enforced.[12] In one case the family issued a sentence of death on a merchant from Ołyka who had dared go to the fair on a neighboring estate, Klewań (Klevan, Ukraine).[13] Such a restrictive approach increased the family's tax revenues in the short run, but the long-term effect could not have been beneficial to the estate economy as a whole.

Some merchants were able to extend their economic range by means of the international river trade, but the Radziwiłłs took care to impose a special charge on that trade too. Levies were imposed not only on all goods originating from the estates but also on those bought in the Baltic ports (principally Königsberg but also Rīga and Gdańsk) and shipped back upriver. This income financed the high costs of the family's own international business.[14]

Jews played a number of key roles in all this mercantile activity. To understand what they were, we will begin by examining two factors that underpinned the Jews' success—the support given them by the Radziwiłłs and the Jews' ability to find sources of mercantile credit. We will then look at the significance of Jewish businessmen for each of the three fields in which trade was important for the estate economy—distribution and sale, supply, and the generation of revenue. After examining all three, we will be in a position to assess the overall significance of Jewish mercantile activity for the estate economy.

THE RADZIWIŁŁS' ATTITUDE
TOWARDS THEIR JEWISH MERCHANTS

The administration, the non-Jewish townspeople, and the Jews were each involved in trade on the estates.[15] The administration marketed its agricultural produce wholesale and bought the goods it needed to supply the Radziwiłł court and maintain estate infrastructure. The non-Jewish townspeople and the Jews, both largely urban groups, competed for the rest of the estate market, including the retail sale of estate produce (bought wholesale from the administration) and supplying the towns and villages.

The non-Jews, invoking their traditional municipal monopoly rights, demanded that Jews not be given free rein to trade, calls that fell on deaf ears. The Radziwiłłs, like other estate owners, supported their Jewish merchants and encouraged their business activities, even exempting them from urban jurisdiction that they felt to be hostile and sending cases between Jews and non-Jews to be heard by their own seigneurial court.[16] Beyond this, if Jewish merchants got into major economic difficulties they could sometimes appeal to their patron for help and protection.[17]

The estate owners' negative attitudes towards the non-Jewish burghers were rooted in the Polish nobility's traditional contempt for commerce, an attitude it shared with the nobility of many other European countries.[18]

The Polish-Lithuanian nobles were also hostile to the townspeople's demand for monopoly rights, which they saw as having a negative impact on their own interests.[19] Jews, forced by the Christian townspeople to work outside the urban monopoly, were perceived more favorably. Still, the estate owners understood that municipal trade was crucial for their estate economies so in their day-to-day dealings moderated their contempt for the burghers.[20]

The Radziwiłłs encouraged commercial activity of all kinds on their estates too.[21] In some cases they stipulated explicitly that Christian and Jewish merchants were to have the same rights, in others their instructions referred simply to "merchants," without any modifier or marker of religion.[22] They even warned their Jewish *arendarze* not to over-collect taxes because it would harm trade.[23]

Jewish merchants seem to have been the main beneficiaries of the family's mercantile policy, and their share of trade grew throughout the eighteenth century until they became the dominant force in the markets.[24] This phenomenon is hard to quantify due to a lack of suitable documentation, so perhaps the best way to get a picture of the Jews' penetration of the urban markets is to look at the changing patterns of their property ownership in the towns. We will here focus on the growth in the number of Jewish-owned houses in central market squares and the increase in Jewish-owned market stalls.

Owning a house on the market square was a marker of a merchant's prosperity and success; conversely exclusion from owning property there was a sign of low status. The Jews in Polish and Lithuanian towns before 1648 had found it difficult to purchase houses in the center of towns, so any increase in their ownership of this kind of house must reflect their penetration of the urban market.[25] Data from the Radziwiłł-owned towns in Lithuania for which we have records track this development over the eighteenth century (Table 6.1).

The table shows a significant growth in the proportion of Jews living around the market squares of these Radziwiłł towns (all of which, with the exception of Korelicze, were important commercial centers). In places such as Mir the growth was the result of an influx of Jewish settlers, while in others such as Birże it was caused by a fall in the total number of houses due to the decline of the urban market.[26] Whatever the reason, the relative number of Jews living around the central markets increased in all the

Table 6.1. Growth in the Number of Jewish-Owned Houses on the Market Square

Town	Year	Number of Buildings on the Market Square	Number of Jewish-Owned Buildings	Percentage	Growth (percent)
Biała	1725	38	20	53	—
Biała	1740	24	15	62	15
Birże	1695	20	6	30	—
Birże	1764	13	7	55	43
Korelicze	1727	38	16	42	—
Korelicze	1762	42	26	62	48
Mir	1712	49	7	14	—
Mir	1757	47	31	66	371
Słuck	1683	31	24	78	—
Słuck	1767	28	27	97	24

SOURCES: AR XXV, 123; AR XXV, 127; AR XXV, 235; AR XXV, 243; AR XXV, 1789; AR XXV, 1811; AR XXV, 1936; AR XXV, 2448; AR XXV, 2455/1; AR XXV, 3834/1, 3837; and AR XXV, 3838.

towns. Even in Nieśwież, where the Jewish population was legally limited to a single street by the terms of its community privilege, Jews were able to acquire buildings on the market square.[27] The dramatic rise in the number of Jews living in the central market square must have been a very clear sign for contemporaries of just how important they now were for the local economy.

The growth in the number of Jewish-owned stalls is a more direct measure of the Jews' penetration of the urban markets.[28] These stalls were usually located in the central market square and served as shops. The difference between a stall and a shop in an eighteenth century Polish-Lithuanian town is not clear. The types of merchandise sold and the total turnover of goods in both were comparable. Stalls were clearly not just for petty trade: Some stall owners had an annual volume of trade in the thousands, even the tens of thousands, of złoty.[29] Nor were market stalls just temporary structures. Many were already built of brick or stone, and if they were wooden, the Radziwiłł family might order that they be replaced with more solid structures.[30] It was probably a matter of architecture: a shop was a room inside an existing building, whereas a stall was a free-standing structure.[31]

Much of the trade in the towns was conducted from these stalls, so changes in their ownership are a sign of developments in the nature of the merchant body (Table 6.2).

Table 6.2. Percentage of Jewish Stall Owners during the Eighteenth Century

Town	Year	Number of Stalls	Jewish-Owned Stalls	Percent
Dawidgródek	1693	4	0	—
Dawidgródek	1760	50	39	78
Głębokie	1704	18	5	28
Głębokie	1752	41	36	88
Kopyś	1694	40	1	2.5
Kopyś	1724	43	10	23
Kopyś*	1732	49	15	31
Kopyś	1747	39	29	74
Kopyś	1755	33	23	70
Kopyś	1773	30	21	70

*In this year, some of the stalls are recorded as deserted. After this is taken into account, the figures are as follows:

Kopyś	1732	26	13	50

SOURCES: AR XXV, 678; AR XXV, 681; AR XXV, 1045; AR XXV, 1046; AR XXV, 1779; AR XXV, 1782; AR XXV, 1788; AR XXV, 1789; AR XXV, 1790; AR XXV, 1811.

These figures show that the both the number and the proportion of Jewish-owned stalls in the towns grew significantly as the century progressed, another good indication of the Jews' growing domination of the commercial life of the estates during these years.[32]

A closer look at the data from Kopyś in eastern Belarus helps clarify this process. The number of Jewish-owned stalls rose from only one in 1694 to 29 by 1747, after which it declined in the third quarter of the eighteenth century.[33] Most of the increase (from 15 to 29 stalls) took place in the 1730s and 1740s, decades when the Radziwiłłs were investing in rebuilding their Lithuanian estates following the Great Northern War, the Russian invasion, and the peasant uprising.[34] The proportional increase of Jews among stall owners in Kopyś was equally marked, from 2.5 percent in the late seventeenth century, to a peak of 74 percent in the mid-eighteenth century, and then steady at about 70 percent thereafter.

The data from 1732 shed some light on the economic processes at work. In that year there were forty-nine stalls in town, but twenty-three of them were deserted. Fifteen of the forty-nine stalls were Jewish-owned, and of those only two were deserted. Thus, while 47 percent of all stalls were not in use, only 13 percent of the Jewish ones were. This seems to have been a reflection of the unsettled times: in this period of wars and their immediate aftermath, many non-Jewish townspeople abandoned trade in favor of a return to subsistence agriculture on the lands they held around the town. Jews, who were not given such land, had little choice but to remain merchants even in the most difficult of circumstances. As a result, their proportion among all the merchants in town grew, and of the 26 active stalls in town, no less than half belonged to Jews. The 1747 figures show the trend continuing. Of only thirty-nine stalls, the number in Jewish hands had risen from thirteen to twenty-nine. Non-Jewish townspeople had continued to move out of trade, leaving Jewish merchants to fill the gap.

Figures from Słuck, the commercial center of the Radziwiłł latifundium in Lithuania, paint the same picture. In 1683, merchants in Słuck numbered 131, of whom 61 (47 percent) were Jews.[35] The 1750 census listed 182 persons engaged in trade, including 141 Jews, or 77 percent of all merchants in the town.[36] This represents a growth of more than 60 percent and shows again the strong Jewish penetration of the urban markets.

Here too, the key factor at play seems to have been the different responses of Jews and the Christians to the devastation in the wars of the early eighteenth century.[37] The Radziwiłłs (and other estate owners) were not troubled by this. Quite the reverse: They saw the return of Christian townspeople to the land as a welcome means of boosting agricultural production. The urban markets could safely be left to the Jews, whose mercantile activity they already knew and welcomed.

So, when in the mid-eighteenth century the estate economy began to revive and more Christian townspeople wanted to return to trade, they ran into two problems: First, the family supported the Jews' commerce and did not really care if the non-Jews continued farming; and second, the Jews, who were already well entrenched in the urban economy, were not inclined to help their non-Jewish competitors break back into the market. The Jews' dominant position must have seemed unassailable.

COMMERCIAL CREDIT

Many estate owners in Poland-Lithuania supported their local merchants by extending credit to those who needed it. Investing in trade as a means of encouraging estate development seems to have become common policy. The Potocki family, for example, loaned a million złoty to the local Jews so they could rebuild the town of Brody after a great fire;[38] the members of the Sieniawski family extended credit to Jews to encourage their economic activities; and the Matuszewicz family made loans to local merchants to develop its estate in Lithuania.[39]

The Radziwiłłs took a different line. They extended credit almost exclusively to merchants engaged in the Niemen River trade, and that just on a personal basis.[40] Others received only indirect credit.[41] In some cases merchants in financial difficulties asked the family to use its influence to hold off a creditor; in others merchants asked to be allowed to defer payments of money they owed to their noble lord himself.[42]

If the Radziwiłłs did not give their Jewish merchants large-scale credit, neither did the Jewish communities.[43] This contradicts the accepted view of many scholars, who argue that the Jewish bodies borrowed large sums at relatively low interest, chiefly from church institutions, then loaned the funds to Jewish merchants at a higher rate of interest.[44] Judith Kalik, however, has found that the communities that took such loans often used them to finance capital projects, such as building synagogues, rather than for investment.[45] In fact the amount of disposable capital held by Jewish communities in Poland-Lithuania seems to have fallen in the eighteenth century, so they simply did not have the money to invest in commerce. Moreover, the difficult security situation in Poland-Lithuania in the years of war and reconstruction made all investments riskier, so such loans were not viable.[46]

The principal source of credit available for merchants on the Radziwiłł latifundium, therefore, was other merchants. In a petition to the family, those engaged in trade in Mir made this absolutely clear: "We, the merchants and stall owners, cannot make a living without credit from foreign merchants. If we are deprived of this credit, we will fall into total bankruptcy and ruin."[47] Michał Kazimierz Radziwiłł himself recognized that merchants were receiving credit from other merchants in various of the orders he issued to his administrators on matters of trade. A common instruction was for the administrator to ensure that merchants from other towns paid their debts on time or they would not be extended credit in the future.[48]

Because the majority of merchants were Jews, most of those giving and receiving credit were Jewish, too. Though Jewish law prohibited Jews from lending money at interest to other Jews, the exigencies of economic life in early modern Eastern Europe had necessitated some adjustments. At the turn of the seventeenth century, when Polish and Lithuanian Jews were already deeply engaged in trade, local rabbis devised a special arrangement to permit the extension of credit (that is, loans) without transgressing the halakhic ban on interest. It was known as the *heter iska*, and it redefined credit as a form of partnership, establishing a kind of promissory note (*mamran*) that made commercial loans legal.[49] So by the eighteenth century there were no legal barriers to hamper the supply of Jewish credit to oil the wheels of commerce on the estates.

Non-Jews also made business loans. In a case from 1713 a Christian woman from Kopyl, who had lent 15,000 złoty to a group of local Jews, complained that she was having difficulties in getting her money back.[50] Nobles on the lookout for good opportunities in which to invest their surplus capital would sometimes make large loans to merchants and stall owners, both Jewish and Christian.[51] Some cases of clergy and church institutions acting as sources of credit for Jewish merchants were also reported. In 1715 Joshua ben Isaac reached a settlement with a priest from the Dominican monastery in Kleck for a debt of 1,125 złoty that he had received from the monks to finance his trade with Königsberg.[52] This was a rarity, however. Priests and monasteries viewed Jewish communal institutions as more solid investments than individuals engaged in trade.[53]

Remarkably the Radziwiłłs remained mostly uninvolved in the credit market on their estates, a departure from their general management policy. As we have seen, their main goal was to ensure that all economic activity on the estates remained inside their borders. In this situation, the family might have been expected to ban loans or other provision of credit to non-residents while encouraging borrowing from outside. In practice however, credit regulation was simply not mentioned in the family's administrative arrangements, and Jews were free to lend and borrow as they pleased. The Jews of Biała for example, were in contact with the Jews of Międzyrzec on the Czartoryski estates and merchants from both communities made commercial loans to each other.[54] Clearly, the Radziwiłłs' economic understanding was not very sophisticated: they focused solely on those transactions that would bring in direct cash income.[55]

Having clarified the sources of credit available to Radziwiłł's Jewish merchants, we are now ready to examine their roles in the estate economy.

JEWISH MERCHANTS
IN DISTRIBUTION AND SALES

Grain

The Radziwiłł administration did not keep consistently organized, latifundium-wide records that would allow an understanding of the extent and structure of the markets. Nor do we have any way of accurately evaluating either the range of the Jews' commercial activities or their importance for the functioning of the estates as a whole. A wealth of sources from different localities have been preserved, however, and they permit us to sketch out a broad picture, in which some of the rather impressionistic generalizations can be balanced by detailed studies of individual markets or sectors.

The sale of alcoholic beverages was the most widespread Jewish marketing activity, the monopoly for which they leased from the Radziwiłłs as we saw in the last chapter. As far as the estate administration was concerned, this was a way of selling the grain from their *folwark*s, but it was done at second-hand: once the *arenda* contract was signed, the actual distribution and sale was taken care of by the *arendarz*.

Of course, the folwarks were not the only source of grain for the *arendarze*, they could purchase it for themselves on the local markets. Sometimes, when the supply from the lords' farms dried up, they had no choice but to do that. On the Radziwiłł latifundium, lessees did not receive a regular supply of grain from the estate, and the ways it was supplied could be changed quite arbitrarily.[56] To the extent that the *arendarze* were forced to buy grain for themselves locally, they should be seen less as Radziwiłł agents than as independent merchants, because they were no longer acting as distributors of *folwark* produce.

Any surplus grain not needed for alcohol production was generally sold by the administration itself, which only rarely used Jewish merchants for the purpose. When Jews who lived on the estate did deal in grain, they did not usually purchase it directly from the *folwark*s.[57] The exception to this rule was when the markets were depressed. At those times the Radziwiłłs brought in the Jews to use as mercantile agents for *folwark* produce, providing them with grain on credit for them to resell. However, the price that was set gave the administration a handsome profit and left the Jewish merchants with the problem of selling over-priced grain on a depressed market.[58] In much the same way the family used Jewish merchants to absorb any surplus agricultural produce it might accumulate by paying them in kind, again setting advantageous prices for itself.[59]

In these cases, the Jewish merchants were not involved in the family's regular distribution of surplus grain but rather served as an additional resource to be exploited where necessary, giving the administration greater flexibility when market conditions were unfavorable.

Hemp

In the eighteenth century extremely favorable terms of trade for hemp and flax developed on the international markets of Königsberg and Riga.[60] The conservative Radziwiłłs, though they wanted to take advantage of this new opportunity, were not willing to adjust their agricultural policy and use their *folwarks* to grow these crops for themselves. So the hemp and flax they needed had to be found elsewhere. The best place proved to be the peasant farms of eastern Belarus, where the system of corvée labor was not well developed. Peasants there continued to pay much of their feudal dues in the form of cereal grains and foodstuffs (eggs, meat, dairy products, and so on) rather than in labor. This left them the time and resources to grow flax and hemp for profit. Here was the source the Radziwiłłs needed; all they had to do was buy it up.[61]

To do so Anna Radziwiłł turned to the most mobile commercial group among her subjects, the Jews. In the mid-1720s she set up a new system on the Łachwa estate in eastern Belarus in which Jewish merchants were tasked with making the rounds of the villages to purchase flax and hemp from the peasants, who were forbidden to sell to anyone else.[62] Once they had finished in the villages, the Jews went to the urban markets and bought whatever was offered for sale there. In a quite extraordinary move, they were even allowed to travel to towns and villages outside the Radziwiłł estates to buy flax and hemp there too.

The estate manager provided the cash for these purchases, based on weekly reckonings submitted by the merchants. The ledgers were carefully audited. Amounts purchased on the estate were checked against the records of the headman (*wójt*) of every village, while purchases from outside the estate were assessed by the estate manager himself. A special warehouse was opened to which the Jews were required to deliver their purchases.[63]

Non-Jewish merchants were apparently not involved in the hemp and flax trade. The *arendarze* in the villages, however, do seem to have got in

JEWS AND TRADE IN THE ESTATE ECONOMY 157

on the act. The profit margins, which derived from gap between the price paid to the peasants and that received from the administration, made it well worth their while. They were also keen to deal in these profitable commodities on their own account.[64] As the trade developed, the estate managers preferred to deal directly with the *arendarze* rather than with the network of individual merchants and so made them responsible for the business.[65] In 1764 the leaseholders in Kopyś were allowed to pay both their *czynsz* and *arenda* dues to the administration in flax and hemp.[66]

The development of this trade exemplifies the ways in which Jewish merchants contributed to the distribution and sale of estate produce in the eighteenth century. When the new business opportunity arose, the Radziwiłł family was unwilling to change the way things were traditionally done in order to take advantage of it. Instead they turned to the Jews, in whose flexibility and business mobility they had great confidence, to find a solution. The Jews for their part were happy to exploit the new business opportunity, which not only gave them an advantage over their non-Jewish competitors but also allowed them to serve as agents of the Radziwiłłs.

In fact this was not only how the flax and hemp trade developed, it was also, as we discussed in the last chapter, the way the sale of grain as alcohol flourished. This would suggest that one of the most important roles of the Jewish merchants in distribution and sale on the Radziwiłł lands was to help the family restructure the estate economy to meet the changing conditions of the eighteenth century without causing any major upheavals.

Manufactured Goods

Early forms of factory (called here "manufactories") began to be set up on the magnate estates of the Commonwealth in the mid-eighteenth century. The motivation for this seems to have been twofold: first, home production saved the expense of importing manufactured goods; second, these primitive factories were quite an efficient way of exploiting estate resources, whether natural or in the form of peasant labor.[67] The lure of easy profits surely influenced the decision to set them up, though they should not be viewed as proto-capitalist enterprises because they remained firmly embedded in the seigneurial economy of the estates.[68]

This was certainly the case on the Radziwiłł latifundium. In the years before 1764 members of the family founded several manufactories on their Lithuanian estates, including a glass and mirror factory in Urzecz, a textile mill in Nieśwież, a glass works in Naliboki, and a porcelain factory in Nowy Świerżeń.[69] The construction of these buildings used timber and other materials from the estates as well as laborers and craftsmen drafted from among the family's subjects.[70] The outlay of cash was kept to a minimum. In his study of the textile mill in Nieśwież, Kula found that the only money expended was for the purchase of dyes in Rīga.[71] Once the mill was running, most of the workforce consisted of peasants fulfilling their corvée obligations. On one occasion, when the mill found itself shorthanded, the manager instructed that young women be conscripted not only from the Nieśwież estate, but also from the family's estates in Mir and Korelicze.[72] Expert craftsmen and artisans were mostly brought from outside, sometimes even from abroad (usually Germany).[73] They, as well as the managers, were paid salaries.

Jews were barely involved in the construction and operation of these manufactories.[74] In Poland-Lithuania, until at least the 1780s, Jewish businessmen tended to avoid this new economic sector, acting neither as investors (which would have been quite implausible on magnate estates) nor as lessee-operators.[75] Only later in the century, when improved management methods, greater efficiency, and market profitability made the industrial sector more attractive, did Jews begin to see manufacturing as a possible source of income.[76] This was true too of the Radziwiłł estates, where few if any Jewish artisans and craftsmen were employed in the manufactories, including the Nieśwież textile mill.[77]

Jews were, however, involved in the economic arrangements that linked the factories with the overall estate economy. They supplied raw materials, expedited matters of finance, and helped distribute finished goods on the market. Here too, though, they were hardly exclusive players and their role was only secondary.

The lion's share of supply was undertaken by the estate administration itself. Raw materials were brought from the estate, and many of the special materials and tools were purchased from abroad, often in Königsberg.[78] Jewish merchants were not needed in either of these supply channels, which had been in place before the manufactories were established, and only became involved when the plants needed goods from the local market. For example, in the 1740s Jewish merchants provided the glass works in Naliboki with a range of items such as iron, wax, sodium nitrate, arsenic, lead, tin, and paper, as well as food for the laborers.[79] The local *arendarz* sold beer and vodka to the workers.[80]

Jewish businessmen also played in a role in factory finances. As we have seen, these plants were deeply embedded in the estate economy, which kept its use of cash to a minimum, preferring wherever possible to exploit existing resources, corvée labor and payments in kind. Consequently, the factory managers often faced problems of liquidity and were hard-pressed to pay wages to the managers, expert craftsmen, and laborers whose work was not fully covered by their feudal dues.[81] To overcome this problem, they would make payments in scrip that could be redeemed with the local *arendarz*. In return for these notes it was not cash that was given but merchandise (mainly food and drink), and that at prices always favorable to the *arendarz*-vendor (which, of course, was a constant source of friction between the *arendarze* and those who worked in the manufactories).[82]

Perhaps the most important role played by Jewish merchants in the operation of the estate manufactories was in product distribution, though again their participation was minor. The main customers of the manufactories were the estate owners themselves, who wanted to economize on importing expensive goods. The account books of the textile mill in Nieśwież show that 57 percent of its production was sent directly to its owner, Michał Kazimierz Radziwiłł, while only a quarter was sold to other customers (among whom were a number of Michał Kazimierz's relatives).[83] Still, it would be a mistake to conclude that the Radziwiłłs were totally uninterested in selling the factory's products on the local market. In Urzecz they even employed a factory agent, a non-Jew named Jan Wilhelm Rosenbaum, to be responsible for distribution.[84]

The Radziwiłł manufactories had three main venues for marketing that part of their products that they did sell: at the factory itself, on the estate markets, and in towns and cities outside the estate. Sales at the factory required no special effort by the management other than providing efficient service.[85] The nature of this "factory-door" trade can be seen from the monthly sales of the Naliboki glass works during 1746 (Table 6.3).[86]

A total of 673 transactions were made at the factory during 1746, bringing in 19,143 złoty and 25 groszy at an average value per sale of 28 złoty, 13 groszy. The majority of these sales (86 percent) were made to non-Jews. Jewish buyers averaged only eight purchases a month as against forty-eight by non-Jews. In terms of factory income, the significance of the non-Jewish purchasers was even greater; they accounted for more than 90 percent of the total volume of trade. In addition, the average value of purchases by Jewish buyers was some 30 percent smaller than those by others.

Table 6.3. Monthly Sales at the Naliboki Glass Works, 1746

	To Jews				To Non-Jews		
Month	No. Sales	Value of Sales	Ave. Value		No. Sales	Value of Sales	Ave. Value
January	7	92 zł., 8 gr.	13 zł., 5 gr.		41	1,387 zł., 21 gr.	33 zł., 24 gr.
February	10	71 zł., 5 gr.	7 zł., 3 gr.		60	1,998 zł., 10 gr.	33 zł., 10 gr.
March	24	809 zł., 18 gr.	33 zł., 22 gr.		99	2,538 zł., 24 gr.	25 zł., 19 gr.
April	2	28 zł., 25 gr.	14 zł., 13 gr.		19	339 zł., 26 gr.	17 zł., 27 gr.
May	4	257 zł., 29 gr.	64 zł., 15 gr.		42	1,316 zł., 28 gr.	13 zł., 11 gr.
June	8	136 zł., 26 gr.	17 zł., 3 gr.		45	864 zł., 26 gr.	19 zł., 6 gr.
July	11	97 zł., 13 gr.	8 zł., 26 gr.		41	1,639 zł., 9 gr.	40 zł.,
August	11	155 zł., 20 gr.	14 zł., 5 gr.		50	3,689 zł., 8 gr.	73 zł., 24 gr.
September	5	46 zł., 8 gr.	9 zł., 8 gr.		36	1,040 zł., 29 gr.	28 zł., 28 gr.
October	5	141 zł., 13 gr.	28 zł., 9 gr.		50	1,199 zł., 13 gr.	24 zł.,
November	2	6 zł., 24 gr.	3 zł., 12 gr.		44	545 zł., 6 gr.	12 zł., 12 gr.
December	3	11 zł., 1 gr.	3 zł., 20 gr.		54	727 zł., 25 gr.	13 zł., 14 gr.
Total	92	1,855 zł., 10 gr.	20 zł., 5 gr.		581	17,288 zł., 15 gr.	29 zł., 23 gr.

SOURCE: AR XIX, NSZ II 1: 234–316.

This disparity can be explained by the fact that the non-Jewish buyers mostly came to shop for personal needs, their own or their noble patron's, and only a small fraction were buying for resale. So for the most part these records do not reflect the activities of professional merchants. The majority of the non-Jewish customers were lords and clergymen or their servants. Only two merchants specializing in glassware can be identified, both from Wilno.[87] Nor were all the Jews independent merchants; some were buying on behalf of noblemen.[88] Other of the Jewish customers, particularly those buying a few low-priced items, might have been local tavern keepers supplying their own needs.

The problem with the on-site sales at Naliboki was that the plant was situated in a remote village accessible just via bad roads so only a few people actually took the trouble to go there.[89] When merchants did come, the factory management extended them goods on credit, perhaps as an encouragement to return.[90] The records note that those few merchants who did buy at the factory door in the mid-eighteenth century took their purchases for resale all over Lithuania and Poland: Wilno, Grodno, Nowogródek, Kojdanów, Mohilew (Mahiliou, Belarus), Torczyń (Torchyn, Ukraine), and

Zasław (Iziaslav, Ukraine), among other places,[91] though this trade was not very brisk.

To supplement these sales, the Radziwiłłs set up their own marketing system in the large towns of Lithuania by acquiring warehouses from which to sell their stock. This arrangement was simple enough to be organized directly by the administration without the help of Jewish agents.[92]

The Jewish merchants came into their own in the sale of the manufactured products on the local markets. Though only a small proportion of the output was disposed of in this way, the administration did lease out special stalls in some of the estate towns, where merchants could sell the goods on commission.[93] Protectionist policies were also put in place to ban the sale of competing goods by Jew or non-Jew alike.[94] The Jews were as dominant in this sector as they were in the urban markets as a whole.

Conclusions

Judging only from the ways the Radziwiłł administration marketed its surplus grain and manufactured goods, one would conclude that Jewish trade was marginal to the estate system of distribution and sale. That would, however, be misleading.

The direct sale of grain, like selling the goods produced by the manufactories, was a relatively simple transaction. So much so, in fact, that the administration had no need of Jewish merchants. It functioned perfectly well on its own. Jewish experience and expertise became important really only when economic conditions demanded more sophistication. The estates' traditional system of marketing, simple and inflexible, found adapting to new conditions really very difficult. It was to overcome this problem, when it arose, that the Radziwiłłs turned to the Jewish merchants on their estates.

So, for example, when the market for direct grain sales declined in the eighteenth century, the administration used Jewish businessmen to keep revenues growing by ever greater exploitation of the *propinacja* leases. This was an incredibly successful policy and it made Jews key figures in the distribution and sale of estate grain.

Changing economic circumstances also determined the role Jews played in the trade with the Baltic market. The Radziwiłł administration continued to sell most of its goods there as it had always done. However, when the terms of trade for flax and hemp improved, it did not have a means of growing these crops for itself without changing the way the estates and their farms were run. To acquire the commodities it wanted, it turned to Jewish merchants for help, having them purchase these crops from the peasants and stockpile them for export. This was an entirely new form of economic activity that brought the family greatly increased profits by taking advantage of the Jewish businessmen's willingness to accept change and enter into new markets.

So, in their roles both as *arendarze* and traders in hemp and flax, Jewish businessmen introduced an element of flexibility into the estate economy that allowed it to benefit from the new opportunities of the eighteenth century without having to go through turbulent upheavals. Interestingly, the two roles were, to some extent at least, complementary. The money that the Jewish merchants paid the peasants to buy their flax and hemp for the Radziwiłłs was recouped by the *arendarze* who sold the very same peasants Radziwiłł grain in the form of alcohol.[95] In this way, the Jewish businessmen helped the magnate estate-owner realize one of the major goals of the seigneurial economy—keeping as much of the money supply as possible in his own hands. Here too, the Jews' role in distribution and sale must be seen as extremely significant for the working of the estates' economic system.

JEWISH MERCHANTS IN SUPPLY

Issues of supply should be divided into two main sectors: supplying the Radziwiłł court and estates (the latter for the upkeep of infrastructure) and supplying estate society with the necessities and luxuries of life. The estate administration was very active in the first of these, while independent merchants dominated the second. Again no comprehensive data exist, so we need to resort to the fragmentary though extensive records that have survived.

The Radziwiłłs preferred to purchase the supplies they needed for their court and latifundium at the great Baltic markets, where they could use the income from sales of their estate produce. Only a few Jewish merchants were active in this trade, so their role was limited.[96] The Radziwiłłs also had extensive business dealings with Polish-Lithuanian merchants both on and off the estate. Jews were a little more active in this type of supply, since they dominated local markets. On the other hand, because their involvement was primarily in small-scale retail trade and the Radziwiłłs chose the wealthier merchants, usually non-Jews, as suppliers, their role here was limited too. The Jewish merchants were mostly important in supplying estate society, where their strength in the retail market was a distinct advantage and was recognized as such by the administration.

This discussion of the Jews' role in estate supply will, then, begin with an examination of the Radziwiłł purchases in the Baltic ports, move on to look at the activities of Polish-Lithuanian purveyors to the court and latifundium, and, finally, attempt to see how the local markets functioned in supplying estate society.

The Radziwiłłs and the Baltic Markets

The Baltic market of choice for the Radziwiłł estates in Lithuania was Königsberg, easily reached via the Niemen River. The administration organized an annual flotilla to take estate products for sale there. With the proceeds, they bought the goods they wanted, principally salt, salt herring, iron, steel, and lead. The family agent in Königsberg also bought French wine, perfumes, coffee, and other luxury goods including a small quantity of fine fabrics, presumably for the family's personal use.[97] Hieronim Florian Radziwiłł's accounts for 1759 also include categories for the raw materials purchased for his factories and his private army. In addition, the family did business at two other Baltic ports, Gdańsk and Rīga. Among the goods they bought at the former were English clocks and various forms of weaponry,[98] while in the latter they even took possession of a shipment of twelve black Africans brought as slaves from London in 1752, evidently to serve in the Radziwiłł palace in Biała.[99]

The volume of the Radziwiłł family trade is impressive. Year after year they bought huge quantities of the three principal imports, salt, salt herring, and iron, to be sent back to the estates from Königsberg. In 1752 alone, Hieronim Florian Radziwiłł purchased 168 łaszt[100] of salt, 200 barrels of salt herring, and 300 ingots[101] of pig iron; in 1754 he bought 40 łaszt of salt and 500 ingots of pig iron; and in 1759, 105 łaszt of salt, 50 barrels of salt herring, and 870 ingots of iron.[102] In cash terms Michał Kazimierz Radziwiłł's expenditures in the summer of 1750 exceeded 25,000 złoty; in 1751 they came to more than 36,000 złoty; and in 1752, 27,500 złoty.[103] The official in charge of the river trade to Rīga reported that, over the course of four years (1754–1757) he took in almost 19,000 thaler—some 152,000 Polish złoty—an average annual revenue of 38,000 złoty.[104] The volume of Michał Kazimierz Radziwiłł's trade in Gdańsk in 1756 exceeded 11,000 złoty.[105] And in 1742, Hieronim Florian Radziwiłł's bills for perfumes and other luxury goods alone topped 14,000 złoty.

The Radziwiłłs were not the only magnates so deeply involved in the Baltic trade. There are figures for the business done by other magnate families in Gdańsk during the eighteenth century too. During the years 1753, 1754, 1756, and 1765–1771, for which records have survived, the Rzewuski family purchased goods worth almost 120,000 złoty at an annual average of 12,000 złoty.[106] In 1771 the Ossoliński family sold 60,000 złoty worth of rye; in 1779, the Potocki family sold potash to the value of 78,000 złoty.[107] Grain sales by the Czartoryski family in Gdańsk in 1715 reached 28,000 złoty.[108] In the first half of the eighteenth century the Lubomirski family sold an average of 140 łaszt of rye in Gdańsk each year.[109] Magnate trade on the eighteenth century Baltic markets was thus common and extensive.[110]

Jewish merchants played an insignificant role in this important sector.[111] From the moment that the shipments of grain reached the Radziwiłł administration until it was sold, all the business was done through an existing estate system, in place at least since the early seventeenth century, in which Jewish merchants were not employed.[112] For example, Michał Kazimierz Radziwiłł's river trade in the 1740s and 1750s was managed by a certain Józef Topolewski (probably a minor nobleman). He organized the storage of the grain at the Niemen River ports, its loading onto rafts, and transport to Königsberg. There he organized its sale, handled the purchase of goods to be sent back to the estates, and supervised their shipping to Lithuania.[113] Jews were hardly involved in any of this (except for Topolewski's agent, Lejzer, whose main role was organizing the flotilla itself and keeping the accounts).[114] In Königsberg, Topolewski did most of his business with the brothers Adolph and Friedrich Saturgus, local non-Jewish merchants who served as Radziwiłł agents for many years.[115]

Polish-Lithuanian Suppliers to the Radziwiłł Court

The Radziwiłłs had other sources of supply besides the Baltic markets. Unlike their subjects, who were restricted to buying on the estate markets, they traded wherever they wanted. They bought goods from merchants in Warsaw, Brody, Chelm, and Opatów, among other places.[116] In 1746 for example Michał Kazimierz Radziwiłł issued a payment order for 141,611 złoty for purchases by his wife, including 44,120 złoty to a Jewish merchant called Abraham from Lwów.[117] Inside Lithuania the family's connections extended as far as Wilno, Brześć, and Pińsk.[118] Estate merchants sometimes helped acquire goods from abroad; for example, traders in Newel in eastern Lithuania brought in goods from Russia.[119] In addition, the family patronized merchants from southern Poland who imported wine from Hungary.[120]

Most references to Radziwiłł suppliers appear in payment orders, which do not always note what was being bought. The randomness of the sources also makes it difficult to reach a full picture of the family's purchases or to grasp the role of Jewish merchants in this business. What can be said is that the Radziwiłłs' purchases included a range of goods, including wines, olives, fabrics (both luxury and simple), furs, and copper. The individual payment orders were for sums ranging from a few hundred to tens of thousands of złoty. The merchants selling to the family were both Jews and non-Jews, but it is difficult to determine the relative importance of each. It is clear, however, that Jewish merchants did not dominate this trade as they did the local markets.

Jewish Women Stall Owners

There was one group of Jewish merchants that did play an important role in supplying the Radziwiłłs, women stall keepers (called in Polish *kramarki*; singular, *kramarka*). For the period 1750 to 1760, we know of 14 such Jewish women, resident on the estate, who sold to Michał Kazimierz Radziwiłł, his family, and his court.[121] For those same years, records survive for only five male Jewish stall keepers who supplied the family; regular non-Jewish suppliers, male or female, were even rarer.

These Jewish women supplied the Radziwiłłs mostly with textiles, from plain local cloth to fabrics imported from Italy and Turkey.[122] Some were apparently intended for the uniforms of the family's private army and some for the livery of retainers and servants; the rest may have been destined for clothes for the family.[123]

The second most important merchandise that the Jewish women stall keepers supplied was spices for the family kitchens; they also provided honey and furs. In some cases the *kramarki* even acted as purchasing agents for the family, helping acquire goods such as grain and fodder for the horses.[124]

Michał Kazimierz Radziwiłł's administrative records from the 1750s alone contain accounts of debts to these Jewish women amounting to some 83,000 złoty.[125] The individual bills ranged from just a few złoty[126] to thousands and even tens of thousands. In fact Radziwiłł had ongoing accounts of more than 500 złoty with nine of the fourteen women listed in his account books; the five others appear on the list just once each and for smaller sums.

These debts were sometimes significant. In 1754, Ḥaya, a stall keeper from the town of Biały Kamieniec (Bilyi Kamin', Ukraine), was owed a total of 21,444 złoty.[127] Even this was not the largest debt. That was owed to Nehama from Ołyka, one of the family's most active suppliers, who had a business relationship with them lasting decades. In 1746, Radziwiłł's debt to this Jewish woman already stood at 26,515 złoty; the next year it grew by 648 złoty and 26 groszy. In partial payment, Radziwiłł granted Nehama the lease on the fishing rights in a local lake for a number of years, a monopoly valued at 14,400 złoty. To the remaining balance of 12,763 złoty and 26 groszy, Radziwiłł added purchases of 3,954 złoty and 26 groszy in 1753, bringing his total debt to 16,718 złoty and 20 groszy.[128] His purchases in subsequent years were also for fairly large amounts: 4,232 złoty and 11 groszy in 1754,[129] 7,987 złoty and 26 groszy in 1756,[130] and 11,211 złoty in 1758.[131] During the 1740s and 1750s then, Michał Kazimierz Radziwiłł's account with Nehama totaled at least 54,549 Polish złoty and 27 groszy, a hefty sum.[132]

The presence of such Jewish businesswomen on the Radziwiłł estates was not an isolated phenomenon.[133] Its roots go back to the sixteenth century. With the relocation of the center of Jewish life from Western and Central Europe to Poland-Lithuania, the Jews' business activity shifted from moneylending to commerce.[134] Women's economic activity changed too. In his research on medieval Jewry, Jordan has argued that Jewish women in some parts of France had developed their own economic activities. Alongside their husbands they acted to supplement the family income by quietly lending small amounts of money at interest to Christian women for household purposes.[135]

In sixteenth-century Poland, Jewish women continued to contribute to the family income, though in new ways. According to a responsum by Rabbi Shlomo Luria of Ostróg, "in the present time, our women . . . conduct trade in the home, acting in place of their husbands."[136] He was referring to women who openly engaged in trade and ran the family store while their husbands were away on business.[137] Women as money earners were probably much more important for those poor families that supported themselves by peddling door to door, an activity that women could do as well as men.[138]

A clearly identified group of female economic actors in Jewish society was made up of widows who continued their husband's business after his death.[139] Some women even carried on business independently of their husbands.[140] Whatever their personal histories, most Jewish women involved in commerce dealt in petty trade on the local market.[141] In this, they were not significantly different from non-Jewish townswomen, who also played an important role in local trade in the sixteenth and seventeenth centuries.[142]

The eighteenth century saw no major structural changes in the commercial activities of Jewish women in Poland and Lithuania. As the Jewish population grew, so did the number of female peddlers. In Kraków there were so many of them that they organized into a group along the lines of a guild.[143] The Council of the Lithuanian Land, afraid that women peddlers would harm the livelihood of male storeowners, issued strict orders banning them.[144] Rabbis and religious leaders also expressed their suspicions that these Jewish women were engaging in immoral behavior and failing to observe the strictures of Jewish law such as keeping the Sabbath.[145] Of course none of this put a stop to Jewish women's economic activity, which was for most families an economic necessity.

There were also cases of wealthy Jewish women involved in large-scale trade and even some who worked closely with magnate families such as the Sieniawskis.[146] Thus, the phenomenon of Jewish women stall keepers on the Radziwiłł estates does not seem to have been very much out of the ordinary.

We cannot say much about the social background of our fourteen kramarki. There is only one case in which the record expressly noted that the merchant was a widow; however, because it did not provide her first name, we cannot identify her.[147] Another of the suppliers, Feyga of Mir, was referred to in a second document as Feyga Królewiecka, which might mean that she was the wife of Joseph ben Leib Królewiecki, one of the general arendarze of Mir between 1752 and 1758.[148] In 1754, Feyga provided Michał Kazimierz Radziwiłł with cloth worth 1,000 złoty; in 1755, 700 złoty; and in 1758, 500 złoty. She also supplied the court with a large amount of fabric on credit.[149] This might suggest that she was contributing to her family's income in her role as court supplier. However, the name Feyga Królewiecka can also be translated as Feyga from Königsberg, which could mean that she was quite unconnected with Joseph ben Leib. The sources simply do not allow an unambiguous identification.[150]

The case of the stall keeper named Mirka Libina provides a different perspective. In the 1750s Mirka supplied textiles to the Radziwiłł family court in Mir. Although the quantities were not usually large, Michał Kazimierz

Radziwiłł owed her 875 złoty in 1755.[151] Mirka had established a close relationship with her noble lord, and in his diary for 1739 Radziwiłł recorded, "I stayed in Mir because last year's fire has left the castle a wreck. I stayed with Mirka, an extremely well-to-do merchant lady."[152] This encounter antedates the earliest mention of her economic dealings with the court by a decade or so, suggesting that these women merchants could forge lasting ties with their patrons. Their commercial careers also made them into another of the links between Jewish society and the Radziwiłł court, and certainly contributed to the family's positive attitude towards Jewish economic activity in general.[153]

Even good relations with the magnate were not a guarantee of protection and safety, however. In April 1752 a blood libel accusation led to the arrest of Mirka and another Jewish woman named Ḥaya. The two were tortured and sent to Wilno for trial. One of them broke down, blamed the local *arendarze*, and agreed to be baptized.[154] Unfortunately no further details about the case have survived, and we know only that Mirka continued to supply fabrics to the Radziwiłł court throughout the 1750s.[155]

Though we do not have full economic records, it is clear that the Radziwiłłs' Jewish suppliers played only an incidental role in supplying the family and its court. The women stall keepers' 83,000 złoty turnover seems quite respectable, though it must be remembered that it was spread out over ten years. By way of comparison, Michał Kazimierz Radziwiłł's outlays in Königsberg alone between 1750 and 1753 ranged from 25,000 to 36,000 złoty each year.[156] The Jewish suppliers formed only one, and by no means the largest, channel of supply open to the Radziwiłł family and its court. In fact, their importance lay not in the gross volume of the business they did, but rather in their being a key supplier of cloth and fabric to the court.[157]

Jewish Suppliers to Estate Society

It was only as suppliers to estate society that Jews played the major role. It could hardly have been otherwise, bearing in mind the Jews' domination of local trade. As we have seen, Jews accounted for some 80 percent of the merchants in the large town of Słuck in 1750; in the small town of Kopyl that year, all the merchants were Jewish. Other indices, too, such as the number of Jewish-owned houses on the central market square and the number of Jewish-owned stalls, give the same picture.[158]

Foreign visitors to Lithuania in the eighteenth century reported that Jews dominated all forms of trade. The Count de Lyra, a courtier from St. Petersburg, writing about his journey from Smolensk to Warsaw in 1730, noted that it was impossible to buy anything from locals if not from Jews.[159] The German writer Friedrich Schulz, describing his experiences on the way from Rīga to Warsaw also gave the impression that almost all trade in Lithuania was in Jewish hands.[160] The English traveler of the 1780s, William Coxe, put it bluntly: "In our route through Lithuania we were struck with the swarms of Jews, who, though very numerous in every other part of Poland, seem to have fixed their head-quarters in this duchy. If you ask for an interpreter, they bring you a Jew; if you come to an inn, the landlord is a Jew; if you want post-horses, a Jew procures them, and a Jew drives them; if you wish to purchase, a Jew is your agent."[161] The existing records do not offer hard data to confirm these impressionistic accounts, though they do provide more detail and give various insights into the nature and scope of Jewish trade.

At the prompting of the nobility the Jews of Poland and Lithuania had moved into wholesale trade during the sixteenth century,[162] initially because it had been difficult to penetrate the retail market. Jews continued as wholesalers even after they began to dominate urban retail trade in the eighteenth century.[163] This was true for almost all the towns of Poland and Lithuania, including those on the Radziwiłł latifundium in Lithuania. Jewish merchants on the estates had commercial ties extending across Lithuania and Poland and even reaching foreign countries. In the Commonwealth, they traded with Wilno, Grodno, and Kowno in Lithuania, and Warsaw, Gdańsk, and Lwów in Poland, among other places.[164] The Radziwiłłs' *jurydiki* (enclaves) in the large royal towns, which were excluded from restrictive municipal jurisdiction, made very convenient venues for these commercial interactions. Their most important international market was Königsberg, but Jews from the latifundium also traveled to Frankfurt a.M., Breslau, and Berlin[165] and even to the international fair in Leipzig.[166] Some even maintained contracts with merchants from Moscow, who gave them access to the important Russian markets.[167]

Urban merchants such as those in Słuck sometimes took a jaundiced view of these Jewish wholesalers and complained about them to the administration.[168] Their major concern was that they were contravening the restrictions on trade carried out inside the city.[169] Słuck had been granted municipal privileges (including a trade monopoly) by the Radziwiłłs in the seventeenth century, among whose terms was a ban on nonresident merchants, which in practice meant mostly wholesalers, trading among themselves within the town limits.[170] The Jewish Council of the Lithuanian Land referred to this privilege in 1633–34, when it issued regulations about the rights of out-of-town Jewish merchants to trade with local Jews: "Should the *kahal* in Słuck find that their lord has given a privilege to the non-Jewish residents of Słuck that visitors may not trade among themselves in Słuck, then no Jewish visitor may conduct any trade with any [other] visitor, whether Jew or non-Jew, even on the market day."[171]

Some Jewish merchants seem to have ignored this regulation, as evidenced by a petition by the non-Jewish burghers of Słuck in the late seventeenth or early eighteenth century: "His Highness the Prince, our most benevolent Lord, has graciously issued a number of decrees forbidding visitors to conduct any commerce among themselves. But the Jews pay no attention to this and conduct various commercial transactions and harm the poor."[172] By the turn of the eighteenth century, then, the Jewish wholesalers in Słuck were powerful enough to violate both the commercial privileges of the non-Jewish burghers and the regulations of the Jewish Council of the Lithuanian Land itself.[173]

Tensions were much higher in the field of retail trade, which Jews dominated. The vast majority of the Christian townspeople's complaints about Jewish trade dealt with the Jews' roles in the retail market. There was not much new about them. The eighteenth-century burghers tended just to repeat the same complaints against Jews that had been made by their fathers and their fathers' fathers: the Jews did not limit their trade to the market place but made their deals throughout the city; they did not restrict their sales to standard business hours; and, worst of all, they traveled outside town to purchase goods from potential sellers.[174] Another bone of contention was Jews doing business on Sundays, when Christians closed their businesses. In Słuck, Sunday trading was forbidden even in the synagogue courtyard within the Jewish quarter.[175]

These laws were obviously not very effective, because the non-Jewish burghers went on complaining time after time, hammering away at the same points. Certainly, the administration did not take the side of the burghers against the Jews, whose position was so strong that they were probably unmoved by their competitors' threats.[176]

Relations between Christian townspeople and Jewish merchants in the eighteenth century were not always marked by serious friction, especially in the small towns.[177] A petition submitted to Michał Kazimierz Radziwiłł in 1746 by the non-Jewish townspeople of Żagory on the Szawle *ekonomia*, exemplified a different kind of relations that could develop:

> We, the burghers of Żagory . . . have [until today] been resolute in our determination . . . not to permit Jews to live in the city and hold leases. Nevertheless, because we pursue our own advantage and the benefit of our lord's treasury . . . from which the city may flourish and its markets grow, we hereby humbly request and petition our Lord . . . that he take under his august protection the Jew, Ber ben Meir, an honorable merchant, well known to us for his benevolence, and permit him to transfer his home and stall from the other side of the city to this [side], to build himself a house [here] and live in it. . . . We all guarantee that he has no debts and is not suspected in any matter. On the contrary, we attest that he has long been an honorable merchant and that his stall offers a range of wares as wide as that found in the large towns.[178]

The people of Żagory seem to have concluded that getting rid of all the Jewish merchants had had a negative impact on trade and so asked Radziwiłł to grant special privileges to an important Jewish merchant to allow him to do business there. Their positive attitude was shown in their request that the Jew be permitted to live in their part of town (meaning the market square) and not be isolated in a distant suburb.[179] This was an acknowledgment on the part of the townspeople that they found it difficult to conduct trade at a level appropriate even for a provincial town in Lithuania and needed Jews to do it for them.[180]

For this small town, as for many other like it, life without Jewish merchants was difficult to the point of impossibility. The Jews turned this to their advantage. According to a house list from 1742 (four years before the petition), there was not a single Jewish-owned house in Żagory; by 1756, Jews owned sixteen houses in town.[181]

It is often claimed that the Jews' success in dominating local trade was because they adopted proto-capitalistic business methods.[182] This was not the case. Jewish merchants had indeed rebelled against their exclusion from the medieval trading monopolies in the sixteenth and seventeenth centuries and it was this that had initially won them the support of the nobles, who were also disadvantaged by that system. However, once they had succeeded in overcoming the competition of the non-Jewish burghers and established themselves as the dominant force in urban trade, the Jews had no qualms in reverting to precisely those monopolistic trading practices they had previously challenged.[183] Thus their success had little to do with any inclination toward capitalism but was instead based on a commonality of economic interests with the nobility. It was with noble support that the Jews initially overcame competition by subverting the trading monopolies, and it was with noble support that they retained their dominance when they adopted precisely the same monopolies for themselves.

All in all, the Jews on the Radziwiłł estates were deeply involved in urban trade, both wholesale and retail. In the large towns Jews were neither the only merchants nor, on many occasions, the richest. They were nonetheless extremely active in the local markets, which led the non-Jewish burghers to try to to limit them, though without much success. In the provincial towns (the majority of settlements on the estates), Jews were often the only merchants, a situation the family and the estate administration seem to have viewed with favor.[184]

Conclusions

To supply the magnate court and the administration of a huge latifundium, the Radziwiłłs needed a variety of goods in large quantities. What they could not grow or produce on the estates, they would obtain either on the international markets or from local suppliers. Commodities available on the international market were more varied than what could be bought locally in Lithuania, so every year the family shipped its produce down the Niemen for sale in Königsberg and used the proceeds to make its purchases there. This was nothing new, the family had engaged in the river trade for well over a century. The Jews' role in this well-established sector had never been great, so their significance in international supply remained negligible.

The family could also buy the goods it needed from local dealers. Jewish businessmen played a more important role here, though their influence was limited because they were not, by and large, among the wealthiest merchants, with whom the family preferred to do business. There were some Jewish purveyors to the Radziwiłł court, but the volume of their trade was not great.

The only sector in which Jewish merchants really competed was textiles. The cloth trade in Poland-Lithuania was dominated by Jewish merchants. On the estates a number of the most active traders were women, some of whom developed close ties with the Radziwiłłs, providing them with large quantities of cloth over many years. Overall, however, Jewish commerce was of only secondary importance in supplying the magnate family.

Jewish trade was much more significant in supplying estate society. This was very important for the Radziwiłłs, because it not only allowed the estate to function but also, as we shall see below, helped generate tax revenue. The family was willing to support the Jewish merchants against their Christian competitors because it shared the nobility's traditional view that the non-Jewish burghers' trading practices were detrimental to its interests.

The relatively large share of retail and wholesale trade that was in the hands of Jewish merchants placed the Christians in a position of inferiority that they found hard to accept. They campaigned against Jewish trade in the larger towns, such as Słuck, but without the support of the estate administration could not achieve much. The situation was different in the provincial towns. There, the weakness of the non-Jewish burghers in the face of a Jewish society supported by the Radziwiłłs and the estate administration, simply left them no choice but to make the best of the situation and accept Jewish dominance of trade. Clearly, then, the Jews' central role in the supply of estate society cannot be called into question.

REVENUE GENERATION

Increased trade on the estates enhanced the Radziwiłł family's income in a number of ways. Not only did wealthier subjects pay higher direct taxes, but the number of transactions on which customs and duties could be charged grew too. Just how much this indirect taxation brought in cannot be precisely determined since it was collected by the general *arendarze*, whose accounts did not distinguish it from *propinacja* income.

It does seem clear, however, that these trade levies could bring in significant sums, particularly during major fairs. Evidence of this can be found in the memoir of Marcin Matuszewicz, a minor nobleman and Radziwiłł family client.[185] Matuszewicz wrote about the fair in the town of Rosna, today in Belarus, owned by his family. This small fair had brought in only 380 złoty until his father decided to encourage trade by making loans to the merchants. As a result, numbers of visitors grew and along with them the volume of trade.

> In Rosna at the time there were small fairs, whose revenues did not exceed 300 tynf [= 380 złoty]. But when my family began to lend money to the merchants so that they could conduct business and trade goods, the number of merchants soon began to increase. . . . There were merchants from

Wrocław who brought textiles, woolen goods, and notions, merchants from Moscow who brought furs, merchants from the city of Chocim [Khotyn, Ukraine] with horses and Turkish goods.[186] So even though the taxes on the fair were collected in a way that made it hard to identify them,[187] the Rosna fair brought in some 10,000 złoty.[188]

There were some major towns on the Radziwiłł latifundium (such as Słuck, Nieśwież, and Biała) that held much larger and more important fairs than this, which presumably brought in much larger sums. Other towns held fairs specializing in specific categories of merchandise that could attract merchants from great distances (the horse fair in Mir is a good example) and they too must have generated a great deal of income.

Of course the customs and duties were charged not just during the fair but on every transaction carried out in the course of the year. With dozens of towns on the Radziwiłł estates, these levies must have brought in a very significant income indeed for the family. Since Jewish merchants dominated local markets, where most of this trade took place, we can assume that they contributed a very great deal to these revenues.

A more detailed picture of trade revenues and an assessment of the importance of Jewish merchants can be gained by looking at a different levy, not included in the general *arenda*s. The Radziwiłł administration imposed such a levy on estate merchants who sent their goods to the international market in Königsberg via the Niemen river.[189] It took the form of a payment for shipping cargo on the magnate's rafts, and its amount was determined by the value and quantity of the freight.[190]

This kind of revenue was not unique to the Radziwiłł family nor to the Niemen river trade. Merchants had shipped goods to the Baltic ports on rafts belonging to estate owners as far back as the first half of the seventeenth century. By the early eighteenth century incomes from the traffic of freight on the San and Vistula rivers from southeastern Poland to Gdańsk were substantial.[191] The eighteenth-century river trade along the Dwina from eastern Belarus to Rīga was also largely financed by merchants who paid estate owners to transport goods on their rafts.[192]

In what follows we will therefore examine the revenues from shipments by private merchants on Radziwiłł rafts along the Niemen. The river trade on the Königsberg route was more important for the Radziwiłł lands examined here than that to either Rīga or Gdańsk. In fact, the administration of the Lithuanian estates often preferred to send merchandise from its holdings in eastern Belarus to ports on the Niemen rather than those on the Dwina (which led to Rīga), even though the latter were much closer.[193] In addition more private freight was shipped on the Niemen route than on the others, yielding significantly more revenue.

The Evolution of the Freight Shipments

Documentation of the river trade between the Radziwiłł estates in Lithuania and Königsberg dates back to the beginning of the seventeenth century. As early as 1608 and 1609 Marcin Kulicki, the Radziwiłłs' pilot, transported private freight to Königsberg along with his patron's merchandise.[194] Documentation has survived from the river trade for six years in the 1620s and 1630s. In 1625 and 1633 there were no freight shipments at all, but in 1626 they accounted for 10 percent of the total revenues of the flotilla, rising to 50 percent in 1627, 1631, and 1634.[195] Most of those paying for shipments in these years were noblemen (apparently those who lacked the means to organize their own flotillas) and non-Jewish merchants. No Jews were involved. In the second half of the seventeenth century, members of the family, notably Bogusław Radziwiłł, whose Protestant allegiances during the wars of the mid-seventeenth century led to his appointment as governor of East Prussia, began to use the Jews of their estates as a source of revenue for the river trade, but there are no data about this activity or the Jews' share in it.[196]

Freight payments on the two major river routes between the Commonwealth and the Baltic ports did not expand significantly until the eighteenth century, and each took its own path of development.[197] The freight trade on the San and Vistula rivers to Gdańsk became more extensive towards the end of the seventeenth century and blossomed during the Great Northern War, probably due to the devastation of agriculture and consequent decline in the volume of goods that the estate owner had to ship.[198] Starting in the mid-1730s, as agricultural productivity improved, freight shipments dwindled until they virtually disappeared.[199]

In contrast, it was only in the mid-1720s that the Radziwiłłs began intensively to exploit freight charges to finance their flotillas on the Niemen River, perhaps as part of their attempts to revive their fortunes after the Great Northern War. So successful were they that this business flourished for the next fifty years or more, long after it had disappeared from the San and Vistula.[200] By 1760 the freight trade had become so important to the estate economy that, in addition to renting out space on the rafts that carried their own goods, the Radziwiłłs outfitted additional rafts meant only to carry freight. That year Hieronim Florian Radziwiłł sent eighteen rafts to Königsberg— seven with his own merchandise and eleven loaded with freight of others.[201]

Freight Shipments in the Eighteenth Century

Goods traded between Lithuania and Königsberg on the Niemen were different from those traded between Poland and Gdańsk on the San and Vistula. The market in East Prussia was small, which meant that the variety of goods there was relatively limited. One freight manifest mentioned twenty-eight products, mainly raw or semi-processed agricultural produce, shipped downriver to Königsberg, while a similar document for the Gdańsk trade listed fifty-seven commodities. Goods sent from Lithuania to Königsberg included flax seed, flax fiber, linen cloth, hemp, canvas, thread, cane, milk, waxes, oil, rye, wheat, millet, buckwheat, potash, copper, hay, kettles, vodka, hog bristles, hides, tobacco, anise, and flour.[202] The vast majority of the Königsberg trade, however, was in just four goods: flax seed, flax fiber, canvas, and rye. These alone could sometimes account for 90 percent or more of the entire volume of trade in any given year (Table 6.4).

In Königsberg the merchants purchased a variety of processed goods for freight shipment to Lithuania, including salt, salt herring, codfish, wines of various types, eau de vie, iron, steel, lead, sheet metal, wire, small shot, boxes, copper flasks, saws, porcelain ware, paper, glass, amber, gunpowder, white lead, alum, sulfur, arsenic, sugar, pepper, cumin, rosemary, orange peel, capers, anise, spices, lemons, olives, rice, coffee, cheese, dyes, woolen fabric, millstones, gravestones, weights, carriages, bullets, and various types of soap.[203] Compared with the 130 types of goods purchased in the larger and more active Gdańsk market, the selection of 57 varieties of goods from Königsberg was relatively limited.[204] In terms of the upriver trade, the major differences between the two ports lay in the salt and cloth businesses. The salt trade, quite significant in Königsberg, was almost nonexistent in Gdańsk,[205] while trade in cloth, well developed in Gdańsk, was marginal in Königsberg.[206]

Income from shipping salt, which seems to have originated largely from the Low Countries and France, accounted for more than 80 percent of the Radziwiłłs' revenues from their Königsberg trade. Salt herring from the Low Countries and Scotland on the North Sea, wine largely from France and Germany, and iron from Sweden were also prominent commodities (Table 6.5).[207]

Table 6.4. The Four Major Types of Freight Shipped to Königsberg
(as a percentage of all the freight trade with Königsberg)

Year	Flax Seed	Flax Fiber	Canvas	Rye	Total
1738	56%	14%	14%	10%	94%
1746	79%	7%	1%	—	87%
1760	35%	1%	8%	13%	57%

SOURCE: AR XX, 52
NOTE: An unusually large consignment of flour belonging to merchants from Moscow shipped on the 1760 flotilla, which caused a 20 percent reduction in the proportions of the normal staples of trade.

Table 6.5. The Four Major Types of Freight Shipped out of Königsberg
(as a percentage of all the freight trade from Königsberg to Lithuania)

Year	Salt	Salt Herring	Wine	Iron	Total
1738	86%	2%	8%	2%	98%
1746	80%	1%	4%	—	85%
1760	82%	5%	10%	—	97%

SOURCE: AR XX, 19

The Merchants

At the start of each year those members of the Radziwiłł family who were planning to organize a flotilla of rafts published an announcement that it would sail to Königsberg in the spring, along with the shipping rates.[208] The announcement was likely distributed in the towns of the estate, especially those near the Niemen (the Radziwiłłs' main port was at Nowy Świerżeń).[209]

Merchants from outside the latifundium also came to ship their goods. The lists of shippers did not usually indicate where they came from, making identification, particularly of one-time shippers, almost impossible. Merchants whose place of residence can be identified typically came from the towns on the latifundium that were close to the port: Nowy Świerżeń, Nieśwież, Mir, Słuck, and Kopyl. Others came from small towns near the river, such as Korelicze, Delaticze, Niehniewicze, and Jeremicze (Yaremichy, Belarus).[210] Still others came from more distant towns on the estate, such as Kiejdany (Kėdainiai, Belarus), Kopyś, and Romanów.

It was also possible to join the flotilla in the large towns such as Kowno and Grodno through which the rafts passed, though most traders, including those from the major towns of Belarus—Mińsk, Mohilew, and Nowogródek—came to its port on the Niemen. Having said all that, the vast majority of the merchants who shipped freight on the Radziwiłł flotilla lived near Nowy Świerżeń.[211]

Who were the shippers? A total of 245 merchants can be identified in the full and partial lists for 1738, 1746, 1747, 1748, 1754, 1760, and 1761, including 115 Christians (47 percent) and 130 Jews (53 percent). Only 38 of these (16 percent) were listed in more than one year, and only twelve (5 percent) in more than two years. Noblemen were prominent among the non-Jews, accounting for some 60 percent of all non-Jewish shippers. Christian townspeople accounted for another 25 percent and clerics for 7 percent.[212] The status of the remaining 8 percent cannot be determined.[213]

The noblemen were presumably acting in the same way as the Radziwiłłs. They shipped produce from their estates for sale in Königsberg, and used the money they received for purchasing various necessities and luxury items to send back home. The small number of Christian urban merchants presumably reflects the weakness of the group in estate society.

Clearly, the majority of the professional merchants (that is, those who made their living from trade) who shipped freight on the Radziwiłł family flotilla were Jews.[214] The freight trade brought them two major benefits: it gave them relatively easy access to the international market, and it meant that they were automatically covered by the Radizwiłłs' exemption from Commonwealth taxes and customs, leaving them to pay only the Prussian duties.[215] The Jewish merchants' role in the freight trade is illustrated in Table 6.6. The figures show that the Jews contributed a significant proportion of the Radziwiłłs' income from freight shipments. Even in 1738, when they participated less in the flotilla, Jews accounted for some 40 percent of the revenues; in other years the figure came to above 60 percent.

The Jewish merchants' significant contribution to these revenues was due to the volume of their trade. Breaking down the payments for freight shipments in 1738, 1746, 1747, 1752, 1760 by shipper (Jews and non-Jews) and by amount, it becomes clear that there were more Jews among shippers who paid freight charges greater than 1,000 złoty (Table 6.7). This suggests that the Jews' importance for the Radziwiłł family's revenues from freight shipments was attributable to large-scale merchants.

To sum up, most of the Radziwiłł family's revenue from freight shipments was generated by nobles and Jewish merchants. The nobles generally traveled to Königsberg, where they had agents to sell the produce from their estates, the income from which they used to purchase goods for their private

Table 6.6. The Role of Jewish Merchants in the Freight Shipments

Year	Merchants	Jewish Merchants	Total Revenue from Freight Shipments	Total Revenue from Jews	Percent of Revenue from Jewish Merchants
1738	43	17	47,108 zł., 3 gr.	17,731 zł., 6 gr.	38
1746	54	37	44,775 zł., 11 gr.	27,065 zł.	60
1747*	41	21	32,928 zł., 7 gr.	22,685 zł., 10 gr.	69
1760	94	53	83,198 zł., 12 gr.	55,689 zł.	66

SOURCES: AR XX, 19; AR XX, 20.
*Data for shipments from Königsberg to Lithuania only

Table 6.7. Breakdown of Freight Shipments by Size of Payment

Shipper	Freight Payments (% of all revenues from each group)		
	Up to 100 złoty	101–1,000 złoty	More than 1,000 złoty
Jews	43 (28%)	76 (49%)	35 (23%)
Non-Jews	30 (30%)	71 (53%)	23 (17%)

SOURCES: AR XX, 19; AR XX, 20.

consumption. The Jews were mostly professional merchants who bought up agricultural produce in Lithuania for resale on the international market. In Königsberg they purchased mainly salt, which they shipped back to Lithuania for resale there.

Jewish merchants accounted for slightly more than half of all shippers, but sometimes paid up to 70 percent of the freight charges collected by the magnate. In most cases, Jews and non-Jews alike sent freight on a relatively small scale (paying charges less than 1,000 złoty). However, the majority of those who sent larger shipments (paying more than 1,000 złoty) were Jews. This explains why the Jewish merchants' share in the Radziwiłłs' revenue from freight charges was often greater than their proportion among the shippers.

The Importance of the Revenue from Freight Shipments

The economic logic behind the freight charges was quite clear: The Radziwiłłs needed the extra revenue to finance their own trade with Königsberg. The arrangements that needed to be made in order to do business there were neither simple nor cheap, and the family's outlay was huge. Assembling the flotilla of rafts was an expensive business: the hemp and flax for export had to be bought and then stored, the crews had to be paid, and the Prussian customs duties needed to be taken care of (the family enjoyed tax exemptions in the Commonwealth). Costs could reach tens of thousands of złoty a year. Income from selling the cargos mostly covered the family's purchases, which also ran to tens of thousands of złoty, though not infrequently purchases exceeded sales. Income from freight was therefore crucial if the family wanted its river trade to turn a profit. To judge from the records kept by the administration, the family usually succeeded in collecting the large amounts needed to make the enterprise worthwhile (Table 6.8).

The sums in the table include the family's purchases in Königsberg, giving the impression that the freight charges almost always allowed it to buy everything it wanted without having to pay out of pocket. Though the accounts showed a deficit for three years, most of the time the balance was positive. These figures do not, however, show the relative importance of the freight charges for the overall income from the river trade. Were they really the factor that made the difference between profit and loss? The detailed accounts surviving for the river trade in 1760 provide enough data to allow an answer this question (Table 6.9).

Note that 1760 was not a typical year: Hieronim Florian Radziwiłł died in late spring so his brother Michał Kazimierz took it upon himself to run his brother's flotilla (as well as his own) and to settle his affairs in Königsberg. He also took the opportunity to liquidate his own debts (he himself died shortly thereafter). The downriver shipment was, therefore, much larger than usual.[216]

Table 6.8. The Balance for the Radziwiłł Family's River Trade

Year	Expenditures*	Income**	Profit
1739	67,349 zł., 8 gr.	73,041zł., 27 gr.	5,692 zł., 19 gr.
1750	50,923 zł., 27 gr.	54,578 zł., 25 gr.	3,654 zł., 28 gr.
1751	65,128 zł., 2 gr.	60,439 zł., 2 gr.	–4,689 zł.
1752	44,527 zł., 9 gr.	59,351 zł., 29 gr.	14,824 zł., 20 gr.
1756***	36,292 zł., 22 gr.	30,547 zł., 21 gr.	–5,835 zł., 1 gr.
1757	89,235 zł., 20 gr.	90,461 zł., 27 gr.	1,226 zł., 7 gr.
1760	278,961 zł., 19 gr.	280,736 zł., 24 gr.	1,775 zł., 5 gr.
1763	89,228 zł., 17 gr.	85,971 zł., 15 gr.	–3,257 zł., 2 gr.

SOURCES: AR XX, 58; AR XX, 62.
* Includes the costs of the flotilla, customs duties, and all the purchases in Königsberg for court and estate.
** Includes income from sales in Königsberg and the receipts from freight payments.
*** The detailed records for 1756 cover only the upriver trade from Königsberg to Lithuania. Surviving records of profits on the downriver trade have been included as income.

Table 6.9. The Balance Sheet for the River Trade in 1760

Expenditures		Income	
Family Purchases	54,579 zł., 4 gr.	Family Sales	198,788 zł., 22 gr.
Expenditures on the flotilla*	41,729 zł., 3 gr.	Freight Payments	81,226 zł., 1 gr.
Prussian customs (1759–1760)	14,494 zł., 8 gr.	Miscellaneous	722 zł.
Individual payments to merchants and legal fees	10,579 zł., 11 gr.		
Payment of previous debts	121,220 zł., 15 gr.		
Obligations to church institutions**	13,933 zł., 20 gr.		
Unpaid Debts	22,331 zł., 18 gr.		
Total	278,867 zł., 19 gr.	Total	280,736 zł., 23 gr.

SOURCE: AR XX, 58
* Including the bribes usually paid to customs officials.
** Michał Kazimierz Radziwiłł pledged to donate some of the income from his river trade each year to the Basilian monastery in Żółkiew. The amount given here is the payment for two years.

As Table 6.9 shows, freight charges made up almost 30 percent of the family's total income from the river trade that year. These charges covered all the expenditure on the flotilla including customs duties, and cleared a tidy profit, enough to cover nearly half of the family's shopping bill. Because the family's own shipment was particularly large on this occasion, there may have been less available space on the rafts, with the possibility that freight charges may have been less significant than usual. Whether or not this was the case, they certainly covered a highly significant part of the family's expenses for the river trade. Without them the whole enterprise would not have been economically viable.

The Radziwiłłs and the Jewish Shippers

The family certainly recognized the importance of those Jewish merchants who shipped freight on their flotillas. Perhaps the best indication of this is that the Jews were almost the only merchants to whom the Radziwiłłs were willing to extend credit. Although cash loans were sometimes offered, credit more frequently took the form of extended repayment dates.[217] This was of most benefit to the large-scale merchants who were allowed to reschedule their debts from year to year.[218]

The recipient of the largest amount of credit was Joshua ben Michael (in Polish, Howsiej Michajłowicz), the *arendarz* from Nowy Świerżeń who later also held the general *arenda* for Mir.[219] Joshua also acted as a supplier of wines and other goods to Michał Kazimierz Radziwiłł and was on good terms with his patron. He managed accounts for the warehouses in Nowy Świerżeń in which goods were stored before they were loaded onto the rafts.[220] A very active shipper of freight, his annual payment to the Radziwiłłs amounted to thousands of złoty.[221] Joshua had a range of accounts with the family and was not expected to pay each bill separately. He was allowed to discount some of his debts against services rendered and to roll others over from one year to the next.[222] In 1761, when he found himself in serious financial difficulties and could not pay his debts in Königsberg, he wrote to his patron (in Polish in his own hand) to ask for help, presumably some kind of loan.[223]

Michał Kazimierz Radziwiłł viewed Joshua with favor, valued his commercial skills, and trusted his loyalty. This relationship was expressed in the instructions that the magnate sent to Königsberg to settle affairs after his brother's death: "To the Jews, Joshua ben Michael and the leaseholder of Świerżeń,[224] who are utterly faithful to my administration [literally "to my treasury"]. Please provide the commissioner with the best ideas [you can] as to how he should proceed."[225]

As with any connection between a Jew and a magnate, however, there was another side to the relationship. On one occasion, when Radziwiłł thought that Joshua had delayed repayment too long, he ordered him to pay off his debts immediately, threatened him with severe penalties for noncompliance, and even had him arrested. Eventually he set up a commission of inquiry to investigate Joshua's affairs.[226] A particular irritant for him was the Jewish merchant's decision to acquire a number of rafts for his own use in shipping goods to Königsberg. Although Radziwiłł did not prevent Joshua from doing so, he issued strict orders that no merchandise be loaded onto them until the family flotilla was completely full.[227]

Much more problematic for Joshua was his relationship with Józef Topolewski, the member of the Radziwiłł administration who ran the flotilla for Michał Kazimierz. Topolewski wanted to receive all shipping fees up front because he had to pay the current expenses of the flotilla, but Joshua, with Radziwiłł's backing, could pay as and when he wanted. Topolewski also seems to have resented Joshua's easygoing business dealings with his patron and took out his frustration by having the Jewish merchant's goods confiscated in Königsberg to pay his debt. He even denounced him to Radziwiłł in 1753 for committing fraud.[228] Joshua, who was clearly a tough business-man,[229] submitted countercharges of corruption against Topolewski and his Jewish agent Lejzer.[230] Such was Joshua's standing that in the end it was Topolewski who was arrested. The noble flotilla manager was reduced to begging Radziwiłł for mercy and shortly thereafter resigned his post. Joshua continued to do business with the family until at least the mid-1760s.[231]

Of course Joshua was not the only Jewish merchant who tangled with the flotilla managers and other noblemen. In his memoirs Solomon Maimon wrote about a similar case involving his father. In fact, Jewish merchants across the latifundium suffered various kinds of harassment from the nobil-ity.[232] They were not totally helpless, however. They filed complaints about their mistreatment to the administration or even to Radziwiłł himself in the reasonable expectation that he would intervene on their behalf.[233] Both the family and its merchants understood that the Jews' importance in bringing in revenues made them worth protecting because they were indispensable to the estate economy.

CONCLUSION

A number of factors contributed to the Jews' success in the commercial sys-tem of the latifundium. Like the estate owner, they had a strong interest in responding to the changing economic conditions of the eighteenth century. The old order had not been particularly beneficial for them. As social and religious outsiders excluded from the urban cartels, Jews had been forced to be always on the lookout for new opportunities. It was only by grasping the possibilities that changing circumstances offered them, in the form of close economic relations with the nobility, that the Jews had been able to over-come the competition from the Christian townspeople (who were invested in maintaining what they saw as a very positive status quo). So for the Jews, change was less of a threat than an opportunity.

The Radziwiłłs, who did not think that way, were caught in something of a bind in the eighteenth century. On the one hand they wanted to exploit new economic possibilities that were opening up, but on the other they did not want to change the organization of their latifundium in order to do so. They extricated themselves from their dilemma by harnessing the Jews' flexibility and willingness to ignore accepted practices. So it was that Jewish businessmen found themselves working for the family in new ways and becoming key figures in the drive to make the estate economy more profitable.

Their new roles were generally ancillary to the old and well-established ways of doing things, which had no place for Jews. However, it was precisely by moving into these new areas that the Jews allowed the existing economic system to take advantage of changing conditions without having to make too many drastic changes. Incomes soared.

Most important was their role in the distribution of grain grown on the *folwarks*, which increasingly relied on the ever greater exploitation of the *propinacja* leases by Jewish *arendarze*. Beyond that, when the changing terms of trade in the Baltic markets meant that hemp and flax needed to be bought by the family for sale there, it was Jewish merchants who moved into the new business. And finally, as shipping expenses grew, Jewish merchants became important players in the freight trade and so played a major role in providing the family with the revenues it needed to finance its purchases in Königsberg.

The sectors in which the Jews' importance was not felt, were precisely those where traditional methods sufficed. Jewish merchants played little or no role in either the distribution of the surplus grain that was not used for *propinacja* or the marketing of the goods produced by the estate manufactories. Both of these involved simple transactions that demanded nothing beyond the traditional ways of selling goods on the market. For that, the administration did not need Jewish expertize. In supply, too, the family and the administration managed very well on their own for the most part, though there was one, telling exception. The textile trade was a niche populated by Jews throughout the Polish-Lithuanian economy and was especially important for the Radziwiłłs since the cloth market in Königsberg was weak. Once again, Jewish merchants—in this case, women stall keepers— were able to flourish because they could meet a need that could not be met by established trading practices.

There was every sign that the Radziwiłłs understood the importance of the Jews' mercantile activity and were willing to translate their appreciation into active support for Jewish merchants, as and when they requested it. This was sometimes when minor members of the administration took out on them various personal, ethnic, or religious frustrations, but was much more common in their dealings with the Christian townspeople. Jewish and non-Jewish merchants had competed over the Polish-Lithuanian urban markets for nearly two centuries. Now, with the support of the Radziwiłłs, Jewish businessmen were finally in a position to assert themselves in the estate towns. It is no surprise then that they moved into the market squares in most places and began to dominate trade. In the larger towns, such as Słuck, the non-Jewish merchants continued to struggle against their Jewish competitors, but in the smaller, provincial towns, Jews were often the only merchants to be found. There was simply no trade without them.[234]

As far as the estate economy was concerned, Jewish merchants became the most important group supplying estate society. This further endeared them to the administration, which exploited local trade and the wealth it created in order to increase its revenues from direct and indirect taxation. The Jews' control of the markets thus continued to grow, until even visitors from abroad could see that there was no way to do trade without them.

The picture that emerges, then, is one in which Jewish merchants and businessmen were successful not only because they were able to adapt to the new conditions of the eighteenth century, but also because they put their skills at the service of the Radziwiłłs, who needed to do exactly the same thing. Jewish commerce provided the family with the means to increase its revenues in changing times, and so its significance must not be measured purely by its volume. It was much more important for the functions it fulfilled in the estate economy. In fact, it would probably not be an exaggeration to say that, in providing much needed flexibility, Jewish mercantile activity formed the very basis for the commercial success enjoyed by the Radziwiłł family, its court, and its estates in the eighteenth century.

Conclusion

ECONOMIC IMPLICATIONS

One would be hard put to characterize the Jews' encounter with the late feudal economy in eighteenth-century Poland-Lithuania as anything other than an extraordinary success story. As has become clear from our study of the Radziwiłł latifundium, Jews came to dominate local and regional trade, especially in the country's eastern regions, pushing out their non-Jewish competitors to the point that in many smaller towns all the merchants were Jews. They also monopolized the business of manufacturing and selling alcoholic beverages, a key sector in the estate economy that allowed revenues to increase even as the terms of trade on the international markets for the Commonwealth's agricultural production declined.

The wealth that the Jews created and the revenues it brought their noble lords gave them an importance in the estate economy that they could leverage into positions of power and influence in estate society. This was because the magnates, ever anxious to increase their incomes, were prepared to give their Jews major incentives to move into those areas of the market where they needed them most. For their part, Jewish businessmen were more than willing to accept these offers and so further improve their market position.

Was the Jews' success simply a matter of conjuncture, being in the right place at the right time, or were some more fundamental factors at play? Since the starting point for the processes described here was the magnates' decision to harness the Jews' economic skills to their own needs, perhaps the focus of the discussion should be on those skills, and how it was that Jews came to display them.

In the period of this study the process of bringing estate produce to market and selling it was largely (though never exclusively) in Jewish hands. The

Radziwiłłs, like most magnate families, had come to rely on the mercantile expertise of Jewish businessmen to boost their incomes through more intensive exploitation of the home market. This held true most particularly for the *arendarze*, who were responsible for the sale of grain in the form of alcoholic beverages. Jewish merchants were encouraged to settle in the latifundium towns precisely because their activity enhanced local markets and increased revenues.

The Jews' mercantile skills are sometimes attributed, particularly by the new economic historians, to a range of sophisticated institutions developed by Jewish society, such as contract law, laws of damages, and a court system geared to dealing with business matters.[1] At times when society around the Jews viewed credit and even mercantile activity as at best a necessary evil, the Jews' familiarity with such institutions and their ability to use them, it is argued, gave them an edge in the market place.[2]

Another way of looking at this issue is through the prism of "human capital."[3] In this perspective Jews became better merchants than their non-Jewish competitors because they invested more resources in giving their children the education to do well in business. This argument tends to focus on the levels of literacy in Jewish societies, which laid great emphasis on educating boys and young men how to read and write. This, it is argued, not only prepared Jews for the market, but also made them excellent candidates for working as financial agents and even managers.[4]

In the specific case discussed here, however, the Jews were not acting in their own closed society but as part of estate society and economy, so these arguments have only limited value. Jewish courts and legal institutions certainly existed on the Radziwiłł latifundium and were used in cases between Jews, but on the larger stage Jewish businessmen worked within non-Jewish institutions based on what must have been for them, initially at least, a strange and unfamiliar legal system. Jews would have had no inherent advantage over their non-Jewish competitors.[5]

The issue of literacy raises a similar issue. Traditional Jewish education gave boys a basic grasp of Yiddish and Hebrew, both of which use Hebrew characters, but did not teach them Polish. One may assume that literacy levels in Jewish society were high from the fact that most Jewish businessmen seem to have been able to sign their names in Hebrew characters. However, since success in business on the estates usually involved extensive dealings with the administration, whose documentation was almost entirely in Polish, literacy in Hebrew and Yiddish was not helpful. Only the poorer and less successful merchants and *arendarze*, whose contacts with the administration were limited, would have been able to function exclusively in Jewish languages. In order to be successful, then, it was crucial to be able to read Polish-language documents. Jewish literacy gave Jewish businessmen little or no direct advantage over their competitors.

The human capital argument is sometimes taken a little more broadly, suggesting that it was the Jews' long centuries of experience in the money and commodity markets of medieval Western and Central Europe that gave them the edge over their competitors. From this viewpoint any innate reasons for the Jews' mercantile success were not important in the period under discussion. It was their centuries of experience in exploiting market conditions that counted most in their continued success. Those who study the Jews' encounter with capitalism in the late nineteenth and twentieth centuries have even suggested that the Jews' centuries long mercantile experience fitted them for the kind of entrepreneurial activity that was so important in a capitalist economy.[6]

This argument is a little more helpful for understanding how the Jews did so well on the magnate latifundium. Clearly, owners like the Radziwiłłs valued Jewish economic activity, otherwise they would not have invited them to settle on their estates and encouraged them to do business there. It is also reasonable to assume that the Jews' mercantile skills were indeed the result of European Jewry's long association with the markets in money and commodities. Still, they had these skills both before the eighteenth century, when their roles were restricted, and in the years examined here when they became a dominant force. This alone cannot be the explanation of their success.

To find that, we need to consider the economic flexibility of Jewish society. As conditions changed in the later seventeenth and eighteenth centuries, Jewish businessmen were able to adapt their business strategies to accommodate them. This was the case particularly in the urban markets as they underwent reconstruction after wars or other periods of destruction. Jewish merchants succeeded in rebuilding their businesses more quickly than their non-Jewish neighbors and used that fact to their advantage in taking over key positions (such as the houses around the market squares) and excluding competitors.

On the Radziwiłł estates, the Jews also played key roles in helping the estate economy adapt to changing conditions. Though it was the family that determined how this was to be done, the effectiveness of its policy depended to a very great extent on the Jews' business skills. The massively increased exploitation of the home market for grain in the form of alcohol, perhaps the most important shift in the estate economy in this period, was wholly reliant on the business acumen of the Jewish leaseholders, from the richest, who took the newly created general *arendas*, to the poorest, who took leases on the hundreds of new taverns the administration built.

Equally, when pressure had to be brought to bear on other sectors of the estate economy to boost revenues, Jewish businessmen soon came to the fore. The economic success of the Ickowicz brothers, for example, was a result of their ability to increase estate incomes, often by altering the traditional forms of direct and indirect taxes paid by residents. The prominence of Jewish merchants as renters of freight space on the Radziwiłł flotillas and as purchasers of hemp for sale in Rīga directly from peasants also attested to their willingness to participate in the processes of reshaping the estate economy.

It is not unreasonable to assume that the Jews' adaptability was grounded, to some extent at least, in their long experience of market conditions. If so, then the question of their entrepreneurial skills needs to be raised, for the ability to read markets and identify new possibilities is often viewed as one of the major characteristics of the successful entrepreneur. Others include an openness to innovation, particularly in finding new ways to combine resources, skill in management, and a willingness to take risks in the pursuit of profit while at the same time acting as an agent of economic change.[7]

At first glance it would seem that the Jews on the Radziwiłł estates in eighteenth century Lithuania did indeed exhibit such characteristics. On closer examination, however, this view needs to be qualified. Though Jewish businessmen did play key roles in the adjustment of the latifundium economy, they were doing so in response to the demands of the estate administration. It was not the Jews' economic activity that was innovative, but the uses to which it was put. Most Jewish merchants in the towns of the latifundium continued to do business in precisely the same way as their fathers and grandfathers. Likewise, the *arendarze* did not invent new ways of running the taverns more profitably. Nor did moving into the sale of alcohol involve taking any kind of entrepreneurial risk. Quite the reverse: Jews who became merchants or *arendarze* (even if they were the first to do so on Radziwiłł lands) were really just walking down well-trodden paths. For the most part, their "entrepreneurship" simply entailed going into business for themselves and engaging largely in buying and selling.

The exception that proved this rule was the career of the Ickowicz brothers. They did show signs of being something close to genuine entrepreneurs. Having started as merchants, they branched out into estate leasing, an unusual choice in their time. As skilled administrators, they ran the leases in an innovative fashion, always searching for new ways to make them more profitable. So successful were they that they ended up managing all Hieronim Florian Radziwiłł's revenues. They assumed the risks of their business choices and rode out a peasant uprising aimed against them, before running afoul of their capricious master. Agents of change, the Ickowiczes certainly made the estates they leased more profitable for their master, though whether, given time, they would have had an even greater effect on estate economy and society, it is impossible to tell. Having said all that, however, even if the brothers did fit the model of Jewish entrepreneurs on the Radziwiłł latifundium, they were a one-off phenomenon. The entrepreneurial qualities they displayed were rarely found in Jewish society.

It would seem more profitable to look for the reasons for the Jews' success in the actual economic choices they made, rather than in any innate characteristics they displayed. In the towns of the latifundium, between 50 percent and 60 percent of the Jewish population chose to make its living from trade, whether in alcoholic beverages or other commodities. Taking the rural populations into account as well, it would seem that between two-thirds and three-quarters of the Jews on the estates had made that choice.

This might suggest that what we see here is the creation of a kind of ethnic economy. A number of different types of these have been identified (usually in a capitalist setting), but the most useful for us is probably the "ethnic-controlled economy" proposed by Light and Gold. They write, "[an] ethnic-controlled economy refers to industries, occupations, and organization of the general labor market in which co-ethnic employees (not owners) exert appreciable and persistent economic power. This power usually results from their numerical clustering, their numerical preponderance, their organization, government mandates, or all four."[8]

Once the differences between a capitalist setting and the conditions on the eighteenth-century Radziwiłł latifundium are taken into account, it seems reasonable to claim that its Jewish residents did create an ethnic-controlled economy that encompassed urban trade and the sale of estate produce in the form of alcohol through the *arenda* system.

A number of factors went into this. They included the Jews' political acuity, their position in latifundium society, their ability to create extensive social and economic networks, their business acumen, and their strategy of leveraging economic success into social capital, which they then exploited to further their economic activity. It was in the combination of these that they managed to carve out the space for an ethnic economy and then take control of it.

Perhaps the most important factor was the ability of leading Jewish businessmen to read the political map of the country and understand the implications for themselves and their businesses. This development had begun a century and a half before the starting point of this study, when it became clear to the Jewish business elite that the central authority of the king was being replaced by that of the nobility. They began to align themselves with the nobles, especially the magnates, pressing their economic skills into the service of their lords and eventually moving to the towns on their estates. This setting proved largely congenial for Jews, who moved to noble-owned lands in great numbers.

The Jews' position in Polish-Lithuanian society had also begun to change. Essentially an urban group, Jews, initially concentrated in the royal towns, were in constant competition with their Christian neighbors for control of local markets. Christians enjoyed an official monopoly on economic activity in the towns, but the Jews' status as a second legally recognized urban group enabled them work round the restrictions.[9] This recommended them to the nobles, whose political rise had been at the expense of the burgher estate as well as the king. Unwilling to strengthen the Christian townspeople, whose trade cartel they despised, the nobility used the Jews as financial and mercantile agents and the economic relations between them blossomed.

This was the basic push and pull of economic forces at work when the Radziwiłł administration began the task of improving estate revenues. It explains why the family opened the latifundium to Jewish settlement and why Jews responded in ever-growing numbers. In the early years, the Jews still had obstacles to overcome. Most problematically, many of the restrictions on Jewish housing and trading in the towns that had been enacted decades earlier still remained in place.

Jews were freest to act in the area of *arenda* on *propinacja* rights. Their ability to contribute to estate revenues in this sector had become clear across the Commonwealth almost a century earlier, so they were an obvious choice for the family in its search for ever greater incomes. The leases on the Radziwiłł latifudium were rolled up into a single general *arenda* for each estate, and that was taken up by a wealthy Jewish businessman or consortium of businessmen. They then broke the *arenda* into its constituent parts and leased each one out separately to less wealthy Jews. In this way, the field of *arenda*s seems to have become an ethnic economy in which the Jewish elite provided work for their less fortunate brethren in a single sector (the sale of alcohol) that was more-or-less entirely populated by Jews.

As time went on, more taverns were built, more Jews became *arendarze*, and the ethnic economy expanded. Its significance for overall latifundium income grew, giving it, and the Jews who made it up, even greater significance in the eyes of the Radziwiłłs. This increased appreciation of Jewish business activity translated into a shift of policy towards the towns. Previous restrictions on Jews were either removed or allowed to fall into abeyance, making it easier for them to make a living, particularly in trade. As their population grew, Jews began to dominate the urban markets. The ethnic economy thus expanded to include local and regional trade, making its importance for estate revenues still greater.

This was a virtuous circle that allowed the Jews on the estates to continue improving their position throughout the period discussed here, leveraging their economic success into added security in their dealings with their Christian competitors. Though still despised for their religion, Jews enjoyed an enhanced status as a crucial element in the estate economy, one that the Radziwiłł family and their administrators wanted preserved. This made their control of the markets and so their importance for estate revenues even greater, effectively turning these sectors into an economic niche dominated by Jews.[10]

This had the added benefit of transforming literacy limited to Jewish languages from a drawback into an advantage. In many ways, the Jews' ethnic economy can be seen as an extended socioeconomic network whose members were connected by links of blood, trust, and economic relations. Communications within the network were carried out almost exclusively in the Jewish languages, which promoted internal cohesion and effectively excluded non-Jews. The Jews' unique cultural, social, and even legal institutions had the same effect.

This is not to say that it was a completely closed system. In trade, especially in the larger towns, there were always non-Jewish merchants competing

with Jews. Jewish *arendarze* dealt with non-Jews working in alcohol production, and often employed Christians to help run their taverns. In the higher
echelons of business, contacts with the estate administration were a matter of
course, and many suppliers and most customers were also non-Jews.

Still, it was the existence of their own economic niche within the estate
economy that allowed the Jews on the Radziwiłł lands to flourish and gave
them such importance in the economic system as a whole. Its development
owed less to any putative economic superiority on the part of Jews than to
the exigencies of their situation, their ability to grasp the significance of
changing conditions, and their success in adapting their responses.

The phenomenon of Jews creating their own economic niche was not
unique to the late feudal Polish-Lithuanian Commonwealth. Similar processes can be identified in settings as far apart as the garment trade in late
nineteenth- and early twentieth-century New York, state finance in the
eighteenth-century Holy Roman Empire, early modern transatlantic trade,
and some parts of the credit market in medieval Western and Central
Europe.[11] In each case specific conditions determined the nature and size
of the niche, its importance for the broader economic system, and even the
degree to which it was open or closed to non-Jews.[12] Nonetheless, the phenomenon of Jews identifying and exploiting the possibilities open to them
in order to create an economic niche for themselves was not an uncommon
one. Where they were then able to leverage the importance of their niche
for the general economy into the kind of social standing that would allow
to expand it and further exploit its possibilities, as they did on the Radziwiłł
estates, they seem to have been able to achieve enormous success.[13]

SOCIAL IMPLICATIONS

What was the nature of the social standing that the Jews living and working on
the Radziwiłł latifundium enjoyed? What were its limitations, and what were
its implications for the development of Jewish society there? The Jews' position grew out of the economic services they provided the Radziwiłłs and their
administration. It was clear that the Jews, particularly those in the *propinacja*
business, were acting on the family's behalf and so would receive its support.
Moreover, the Jews proved quite adept at leveraging their economic activity
into improved status in the towns where they lived. As a result they came to
enjoy an unprecedented degree of authority, even power, in estate society.

Such was strikingly the case with the general *arendarze*, whose financial and administrative services to the estate administration, made them the unofficial equivalent of senior officials in Radziwiłł employ. Their improved status was most obvious when they executed payment orders given by the family. Recipients included suppliers of goods and services, estate functionaries receiving their salaries or expenses, and beneficiaries of Radziwiłł largesse. In order to receive the cash, these individuals had to visit one or other of the general *arendarze*, who functioned very much as the lord's private bankers. As a result, a whole range of people, including nobles and church officials, had to stand cap in hand (figuratively speaking) before Jewish businessmen when they presented their money orders for payment.

Secondary *arendarze*, too, acting as collectors of taxes and customs on trade, had supervisory power over merchants, Jewish and non-Jewish, and could even control crucial institutions of urban economic life, such as the town scales. Rural leaseholders, who provided the peasants with various services in their roles as tavern keepers, storekeepers, grain merchants, and even moneylenders, became an indispensable part of village life as well as representatives of the estate administration they served.

Estate society reacted to this situation in a number of ways. In many cases, strong business ties and harmonious relations developed between individual Jews and their neighbors, though the antagonism towards Jews that was endemic in Polish-Lithuanian society was felt too. Townspeople, peasants, the local nobility, and the clergy—all gave vent to it from time to time.[14] What had changed by the eighteenth century was their ability to translate their enmity into action. The estate residents knew that the Radziwiłł administration supported the Jews and their economic activity and would allow neither to be seriously harmed.[15]

It is tempting to ascribe the anti-Jewish feeling simply to traditional religious hatred, but this was not the case. Rather it was, in part at least, a reaction to the fact that the Jews were acting on behalf of a feudal lord whose policies were often very unpopular. The Radziwiłłs kept their revenues high by squeezing the home market, even to the extent of curtailing their subjects' traditional rights. Much of the population suffered from creeping pauperization, and a sense of disenfranchisement, which brought on anger and resentment. Open opposition to the Radziwiłłs and their policies could be met with harsh measures—witness the brutal repression of the Krzyczew uprising from 1740–1744—so it was much safer to find a different outlet for these feelings. Jews, identified with the administration's economic policy, formed an obvious target. Thus the popular expressions of anti-Jewish feeling on the estates may well have been intended to camouflage a more fundamental opposition to the magnate regime.

The complexity of the Jews' situation stemmed from the fact that they had no independent source of power on which to base their social authority; that derived exclusively from the backing of the Radziwiłł administration. Since it was given in return for economic and managerial services, when there was no further need for them, the backing vanished, and with it whatever status and authority the Jews had enjoyed. The fate of the Ickowicz brothers is a prime example of this.

The Jews' situation on the Radziwiłł latifundium, as on other magnate estates, was therefore marked by a basic duality. Official support for them assured their standing in society, and even gave them a degree of authority in some economic and social spheres, but their status was really dependent on their ability to give their master the revenues he wanted. Beyond this, the services that guaranteed the Jews the backing of the Radziwiłł administration were precisely those that the non-Jewish subjects blamed for their declining economic position. So, although working for the Radziwiłłs brought the Jews better conditions and created a favorable setting for the growth of Jewish society, it could never entirely protect them from the animus of their non-Jewish neighbors.[16]

A similar kind of duality may be seen in the development of the Jewish communal institutions. On the one hand, the Radziwiłł family supported the Jewish communities on its estates and, like many other nobles, granted them charters—known as "privileges"—that served as the legal basis for their existence.[17] It also unofficially coopted these Jewish bodies, as well as the rabbinate, into estate administration, making them responsible for the smooth functioning of Jewish society and its economic life. As a result, the Jewish communities on the estates flourished and grew in strength.[18]

On the other hand, since they now functioned as part of the Radziwiłł administration, both the communal institutions and the rabbis were not just closely identified with the non-Jewish authorities, their autonomy of action was limited. Any move they made that their lord or his administration felt ran counter to his interests could lead to harsh sanctions. An excellent example of this was the communities' attempts to limit competition over *arenda* leases. Competition drove up prices, which served the

Radziwiłłs by increasing their revenues, but was detrimental to the Jewish businessmen trying to make a profit. The communities tried to limit competition by imposing the principle of possessors rights, "dinei ḥazakah," but were met with fierce rejection and cruel punishments on the part of the administration.[19] In such a situation, their hands were tied.

The backing that the Radziwiłłs gave the Jewish communities could undermine their authority in other ways, too. Members of the economic elite, especially those who provided direct services to the family, would often be granted personal immunity from communal jurisdiction, the better to serve their lords and masters. More commonly, and not only on the Radziwiłł estates, wealthy Jews exploited their ties with the estate administration to buy for themselves, or members of their family, positions of authority within the community, particularly rabbinic posts.[20] As a result, a new Jewish elite began to emerge, whose status and power were based exclusively on its wealth and ties with the magnates, rather than on the traditional criteria of lineage and scholarship. This seems to have had a destabilizing effect on Jewish life and led to much social criticism in the eighteenth century.[21]

In all, however, the Jews on the Radziwiłł latifundium do seem to have perceived their situation as positive, or at least better than the alternatives. By the second half of the eighteenth century, almost one-tenth of all Lithuanian Jews were living on the Radziwiłł estates in the Grand Duchy, attracted by the family's policies that encouraged them to settle and do business on its lands.

POLITICAL IMPLICATIONS

At the beginning of this study, we noted that the seventy-five years it covers corresponded to the period of the Radziwiłł dynasty's recovery from the disasters of the mid-seventeenth century, and its ascent to the pinnacle of power and influence in the Polish-Lithuanian Commonwealth. We have seen how, in the same period, the Jews on the latifundium created a lively and flourishing society, largely on the basis of the economic roles they played in the estate economy—a key factor in increasing the family's revenues from its lands. It remains to ask how these two seemingly parallel processes were connected, and what the significance of that connection might have been for the history of the Commonwealth as a whole.

The rise of the family was contingent on its success in accumulating resources, particularly landed estates. Ownership of a vast latifundium was one marker of magnate status. Others were acquiring enormous wealth, adopting an opulent lifestyle, and holding the highest positions the state could offer, especially a seat in the Senate. These were not separate. Land ownership both improved the family's social status and provided the revenues it needed to take its place among the elite, while the income was used not only to bankroll the Radziwiłłs' luxurious lifestyle, but also to cover the expenses of political life, such as buying the support of lesser nobles.[22]

Since money was of key importance, and the latifundium was the major source of its wealth, the family's attitude towards estate management must hold the key to understanding its rise to power and influence. In the eighteenth century the Radziwiłłs laid great emphasis on increasing the size of their holdings by regaining control of lost estates, purchasing new ones, and acquiring others through marriage in the form of dowries.[23] The acquisition of new lands made available more farms, natural resources, and labor, all of which contributed to increased incomes.

Changes were also made in the administration of the estates, to make them more profitable, with a central pillar of the new approach being the greater exploitation of the home market. It was to this end that the Radziwiłłs made intensive use of their Jewish subjects. They put the Jews in control of the *arenda* system, at the heart of which was the ever-increasing income from *propinacja*, and gave them control over the urban markets which generated further huge sums. So, the Radziwiłł's "Jewish policy" aimed at improving incomes from the estates, and the Jews' economic acumen that succeeded in doing just that, must be seen as key factors in the family's return to greatness.

This development had even broader implications for the history of Poland-Lithuania in the eighteenth century. The period from the later seventeenth century to the end of the eighteenth was a time when a small number of magnate families acquired a huge amount of land, wealth, and power and so became the dominant force in governing the state. That raises the question of whether Jewish economic activity played a role in the rise of other dynasties besides the Radziwiłłs. What is known of conditions on other latifundia, particularly the Sieniawski and Czartoryski lands, suggests that the situation was indeed comparable on all the estates.[24]

If such was the case, then the magnates' rise to power *as a group* was heav-ily dependent on the roles Jews played in their estate economies.[25] And so, far from being a marginal phenomenon, Jewish economic activity in the service of the magnates was of quite central importance in the economic, social, and political development of the Polish-Lithuanian Commonwealth as a whole.

Reference Matter

Notes

INTRODUCTION

1. Goldberg, *Ha-ḥevrah ha-yehudit*, 90–124. For explanations of the Polish terms used in this book, see the Glossary.

2. The magnates were exceptionally rich nobles with extensive landholdings who were also members of the Senate. Their power and influence inside Poland-Lithuania was enormous. For a discussion of the development of the magnates as a group: H. Litwin, "The Polish Magnates"; Kersten, "Problem władzy"; and Czapliński, "Rządy oligarchii," 130–63.

3. For a brief historiographical survey with references to the relevant literature: Kobrin and Teller, "Purchasing Power," 1–24.

4. Sombart, *The Jews and Modern Capitalism*.

5. See, in particular, Muller, *Capitalism and the Jews*; Lederhendler, *Jewish Immigrants;* and Kobrin, ed., *Chosen Capital*. For a refreshingly different view: Karp, "Economic History and Jewish Modernity," 249–66. Another recent study to move away from the focus on capitalism is Trivellato, *The Familiarity of Strangers*.

6. The lack of the medieval legal underpinnings of feudalism in early modern Poland-Lithuania has led some to question the use of the word "feudalism" to describe it. Interestingly, research on medieval Western Europe has suggested that these very legal underpinnings were missing there, too: Reynolds, *Fiefs and Vassals*. Nonetheless, what developed in Poland-Lithuania shares enough of the social and economic structure of what is classically understood as feudalism to justify using the term here, especially if it is qualified as "late feudalism," which can refer only to the system employed in the Polish-Lithuanian Commonwealth.

7. For basic surveys of Polish Jewish history: Baron, *A Social and Religious History*; Weinryb, *The Jews of Poland*; and Hundert, *Jews in Poland-Lithuania*.

8. On the niche as an economic concept: Tisdell and Seidl, "Niches," and Morales, *Ethnic Niches*, 10–56. See also Popielarz and Neal, "The Niche," 65–84.

9. Zenner, *Minorities*. The classic formulation of middleman minority theory can be found in Bonacich, "A Theory." Middleman minority theory has been subject to much criticism. In the context of this study, which understands the Jews as an integral part of the feudal system in Poland-Lithuania, the very idea of a middleman minority is problematic. Since the feudal system was by its nature hierarchical,

the Jews, though indeed middlemen, were by no means the only ones: parts of the nobility, the non-Jewish townspeople and even the wealthier peasants were also middlemen. Thus the definition loses its specificity and so its value.

10. On the issue of Jewish empowerment and its limits: Teller, "In the Land of their Enemies," 431–46.

11. The name is pronounced Rad-ji-viw, with the accent on the second syllable. The final *w* is, actually, a soft *l*.

12. Hundert, *Jews in Poland-Lithuania*, 21–56.

13. Zaremska, *Żydzi w średniowiecznej Polsce*, 108–215.

14. Teller, "Telling the Difference."

15. On the process of colonization: H. Litwin, *Napływ szlachty*.

16. On the Jews' roles in the colonization of Ukraine: Ettinger, "Ḥelkam shel ha-yehudim."

17. In this period the larger magnate latifundia tended to swallow up smaller noble estates, which were less economically viable. Kozłowskij, "Struktura własności," and Mieleszko, "Formy i struktura."

18. For literature of this type on the estates and their economy: Serczyk, *Gospodarstwo magnackie*; Wyczański, *Studia*; Rychlikowa, *Klucz wielkoporębski*; Rychlikowa, *Produkcja zbożowa*; Homecki, *Produkcja i handel*; and M. Topolska, *Dobra szkłówskie*. See also Bergerówna, *Księżna pani*.

19. Of special importance in this regard is Rutkowski's study on the economic activity of royal estates in Poland in the sixteenth century, *Historia gospodarcza*, 132–414. See also the theoretical approach in Kula, *An Economic Theory*. On the importance of Kula for this study, see below.

20. Pośpiech and Tygielski, "The Social Role."

21. On the lifestyle of the Polish-Lithuanian nobility in the seventeenth and eighteenth centuries: Czapliński and Długosz, *Życie codzienne*; and Kuchowicz, *Człowiek*. On the cost of political activity: Zielińska, "Mechanizm sejmikowy."

22. For an overview of relations between the nobility and the Jews: Goldberg, *Ha-ḥevrah ha-yehudit*, and Goldberg, "The Changes."

23. On the Radziwiłł family and their estates: Anusik and Strojnowski, "Radziwiłłowie."

24. Not a great deal of attention has been devoted to early modern Lithuanian Jewry (although many aspects of pre-partition Lithuanian Jewish history are discussed in works on the history of Polish Jewry). The recent doctoral dissertation by Mania Cieśla, "The Jews in the Grand Duchy," offers perhaps the broadest perspective on the social and economic history of Lithuanian Jewry in the early modern period. The only other monograph specifically on this topic is that of Bershadskiĭ, *Litovskiye Yevrei*, which was published in the nineteenth century; it focuses mainly on the Middle Ages and the sixteenth century. Between the two world wars a group of historians in Soviet Belorussia (Belarus), Israel Sosis prominent among them, produced a number of studies on the social and economic history of pre-partition Lithuanian Jewry. They published in the Minsk-based journal *Tsaytshrift*, which was

issued from 1926 to 1930. On this: Alfred Greenbaum, *Jewish Scholarship*, and Yalen, "Red Kasrilevke." Post-Holocaust scholarship has focused mainly on the history of Lithuanian Jewry in the nineteenth and twentieth centuries. For example, in Masha Greenbaum's survey, *The Jews of Lithuania*, the period from the sixteenth century to the late eighteenth century takes up only about eighty of four hundred pages. For an excellent, if dated, Hebrew-language survey, see Kloizner, "Toledot ha-yehudim be-Lita." Also noteworthy among regional studies are two monographs on the history of the Jewish communities in the large royal towns of historical Lithuania: Nadav, *The Jews of Pinsk*, and Kloizner, *Toledot ha-kehillah- ha-'ivrit be-Vilna*.

25. Discussion of the demographic development of Lithuanian Jewry in this period is not extensive. See Stampfer, "The 1764 Census," 91–121. The distinction between conditions in Poland and Lithuania did not go unnoticed by the Jews. For example, the separation of the Lithuanian and Polish treasuries in the 1620s apparently led to the resumption of activity of a separate council of Lithuanian Jewish communities. On the establishment of the Council of the Land of Lithuania in 1623: Michałowska-Mycielska, *Sejm Żydów Litewskich*, 27–37. Simon Dubnow, the editor of the modern edition of the council's record book, *Pinkas Medinat Lita*, did not make the connection between the formation of the council and the re-organization of the Lithuanian treasury. The early history of the institution is unclear. Israel Halperin found a regulation issued by a Lithuanian council before the Union of Lublin (1569), but there is no evidence that the council continued as a regularly functioning body in the years before 1623. See Halperin, *Yehudim ve-yahadut*, 48–54.

26. In the course of the discussion here, details of the activity on the Radziwiłłs' estates outside Lithuania are sometimes given but only to shed light on what was happening on the Lithuanian estates. A special case is the city of Biała Podlaska and the surrounding estate. Although Biała was part of Crown Poland, its proximity to the Radziwiłłs' estates in Lithuania meant that it was managed together with them, and so we treat it here as part of the Lithuanian holdings. See Wasilewski and Krawczak, *Z nieznanej przeszłości*.

27. There is extensive literature on the Radziwiłł family. Basic studies on its history include Kotłubaj, *Galerja nieświeżka*; Eichhorn, *Stosunek*; Zielińska, "Archiwa Radziwiłłów"; Rostworowski, ed., *Polski Słownik Biograficzny*, 30: 132–414.

28. One of his major achievements was commissioning a map of the Grand Duchy of Lithuania from the well-known geographer Maciej Strubicz. This map, which survives in only one copy from that period, is an important source for the history of Lithuania in the early seventeenth century: Alexandrowicz, *Rozwój kartografii*, I: 75–136. The diary of Mikołaj Krzysztof Radziwiłł's pilgrimage, published in Polish and Latin translation, is an important source on the history of Palestine in the late sixteenth century; see M. Radziwiłł, *Podróż do Ziemi Świętej*. Radziwiłł's pilgrimage was remembered in Jewish folklore too. According to a popular tradition, during his travels Radziwiłł met Rabbi Meir ben Samuel Katzenellenbogen in Padua and was so impressed with him that he developed a

highly favorable opinions of Jews in general. The legend tells that Radziwiłł later met Katzenellenbogen's son (Saul Wahl), who was studying in Lithuania, and as a result Wahl came to serve as king of Poland for a day. The story is retold in Pinhas Katzenellenbogen's book, *Sefer yesh manhilin*, 143–50. Zevi Hirsh Edelmann wrote an entire book, *Gedulat Shaul*, about Saul Wahl.

29. Siekierski, "Landed Wealth."

30. In the first half of the seventeenth century Janusz Radziwiłł invited to his court Joseph Solomon Delmedigo, a Jewish physician from Crete, known by the acronym of his Hebrew name as Yashar of Candia. Delmedigo lived in Lithuania from about 1620 to 1624, and in a letter he referred to the place as "my second homeland." He was in touch with the Karaites in Troki and corresponded with Polish intellectuals, such as Jan Brożek of the Kraków Academy. See Barzilay, *Yoseph Shlomo Delmedigo*, 59–76, and Halperin, *Yehudim ve-yahadut*, 388–93.

31. The logic behind the decision to support the king of Sweden was that both Russian and Swedish forces had invaded Lithuania and it was hard to fight on two fronts.

32. Codello, "Rywalizacja." On the administration of Bogusław Radziwiłł's estates in this period: Miluński, "Zarząd dóbr," 195–282.

33. Lesiński, "Spory."

34. See note 23 above.

35. The Radziwiłłs' latifundium was based on three entailed estates (Polish, *ordynacja*): Nieśwież, Ołyka (Olika, Ukraine), and Kleck (Kletzk, Belarus). These were estates that family members were not allowed to sell or divide; each had to be passed down complete from generation to generation within the family. Karol Stanisław's preeminent position within the family was based in no small measure on the fact that he held two of them. When Marcin Mikołaj Radziwiłł was imprisoned without heirs (see note 46), the third, Kleck, passed into the hands of Karol Stanisław's sons too. On the institution of the *ordinacja*: Zielińska, "Ordinacje," 17–30.

36. Karkucińska, "Działalność gospodarcza i kulturalna," 229–41. For more on the manufactories and the Jews' roles in them, see Chapter Six.

37. They remained in her control even after the wedding was called off: Lesiński, "Spory." For a biography of this fascinating character: Karkucińska, *Anna z Sanguszków Radziwiłłowa*.

38. The last payment was made after just fourteen years. Afterwards Hieronim Florian estimated that the entire transaction had cost more than 6 million złoty. See Kotłubaj, *Galerja nieświeżka*, 427.

39. On this: Zielińska, "Przyczynek do kwestii konfliktu," 132–39.

40. Sajkowski, *Od Sierotki do Rybeńki*, 133–74.

41. This latifundium contained approximately eighty cities, towns, and villages along with extensive agricultural land: Anusik and Strojnowski, "Radziwiłłowie," 45–46.

42. Falniowska-Gradowska, *Królewszczyzny*, 23–52, and Zielińska, *Magnateria polska*, 86–93.

43. Not much has been written on him. See the entry by Hanna Dymanicka-Wołoszyńska in Rostworowski, ed., *Polski Słownik Biograficzny*, 30: 187.

44. His brutality also manifested itself towards Jews. Memoirs from the time tell of him holding target practice in which the targets were Jewish-looking dolls tied to pigs' backs: Matuszewicz, *Diariusz*, I: 572. On Hieronim Florian's army, see Kitowicz, *Opis obyczajów*, 387–88, and Lech, "Milicje Radziwiłłow," 33–60. See also Pasztor, "Milicje magnackie," 140–46.

45. On this affair, see below, Chapter Four.

46. Marcin Mikołaj Radziwiłł was a scandalous figure. He seems to have been a psychopath and was accused of having committed a number of murders. He took an interest in religious issues, particularly connected with Judaism, eventually adopting a Jewish way of life (observing the Sabbath on Saturday and eating only kosher food). He even had a Jewish advisor and confidant named Szymon. In 1748 Marcin Mikołaj was declared insane and was imprisoned in the family palace in Słuck; he remained there until his death in 1782. (Szymon was also arrested in 1748 but his fate is unknown.) See Matuszewicz, *Diariusz*, I: 251–52 and 284–86; and Kotłubaj, *Galerja nieświeżska*, 518–22.

47. All the figures are drawn from Anusik and Strojnowski, "Radziwiłłowie," 45–46.

48. A thaler was worth eight złoty at the time.

49. Anusik and Strojnowski, "Problemy majątkowe," 79–112; Anusik and Strojnowski, "Radziwiłłowie," 29–57.

50. There is a vast literature on this character. See the entry by Jerzy Michalski in Rostworowski, ed., *Polski Słownik Biograficzny*, 30: 248–62. For a contemporary description of the man and his behavior by one of his Jewish subjects, see Solomon Maimon, *An Autobiography*, 80–88.

51. The battle between the Russian army and Radziwiłł's forces at Slonim in 1764 is described in a Hebrew document, Kamenetskiĭ, "Yevreĭskiĭ dokument," 311–17.

52. Karol Stanisław returned after a few years and took part in the Confederation of Radom in 1767. He fought against the granting of rights to Protestants and to Greek Orthodox clergy and collaborated with Russia to achieve these goals. Shortly thereafter, in the Confederation of Bar, he turned against Russia. In the late 1760s he returned to exile.

53. On the period as a whole, see Lukowski, *Disorderly Liberty*.

54. Archiwum Główne Akt Dawnych w Warszawie (AGAD), Archiwum Radziwiłłow. On the history of the archive there is an unpublished essay by the man who was the family archivist in the interwar period: Taurogiński, "Geneza." For a description of the archive and its structure: Zielińska, "Archiwa Radziwiłłów," 105–29, and Zielińska, *Informator*, 195–203. In what follows, the name of the archive is abbreviated to AR, the numbers of the different *fonds* (collections) are given in Roman numerals, and the file numbers in Arabic numbers. Page numbers follow, after a colon.

55. Natsional'niĭ Arkhiv Respubliki Belarus', Minsk (NABRM), Fond 694. Most

of the materials date from after 1764, particularly the nineteenth century, but there are records from the eighteenth century and even earlier. The Central State Historical Archives in Kiev have a division of records from the Radziwiłł family archives, but most of them concern the family's estates in Ukraine: Bańkowski, "Polskie archiwa," 172–73. The documentation pertaining to the Radziwiłłs in the Lithuanian State Historical Archives in Vilnius deals mainly with the activity of various family members as *wojewody* of Wilno and therefore shed no light on estate administration. I thank Ewa Lechniak of Poznań for bringing this to my attention. The documents concerning the management of the Radziwiłł *jurydika* in Wilno during the eighteenth century can be found in AR XVIII, 261 and AR XVIII, 266.

56. From our period, the Radziwiłł collection in Warsaw holds the diaries of Karol Stanisław (the grandfather), Hieronim Florian, and Michał Kazimierz Radziwiłł: AR VI 79–II, 80–II, 81–II. Excerpts from the diary of Hieronim Florian and a selection of his other writings have been published as *Hieronima Floriana Radziwiłła diariusze i pisma różne*. Another manuscript, apparently from his youth, with remarks on a variety of topics, can be found in the Czartoryski family archives in Kraków, MS 1721. On Michał Kazimierz's diary: Zielińska, "Więź rodowa."

57. Some of the economic orders found in the Radziwiłł archives have been published: Baranowski, et al., eds., *Instrukcje gospodarze*, 299–394 and 446–72. These documents, however, pertain to the Nieborów estate, which came into the family only in 1774.

58. As a methodological note, it is worth emphasizing that not only documents that actually mentioned Jews were consulted (though they were extremely numerous). Without reading more general documentation about estate administration, it would have been impossible to understand the context of what was being studied.

59. The National Library of Israel (NLI), Manuscript Division, Heb 4° 103. A few pages of this *pinkas* have been published: Assaf, "Mi-pinkas Zabludova," 307–17. Two *pinkassim* of the Jewish community of Nieśwież containing material from the eighteenth century are held by the Vernadsky National Library in Kiev, but none of the documentation they contain is from the period discussed here; thanks to Prof. Gershon Hundert for this information. Sumptuary legislation of 1751 from the Nieśwież Jewish community (apparently from a different *pinkas*, kept in the city until the Holocaust) has been published: "Litwin, "Mi-pinkasei Nishviezh," 161–62. A few Hebrew and Polish documents from Jewish communities on the estates can be found in the Radziwiłł collection in Warsaw: AR XXV, 240; AR V, 15467.

60. I consulted two manuscript *pinkassim*: AGAD Archiwum Roskie, 321 (Boćki); NLI, Manuscript Division, Heb 4° 920 (Horki). The comparative materials from Włodawa and Tykocin I read in published form: Weinryb, *Texts and Studies*, 221–86, and *Pinkas Kahal Tiktin*.

61. On this institution, see the Glossary.

62. NLI, Manuscript Division, Heb 4° 927.

63. See *Solomon Maimon: An Autobiography*. For an assessment of the reliability of this source see Teller, "Zikhronot." Memoirs of non-Jews who lived on the estates

in this period also contain valuable first-hand accounts of life there. Particularly valuable for this study was Matuszewicz, *Diariusz*.

64. Some of the problems involved in the use of rabbinical literature to study the socioeconomic history of Polish Jewry are discussed in Soloveichik, *Halakhah*, 14: "the [business affairs] of the group of merchants who operated on an international scale from the port of Danzig in the period prior to . . . 1648 are not mentioned in the rabbinical literature from Poland. To a certain extent this was because the wealthiest businessmen were sometimes beyond the control of the *kahal* [the governing body of the local Jewish community], but mostly it was because they preferred to settle their affairs among themselves, and when they had to consult halakhic authorities, they would ask their questions orally. . . . Thus the rabbinical literature often does not reflect the activity of this wealthy elite." This also applies to the period discussed here.

65. Ezekiel Landau was the rabbi of Jampol (Yampil, Ukraine), for ten years until 1756. On his period as rabbi there see Gelman, *Noda' Bi-Yehudah*, 1–14. Ḥaim Ha-kohen Rapoport was the rabbi of Słuck in the 1730s and afterwards the rabbi of Lwów. See Dembitzer, *Kelilat Yofi*, 137–40. Sadly, hardly any of their writings contain first-hand accounts of their life on the Radziwiłł estates. On Rapoport's connections with the Radziwiłł family see AR IV, 470: 16.

66. Williamson, "The New Institutional Economics."

67. Coase, The New Institutional Economics."

68. North, *Understanding the Process*, 11.

69. Greif, *Institutions*, 40–41. All the same, Trivellato, in *The Familiarity of Strangers*, 17, criticizes Greif for falling into the very same trap.

70. This aspect of NIE historical research was the target of one of Boldizzoni's critiques in his sweeping condemnation of the school in general: Boldizzoni, *The Poverty of Clio*, 12–17. For a more balanced view: Cipolla, *Between History and Economics*, 69–70.

71. Greif, *Institutions*. North also devoted much time and effort to this in *Structure and Change*, 71–210. North came under intense (though not always convincing) fire from Boldizzoni for doing so; see the Boldizzoni citation in the previous note.

72. See notes 18 and 19. Even these studies do not adequately address the role of the Jews in marketing processes.

73. Kula defined the Polish-Lithuanian feudalism he studied, as "a socioeconomic system which is pre-dominantly agrarian and characterized by a low level of productive forces and of commercialization," and "a corporate system in which the basic unit of production is a large, landed estate surrounded by small plots of peasants who are dependent on the former both economically and juridically, and who have to furnish various services to the lord and submit to his authority." Kula, *An Economic Theory*, 9.

74. Kula, 165–75.

75. Kula, 18.

76. Goldberg's articles on this topic are to be found in Goldberg, *Ha-ḥevrah ha-yehudit*, 159–70 and 232–50. See also Hundert, *Jews in Poland-Lithuania*, 32–56.

77. Hundert, *The Jews in a Polish Private Town*, 46–68 and 134–55. For an overview of the Jews in private towns: Opas, "Sytuacja ludności," 3–37.

78. Rosman, *The Lords' Jews*. Little has been written on the history of the Jews on the Radziwiłł estates, but see Bardach, "Żydzi w Birżach," 199–220; Halperin, *Yehudim ve-yahadut*, 277–88; Lech, "Powstanie chłopów"; Zielińska, "Kariera i upadek," 33–49. Teller, "Radziwiłłowie a Żydzi" is a Polish-language summary of the main conclusions of the present study.

79. Rosman notes what he describes as negative effects of this situation, especially restrictions on the autonomous activity of the Jewish communities. For the most part, however, in attempting to change the standard picture presented in the literature, he stresses the support that the Jews received and their increased strength. Rosman, *The Lords' Jews*, 64–68.

80. Ibid., 210.

81. Coser's comments on the Court Jews of the eighteenth-century Holy Roman Empire seem apposite here too: "Though the Court Jew performed highly important services for the Prince . . . their relations remained asymmetrical. . . . The Prince expected particular loyalty and gratitude from the Jew. [The Court Jew] was permanently in debt to the ruler who had raised him up from the depths." See Coser, "The Alien," 574–81, especially 577.

82. Anna Radziwiłł was aware of this and wrote in one of her letters: "I know that when our administrators come to the Lithuanian estates, they do whatever they feel like doing—and the Jews are afraid of this." AR IV, 627, letter 582, 13/1/1740.

83. The Tatars, a Muslim group, were another minority group relocated onto the Radziwiłł estates to serve particular needs in administration. See Borawski, "Tatarzy" and "Tatarzy w miastach."

84. For instance Gritskevich's *Sotsiyal'naia borba*, a monograph on social conflict in Belarusian cities in the sixteenth through the eighteenth centuries that includes chapters on "class struggle" within urban society and national-religious conflict in the private towns of the region, does not mention the Jews at all. His other studies are no different; see, for example, his *Chastnovladel'cheskiye goroda*.

85. Kaźmierczyk, *Żydzi*.

CHAPTER ONE

1. Bershadskiĭ, *Litovskiye Yevrei*, 331.

2. Zielińska, "Archiwa Radziwiłłów," 109.

3. AR XV, 5, *plik* 2: 1–5. An eighteenth-century copy of the charter was published in Goldberg, ed., *Jewish Privileges*, II: 142–46. The community was probably relatively new at that time, in view of the fact that it does not appear on a list of Jewish communities in Lithuania drawn up in 1553: Kloizner, "Toledot ha-yehudim be-Lita," 28. On Mikołaj Krzysztof Radziwiłł, see the Introduction.

4. He ordered that the gates be locked every night and on the three holy days

before Easter. This is a highly unusual regulation because, even though the Jews of many communities in Poland-Lithuania tended to live in a particular part of town, the creation of an actual ghetto with gates that could be locked was rare: Teller, "Tarbut ha-diyur," 197–207, and Hundert, "Jewish Urban Residence," 25–34.

5. Radziwiłł's granting the right to determine who could join the community should be considered the establishment of local Jewish autonomous institutions, because the exercise of this right (known to the Jews as *ḥerem ha-yishuv* or *ḥezkat ha-yishuv*) formed the basis for Jewish communal jurisdiction. On *ḥezkat ha-yishuv*: Siemiaticki, "Ḥezkat ha-yishuv," 199–253; Gladstein-Kastenberg, "Ḥezkat ha-yishuv," 216–29; Rabinowicz, *The Herem Hayyishub*.

6. AR XXIII, 132: 26–27. The document was published in: Goldberg, ed., *Jewish Privileges*, I: 300–303. This community also seems to have been founded after 1553. See note 3.

7. AR XXIII, 137: 119.

8. Bardach, "Żydzi w Birżach," 199–220.

9. Aleksander Ludwik Radziwiłł was relying on a privilege given to the Jews of Biała by one of his ancestors, so it can be assumed that Jews had lived there since at least the early seventeenth century: Rachuba, "Biała." There were more Jewish-owned houses in Biała Podlaska at this time than in Słuck, a much bigger town. This is not the only case where smaller towns were home to larger communities. It would seem that noble owners took more seriously the demands of non-Jewish townspeople to restrict Jewish settlement in the major towns than in the smaller ones. See Mahler, *Toledot ha-yehudim*, 142–46.

10. Rachuba, "Biała," 37–66. Aleksander Ludwik Radziwiłł issued a similar order to the Jews of Nieśwież in the 1640s: AR XV, 5, plik 2: 45–46. See the restrictions on Jewish settlement in the privilege granted by Bogusław Radziwiłł to his town of Węgrów: AGAD Komisja Spraw Wewnętrznych 3159E: 119–30. In the terms described in these documents Jewish settlement also caused losses (in tax revenue, at least) to the Radziwiłł treasury. See below for their reaction.

11. Hanover, *Yavein Metsulah*, 58.

12. On this: Pendzich, "The Burghers," 118–61.

13. On Bogusław Radziwiłł's administration in these years: Miluński, "Zarząd dóbr," 208–12.

14. See note 8.

15. AR XXV, 3831.

16. AR XXV, 3834/1.

17. This was not universal, however. Though the Słuck Jews enjoyed the family's support, those in Biała Podlaska still labored under a number of restrictions, mainly caused by the family's granting of Magdeburg law (i.e. full urban status) to the town. This strengthened the town council, which was hostile to Jewish settlement.

18. One major addition was the Neuburg estates, which were finally restored to the Radziwiłłs in 1745, though they had held them since 1731. Another was the estate of Marcin Mikołaj Radziwiłł (of a different branch of the family), whose estates

were transferred to his cousin Hieronim Florian in 1748 after he had been imprisoned as insane. When Hieronim Florian died in 1760, the two latifundia—Marcin
Mikołaj's and Hieronim Florian's—fell to Michał Kazimierz, increasing his already
huge latifundium. It was this that his son Karol Stanisław inherited when his father
died in 1762. See the Introduction.

19. These inventories (in Polish, *inwentarze*) were detailed lists of the Radziwiłłs'
properties and the revenues they brought the family. On some of the problems
involved in using them, especially for the history of agriculture: Leskiewoczowa,
"Inwentarze."

20. The inventory for Nieśwież counts the non-Jewish population according to
the plots of land they owned rather than the chimneys in their houses, so the two
populations there cannot be compared. Jews can usually be identified in the inventories because they are called as such or because there is a separate section devoted
to the Jewish population. In other cases, the appearance of characteristically Jewish
names makes the identification quite clear.

21. See the studies by Hundert and Teller cited in note 4. The townspeople of
Słuck complained about the overcrowding in Jewish-owned houses: AR XXIII, 137:
passim and AR XXIII, 120: passim.

22. One place for which there are satisfactory data is Słuck. According to a 1750
inventory, the Christian population stood at 3,391 in 755 houses, making an average
of 4.5 people per house. The Jewish population of the town was 1,639 in 230 houses,
an average of 7 people per house. Thus the proportion of Jews in the urban population was fully 50 percent greater than the proportion of Jewish-owned properties;
see AR XXV, 3537 and AR XXV, 3538. Though it remains unclear just how representative this figure is, it does receive some support from Opas's study of Jewish settlement in the towns of the Lublin region in the eighteenth century. He too found
an average of seven persons per Jewish-owned house: Opas, "Sytuacja ludności," 11.

23. For example, in a highly detailed and persuasive study ("Zaludnienie," 50–
55), Alexandrowicz calculated an average of seven people per house in the small
towns of Lithuania in the mid-seventeenth century, which looks excellent until we
see the figures from Słuck above. See also Bogucka and Samsonowicz, *Dzieje miast*,
384–85.

24. Before we can estimate the size of the Jewish population on the Radziwiłł
estates, we also need to know how many Jews lived in villages as tavern keepers with
their families. Though the inventories do list the taverns, they tend not to mention
the people who ran them. With no way to determine how many people lived in
each one, even a rough estimate is not possible. Other sources may help to fill the
gap; based on the census of Jews from 1764–65, Raphael Mahler determined that
a third of the Jews of Poland lived in villages, and showed that in the eastern parts
of the country where the economic structure was more like that of Lithuania, they
numbered 30 percent. Because Mahler's data did not include Lithuania nor cover
the late seventeenth century, and because the leasing system on the Radziwiłł estates
was not yet well developed, we should assume that fewer than 30 percent of the

Jews lived in villages at the time Still, we have no way of estimating the actual number. See Mahler, *Yidn in Amolikn Poyln*, 50–51. Kalik reaches similar conclusions in her study of the Jewish population of Crown Poland in the seventeenth century, Kalik, *Scepter of Judah*, 39–48 and Chapter Five in this study.

25. See note 24.

26. Frost, *The Northern Wars*, 226–300.

27. Ochmański, *Historia Litwy*, 157–59, and Kosman, *Historia Białorusi*, 170–72.

28. See Karol Stanisław's diary, AR VI, 79–II: 70. The family's castle in Mir also burned down that year, though the town seems to have survived, only to be hit by the war a few years later. Ibid.

29. AR XXV, 1929: 45–46. The nearby Kopyś estate was also destroyed at that time: AR XXV, 1727.

30. On the impact of the Great Northern War on the Jews of Poland-Lithuania: Nadav, "Iyun," 89–96.

31. On the effects of the war in general, especially in Poland: Gierowski, *Między saskim absolutyzmem*, 9–78, and Hyczko, "Straty i zniszczenia," 33–54.

32. For Słuck: AR XXV, 3835/1 and AR XXV, 3836; and for Kopyś: AR XXV, 1775 and AR XXV, 1777. These are not the only examples. The pattern in Birże was slightly different: though the number of Jewish homes there fell (from 53 to 43), the total number of houses dropped much more (from 211 to 90), meaning a net growth in the proportion of Jewish owned properties from 25 percent to 48 percent. See AR XXV, 235 and AR XXV, 236.

33. Mordekhai Nadav (*Pinsk*, 180–209) reached a similar conclusion regarding the recovery of the Jews of Pińsk following the mid-seventeenth century wars.

34. AR V, 12424, n.p., 2/5/1753; see also AR XXIII, 137: 65.

35. Roman Rybarski, a leading Polish historian in the interwar period who held openly anti-Semitic views, noted that Jewish society had grown in this period when the Polish towns had shrunk and assumed that the Jews had caused the decline. The data here suggest the opposite: it was the decline of the towns and the decrease in their population that opened up possibilities for the Jews that had not previously existed. In fact, it would seem that, far from causing decline, Jewish economic activity helped the towns survive and recover more quickly than they might otherwise have done. See Rybarski, *Handel i polityka handlowa*, 226–27.

36. In similar vein, Jonathan Israel ("Central European Jewry," 3–30) noted positive effects of the Thirty Years War on the development of German Jewry, which he attributed to the importance of the financial services that the Jews provided to the various sides.

37. Demographic shifts among the Jewish population in this decade were probably not great. While these were years of natural increase in the Jewish population, they were also a time of intensive military activity in both Poland and Lithuania. Wartime conditions naturally reduced or even halted population growth. It would not be unreasonable to assume that the data from 1775 are also valid for 1764. The 1775 document, which forms the basis for the calculations here, summarizes

a census of Lithuanian Jewry that was based on the 1764–65 listing but was partially updated after the first partition in 1772. This manuscript, can be found in the Lithuanian State Archives in Vilna: Lietuvos TSR Centrinis Valstybęs Istorijos Archyvas, Vilnius, SA, b. 3739. I should like to thank my friend Prof. Shaul Stampfer of the Hebrew University in Jerusalem for bringing this important source to my attention. See also Stampfer, "The 1764 Census," 91–121.

38. Mahler, *Yidn in amolikn Poyln*, 29–39. On the problems involved in the use of this kind of census as a source for the demographic history of early modern Polish Jewry: Guldon, "Źródła," and Guldon and Krikun, "Przycyznek do krytyki."

39. See Mahler, *Yidn in amolikn Poyln*, 37.

40. For comparison's sake, there were twenty Jewish communities on the estates of the Czartoryski-Sieniawski family in southeastern Poland in 1764, including twelve with at least a thousand Jews: Rosman, *The Lords' Jews*, 213–14.

41. This was not a pattern unique to the estates: Mahler, *Yidn in amolikn Poyln*, 238–44. Of the large Jewish communities on the estates, only Słuck was of great importance for Lithuanian Jewry as a whole because it was one of the five principal Jewish communities in the Council of the Land of Lithuania. On this: Teller, "Radziwill," 251–56.

42. The relatively large number of Jews leasing village taverns further increased this penetration of the countryside.

43. AR XV, 24, plik 4: 1. The only clause relevant to the Jews was the tax exemption, because the other obligations did not apply to them.

44. Kulejewska-Topolska, *Nowe lokacje*, 143–44; Ettinger, "Helkam shel hayehudim," 110–11; and Goldberg, ed., *Jewish Privileges*, I: 141–43, 218–20, and 320–29. For other examples on the Radziwiłł estates in the eighteenth century: NABRM 694, opis 4, 1163: 16 and AR XXIX, 9, n.p., 28/I/1751.

45. The term *ekonomia* refers to a particular kind of royal estate (also called a "table estate"). Unlike the many *starostwa*, which the king distributed to his noble supporters, the few *ekonomii* were supposed to remain in his possession. In practice, however, kings tended to lease them to magnates, who simply made them one of their own estates. The fee involved was often nominal. An *ekonomia* could sometimes even be bequeathed to the son of the magnate who held it. See Stańczak, *Kamera saska*, 87–115; Falniowska-Gradowska, *Królewszczyzny*, 37–46; and Zielińska, *Magnateria*, 79–88.

46. AR XXV, 4167; AR XXV, 4168; AR XXV, 4169; and AR XXV, 4172. Very little has been written about the Szawle *ekonomia*; see Kula, *Szkice* II, 309–41, and the details included in Kościałkowski, *Antoni Tyzenhauz*, I: 523–659 and II: 5–125.

47. AR XXV, 4169: 2–9.

48. AR XXV, 4168: 2–4 and AR XXIX, 5: 23–25. It should be noted that the order did not apply to those Jewish individuals who held personal privileges permitting them to live and trade on the estate.

49. Complaints about this from the city of Szawle are noted in one of the inventories (AR XXV, 4168): "In the realm of commerce, a loss of 44 złoty and 10 groszy

resulted because the Jews were expelled." See also AR XXV, 4169: "Customs [revenues] on commerce used to be 120 złoty; now [they come to] only 60." Collecting these customs duties was one of the leaseholder's responsibilities. See Chapter Three. In 1746 the townspeople of Żagory went so far as to ask Radziwiłł to bring a Jewish merchant to the city to improve commerce. See AR XXIII, 33, plik 6.

50. AR XXV, 4169.

51. See AR XXV, 4636. The 1756 inventory also mentions thirty Jewish families that rented properties in Żagory.

52. AR XXV, 4172. See also AR XXIX, 5: 188 and AR XXIX, 7: 487.

53. AR XXV, 4172. These figures are so high that one wonders about their accuracy. Although they come from the accounts of the *ekonomia* that appear in the estate inventory, they should perhaps be taken with a grain of salt. See the discussion of leasing in Chapter Five.

54. AR XXIX, 5: 71–72 and 142.

55. AR V, 2190: 27 and 37. A reference to the incident is found in a document from the 1780s (published in the nineteenth century by Shmuel Yosef Fünn) describing the expulsion of the Jews from Kowno in that decade. The Jews' response is given there in the following terms: "We shall set our minds to settle across the River Wilia under the government of the distinguished and mighty Duke, wojewoda of Wilno, His Highness Karol Stanisław Radziwiłł, where a few [Jews] have settled since the first expulsion." Fünn, *Kiryah ne'emanah*, 195. The document was dated 1783 and its author noted that the first expulsion had taken place thirty years earlier. Thus, the first expulsion and initial settlement on the Radziwiłłs' land can be dated to 1753. For further discussion: Lipman, *Le-Toledot ha-Yehudim*, 139–40.

56. AR V, 2190: 27 and 37. The Christian townspeople of Kowno reacted with fury to Radziwiłł's decision, which both undermined their municipal sovereignty and foiled their attempt to get rid of their Jewish rivals.

57. A well-known example of a *jurydyka* established to attract Jewish settlement in the face of opposition from local townspeople was Nowa Jerozolima (New Jerusalem), founded in Warsaw in 1774 by August Sułkowski. In that case the townspeople of Warsaw proved strong enough to cause the abolition of the *jurydyka* within two years. See Zienkowska, "Spór."

58. On the legal basis for the relations between Jews and their lords in private towns: Goldberg, "Bein ḥofesh le-netinut," 108–11.

59. Wyrobisz, "Polityka Firleyów."

60. This policy was in no way unique to the Radziwiłłs since it had formed the basis for Jewish settlement in Poland for centuries. See Teller, "Telling the Difference." On the noble estates these bodies enjoyed the same degree of autonomy as the corresponding non-Jewish institutions: Hundert, "Kahal i samorząd miejski."

61. AR XXIX, 5: 519; NARBM 694, opis 7, 457; and Goldberg, ed., *Jewish Privileges*, I: 301. Such regulations did not exist only in the Radziwiłł towns; see Goldberg's introduction to *Jewish Privileges*, 22–23. Though this seems to have been the general principle, there were always exceptions, even on the Radziwiłł estates. In

Nieśwież, for instance, a lawsuit filed by a Jew against a Christian was heard by the municipal court. AR XXIX, 5: 611.

62. NARB 694, opis 7, 457: 4; AR XXIX, 9, n.p., 10/9/1757.

63. A privilege for the Nieśwież Jewish community dating from the period in question has survived. It comprises Michał Kazimierz Radziwiłł's confirmation of the privilege granted to the community by Mikołaj Krzysztof Radziwiłł in 1589 (see note 3). Privileges for the Jews of Kopyś and Romanów Ruski (Ramanaŭ, Belarus) were copied into an estate inventory of 1732 (AR XXV, 1782/1) as was a privilege for Krzyczew in 1727 (AR XXV, 1932: 8–10). A privilege for the Słuck Jewish community exists in a seventeenth-century copy (note 6). Outside Lithuania there were confirmations of privileges from Biały Kamień (Bilyi Kamin', Ukraine) and Jampol (Yampil', Ukraine)—copies dating from 1753, AR XXIX, 7: 306–10—as well as a privilege from Pomarzany (Pomoryany, Ukraine), confirmed in 1747 (Ossolineum, rkps. 2540).

64. For example, Michał Kazimierz Radziwiłł asked the bishop of Wilno to give a license to the Jews of Dawidgródek (David-Haradok, Belarus) to build a new synagogue after the old one had been destroyed in a fire. The bishop acquiesced: NARB 694, opis 4, 905: 1. For a similar case involving the construction of a synagogue in a new community: AR XXIX, 5: 493–94.

65. AR XXIX, 7: 217 and 218; AR XXIX, 9, n.p., 12/8/1756; and AR XXIII, 150, n.p., 9/9/1708. See also AR XXIII, 91, n.p., 9/3/1730. On the types of building: Kalinowski, "Zabudowa," 7–63, and Baranowski, Życie codzienne, 82–90. In the last quarter of the eighteenth century conditions in the towns of Poland-Lithuania improved thanks to the activity of the Commission for Good Order (Komisja Boni Ordinis). On this see Baranowski, Życie codzienne, 248–52.

66. AR XXV, 3836.

67. AR XXV, 1936. Rosman, The Lords' Jews, 48–49, notes a similar pattern on the Czartoryski-Sieniawski estates. The data here and those of Rosman contradict the assertions in Kalinowski, "Zabudowa," 57, and Baranowski, Życie codzienne, 86–87, that the quality of construction of the Jews' homes was worse than that of their neighbors.

68. Little has been written on the housing patterns of early modern Polish Jewry. See Goldberg, "O budownictwie," 107–21.

69. For a fuller discussion of this see Chapter Six.

70. AR XXV, 2029; AR XXV, 2457/1; AR XXV, 4301/1. In Birże, which ran according to Magdeburg law, the Jews had to pay a higher czynsz for not being subject to the municipal council: AR XXV, 236; Akty izdavayemye vilenskogo komissieĭ XXIX: 297–99. On this phenomenon in the private towns of the Lublin region: Opas, "Sytuacja ludności," 29–32.

71. AR XXV, 2457/1: 12.

72. Ibid.

73. AR XXV, 123. In Łachwa (Lakhva, Belarus) the Jews paid three zloty and ten groszy per house, twice as much as Christians: AR XXV, 1730.

74. AR XXV, 2029.

75. In the seventeenth century noble owners of private towns had been hesitant to encourage Jewish settlement because they received nothing in exchange for the Jews' exemption from the corvée labor that non-Jewish townspeople were required to perform. For example, in 1650 the noble lord of Świętojerska explained his decision to limit Jewish settlement as follows: "Because the Jews who have bought lots from the townspeople of Świętojerska pay [my] Court for the lots but do not fulfill any of the other duties to the Court that the townspeople [i.e., the previous owners] do." The original text is published in Alexandrowicz, "Zaludnienie miasteczek," 49, note 61. Once the higher taxes for Jews were established they not only gave Radziwiłł a good reason to encourage Jewish settlement, they were also an added incentive for him to oppose attempts of various municipal councils to expel the Jews from their towns: AR XXV, 2457/1; AR XXV, 3672.

76. AR XXV, 127; AR XXV, 1046; AR XXV, 1932; AR XXIII,146: 110; and NARBM 694, opis 4, 1163: 11. On Jews serving in the town militias: Gritskevich, "Milicje miast magnackich," 56–57. For cases in which Jews did not fulfill labor obligations for the towns: AR XXV, 2029; AR XXV, 2693; and NARBM 694, opis 2, 1701.

77. AR XXIX, 5: 248 and 621; AR XXIX, 7: 35; AR XXIX, 7: 281; AR XXIX, 7: 632; AR XXIX, 7: 641–42; see also AR XXIX, 9, n.p., 1/10/1760.

78. This was apparently unique to the Radziwiłł estates. On other estates every effort was made to bring back non-Jewish townspeople who had fled too: Codello, "Zbiegostwo mieszczan," and Opas, "Wolność osobista."

79. This conclusion is based only on the fact that surviving sources do not mention such restrictions, so it must remain an assumption until additional evidence is found.

80. The towns are Birże, Głębokie (Hlybokae, Belarus), Newel (Nevel', Russia), Słuck, Kopyl (Kapyl', Belarus), Kopyś, Romanów Ruski, and Siebież (Sebezh, Russia). See AR XXV, 235; AR XXV, 243; AR XXV, 1045; AR XXV, 1047; AR XXV, 1775; AR XXV, 1789; AR XXV, 2617; AR XXV, 2624; AR XXV, 3552; AR XXV, 3557; AR XXV, 3686; AR XXV, 3693; AR XXV, 3833; AR XXV, 3834/1; AR XXV, 3837; and AR XXV, 3838. The fact that these towns were administered by the Radziwiłłs beginning in the 1730s strengthens the impression that the family's policy was the cause of the increase in the Jewish population, because at least some of the growth of the Neuburg towns between the 1730s and 1760s must have been due to that. Presumably, without the Radziwiłłs' administration the disparity between the groups of towns would have been even larger.

81. Based on these data it would seem that natural increase accounted for only half of the Jewish population growth on the Radziwiłł estates.

CHAPTER TWO

1. Towns on noble-owned estates were known as "private towns."

2. This attitude was rooted in the practice of the medieval kings of Central and East-Central Europe: Stow, *Alienated Minority*, 89–101.

3. Goldberg, *Ha-ḥevrah ha-yehudit*, 90–124 and 144–58.

4. On the various customs and levies on trade see Chapter Five.

5. *Shtetlach* is the plural form of the Yiddish word *shtetl*, which means "small town."

6. On the differences between the two types of town: Wyrobisz, "Typy funkcjonalne," 25–49.

7. The inventories generally contain data only on people in certain prominent occupations but give no details about the others. Mahler (*Yidn in amolikn Poyln*, 83–84) notes a similar problem in his analysis of the 1764–65 census of Polish Jewry. Another problem with them is that they usually list homeowners only, leaving out renters. Because a sizable portion of the urban population rented their homes, this makes most inventories a very partial record indeed. Data from Biała, Słuck, and Kopyl in the mid-eighteenth century indicate that over a third of the Jews rented their homes: in Biała there were 108 Jewish homeowners and 88 renters; in Słuck there were 230 Jewish homeowners and 137 renters; in Kopyl there were 53 Jewish homeowners and 25 renters. See AR XXV, 127 and 3837.

8. In fact, two separate inventories were made—one of the Christian population in the two towns and one of the Jews there. They detail not only homeowners but renters too. Next to each name is the person's occupation, even if that person was simply engaged in trade or some other occupation not usually noted in this type of record. For the file of the Jews in the two towns: AR XXV, 3837. For the Christians: AR XXV, 3838.

9. In fact, though it was one of the largest settlements in the region, Słuck was not a big town on a national scale.

10. See Wyrobisz, "Typy funkcjonalne," 36–38. On the development of crafts in Słuck: Gritskevich, *Chastnovladel'cheskiye goroda*, 70–75.

11. See the detailed guide to the duties charged on commerce (*instruktarz*) attached to the lease for Słuck in 1762: AR XXIX, 10, n.p., 25/12/1762. Despite this, Wyrobisz ("Typy funkcjonalne," 42–45) has argued that these factors did not substantially change the economic structure of towns such as Słuck.

12. These inventories include details not only of heads of household but also of family members, allowing us to estimate the total population of the town. Unfortunately, the one group they do not describe in detail is the wives of household heads, which drastically reduces the value of the data for research into social structures.

13. This category includes those employed by the town council or *kahal*, as well as clergymen, teamsters, musicians, teachers, servants, and day laborers.

14. On the overall importance of *propinacja* for the estate economy, see Chapter Five.

15. On the terminology used for merchants and craftsmen: Goldberg, "Ha-mishar ha-kimona'i," 12–13.

16. The Jewish communal authorities in Poland-Lithuania took a dim view of these brokers, whom they felt interfered with the smooth running of trade. See *Pinkas Ha-ksherim*, nos. 48, 703, 1317, 1318, 2256; *Pinkas Medinat Lita*, nos. 44, 45; and Weinryb, *Texts and Studies* 229, no. 14.

17. Jewish women also worked in trade. Fourteen of the Jewish merchants (11 percent) were women. Although no female Jewish peddlers are listed in the Słuck *inwentarz*, this does not mean there were none. Wives of Jewish petty merchants often worked as peddlers but were not listed in the *inventory*. On female peddlers in Lithuania in general: *Pinkas Medinat Lita*, no. 947.

18. For a more extensive discussion of Jewish commerce, including women's roles, see Chapter Six.

19. In his discussion of the formation of the local market, Rusiński hardly mentions the importance of Jews: Rusiński, "O rynku wewnętrznym."

20. Kula, *An Economic Theory*, 134–37.

21. The inventories show that small towns often did not have physicians but rather barber-surgeons, known in Yiddish as *feldshers*. In many cases these were Jews. See Ringelblum, "Yidishe feldshers," 351–52. For a broader view of the history of Jewish *feldsher*: Kossoy and Ohry, *The Feldshers*, especially 132–59.

22. These were one cavalryman (*huzar*), two corporals (*kapral*), and forty soldiers (*żołnierz*). On the Radziwiłłs' private army: Lech, "Milicje Radziwiłłów," 33–60. See also Pasztor, "Milicje magnackie," 140–46.

23. Ochmański, "W kwestii."

24. Ochmański (ibid., 290–92) claims that the plots of land received by townspeople before 1648 were too small to support them. In his work on Biała Podlaska near the Lithuanian border, Rachuba ("Biała," 47–56) has calculated that the plots of land that townspeople received were, in fact, large enough to support them.

25. On Jewish craftsmen in Lithuania: Sosis, "Yidishe balmeloches," 1–29. Sosis's Lithuanian and Belarusian sources are from the late eighteenth century and so do not deal with the period discussed here. On Jewish craftsmen in Poland-Lithuania in general: Kremer, "Le-ḥeker ha-mela'chah," 294–325; Halpcrin, *Yehudim va-yahadut*, 163–80; Kramerówna, "Żydowskie cechy," 259–98; and Horn, "The Chronology and Distribution," 249–66.

26. Of course, despite their ritual functions, their clientele was not limited just to Jews. For a historical survey of Jewish craftsmen in general: Wischnitzer, *A History of Jewish Crafts and Guilds*.

27. On the development of guilds in the private towns of Belarus: Gritskevich, *Chastnovladel'cheskiye goroda*, 70–75. On the guilds' war against Jewish skilled craftsmen: Kremer, "Le-ḥeker ha-mela'chah," 308–13.

28. These joint guilds were found in many towns at the time; for instance, the furriers and butchers organized in this way in Nieśwież: AR XV, 18, plik 3, n.p., 11/4/1703; and AR XXIX, 9, n.p., 4/11/1758. See Kremer, "Der anteil," 3–32, and Pendzich, "The Jewish Community," especially 177. In contrast to the accepted view, it seems that Jewish guilds did not develop widely in Poland until the eighteenth century, and in Lithuania they were not common until the very end of the century. Even Wischnitzer ("Di struktur") does not present sources from Lithuania before then. On the development of Jewish guilds in Poland-Lithuania as a whole: Horn, "The Chronology and Distribution."

29. AR XXIII, 137: 102.

30. AR XXIII, 137: 79.

31. AR XXIII, 131, n.p., n.d., *suplika* of Szawel Zorochowicz and Frydman Mowszowicz, haberdashers.

32. It should be noted that both the teamsters in Kopyl were Jews.

33. There were eight Christian and no Jewish day laborers.

34. See NARBM, 694, opis 3, 38: 1–6.

35. Wyrobisz ("Polityka Firleyów," 603) notes that the estate owners encouraged only those craftsmen who served the court. The Radziwiłłs too employed Jewish craftsmen for various jobs at court and on the estate, including silversmiths, glaziers, furriers, bookbinders, painters, potash makers, and saltpeter makers. See AR XXIX, 5: 377–78; AR XXIX, 6: 426; AR XXIX, 7: 195; AR XXIX, 9, n.p., 23/9/1756; AR V, 7170: 157; AR XIX, U III: 1; and AR IV, 237: 60. In this last letter, from 1717, Karol Stanisław Radziwiłł mentions having ordered a goblet from a Jewish silversmith from Biała for the local Orthodox church.

36. There were also a few extremely wealthy merchants with connections outside Poland, such as the Ickowicz brothers (see Chapter Four) and Joshua ben Michael (see Chapter Six). The Jews' domination of the urban markets was not limited to the Radziwiłł estates, but was general in eighteenth-century Poland-Lithuania.

37. It is not clear how involved Jews were in marketing the finished products of craftsmen, since in many cases the latter tried to market their products themselves. Craftsmen also tried to keep the Jews out of the market for their raw materials, but here too the extent of their success is not clear. See AR XXIX, 7: 23–24 and 304–6. See also Hundert, *The Jews in a Polish Private Town*, 47 and 60.

38. Urban taverns were just part of a network of taverns that extended to the villages as well. For an extensive discussion of the importance of taverns in the estate economy see Chapter Five.

39. See, for example, AR XXV, 2457/1: 12. According to this order, the *wójt* (town official) was responsible for collecting the tax from the Christian townspeople and transferring it to the estate administration. The *kahal* was responsible for doing the same in the Jewish community.

40. This may not always have been the case in the royal towns: Bałaban, *Historja Żydów*, 187–207.

41. AR XXIX, 9, n.p., 4/11/1758; AR XXV, 1046; and AR XXV, 2071: 42.

42. See, for example, AR XXIX, 9, n.p., 22/7/1756.

43. AR XXIX, 11, n.p., 18/5/1764.

44. This special levy was not the same as the new Jewish poll tax instituted in 1764. The census on which the poll tax was based was only conducted later that year.

45. For a description of Jewish communal administration and elections: Balaban, "Ha-'otonomiyah ha-yehudit," 44–65.

46. Hundert, "Kahał i samorząd miejski," 66–74.

47. AR V, 6943 II: 70–73; AR XXIX, 7: 191–92; and AR XXIX, 9, n.p., 25/12/1755. See also Weinryb, "Beiträge zur Finanzgeschichte," II: 187–214, especially 196–207.

48. NARBM 694, opis 2, plik 2281: 101; AR V, 6943 II: 66; AR V, 12424, n.p., 27/11/1753; and AR XXV, 3538/1: 13.

49. AR XXIX, 6: 427, and AR V, 7170: 142.

50. AR V, 15467, n.p., n.d.

51. For examples: AR XXIX, 5: 716–17; AR XXIX, 6: 299–300; AR XXIX, 7: 507–8; AR XXIX, 8: 2 and 5; AR XXIX, 9, n.p., 27/5/1760; and L'vivs'ka Natsional'na Naukova Biblioteka Ukraïny imeni V. Stefanika, fond 103, opis 1, teka 6801.

52. AR XXIX, 6: 296; AR XXIX, 7: 861; AR XXIX, 9, n.p, 17/6/1760 and 29/6/1760.

53. AR XXIX, 9, n.p., 25/7/1760. The rabbi's name was Yosef ben Mendel. Less than a month later the kahal received a rebate of 200 czerwony złoty: AR XXIX, 9, n.p., 21/8/1760.

54. See, for example, AR XXIX, 9, n.p., 2/8/1756, 20/11/1760, and 2/4/1761.

55. A letter from one of Anna Radziwiłł's administrators read in part: "I ordered the members of the local kahal to be jailed for not having yet appointed a rabbi as they promised; once they have been put in prison, they will immediately intensify their efforts [to find] a rabbi, and [pay] the fee for [his appointment] to Her Highness, the Gracious Princess." AR V, 6943: 110. See also AR XXIX, 9, n.p., 29/6/1760. This was an extreme case. Usually the communities, that presumably wanted a rabbi anyway, gave in to the pressure from the estate owner and appointed one immediately.

56. In some cases the kahal charged the applicant more than the estate owner was paid and so profited from the appointment: Balaban, Le-Toledot ha-tenu'ah, 83.

57. AR IV kopie, 7: 363, no. 24. See the order by Michał Kazimierz Radziwiłł to his Jewish communities to help the Jews of Korelicze after their synagogue burned down: AR XXIX, 9, n.p., 25/9/1759.

58. AR XXIII, 137: 43–46.

59. AR XXIX, 9, n.p., 18/6/1758 and 1/10/1760. See also AR IV, 627, letter 596; Goldberg, Ha-ḥevrah ha-yehudit, 133–34; and Teller, "Radziwiłł."

60. For requests of this sort: AR V, 15467, n.p., 7/6/1756; AR XXIII, 131, n.p., n.d., suplika of the Bielica community.

61. The budget of the Słuck Jewish community for 1732–33 opened with the following statement: "This register is an accounting of the community's expenditure and income from Passover 5492 until Passover 5493 . . . and to show the accounts to the noble . . . gubernator, Pan Szyszka . . ." AR XXV, 240. See also AR XXIX, 5: 609; AR XXIX, 6: 367–68; AR XXV, 3538/1: 13; and AR XXV, 1921: 35. See also Instrukcje gospodarze, 424.

62. See the sums that community leaders in Mir were required to repay between 1723 and 1726: AR XXIII, 93, plik 2, n.p., 1726. See also Bergerówna, Księżna pani, 311–14.

63. AR XXIII, 54: 1, and AR XXIII, 154: 1018. One of the few regulations in Polish in the record book of the Jewish community of Boćki refers specifically to the community chest. See Archiwum Glowne Akt Dawnych we Warszawie, Archiwum Roskie, 321: 82.

64. AR XXIII, 137: 48, and AR XXIII, 146: 117; AR XXIX, 5: 519; and AR XXIX, 6: 609. On the communal system of taxation see Weinryb, "Kavim le-Toledot ha-kalkalah," 90–113; and Weinryb, "Beiträge zur Finanzgeschichte," II: 187–214.

65. See Chapter Five.

66. Kalik, "Patterns of Contact." For general literature on the subject of community debts, see Rosman, "The Indebtedness"; Galant, "Zadolzhennost'"; Sobczak, "Zadłużenie"; and Morgensztern, "Zadłużenie gmin," See also Kalik, "Hafkadah ve-viderkaf."

67. The annual payments were higher than the average (which was 7 percent) owing to one loan of 20,000 złoty on which the annual rate of interest was 30 percent, i.e., 6,000 złoty.

68. AR XXV, 240.

69. Ibid.

70. See the Zabłudów community *pinkas*: "regarding the matter that is well known to everyone due to the magnitude of the scandal . . . it was therefore agreed by the whole community council and all the taxpayers that a loan should be taken out for our community as a whole, . . . so that it will always be possible to redeem captives." National Library of Israel, Manuscript Division, Heb 4°, 103: 425. See also AR XXIII, 131, n.p., n.d., *suplika* of the Bielica community.

71. Kalik, "Patterns of Contact." This custom had a parallel in Jewish society: wealthy people gave standing loans to communities and regional councils in exchange for promises that prayers would be said for their souls after their death. *Pinkas Medinat Lita*, 449, no. 287.

72. There are several agreements of this sort: AR VIII, 376, passim.

73. AR XXIX, 5: 298; AR XXIX, 6: 67–76; and AR VIII, 376: 41–42.

74. AR XXIII, 137: 118; AR XXIII, 9, koperta 3: 33; AR V, 15782: 71–73; and AR XXIX, 9, n.p., 4/1/1756. See also Hundert, *The Jews in a Polish Private Town*, 136–37 and 142–43.

75. AR XXIX, 6: 414–15; and AR V, 12424–II, n.p., 15/5/1758.

76. AR V, 15984, n.p., 23/5/1745; and AR IV, 131: 28–29.

77. AR XXIX, 5: 401; and AR XXIX, 7: 647 and 836–37.

78. See note 51; also AR XXIX, 9, n.p., 10/9/1757, no. 3. The rabbi's power came from his authority to wield the *ḥerem* (excommunication) against Jews who refused to comply with instructions. See Lewin, *Klątwa żydowska*, 17–35, and for a full discussion of these issues, Kaźmierczyk, *Żydzi*, 135–56.

79. AR XXIX, 8: 65.

80. AR XXIX, 7: 679.

81. AR XXIX, 7: 511–12, 679 and 794. Non-Jewish townspeople were also required to take part in commissions of inquiry: AR XXIX, 9, n.p., 25/5/1756. In this case Michał Kazimierz Radziwiłł established a commission of inquiry in Ołyka comprising the *wójt* and town councilors in order to investigate a blood libel against the Jews of Jampol. Other such commissions of course had nothing to do with Jews.

82. See the papers of the Jewish committees that investigated the accusations ex-

changed by Joshua ben Michael (Howsiej Michajłowicz), a merchant and *arendarz*, and Józef Topolewski, manager of Michał Kazimierz Radziwiłł's river trade: AR XX, 18. On these issues, see Chapter Six.

83. NABRM 694, opis 4, teka 1163: 118; AR XXIII, 9, plik 1, n.p., 14/8/1755; AR XXIX, 5: 401; AR V, 15984 (VII); AR XXIX, 7: 659; AR XXIX, 8: 41; and AR XXIX, 9, n.p., 18/4/1759.

84. On this phenomenon and its socioeconomic significance, see Chapter Five.

85. AR XXIX, 7: 669; AR XXIX, 8: 81; and AR XXIX, 11, n.p., 22/2/1764. See also AR XXIX, 5: 725. This kind of privilege was first granted by the royal court. Jews of course were not its main beneficiaries. See Hundert, "Was there an East European Analogue to Court Jews?"

86. *Icones familiae ducalis Radivillianae*, Nesvisium (Nieśwież), 1758.

87. AR XXIX, 7: 102. See also AR XXIX, 5: 725. Although Hirsz is considered one of the Poland's leading graphic artists of the eighteenth century, his name is unknown in Jewish historiography (on Jewish artists of the period: Landsberger, "The Jewish Artist"). He is not even mentioned in the *Encyclopaedia Judaica*. On Hirsz: Widacka, "Działalność," 62–69.

88. See Rosman, *The Lords' Jews*, 70, 177–78, and Lederhendler, "The Decline."

89. See Goldberg, *Ha-ḥevrah ha-yehudit*, 90–124; Goldberg, "Tlutan ve'atzma'utan," 141–46. For an attempt by the Radziwiłłs to strip the *kahal* of Słuck of basic powers (*ḥerem*, rabbinical court), see AR XXIII, 137: 2. This order was local in nature and was related to a local dispute: Michałowska-Mycielska, "Władza dominialna," 59–71.

90. See Dinur, "Reshitah shel ha-ḥasidut," 104–6.

91. Rosman, "An Exploitative Regime," xi–xxx.

92. The two sons of the *arendarz* and merchant Joshua ben Michael were rabbis on the Radziwiłł estates; see AR V, 15467, n.p., 14/3/1749. Szmojło and Gedalia Ickowicz exploited their connections with magnates in Poland and Lithuania to obtain rabbinical positions for their sons-in-law (see Chapter Four). For additional cases: AR V, 6943–II: 167; and AR V, 7170: 91 and 120.

93. *Pinkas Medinat Lita*, nos. 207, 439, 840, 882, and 915. In Poland this problem first arose in the late sixteenth century: *Pinkas Va'ad Arba Ha'aratzot, no.* 178. See also Teller, "Tradition and Crisis?" 1–39.

94. This could also be seen throughout Poland-Lithuania in that period. See Goldberg, *Ha-ḥevrah hayehudit*, 12–30, and Wyrobisz, "Materialy," 715.

95. See Chapter Three; also Levine, "Gentry, Jews, and Serfs."

CHAPTER THREE

1. Much has been written on this. See, in particular, Z. Zielińska, *Walka "familii."*

2. T. Zielińska, "Mechanizm sejmikowy."

3. North, *Structure and Change*, 3–19 and 33–44.

4. On the organization of agriculture in early modern Lithuania: Wieczorek, *Z dziejów ustroju*, and Żabko-Potopowicz, *Praca najemna*.

5. Many of the titles differed from estate to estate. The ones given here are those that were in use on the Radziwiłł latifundium.

6. The most comprehensive description of the structure of estate administration in the eighteenth century is still Bergerówna, *Księżna pani*, 176–243 and 271–86. See also Szkurłatowski, "Organizacja administracji."

7. In his study of the agricultural structure of Lithuania in the eighteenth century (*Z dziejów ustroju*, 25–26), Wieczorek calculated the annual income of an *ekonom* as follows: 50–200 złoty, plus 3–6 barrels of rye, the same quantity each of barley and oats, 0.25–1.5 barrels of buckwheat, 20–36 gallons of peas, about 40 pounds of pork, 6 gallons of butter, 20–30 złoty to purchase meat, 20–25 pounds of wax, up to 12 dozen herring, and 10–20 pounds of salt. A *gubernator* earned almost double the amount of produce, and apparently more money as well.

8. These letters are scattered among the Radziwiłł correspondence (letters written by members of the family [AR IV] and letters written to the family [AR V]), as well in their economic instructions (AR XXIX) and among the general documentation from various estates (AR XXIII and NABRM 694, opisy 3, 4). Some can also be found in other parts of the collection (AR XI and AR XX). They have a fixed format. The administrator entitled his letter "Points for the lord's decision" and wrote only on the left-hand side of the page. Radziwiłł's responses were written in on the right-hand side opposite the questions.

9. Though some Jews held high-ranking positions on the Sieniawski and Czartoryski estates in this period (Rosman, *The Lords' Jews*, 143–84), there were almost no Jewish administrators on the Radziwiłł estates.

10. On estate bookkeeping methods see Łukasik, *Rachunkowość*, 42–47. Also Kula, *An Economic Theory*, 28–36.

11. Administrators did not always work efficiently even given this supervision. In one instance, the *gubernator* of Birże made money from selling alcohol in collaboration with the priest in Wiżuny (Vyžuonos, Lithuania) without making the requisite payments to the local leaseholder. Hieronim Florian Radziwiłł sent his administrator a stern letter warning him to make sure that the revenues from the local alcohol lease were not affected. See AR IV kopie, 6, plik 6: 573.

12. This kind of job was not enough to buy the loyalty of the upper nobility. The Radziwiłłs had to find more lucrative public positions for them. Zielińska, "Mechanizm sejmikowy."

13. Dąbkowski, *Prawo prywatne*, 72–73. On the structure of property rights as evidence of the economic nature of any society: Eggertsson, *Economic Behavior*, 33–58, and North, *Structure and Change*, 17–18 and 128–32. In the Radziwiłł archive most of the legal documentation dealing with mortgages and estate leases is to be found in AR XXIII and NABRM 694, opisy 3, 4. The economic instructions (AR XXIX) contain many contracts of monopoly leases as well as one or two contracts of other types.

14. Bardach, *Historia państwa i prawa*, 303 and 503–4; Kalik, "Hafkadah ve-viderkaf," 25–47.

15. On the situation in this regard in the Grand Duchy of Lithuania in the second half of the eighteenth century: Kozłowskij, "Struktura własnośći," 81–82 and particularly his Table 4.

16. The member of the family who most heavily mortgaged estates to raise money was Karol Stanisław ("Panie Kochanku") Radziwiłł. See Anusik and Strojnowski, "Problemy majątkowe," 91–95.

17. In his study of the development of the Radziwiłł estates in the sixteenth century, Siekierski ("Landed Wealth," 68–88) notes that Mikołaj Krzysztof Radziwiłł acquired several of his estates in this manner.

18. Although the contracts usually included a clause stating that those who took possession of real estate as a mortgage had to return it in the same condition in which they received it, their desire to make a quick profit often led to overexploitation, sometimes ruinous.

19. The Radziwiłłs remained a major social economic, and political force in these years, and even when they did mortgage various estates, the mortgage holders could not really compete with them. The discomfort was likely to be more of a local irritant than anything else.

20. The topic of the estate lease in Poland-Lithuania has not yet received the scholarly attention it deserves. The discussion here is based mainly on various references in the literature and the examination of the documentation in the Radziwiłł archives.

21. This form of leasing was known as *arendowna posesja* (leasehold) or *dzierżawa* (lease). In *The Lords' Jews*, 110–13, Rosman argues that there is a clear distinction between the use of *dzierżawa* to mean an estate lease and *arenda* to mean the lease of incomes derived from estate monopolies. Though this was the case on the estates that he studied, the distinction does not apply to the Radziwiłł latifundium.

22. The flip side of this was that he had to cover any losses he might sustain.

23. Many Jews made their living by leasing estates in this period. See Ettinger, "Helkam shel ha-yehudim," 128–29, and Mahler, *Toledot ha-yehudim*, 115–24. Rabbi Meshulam Feivish of Kraków (writing in 1590) and the leaders of the Jewish communities in the Włodzimierz (Volodymyr, Ukraine) region, writing in 1602, legislated on the issues of Jewish law that arose when Jews who leased estates had to exploit corvée labor done for them by peasants on the Sabbath. See *Pinkas Va'ad Arba Ha'aratzot*, 483–87, para. 12; Ben Sasson, "Takkanot," 204–5.

24. Kula, *An Economic Theory*, 36–37.

25. This did not include gifts, bribes, and other payments, which remained with the leaseholder.

26. For an example, see the lease for the County of Mir given by Michał Kazimierz Radziwiłł to the noble Antoni Przeździecki for 205,377 złoty and 18 groszy (AR XXIX, 5: 457–65): "If there is a clear profit beyond the sum of 205,377 złoty and 18 groszy, the three-year income, then the honorable lord Przeździecki . . . must repay this extra amount to my treasury at the end of the three-year term of the lease. If,

however, the honorable lord . . . cannot collect the sum stated above in accordance with the inventory, then . . . I, Prince Radziwiłł, undertake to help . . . and pay . . . the entire amount to the honorable lord."

27. The files of the economic instructions contain many announcements of such commissions visiting estates on the expiration of leases. They also contain the instructions to the commission members, for example: AR XXIX: 7, 86–87, 292–96, and 866–68. Subjects' complaints are referred to in the documents as *pretensyje*. See, for example, NABRM 694, opis 4, 1154: 70 and NABRM 694, opis 2, 1700: 6–10.

28. Estate leaseholders were not usually allowed to choose monopoly rights leaseholders. See Chapter Five.

29. The new approach to estate leasing was the likely cause of Jews moving away from this sector in the later seventeenth and eighteenth centuries. See Mahler, *Toledot ha-yehudim*, 247. This is sometimes attributed to the legal prohibition on leasing rural properties to Jews, but Goldberg (*Ha-ḥevrah ha-yehudit*, 159–70) has shown that the ban was not actually enforced.

30. On this aspect of choosing leaseholders see Stashevskiĭ, *Istoriia*, 157. Kalik, "Szlachta Attitudes," discusses the nobility's attitude towards leasing in general and Jewish leaseholders in particular.

31. The Ickowicz brothers, Jews who leased Hieronim Florian Radziwiłł's estates in the 1740s, were a clear exception. They took on the leases with the clear intention of maximizing income rather than preserving the status quo. Radziwiłł was delighted with this, though he was not prompted to encourage noble leaseholders to do the same.

32. See Kutrzeba, *Historia ustroju*, I: 88–96; Baron, *A Social and Religious History*, 28; Opas, "Miasta prywatne," 28–47. The growth of the nobles' power in Lithuania had a somewhat different history: Kutrzeba, *Historia ustroju*, II, 33–48 and Ochmański, *Historia Litwy*, 97–100. The Union of Lublin in 1569 made the rights of Lithuanian nobles the same as those of the Polish nobility.

33. Corvée labor is known to have existed in Poland since the fifteenth century, but was institutionalized only in the second half of the sixteenth century. In Lithuania corvéc labor and its institutionalization were linked with the agricultural reforms instituted by Zygmunt II August on the ducal estates between 1547 and 1566. The reforms spread to the noble estates during the decades that followed: Ochmański, "Reforma włoczna na Litwie" and Kosman, "Pomiara włoczna." On agricultural reform on the Radziwiłł estates in the sixteenth century: Ochmański, "Reforma włoczna w dobrach." In fact corvée labor never became as widespread in Lithuania as it did in Poland.

34. Rutkowski, *Badania*, 344–53; Burzyński, "Struktura dochodów," 41–44; and Serczyk, *Gospodarstwo magnackie*, 150–51.

35. Almost the only exception to this was the freedom given to residents to produce their own alcohol at times of family celebration, particularly weddings.

36. Bobrzyński, "Prawo propinacji," 234–52 and 260–71. On this process in Lithuania: Alexandrowicz, "Miasteczka Białorusi i Litwy," 97–104. Alexandrowicz (100

and 103) dates the switch to leasing in Lithuania to the last decades of the sixteenth century.

37. The sale of grain in the form of alcohol was thus particularly well suited to areas distant from the major trade routes to the Baltic coast: Rutkowski, *Badania*, 301–16. For a slightly different view: Wyczański, *Polska*, 20–22 and 37.

38. Hoszowski, "The Polish Baltic Trade," especially 144–46.

39. Topolski, *Gospodarka polska*, 39–40; Goldberg, *Ha-ḥevrah ha-yehudit*, 232–33.

40. For a comprehensive analysis of milling arrangements on Polish estates in the sixteenth century: Rutkowski, *Badania*; Serczyk, *Gospodarstwo magnackie*, 120–21; and Rychlikowa, *Klucz wielkoporębski*, 136–38. Payments in kind, though prevalent on the Radziwiłł latifundium, were not used in every case.

41. Alexandrowicz ("Miasteczka Białorusi i Litwy," 77–82) notes that these duties were sometimes included in the propinacja lease in the sixteenth and seventeenth centuries too. Research on the economic structure of the estates has focused mainly on agricultural production and has largely ignored these revenues. For more details see Chapter Five. Almost the only study to mention customs and duties is Rutkowski, *Badania*, 352–53.

42. Kalik, "Szlachta Attitudes."

43. In these leases, as in the estate leases, the owners did undertake to cover losses stemming from natural disasters or war.

44. In extreme cases this could lead to peasant revolt, as happened on the Radziwiłł estates in 1740 when the peasants and local nobility violently rebelled against the Ickowicz brothers, who had leased the Krzyczew *starostwo*. Though the peasants complained of exploitation, Hieronim Florian Radziwiłł sided with his leaseholders because their activity had significantly boosted his revenues. In the end he brutally suppressed the uprising and continued to work with the leaseholders. See Chapter Four and also Rosman, *The Lords' Jews*, 64–68.

45. See the stories told in *Solomon Maimon: An Autobiography*, 6–18.

46. On the Radziwiłłs' attitude towards trade and their attempts to encourage it see Chapter Six. The use made of Jews to stimulate local commerce can be seen in a whole range of community privileges. See Goldberg, *Jewish Privileges*, passim.

47. Towards the end of Michał Kazimierz Radziwiłł's lifetime, lists were drawn up of estates that were either mortgaged or leased out: AR XXIX:11, passim.

48. Michał Kazimierz Radziwiłł made this condition explicit in many of the lease contracts he signed. See Chapter Five.

CHAPTER FOUR

1. Rosman, *The Lords' Jews*, 110–13 and 144–45; Goldberg, *Ha-ḥevra ha-yehudit*, 159–70.

2. Ibid. On the nobility's attitude towards estate leasing by Jews: Kalik, "Szlachta Attitudes," 15–26. See also Krupa, *Żydzi*, 160–64.

3. On this phenomenon in the Sieniawski-Czartoryski estates: Rosman, *The Lords' Jews*, 143–84.

4. On the Ickowicz brothers: Halperin, *Yehudim ve-yahadut*, 277–88, and Zielińska, "Kariera i upadek." On the peasant revolt against the brothers in Belarus: Lech, "Powstanie chłopów," and also below.

5. In pre-modern Jewish culture, patronymics tended to be used rather than surnames, though there were some exceptions, particularly in elite groups. In this case the Polish "Ickowicz" is an exact translation of the Hebrew, "ben Yitzḥak," meaning son of Isaac. The Polish form of Shmuel, "Szmojło," is pronounced Shmoywo in English, with the stress on the first o.

6. Their Hebrew signatures appear on the Mir inventory from 1727 as follows: "Gedaliah the son of our master and teacher, Yitzḥak Segal of Olik, Shmuel the son of our master and teacher, Yitzḥak Segal of the holy community of Olik," AR XXV, 2451/1: 58. See also their signatures on the instructions they received from Anna Radziwiłł on November 14, 1726 in AR XXIII: 91, n.p., On the identification of Olik as Ołyka, see Mahler, "Shmoteihem shel mekomot," 146–61. Volhynia is today in northern Ukraine.

7. See the letter by Anna Radziwiłł's administrator in Ołyka, dated August 6, 1721. AR V, 6943 V: 138–41.

8. AR V, 6943 V: 92–95, letter from the Ołyka administrator to Anna Radziwiłł, October 10, 1720.

9. The administrator (Kochanowski) had a particularly unfavorable opinion of Gdal, describing him and his colleague Jakób as thieves and cheats: AR V, 6943 VI: 47–49.

10. AR XXIII, 91, n.p.; AR XXIII, 93, plik 2, n.p.

11. Szmojło Ickowicz's name first appears among the residents of Biała in the inventory from 1728 (AR XXV, 124). It does not appear in the previous inventory from 1725 (AR XXV, 123). Since he took the Mir lease in 1726, we can assume that was the year he moved.

12. On Anna Radziwiłł's economic activity, see Karkucińska, *Anna z Sanguszków Radziwiłłowa*, especially 41–56.

13. Most estate leases in the eighteenth century limited receipt of incomes to those registered in the inventory, which suggests that Anna Radziwiłł was expecting the brothers to make this lease more profitable. Other members of the family were equally generous in the leases they gave the Ickowiczes, presumably for the same reason. See the 1740 lease of Hieronim Florian Radziwiłł's latifundium: "Szmojło Ickowicz, my general accountant, has taken a three-year lease on all my aforementioned estates and may manage them in the best way possible, deriving for himself all the benefits and profits." AR XI, 140: 18–21.

14. Ibid.

15. See, for example, the letter from Antoni Kazimierz Sapieha to Szmojło Ickowicz, dated August 1, 1727: AR V, 13817, n.p.

16. See, for example, AR V, 18655: 144–45 and 146–48; and Goldberg, *Ha-ḥevrah ha-yehudit*, 164.

17. Note 10.

18. AR XXXIII, 3: 3, no. 3. See Goldberg, *Ha-ḥevrah ha-yehudit*, 165–67.

19. See, for example, AR XX, 94.

20. AR V, 15782: 5.

21. AR XX, 86: 2; AR V, 5598: 1–2.

22. AR V, 4041: 1; AR V, 15782: 1–2, 4, 6–8, and 13; AR XX, 94: 1–15; AR XX, 87: 2–7; NABRM 694, opis 4, 2021: 49.

23. Ibid. On the purchase of diamonds: AR XXIII, 91: n.p.

24. Zielińska, "Kariera i upadek," 41. See also AR XVII, 123: 39–95.

25. For the accounts from 1733: AR XXIII, 150. The other accounts can be found in AR XXIII, 91; AR, X, "Ickowicz": 20.

26. *Pinkas Va'ad Arba Ha'aratzot*, 271–73, and Kalik, *Scepter of Judah*, 153–356.

27. Szmojło first complained about the damage that the Russian army had done to the Mir estate (adding that the Radziwiłłs' own private militia had caused just as much destruction) in two letters written in October 1733. AR V, 15782: 3–35. In 1734 sub-leaseholders on the Mir estate also submitted claims for compensation, some of which were answered: AR XXIII, 91, n.p.

28. A notebook containing copies of all Szmojło's real estate contracts in Słuck between 1733 and 1737 has survived: AR XXIII, 55.

29. The story survived in two versions, one in the collection of hagiographic legends about the Baal Shem Tov (*Sefer Shivḥei Ha-Besht*, 267–75), and the other, much abridged, in the writings of the preacher David of Maków (Wilensky, *Ḥasidim u-mitnagdim*, II: 242). See Teller, "Masoret Slutzk," 15–38, and Halperin, *Yehudim ve-yahadut*, 277–88.

30. AR XXIII, 155.

31. See the contracts between the Ickowicz brothers and various merchants to supply hemp and potash to Rīga from Birże and Krzyczew, AR XX, 87. For trade along the Dwina (Daugava) River from Belarus to Rīga, see Topolska, "Związku handlowe," 9–31; Mieleszko, "Handel," 675–713; Handrack, *Der Handel*, 81–83.

32. On the relations between the Ickowicz brothers and the Saturgus brothers, see the correspondence between them: AR V, 13955, passim and AR V, 15782, passim. The first letter by Adolph Saturgus that mentions Szmojło's name is dated September 1, 1733. On the Saturgus brothers: Gause, *Der Grundbesitz der Familie Saturgus in Königsberg*.

33. AR XX, 87: 4–7.

34. This is mentioned frequently in the Saturguses' correspondence: AR V, 13955, passim.

35. Zielińska, "Kariera i upadek," 36. Szmojło received the title in the mid 1730s, but the lack of consistency in the documentation makes it difficult to date precisely. The first time the title appeared in his real estate contracts in Słuck was in July 1736, so this might have been the year in which it was granted. See AR XXIII, 155.

36. Marcin Radziwiłł also had a Jewish "cashier" named Szymon, whose function and title were comparable to Szmojło's. In memoirs of the period Szymon is described as a person "who controlled everything in general." Matuszewicz, *Diariusz*, 286.

37. On the issue of granting appropriate titles to Jewish estate functionaries: Rosman, *The Lords' Jews*, 156–57.

38. AR XIX, U-VII: 1; NSZ VII, 2: 1–7; and AR V, 15782 all contain correspondence between Szmojło and the managers of the Radziwiłł-owned manufactories in the towns of Naliboki (Nalibaki, Belarus) and Urzecz. See Karkucińska, *Anna z Sanguszków Radziwiłłowa*, 155 and 354–56. On the Radziwiłł manufactories see Chapter Six.

39. See, for example, AR V, 15782: 15–18, 51–57.

40. AR IV, 44, kop. 626, letters 471 and 472; AR V, 15782: 22–25. This correspondence is evidence of Szmojło's close acquaintance with political life inside and outside Lithuania and of his ties with non-Jewish society. See also AR V, 18655: 146–48.

41. AR V, 15782: 9–11, 26–29, and 33–35. Szmojło's personal credibility seems to have been very important to him. When someone on the estate accused him of failing to honor a payment order signed by Anna Radziwiłł, he wrote to her in agitated Polish, "Never, God forbid! It is not my way to receive orders from her Grace, my Lady the Princess, and not to fulfill them immediately and do what must be done. This has never happened. I would never detain a person bearing a payment order from my Lady the Princess for an entire day and not do as mandated; on the contrary, I pay at once whatever each one is due." AR V, 15782: 58–61. This does not mean that the duchess accepted with equanimity everything that Szmojło did. Her correspondence with the "cashier" also includes letters in which she expresses harsh anger at actions by Szmojło that displeased her: NABRM 694, opis 7, 712: 96; AR IV, 44, kop. 628: 34–36.

42. AR X, "Ickowicz": 16. This was a particularly generous deal because Radziwiłł also agreed to cover any losses that might accrue to Szmojło.

43. See AR XXV, 1935 and AR XXV, 1936.

44. Lech, "Powstanie chłopów," 323–24.

45. This was standard practice: Kula, *Measures and Men*, 127–46.

46. On the resurveying: *Regesty i nadpisy*, II, nos. 1869 and 1875, and Halperin, *Yehudim ve-yahadut*, 283. On boundary changes during the survey: AR XVII, 17: 71; NABRM 694, opis 4, 1159: 70.

47. Ibid.

48. *Regesty i nadpisy*, II, no. 1765, and AR V, 15782: 68–69.

49. Halperin, *Yehudim ve-yahadut*, 282–83. On relations between the Radziwiłł administration and the Orthodox Church on its estates in the seventeenth century: Degiel, *Protestanci i prawosławni*, 42–53.

50. See Chapter Two.

51. AR XXIII, 9, kop. 3: 33. See also Hendel, "Ha-yehudim ba-Biala," 10–11.

52. AR V, 15782: 71–76.

53. It was this above all that distinguished the brothers' economic strategy from that of the noble estate leaseholders. Nobles too had to have their produce marketed, but it was the brothers' ability to integrate the two branches and dramatically increase their profitability that made them so successful. Anna Radziwiłł recognized

the importance of Szmojło's commercial activity and granted him a general letter of protection on April 3, 1736. AR XI, 122: 36.

54. See the supply contracts, especially to Rīga, in AR XX, 87. See also AR V, 13955, letter dated 8/3/1736.

55. On the economic structure of eastern Belarus see Topolska, *Dobra szkłowskie*. On the links with the Baltic ports see Mieleszko, "Handel," 53–91.

56. AR XVII, 123: 2 and AR XXIII, 93, teka 1, no. 5. See also two complaints by Jewish merchants against another by the name of Haim who tried to adopt the monopolistic methods reserved for the brothers: NABRM 694, opis 4, 1159: 337–38.

57. AR IV, 628: 54–55; AR IV, 629: 1–2; and AR IV, 630: 113–14. See also Karkucińska, *Anna z Sanguszków Radziwiłłowa*, 36.

58. AR V, 15782: 117. For other records of her business activity: AR XIX, NSZ V: 8–15.

59. NABRM 694, opis 4, 2201, passim.

60. AR V, 4273, passim. See also AR V, 3689: 1–2.

61. AR XXIII, 122, teka 6, and AR XXIII, 9, teka 3: 34.

62. AR XXIII, 93, teka 1, no. 5; AR XVII, 123: 2–3.

63. AR XVII, 123: 4, no. 3.

64. Ibid.; AR XVII, 11, no. 13; and AR XXIII, 93, teka 1, no. 7.

65. AR XXIII, 146: 75; AR IV kopie, 6, plik 9: 521; and AR XXIII, 93, teka 1, no. 2.

66. The granting of secondary leases to relatives was by no means unique to the Ickowicz brothers: *Solomon Maimon: An Autobiography*, 6–7.

67. See the complaint about this in AR XVII, 123: 12, nos. 12, 13.

68. A large number of contracts (written in Hebrew) between the brothers and Jewish merchants can be found in NABRM 694, opis 4, 2201.

69. *Pan* (plural, *panowie*) is a title similar to the English "mister," though it was mostly used in this period for noblemen.

70. AR XXIII, 93, teka 1, no. 2. On the violent treatment of both Jews and non-Jews by a rich and well-connected leaseholder from Drohobycz (Drohobych, Ukraine), see Balaban, "Zalmen der rosh kahal," 75–77. See also Nadav, "Ma'asei 'alimut," 41–56.

71. This was a common problem in Poland-Lithuania in the eighteenth century: Dinur, "Reshitah shel ha-hasidut," 100–110, and Rosman, "An Exploitative Regime," xi–xxx.

72. The minutes of this session of the *Sejm* were published in *Teki Podoskiego*, IV, especially 450–53.

73. AR XXIII, 146: 79–95. On the plot to murder Szmojło: AR XXIII, 146: 81.

74. For petitions submitted by peasants from the Krzyczew *starostwo*, see AR XVII, 123.

75. At the start of her withdrawal from active involvement in managing the estates, on August 6, 1739, Anna granted Szmojło a release stating that he had fulfilled all his obligations towards her and her family. AR XI, 122: 51–53.

76. See the Introduction.

77. For a general discussion of the period, including how the Radziwiłł family was affected, see Skibiński, *Europa a Polska*.

78. This question of the restoration of the Neuburg estates to the Radziwiłł families is a complex one and has not yet received the full scholarly attention it deserves. See Lesiński, "Spory," 95–132.

79. AR XI, 140: 18–20. There is some discrepancy as to the precise figure involved. See AR XXIII, 122, teka 6.

80. AR X, "Ickowicz": 112–18.

81. See note 25.

82. AR XI, 222: 20–26, 28–31, and 102–4. In 1742, Ickowicz paid Marcin Mikołaj an additional 1,000 złoty to lease the *starostwo* of Grabów in Great Poland: AR XI, 222: 108–10.

83. AR IV kopie, 6, teka 6: 197.

84. NABRM 694, opis 7, 712: 23; AR V, 13955–II, n.p., 26/11/1740.

85. NABRM 694, opis 4, 2201, 57 and 80. The original is in Hebrew.

86. AR V, 13955–II, n.p., 1/9/1742. On Ephraim see Schnee, *Der Hoffinanz*, I: 143–69. Schnee (153) discusses the business deals that Szmojło and Ephraim made, but his main focus is on the competition between them. He also notes that Szmojło's son, Abraham, traveled to Teplitz in Bohemia to take the cure. Gdal had ties with the town of Dessau, but these do not seem to have been of a commercial nature. See AR IV, 45, kop. 629: 86–90.

87. For the lease of the forests, see NABRM 694, opis 3, 35: 1. On his trade in these products with Riga and Königsberg: AR IV kopie, 6, plik 4: 107.

88. AR XX, 88. This file contains individual accounts and miscellaneous records, which makes it very difficult to reach a comprehensive picture of the brothers' commercial activities in Königsberg.

89. AR X, "Ickowicz": 148.

90. AR XX, 95: 1–4.

91. We cannot be certain whether these goods actually belonged to the Ickowicz brothers or whether they traded in them for the Radziwiłłs. All of the business documents are addressed to the brothers, but this is no proof one way or the other. See AR XI, 140: 66.

92. AR IV kop. 126: 28. Hieronim Florian also asked Szmojło to use his contacts in Berlin to locate a court official or minister who would represent his interests for a fee: AR XI, 140: 60. See Karkucińska, *Anna z Sanguszków Radziwiłłowa*, 101.

93. Lipman Levy was the Court Jew of Ernst Johann von Biron, Duke of Courland (Latvia), from 1737. He was also an intimate of Prince Dmitriĭ Golitsyn, another influential figure at the court of Tsarina Anna Ivanovna. In the 1730s Lipman Levy (also known as Isaac Lipman) was granted the title Ober-Hof-Komissar and performed various services for the Russian court. He was expelled from Russia with the rest of its Jews in 1744 on the orders of Tsarina Elizabeth and the Senate. His commercial activities in Courland and on the Baltic coast brought him into contact with the Ickowicz brothers, who traded with him directly in St. Petersburg.

NOTES TO CHAPTER FOUR   233

This suggests that there might have been a small circle of Court Jews from Prussia eastward across the Baltic, a topic that is worth some study. The Radziwiłł archives contain correspondence between Anna Radziwiłł and Lipman (who appears under the name Liebman): AR IV, 45 kop. 627, letter 452; AR V, 8470. See also Zielińska, "Kariera i upadek," 39. On Lipman Levy see Gessen, "Lipman, Levi"; Wunderbar, *Geschichte der Juden*, 23. For a description of his career in the context of the activities of other Jews at the court of St. Petersburg in those years: Meisl, *Geschichte der Juden in Polen und Russland*, 74–80.

94. AR XI, 140: 69–70.

95. Ibid., 61.

96. See note 77.

97. See the letters of those years from Hieronim Florian to Szmojło in Königsberg: AR IV, 45, kop. 629. See also AR V, 13955–III, 8.7.1744.

98. AR IV, 45, kop. 628, 19–23; AR IV, 45, kop. 629: 31–32; and AR IV, 45, kop. 630: 124–25.

99. The contract dated November 23, 1739 can be found in AR X, "Czartoryski," n.p.

100. AR V, 2578: 15–18. The vast majority of the contracts and letters related to the brothers' river trade in Lithuania (to be found in AR XX) were signed in Stołpce.

101. AR V, 2578: 28; Biblioteka Czartotyskich, rkps. 5835, letter 15291. Szmojło also supervised the building and restoration of the Radziwiłł residences in Iwań (Ivan, Belarus), Niehniewicze (Niahnevichy, Belarus), and Słuck. Karkucińska, *Anna z Sanguszków Radziwiłłowa*, 66–75.

102. AR X, "Sanguszko": 98–110.

103. AR XX, 85: 9–11 (October 21, 1740). I should like to thank Ms. Silvia Noll for help in deciphering this text. Gdal Ickowicz does not appear on the list of the Court Jews of the king of Prussia given in Schnee's *Der Hoffinanz* or in Stern's *Court Jew*. On Szmojło's status see Schnee, *Der Hoffinanz*, 153. A Schutzjude was a Jew in possession of a personal privilege giving him the right to settle in a certain German town.

104. Heinrich von Brühl, the influential first minister and confidant of Augustus III, king of Poland and elector of Saxony.

105. These were royal domains near Kraków in Lesser Poland. There seems to have been a plan to lease the revenues of these estates to Gdal, perhaps with the goal of increasing them.

106. AR IV, 45, kop. 629: 115. The nobleman mentioned here seems to have been Jakub Wilczewski (1697–1780), a member of a prominent local noble family.

107. The last Jew to have reached the heights of acting as financial advisor to the royal family had been Ya'akov Betsal'el ben Natan, known in Polish as Becal. He had served King Jan III Sobieski in the early 1690s, before going bankrupt following a number of trials for corruption (he was acquitted). Kaźmierczyk, "Jakub Becal."

108. We know that Szmojło lived in Biała and Słuck, while Gdal and his family moved to Wołożyn in the early 1740s. No records of the composition of the community councils in these places have survived for these years. There are only two documents issued by the Lithuanian Jewish Council during the brothers' active period still extant, and they do not mention the names of its members. See Halperin, *Tosafot u-milu'im*, 63–64 (documents from 1739 and 1740).

109. AR XXIII, 9, kop. 3: 33; and AR V, 15782: 71–73.

110. See note 4. In an article that examined an outbreak of street violence in the community of Opatów in the mid-1740s, Hundert hypothesized that it was organized by the brothers (or those close to them) in opposition to the Landau family who controlled the local *kahal*. See Hundert, "Shkiy'at yira't kavod," 41–50.

111. February 27th, 1736.

112. For the Hebrew original, see NABRM 694, opis 4, 2201: 48. For a history of the Ginsburg family see Maggid, *Toledot mishpahat Ginsburg*. There is no reference to Shimon ben Yitzhak Ginsburg in that volume, so he may not, in the end, have received the post he wanted.

113. On the significance of the rabbinate for the estate administration, see Chapter Two.

114. Rabbi Naḥman Katz has not received much attention in the scholarly literature on the history of the Jews of Wilno, simply mentioned as a candidate for the post of rabbi of Wilno in 1750. Documents in the Radziwiłł archives indicate that he was appointed to the position for only a short time, in the mid-1740s, and that he was dismissed after the fall of the Ickowicz brothers. His litigation with the Wilno community over his financial losses evidently continued until 1750, which explains why some scholars assumed he was a candidate that year. See the letter referring to Naḥman's claims dated 1750: Fünn, *Kiryah ne'emanah*, 268. See also Maggid, *Vilna*, 17; Kloizner, "Yehudah, safra' ve-dayna'," 142–43. Naḥman's wife Deborah did not move to Wilno in the mid-1740s, but continued to live in Wołożyn, where she received letters addressed to the "wife of the rabbi of Wilno." AR V, 2473, passim, and AR XXIX, 5: 217.

115. Te'omim-Frankel received a royal confirmation that guaranteed him immunity from the *kahal's* debts: AGAD, Metryka Korona, Sigillata 25: 149v (12th March, 1744). The expenses undertaken by the Ickowiczes to obtain the post were extremely high. Szmojło gave Yeḥezkiel ben Binyamin Ze'ev Wolf of Tarnów a promissory note for 600 red złoty (equal to 10,800 złoty) to cover his expenses in procuring the rabbinate. It can be found in NABRM 694, opis 4, 2201: 57 and 80. For more on the affair: Balaban, *Theomim Fränkel*; and Bałaban, *Historja Żydów*, 273–90.

116. Bałaban, *Historja Żydów*, 283.

117. AR XX, 85: 50–51. On the existence of these private synagogues in Königsberg: Storm, "Culture and Exchange," 81–114.

118. AR IV, 45, kop. 629: 86–90.

119. Balaban, *Joseph Jonas Theomin-Fränkel*, 43.

120. See note 86.

121. "Madam Henia, [Szmojło's] wife, may she live a long life, also performed good services with His Highness the Duke, like Queen Esther." This document has been published a number of times. For a bibliography: Halperin, *Yehudim ve-yahadut*, 277 note 4.

122. AR V, 1334: 222 (7/8/1738). On Branicki's relations with Jews: Halperin, *Yehudim ve-yahadut*, 152–54; and Bałaban, *Historja Żydów*, 273 and 289–90.

123. AR IV, 45, kop. 637: 171–72; AR IV, 45, kop. 638: 445.

124. AR IV, 44, kop. 628: 84–86; AR V, 2578: 30.

125. AR V, 2578: 32. On August 20, 1741, August Czartoryski ordered the brothers to help the residents of his town of Wołożyn, which they were leasing, because it had burned to the ground.

126. See note 48.

127. AR V, 2578: 33–34.

128. AR V, 5597, n.p., 20/5/1742. The priest does not seem to have been removed immediately, because in August of that year he made a blood libel accusation against the brothers (i.e. accused them of killing a Christian child for ritual purposes) and tried to extort 200 thalers from them. See AR, 2578: 40.

129. AR XVII, 123: 21–23.

130. AR V, 2578: 24–25. See also Branicki's complaint that Szmojło had abused one of his Jewish traders and confiscated his merchandise: AR V, 1334: 205.

131. *Sefer Shivḥei Ha-Besht*, 274–275.

132. Jews on the Radziwiłł estates were likely ambivalent about the brothers, who, despite their obnoxious behavior, would sometimes help communities and individuals if they needed it. See, for example, Szmojło's letter to Anna Radziwiłł, in which he begs her to commute a death sentence given to a Jew: AR V, 15782: 89. See also Salomon Maimon's highly positive opinion of the brothers: *Solomon Maimon: An Autobiography*, 3.

133. AR IV kopie, 6, plik 6: 198.

134. Bałaban, *Historja Żydów*, 277–88. Conflict and competition over rabbinic posts was commonplace in the eighteenth century: Teller, "Tradition and Crisis?" 1–39.

135. Hedeman, *Dzisna and Druje*, 350.

136. AR IV, 30, kop. 417, letter 981; AR IV, 29, kop. 129: 33–35.

137. AR IV,128: 19–20; AR IV, 129: 31–32.

138. The rebellion has been studied by a number of historians, notably Israel Halperin (*Yehudim ve-yahadut*, 277–88) and Marion Lech ("Powstanie chłopów"). Halperin, who used both Jewish and non-Jewish sources, focused on the Ickowicz brothers as the cause of the uprising. Lech examined the affair in its specific Belarussian context, focusing on changes in the peasants' socioeconomic situation and the balance of power among the local nobility; he largely ignored the brothers. I shall here integrate both approaches and use a range of archival sources not examined in previous studies.

139. On this: Topolska, *Dobra szkłowskie*.

140. Zielińska, *Magnateria polska*, 81–82.

141. NABRM 694, opis 4, 1159: 9.

142. It was called the *sąd referendarski*. See Kaczmarczyk and Leśnodorski, *Historia państwa i prawa*, II: 203 and 459.

143. See *Historia chłopów*, I: 294.

144. Lech, "Powstanie chłopów," 317–19. Lech (320–22) sees the Radziwiłłs' harsh treatment of the local militia as another factor behind the revolt.

145. This was common across the Grand Duchy of Lithuania after the Great Northern War. Żabko-Potopowicz, *Praca najemna*, 70–112.

146. AR XXV, 1935.

147. See note 43.

148. The custom of *kolendy żydowskie*, based on a feudal obligation, is described in the memoirs of the nineteenth-century mayor of Dzików, Jan Słomka: "I recall that the custom still was in our village for the tavern keepers to make the rounds 'for presents,' each one calling on his customers—the ones who regularly sat and drank in his bar-room. The best known in Dzików was Solomon S. from Tarnobrzeg. On entering the house he would begin, 'God give you good fortune, that success may be yours, that health may favour you, that you may have money so that nothing may be lacking to you! I have come with my Good Wishes.' He would then pour out a tiny glass of vodka—he had plenty with him—and would treat every member of the family (except the smallest children), as well as the servants. . . . And if he expected a liberal gift, he would leave the bottle. For all this the farmer would give him something in his turn: a sack of grain—rye, barley, wheat, oats—whatever he could spare, while the good-wife brought out eggs, buckwheat, fowls, or anything under her hand. The giving of these gifts was held to be a duty, and if anyone gave stingily, Solomon would remind him of it in front of others. Whoever was generous would get praise, so as to encourage others in the good work. This sort of thing went on twice a year—once after Christmas 'for the Carol' and then after Easter 'for the Easter Gift.'" *From Serfdom to Self-Government*, 92–93.

149. AR XVII, 123: 5–12.

150. See AR IV kopie, 6, plik 7: 323, no. 23.

151. Kosman, *Historia Białorusi*, 136–41 and 193–94.

152. The Jews of Krzyczew received their community privilege from King Jan Kazimierz in 1664: AR XXV, 1932: 8–10 (confirmation from 1681). Jews had been living in eastern Belarus since at least the beginning of the seventeenth century. The privilege granted to the Jews of Kopyś by Bogusław Radziwiłł in 1645 noted that there had been a synagogue there for some time already: AR XXV, 1782/1: 383–85; and Goldberg, *Jewish Privileges*, II: 100–101.

153. AR XXIII, 33.

154. AR V, 7132: 5–7.

155. NABRM 694, opis 1159, 30.

156. On the changing attitudes towards the Cossack uprising, see Raba, *Between*

Remembrance and Denial, especially 201–41. Raba does not mention the uprising in Krzyczew.

157. The entire proclamation, found in AR V, 10725, was published by Lech, "Powstanie chłopów," 326.

158. Ibid.

159. Leviticus 26:44.

160. Halperin, ed., *Bet Yisrael be-Polin,* II: 272.

161. AR X "Gdal"; and Zielińska, "Kariera i upadek," 41.

162. AR IV, 45, kop. 628, 148.

163. AR IV kopie, 6, plik 7: 363–64.

164. AR VI:81–II. On the military aspects of the action see Lech, "Milicje Radziwiłłów," 33–60, especially 54–55.

165. See note 121. On "Little Purim" memorial days: Yerushalmi, *Zakhor,* 46–48.

166. AR XVII, 121. See AR IV, 45, kop. 628: 147.

167. AR IV kopie, 6, plik 7: 363–64.

168. AR IV kopie, 6, plik 9: 608–9.

169. NABRM 694, opis 4, 1163: 26a. There is no evidence that Karpatowicz succeeded in expelling the Jews.

170. See his letter (in French) dated March 19, 1748, to Hieronim Florian Radziwiłł: "Your sharp sight, my lord, will not allow you to ignore the fact that for around eight years, I have not held a single one of His Highness's estates." AR V, 5596: 1–3.

171. See the letters from his agent, Głębocki: AR V, 4273.

172. Radziwiłł wrote a note in his own hand and appended it to a stern letter to Szmojło: "Even though I gave orders to write you a letter of reproach, treasurer, I am doing so only for appearance's sake, so that people will not be suspicious." AR IV, 128: 24–25.

173. AR IV kopie, 6, plik 7: 308; AR IV, 128: 5–7.

174. AR IV kopie, 6, plik 8: 459.

175. AR V, 15782: 195–97, and AR IV, kopie, 425: 22–23.

176. In Polish, *kochany dzierżawco.* AR IV kop. 356: 8–11 and 16–18.

177. For the letters, see AR IV kop. 218, 425, 570, 637, 638, and 662.

178. AR IV, kop. 356: 36; AR IV, 630: 108–11, and NABRM 694, opis 7, 712: 96. Anna Radziwiłł even began one of her letters of censure to Szmojło as follows: "Treasurer, I am already cursing you in body and soul because there is no money to complete the church in Birże." AR IV, 628: 84.

179. AR IV, kop. 417, letter 978; AR IV kop. 630: 33–35.

180. See among others the correspondence with Jan Klemens Branicki and the *wojewoda* of Sandomierz: AR IV kop. 129: 1–10, 19; AR V, 1334–III: 260–61.

181. See notes 184 and 185. On the visit with the Radziwiłł family, see AR IV, kop. 630: 124–25. According to the letter Szmojło and his daughter spent the Sabbath in the family's palace.

182. AR V, 2578: 48.

183. AR X, "Sanguszko": 98–110.

184. See Schiper, "Żydzi w Tarnowie," 233. See also note 115. Arrests for nonpayment of debt were not unusual in this period.

185. AR IV kopie, 6, plik 8: 431 and AR IV kop. 630: 124–25. In this letter Anna Radziwiłł asks her son Michał Kazimierz to intercede with Sanguszko (her brother) for the release of Szmojło's daughter: AR IV kopie, 6, plik 9: 466.

186. Rosman, *The Lords' Jews*, 179–81; Zielińska, "Kariera i upadek," 48.

187. AR IV, kop. 630: 8–10, 64–66.

188. AR IV, 127: 75–77; AR IV, 129: 20–22 and 27–28.

189. See the report by Ludwig Schilling, Radziwiłł's agent: AR V, 15984–1, n.p., 13.4.1745.

190. AR IV, kop. 630, letters 876–78.

191. AR IV, 131: 22–24.

192. AR XXIII, 155: 59–60. The Hasidic text, *Sefer Shivḥei ha-Besht,* says that Szmojło and his family were planning to run away from Radziwiłł when they were arrested. Teller, "Masoret Slutzk," 15–38.

193. This is clearly suggested by Hieronim Florian's statement that recovering Słuck and the Neuburg estates cost him a total of 6,051,400 złoty—almost precisely the amount he demanded from Szmojło. Kotłubaj, *Galerja nieświeżka*, 427.

194. AR XXIII, 155: 59–60. The date that appears on both the document and the copy, June 15, must be a mistake. Zielińska argued that the actual date was July 5, but July 15 seems most likely.

195. AR IV kopie, 6, plik 9: 519–21, 541, 554, and 625; AR IV kop. 131: 40–42. On Szmojło's papers: AR IV kopie, 6, plik 9: 599.

196. AR IV kopie, 6, plik 9: 519.

197. Lists of those arrested can be found in AR VII, 707. On February 28, 1747, ninety-seven people were in detention. See Halperin, *Yehudim ve-yahadut*, 281.

198. AR V, 15984–II: 281.

199. AR IV kopie, 6, plik 9: 542, 556, and 629; and AR XXIX, 5: 217.

200. Balaban, *Joseph Jonas Theomin-Fränkel*, 43.

201. On this see Storm, "Culture and Exchange," 143.

202. Extensive documentation on the case can be found in NABRM 694, opis 14, 278. There are many letters about the case sent to Radziwiłł from Königsberg and Berlin by his agent, Ludwig Schilling: AR V, 15984.

203. December 19, 1746.

204. The Jewish National Library, Jerusalem, Manuscript Division, Heb 4° 927, 75a.

205. Ibid., 75–79. The entry on Yitzhak is at page 76b.

206. See the Glossary.

207. Emden, *Va-yakem 'edut*, 68a.

208. AR V, 8470.

209. AR V, 5596: 1–3.

210. During these same years, many European Court Jews were intensively engaged in efforts to persuade Maria Theresa to rescind her 1744 edict banishing the

Jews from Prague, Bohemia, and Moravia: Mevorah, "Ma'asei ha-hishtadlut," 125–64. However, this network of highly influential Jews did not attempt to intercede on Szmojło's behalf.

211. On Shmuel Zbytkower: Ringelblum, "Shmuel Zbytkover," 246–66, and 337–55; and Aust, Commercial Cosmopolitans," passim. On the career of Ya'akov Betsal'el ben Natan, a similar figure from the end of the seventeenth century, see note 107.

212. The Court Jews, on the other hand, enjoyed relative safety as long as the monarch they served was alive. Only when he died did their situation become precarious, as happened with Joseph Süss Oppenheimer. Stern, *The Court Jew*, 87–90.

213. While this more aggressively interventionist policy had much in common with that taking place in the Central Europe of the day, the goals were not the same. No attempt was made to restructure the estate economy as was happening in the German lands. The seigneurial economy served the Polish-Lithuanian magnates well and they were not interested in changing it, just exploiting it more intensively.

214. This does not mean that nobles totally rejected commercial activity. The very fact of being leaseholders forced them to engage in trade. Nonetheless, their basic antipathy to this form of economic activity meant that in most cases they did not develop the skills and expertise in it that the Jews did. See Gierszewski, "Magnaci i szlachta."

215. *Solomon Maimon: An Autobiography*, 3.

216. He paid 59,155 złoty and eight groszy for a two-year lease. AR XXV, 1624: 65–67. See also AR XXIX, 5: 100, 105, 203, 245–48, and 306. It seems likely that he signed the lease just before Szmojło was arrested.

217. The situation was different on the estates of the Sieniawski and Czartoryski families, who did employ a few Jews in administrative capacities: Rosman, *The Lords' Jews*, 143–84.

CHAPTER FIVE

1. If the estate was mortgaged to another noble, the owner lost all control over the monopoly leases derived from it, often treating it as if it formed part of a different latifundium entirely. NABRM fond 694, opis 4, teka 1593: 85.

2. AR XXV, 3839, no. 9.

3. AR XXV, 3839, no. 78. See also AR XXV, 2675, no. 65, and *Instrukcje gospodarze*, II: 314.

4. AR XXIX, 9, n.p., 11/1/1759.

5. NARBM 694, opis 7, teka 457: 4.

6. Radziwiłł's detailed plans for the development of the *ekonomia* may be found in AR XXV, 4169: 2–9. On the nature of the *ekonomia*, its inclusion in the Radziwiłł estates, and Jewish settlement there, see Chapter One.

7. Customs and tolls on trade were also key monopolies bringing income to the estate. AR XXV, 4169, nos. 3, 4, 5, 9, 12, and 20.

8. See also AR XXIX, 7: 487. This figure is considerably higher than that given

in Kula, *Szkice*, II: 321. Because Kula presents only estimates however, the figures given here, drawn from the contemporary *inwentarz*, are to be preferred. See AR XXV, 4172.

9. AR XXV, 4172. These figures are startlingly high and so raise questions as to their accuracy. Though they are drawn from the general accounts of the Szawle *ekonomia* as recorded in the *inwentarz*, they are not necessarily accurate. Nonetheless, they cannot but demonstrate a significant increase of some kind in the incomes from Szawle as well a much more intensive exploitation of the incomes from the *arenda*. The high percentages probably reflect the extremely run-down state of the *ekonomia* in the 1740s rather than stunning success in the 1760s. The jump in the proportion of the total income coming from the *arenda* is a faithful reflection of the importance these incomes had for the Radziwiłłs.

10. On the problematic nature of these sources see Kula, *Problemy i metody*, 600–606. See also Leskiewiczowa, "Inwentarze," 363–78.

11. For comparative purposes Rychlikowa brings data from the end of the eighteenth century dealing with eighteen estates in Małopolska. Her figures reveal that income from the *arenda* of *propinacja* made up some 21 percent of total estate income on average. This figure exceeded 30 percent in only five of the estates she studied. In ten estates it was between 10 percent and 30 percent, and in the remaining three, less than 10 percent. See Rychlikowa, *Produkcja zbożowa*, 217–28.

12. AR XXV, 4172: 677–81.

13. In fact even at the end of the period the proportion of the total income from Szawle that came from the *arenda* was one of the lowest to be found on the Radziwiłł estates (23 percent).

14. On this see the Introduction. The estates returned to the family's control in the 1740s.

15. Of the others, Dawidgródek and Dubińka were controlled by a different branch of the family, while the Szawle *ekonomia* was a royal estate and is an exceptional case.

16. For the lack of solid comparative data this can remain only a preliminary conclusion.

17. See note 9.

18. AR XXV, 1774.

19. AR XXV, 1791.

20. AR XXV, 2619 and AR XXV, 2626.

21. Topolska, *Dobra szkłowskie*, 71–75.

22. This kind of *arenda* was not unique to the Radziwiłł estates in this period; many of the magnate families instituted them. See Rapoport, *She'elot ve-teshuvot*, Hoshen Mishpat, no. 19; and Rosman, *The Lords' Jews*, 115–16.

23. NARBM 694, opis 3, teka 38: 1.

24. See the Introduction.

25. Rosman, "Ha-yaḥas," 239.

26. The Radziwiłł archive in Warsaw (AR) holds many such contracts in unit AR

XXIII, arranged by place. AR XI, arranged by family member, also contains some lease contracts. An important collection of this kind of contract from 1745–1764 is found in AR XXIX: 5–11, which contain the copies of the administrative orders, letters, and other materials issued by Michał Kazimierz Radziwiłł and his son.

27. In addition to noting the rights granted, the contracts also note the taverns in which the alcohol was to be sold.

28. These were generally water mills where estate inhabitants came to grind their grain into flour.

29. There are two versions of this schedule, the first from 1736 (NARBM 694, opis 3, teka 4487: 23–24), the second from 1759 (AR XXIX, 9, n.p., 6.2.1759).

30. See AR XXIX, 8: 48–49.

31. Other goods, including wool, leather, millet, mead, tobacco, tar, and oil, sometimes also appeared in this category without any explanation. See AR XXIX, 9, n.p., 8.9.1757.

32. In his regulations on keeping the Sabbath, Rabbi Yehuda Leib Puḥovitzer wrote, "the tax they called targowe, which is when [the merchants] give a little to the arenda from what they bring to market." Puḥovitzer, *Sefer kavod ḥakhamim*, 89–90. Puḥovitzer was born in Pińsk (Belarus) around 1630, served as rabbi and preacher both in Pińsk and in Słuck (which was on the Radziwiłł estates), and died in Jerusalem around 1700. See Nadav, *The Jews of Pinsk*, 233–35. On the regulations see Ben Sasson, "Takkanot," 183–206.

33. On the development of these charges in Lithuania and Belarus (including on the Radziwiłł estates there) during the sixteenth and seventeenth centuries see Alexandrowicz, "Miasteczka Białorusi i Litwy," 78–82.

34. These figures are taken from only two estates for which documentation has survived, and may not be representative.

35. The prohibition on milling outside the estates appears in almost every *arenda* contract. For the ban on the use of hand mills, see AR XXIX, 6: 62. In at least one case the contract instructed the *arendarze* to station overseers at the mills to keep an eye on payment collection: AR XXIX, 9, n.p., 24/6/1757.

36. AR XXIII, 6, n.p., For a similar case: AR V, 7170: 67.

37. AR XXIX, 9, n.p., 23/11/1757. See also AR XXV, 678: 47, no. 5; AR XXIX, 5: 609–12; AR IV kopie, 6, plik 7: 347–48; and *Akty izdavayemye vilenskogo komissieĭ* XXIX, 297–99.

38. See Rosman, *The Lords' Jews*, 115, note 30.

39. Rosman (123) found such cases on the Sieniwaski and Czartoryski estates. This does not mean that the Radziwiłł administration never exerted pressure on hesitant *arendarze* to persuade them to take a lease. See AR V, 15984 (7), n.p., 16.8.1751.

40. See AR V, 3407: 47–50 and 175–76; and AR V, 12424 (1), n.p., 28.12.1756 (since this letter deals with the lease of Mohilna (Mogil'no, Belarus), one of the *arendarze* it mentions might be Solomon Maimon's grandfather); AR V, 12424 (2), n.p., 7/5/1759; AR V, 15984 (7), n.p., 22/7/1755; and AR V, 16039, n.p., 11/9/1731.

41. See, for example, AR IV, kop. 470, list 2321; AR XXIX, 5: 469–70; AR XXIX, 6: 203–4 and 441; and NARBM, 694, opis 2, teka 4187: 24.

42. The series of contracts examined here, consisting of 95 different documents, were reconstructed from the economic instruction books kept by Michał Kazimierz Radziwiłł and his son Karol Stanisław, covering the period 1745–1764 (AR XXIX:5–11). In order to give as full a picture as possible, data were also used from three Radziwiłł estates outside Lithuania: Jampol, Pomarzany, and Żółkiew, all in Ukraine.

43. There was no uniform way of registering *aukcje* in the contracts. In some cases it was simply included in the price given, in others it was noted in a special clause. Since new contracts were simply copied from the old with only the overall price changed, it is often hard to tell whether the separate *aukcja* clauses represented a new rise or simply reflected an old one. This is particularly true when there is a break in the series of contracts.

44. These figures can be compared with those found by Rosman for *arenda* prices in the Sieniawa-Oleszyce estates in southeastern Poland in the period 1708–1726: 47 percent higher, 31 percent stable, 22 percent lower. The relatively large number of decreases may be explained by the fact that for most of this period Poland was involved in the Great Northern War with the attendant physical destruction and economic uncertainty. See Rosman, *The Lords' Jews*, 127.

45. For a list of these *aukcje*: AR XXIX, 9, n.p., 12/12/1758. The price of the *arenda* continued to rise steeply after 1758.

46. "[I]n addition, if on the Feast of John the Baptist in any of the three years of this, someone should offer an *aukcja* and the current *arendarz* is not willing to pay that amount into [Our] treasury, this contract is no longer valid and [the *arenda*] is to be transferred to the man who proposed the *aukcja*." AR XXIII, 4: 248. See also AR XXIX, 6: 376–78. Competition over *arenda*s is known from the sixteenth century, but seems to have become worse in the eighteenth. See Luria, *Responsa*, no. 35.

47. AR XXIX, 7: 173, 468–72 and 683–87; AR XXIX, 9, n.p., 25/6/1756, 9/10/1758 and 19/6/1760.

48. AR XXIX, 7: 115–19, 519, and 687–92; and AR XXIX, 9, n.p., 8/9/1757, 20/11/1758 and 1/8/1760.

49. AR XXIX, 6: 134 and 243–46. See also the two contracts for the Romanów general *arenda*, the first signed on 10/6/1756 after an annual *aukcja* of 166 thaler was offered, the second on 24/6/1756, when the *aukcja* was increased to 266 thaler. AR XXIX, 9, n.p., 10/6/1756 and 24/6/1756.

50. AR XXIX, 9, n.p., 18/6/1756; and NARBM, 694, opis 4, teka 1163: 170a. See also *Solomon Maimon: An Autobiography*, 38–41.

51. AR XXIX, 6: 226, and AR IV kop. 470, list 2321. This case concerns a Jew from Pomarzany in southeastern Poland, who traveled all the way to Biała Podlaska in order to offer an *aukcja*. In another case an *arendarz* tried to prevent a competitor from approaching Radziwiłł directly: AR V, 16039, n.p., 11/9/1731.

52. AR V, 6943 (II): 43–46, 17/6/1723.

53. See, for example, AR XXIX, 5: 229–30, and AR XXIX, 9, n.p., 25/12/1756. The willingness of the *arendarze* to go on paying new *aukcje* on a regular basis, even though their ability to raise prices on the monopoly rights they leased was limited, is a clear sign just how profitable the *arenda* business was.

54. NARBM, 694, opis 4, teka 1163: 70. This kind of wild competition was by no means unique to the Radziwiłł estates and was found everywhere in the Polish-Lithuanian Commonwealth where Jews made their living from *arenda*.

55. The principle of possessors' rights and particularly its use by the Jews of the Polish-Lithuanian Commonwealth awaits detailed study. In the meantime see the discussion of its halakhic sources in Fram, *Ideals Face Reality*, 270–314. See also Katz, *Tradition and Crisis*, 73–76.

56. "Cases concerning *arenda* or [leases] of customs and duties, whether from the King or a nobleman, are to be decided not by the rabbinic court, but by the community leaders." *Pinkas Medinat Lita*, no. 66; also nos. 73–78, 102, 121, 295, 308, 404, 661, and 809. See also Sirkes, *She'elot ve-teshuvot ha-bah ha-yeshanot*, no. 61; Gomer, *Beiträge*, 44–45.

57. This was the situation in the Boćki community, for example. See Archiwum Główne Akt Dawnych, Archiwum Roskie 321 and 137, also 140. See also the announcement published by the Council of Four Lands in 1676: "No Jew, whoever he may be, may . . . lease any rights . . . whether from the nobility or from the Royal Treasury, such as arendas, czopowe, duties . . . and so on . . . without the knowledge and permission of the [local] community." *Pinkas Va'ad Arba Ha'aratzot* 148, no. 352.

58. See Mahler, *Toledot ha-yehudim*, 199 and 359, and Shmeruk, "Ha-ḥasidut," 185.

59. See Nadav, "Le-toledot ha-hityashvut," 717–24.

60. This was not the only issue on which the magnate was interested in weakening communal authority. See Chapter Two. Though the communities did what they could to maintain economic discipline over possessors' rights since it was in the best interests of the Jewish businessmen themselves, they were largely ineffective. See Shmeruk, "Ha-ḥasidut," 182–85.

61. AR XXIX, 6: 310. The Radziwiłłs were by no means the only magnate family opposed to the imposition of possessors' rights: Bershadskiĭ, *Litovskiye Yevrei*, 31–34.

62. AR XXIX, 7: 659; AR XXIX, 8: 41.

63. AR XXIII, 9, plik 1, n.p., 14/8/1755; AR XXIX, 9, n.p., 18/4/1759.

64. AR XXIX, 5–11, passim. It was also not uncommon for the general *arendarz* not to pay his debt to Radziwiłł on the date specified in the lease but to roll it over to the next payment and continue doing so until the end of the lease.

65. The *arendarz* had no say in who was to be paid; this was the sole province of Radziwiłł and his family. Even his most senior administrators could not issue payment orders. AR XXIX, 9, n.p., 19/4/1757.

66. AR XXIX, 9, n.p., 19/4/1757.

67. AR XXIII, 146: 107 and 110.

68. AR XXIX, 9, n.p., 9/4/1756.

69. AR XXIX, 9, n.p., 21/9/1756.

70. AR XXIX, 6: 276.

71. AR XXIX, 5: 86 and 159–60; AR XXIX, 7: 875; AR XXIX, 9, n.p., 23/11/1757; and AR V, 15467, n.p., 18/12/1746.

72. AR V, 7170: 98–101. See Rosman, *The Lords' Jews*, 129, note 73.

73. AR XXIX, 7: 89 and 476; AR XXIII, 4: 277; AR XV, 20, plik 4, n.p.; NARBM 694, opis 2, teka 4187: 4; and NARBM 694, opis 3, teka 4487: 13–22.

74. On this trade, see Chapter Six.

75. AR XV, 20, plik 4, no. 3, n.p.

76. See Bergerówna, *Księżna pani*, 319.

77. AR XV, 20, plik 4, no. 3, n.p.

78. AR XXIX, 7: 449.

79. AR XXIX, 9, n.p., 2/5/1757.

80. Kamieńska, *Manufaktura szklana*, 173.

81. AR XXIII, 4: 292. On the importance of drinking as part of the activities of the *sejmik* (the local noble assembly): Kitowicz, *Opis obyczajów*, 473–75.

82. AR XXIX, 7: 497–506; AR XXIX, 9, n.p., 13/8/1757; AR XXIII, 150, n.p., 10/6/1755; and AR XI, 222: 2–8.

83. See Rosman, "Ha-yaḥas," 239. The paucity of sources about secondary *arendarze* in the Radziwiłł archives is explained by the fact that contracts and all accounts were made with the general *arendarz* and not with Radziwiłł himself, so the documentation was not preserved in the family archive. For a description of this group based largely on Hasidic literature, see Halamshtok, "Der yiddisher lebenshteiger," 86–98.

84. This does not mean that Maimon's grandfather leased the entire estate, but rather that he leased the income from all these installations as part of his arenda. This arenda formed part of the general *arenda* of Mir. I have here corrected the English version of the autobiography, which translates the German term "Pacht" incorrectly as "farm."

85. *Solomon Maimon: An Autobiography*, 6–11.

86. Ibid. On the situation in Żukowy Borek see the report on the Mir general *arenda* from 1733: "two taverns are in a terrible state and totally run-down, one is in Żukowica, the other in Żukowy Borek." AR XXIII, 94, plik 1, n.p., 13/9/1733. For more detail on the historical background to Maimon's descriptions see Teller, "Zikhronot," 1–10.

87. *Solomon Maimon: An Autobiography*, 7.

88. AR XXIII, 150, n.p.

89. Goldberg, *Ha-ḥevrah ha-yehudit*, 232–40. For a social analysis of the village *arendarze* see Mahler, *Toledot ha-yehudim*, 249–53.

90. On this see Chapter Three.

91. Leskiewiczowa, *Próba analizy*, 42–43.

92. AR XXIII, 4: 321. See also Leszczyński, *Żydzi ziemi Bielskiej*, 135–37.

93. AR XXIX, 8: 72 and 76–80, and AR XI, 222: 2–8. See also Ringelblum, *Projekty i próby*, 17–18; Podraza, "Żydzi i wieś," 255–65; and Maroszek, "Żydzi wiejscy," 56–70.

94. AR XXV, 2622: 231–32; AR IV kopie, 6, plik 9: 608–9; and AR XXIII, 149, n.p., no. 10. In many cases the rural *arendarz* did not have enough capital to grant loans, so he borrowed from the local nobles and lent the money at a higher interest rate to the peasants. See also AR XXIX, 5: 469–70, a report that peasants were taking loans directly from the local nobility in the Kamieniec Litewski *starostwo*.

95. See Alexandrowicz, "Miasteczka Białorusi i Litwy," 97–140. On the issue of the connections between the village and the wider market see Rusiński, "O rynku wewnętrznym," 137–40.

96. On this see Kula, *An Economic Theory*, 68–69 and 135–36.

97. Alexandrowicz, "Miasteczka Białorusi i Litwy," 125, and Ringelblum, *Projekty i próby*, 9. Ringelblum mentions a great deal of anger and bitterness among the peasants who were forced into this arrangement.

98. AR IV kopie, 6, plik 9: 608–09; AR XIX, 8: 72 and 76–80; and AR IV, 132: 5–12. See also Bergerówna, *Księżna pani*, 149.

99. Baranowski, *Życie codzienne*, 177–79; Baranowski, *Polska karczma*, 12–45; Burszta, *Wieś i karczma*, 164–65. See also the criticism voiced by the preacher, Zvi Hirsh Koidanover of those who build: "a house or a special room where the goyim can drink, play, and whore—[a sin] that many [Jews] in Poland and Lithuania fail in." The Yiddish version of this reads a little differently: "and obviously when [a Jew], God Forbid, builds a whore house or a tavern for goyim where they can dance and leap, guzzle and swill, as we see for our sins in some places in Poland and Lithuania." *Sefer kav ha-yashar*, no. 24, 52b–53a.

100. Goldberg, *Ha-ḥevrah ha-yehudit*, 347. This duality found expressions in many works of Polish literature from the nineteenth century. See Opalski, *The Jewish Tavern-Keeper*, especially 11–20.

101. NARBM, 694, opis 4, teka 1163: 23. See also AR XIX, U V, 2: 15, and Rosman, *The Lords' Jews*, 115.

102. The dwarf mentioned in the text was brought to the residence of the local administrator, where closer inspection revealed that she had already grown enough not to be considered abnormal. Radziwiłł ordered that she be sent back home: AR V, 7170: 98.

103. The issue of the urban *arenda* has received little attention in the literature. Almost the only study devoted to it is Goldberg, *Ha-ḥevrah ha-yehudit*, 241–50.

104. "[A]s is the custom on my estates, I grant the right of free alcohol sale to everyone, once mutual agreement has been reached on the payment due to the *arendarze*—to the satisfaction of both sides, the mass of the [Christian] townspeople and the *arendarze*." AR XXIX, 8: 70. See also AR XXIX, 9, n.p., 11/7.1760, and AR IV kopie, 6: 435. In Żółkiew the cost of the licenses payment was 1,000 złoty, of which the municipal council paid 400 złoty for the Christian alcohol vendors and the kahal paid 600 złoty for the Jewish vendors. In the small town of Czartoryska the *arendarz* was paid by each of the vendors 15 złoty per hundred quarts of plain vodka they sold. AR XXIX, 7: 385.

105. In Słuck the *arendarz*'s tavern was distinguished from the others by being

called "kabak" (i.e., the Belarusian rather than the usual Polish term for an inn). Normally the beer and vodka sold there were made from grain supplied by the estate.

106. AR XXV, 3837 and AR XXV, 3838; see also Chapter One. Słuck was one of the largest and most important Jewish communities in the Council of Lithuania alongside Brześć, Pińsk, Grodno, and Wilno.

107. AR XXIII, 158, n.p., 24/3/1753. A *miednica* was about 34 liters' and one tynf was equal to one złoty and eight grosze. The price of a *miednica* of plain vodka was fixed at 18 złoty, which means that the tavern's profit margin was about 15 percent.

108. Two years later Radziwiłł ordered the *arendarze* of the *licenty* incomes to do these things. AR XXIII, 158, n.p., 1/9/1755.

109. AR XXIII, 158, n.p., 24/3/1753. This kind of institution was not unique to Słuck. Something similar, called a "kaffenhauz," was to be found in the town of Kock and probably also in other towns where magnate residences were to be found. See Bergerówna, *Księżna pani*, 160–62, and Baranowski, *Polska karczma*, 32–35.

110. See AR XI, 222: 7.

111. "A record of the plain vodka—how much was measured and given to the Słuck tavern." NARBM, 694, opis 2, teka 7421: 18.

112. Celebrated by the locals on May 4 according to the Gregorian calendar.

113. "Detailed daily sales in the Słuck tavern and the amount paid by it to the lord's treasury from the first of January to the first day of July in 1750"; ibid., 25–27. This list contains only details of the plain vodka sold in the tavern, so it reflects only part of its income.

114. At first glance this figure seems very high, but it can be compared with the description of Dov Ber of Bolechów (Bolekhiv, Ukraine) of the takings in one of the best weeks of his time as *arendarz* of that town: "and we took for vodka a few hundred złoty." Birkenthal, *Zikhronot R. Dov Ber*, 99. Bolechów was a much smaller and poorer town than Słuck, so a weekly take of 1,200 złoty in Słuck may not be unreasonable.

115. This is a Yiddish word meaning a tenant. In Polish it can mean a bailiff. The precise sense in which it used here is unclear.

116. On Pohovitzer himself and these regulations, see note 36.

117. AR XXIII, 158, n.p., 24/6/1753.

118. It is called by the usual Polish term, *dom gościnny*, which literally means guest house.

119. That is, the one managed by Mordechai ben Ya'akov.

120. See also Hundert, *The Jews in a Polish Private Town*, 64–67.

121. This was a popular policy among most of the noble owners of towns. See Matuszewicz, *Diariusz*, I: 81, 117, and 365; and Rosman, *The Lords' Jews*, 79–80. Princess Anna Jabłonowska went so far as to advertise the fairs on her estates in a Warsaw newspaper. See Begerówna, *Księżna pani*, 145.

122. "[B]ut as for the secondary *arendarze*, they should not have any business in the surrounding villages, but just in the town, in order to give the markets and the fairs a stronger basis." AR XXIX, 8: 70–74.

123. NARBM, 694, opis 4, teka 1163: 13b–14a; AR IV kopie, 6, plik 9: 608b–609b.

124. "All my subjects on the Jampol estate must travel to the markets and fairs in Jampol and sell there what they have to sell, in order to give its markets and fairs a stronger basis." AR XXIX, 9, n.p., 23/11/1757. See also AR IV kopie, 6, plik 7: 347–48 and AR XXIX, 5: 609–12, no. 4.

125. For example, "that the present—and future—*arendarze* should not receive their contracts from my officials but from me myself." AR XXIX, 9, n.p., 9/10/1758. See also AR XXIX, 11, n.p., 14/8/1763; NARBM, 694, opis 3, teka 38: 1–6.

126. AR XXIX, 9, n.p., 17/10/1756; AR XXIX, 7: 271 and passim. There are also other indications of differences in status between *arendarze* (especially general *arendarze*) and the ordinary members of the Jewish communities. See below.

127. "Those *arendarze*, by virtue of their function, I take under my immediate protection, and free them from every jurisdiction, reserving them for my court alone." NARBM, 694, opis 3, teka 38: 1–6. See also AR XXIX, 7: 394–99, and AR XXIX, 9, n.p., 9/10/1758. Even though the rabbinic courts are not expressly mentioned here, it is hard to imagine that this order did not extend to them too. Even if the *arendarze* agreed voluntarily to use the rabbinic courts in cases between them and other Jews, this order freed them from having to obey a verdict with which they disagreed.

128. NARBM, 694, opis 3, teka 38: 1–6. In all references to this issue it was always made clear that the exemption did not cover taxes imposed by the state authorities.

129. AR XXIX, 8: 65b; AR XXIX, 9, n.p., 8/9/1757; AR XXIII, 131, n.p.; and AR IV kopie, 6, plik 9: 608b–09b.

130. AR IV, 20: 253; AR XXIX, 5: 228–29 and 523; AR XXIX, 7: 687–92; and AR XXIX, 9, n.p, 17/1/1756.

131. See, for example, the complaints about payment difficulties, AR XXIII, 93, plik 1.

132. AR XXIX, 5: 211–17 and 222–27, and AR XXIII, 131, n.p., *Arendarze* engaging in agricultural activity were common in the eastern regions of the Polish-Lithuanian Commonwealth. See Goldberg, "Rolnictwo wśród Żydów," 62–88. The eighteenth-century English traveler William Coxe, who visited Lithuania in the 1770s, commented, "this perhaps is the only country in Europe where Jews cultivate the ground: in passing through Lithuania we frequently saw them engaged in sowing, reaping, mowing, and other works of husbandry." Coxe, *Travels into Poland*, 270.

133. AR XXIX, 7: 866, and AR XXIX, 9, n.p., 1/12/1758 and 20/11/1758. These perks are somewhat reminiscent of the payments in kind that were an integral part of the salary of Radziwiłł's estate administration officials. See Chapter Three.

134. AR XXIX, 7: 641–42, and 767; AR XXIX, 9, n.p., 6/11/1759 and 3/8/1760.

135. AR XXIX, 5: 72–73; AR XXIX, 6: 204–6; AR XXIX, 7: 549; and AR XXIX, 9: n.p., 2/12/1757. When peasants did their corvée labour for the *arendarz* in the manufacture of vodka, the question arose of what was to be done with them on the Jewish Sabbath, when the distilleries were kept closed. Radziwiłł's solution was to have the

peasants work on cleaning one of his palaces on those days. See AR XXIX, 7: 292–96 and 682; AR XXIX, 8: 8b–9a; and AR V, 12424, n.p., 15/12/1752. On the phenomenon of peasant corvée labor for Jewish *arendarze*, see Goldberg, *Ha-ḥevrah ha-yehudit*, 159–70.

136. AR XXIII, 93, plik 1, n.p.; AR XVII, 123: 39–95. See also the discussion on the causes of the 1740 peasant revolt in Chapter Four.

137. AR V, 15467, n.p., 18/12/1746; AR XXIX, 9, n.p., 25/12/1756; and NARBM, 694, opis 4, teka 1159: 70.

138. AR XXIX, 9, n.p., 12/8/1756.

139. AR V, 7132: 5–7. See also the discussion of relations between the *arendarze* and the orthodox clergy below.

140. AR XXIX, 7: 492–97; AR V, 15467, n.p., 18/12/1746; AR XXIII, 137: 113; and National Library of Israel, Jerusalem, Manuscript Department Heb 4° 103: 490. On the use of violence by Jews: "in running their business and managing their affairs, the Jews stood firm on their rights and were not averse to the use of physical force and personal injury." Nadav, "Ma'asei 'alimut," 45 and 51–56.

141. AR XXIX, 9, n.p., 9/12/1758. See also AR XXIX, 9, n.p., 11/12/1756, and 28/6/1758.

142. For a discussion of this, see Kula, *Measures and Men*, 127–55; Mielczarski, *Rynek zbożowy*, 71–87.

143. AR XXIX, 5–11, passim. This was by no means unique to the Radziwiłł estates.

144. The contracts from Dawidgródek and Słuck are exceptional in this regard. The former states explicitly, "the aforementioned *arendarze* must sell the vodka for 12 groszy per marked quart . . . not at a higher price and not in a smaller measure." AR XI, 222: 2–8.

145. "[T]he price of drink in the whole Duchy of Kopyś must be calculated from the rise or fall in grain [prices]": AR XXIX, 9, n.p., 9/10/1758. See also AR XXIII, 150, n.p., 10/6/1750; and AR XI, 222: 2–8. In most cases the instructions do not specify how much grain the *arendarz* should use in the manufacture of vodka, simply stating that the vodka should be "good" or "of good quality." This might have been a loophole for the *arendarz* that allowed him to invest less in manufacturing the vodka and so increase his profit margins on each sale.

146. Kula, *Measures and Men*, 145.

147. See, for example, AR XXIX, 9, n.p., 6/2/1759.

148. AR XXIX, 9: n.p., 25/6/1756 and 25/12/1756; and AR XXV, 3552: 19.

149. Radziwiłł ordered that all the merchants in his town use the municipal scales; the use of any others would lead to a fine. AR XXV, 3553: 19.

150. They were not the only responsible parties, however. The estate administration was charged with supervising both the stamped weights and the Jews who used them. NARBM 694, opis 4, teka 1193: 11; and AR XXV, 2622: 232.

151. In his Sabbath regulations Rabbi Yehuda Leib Puḥovitzer described the process thus, "Those who hold the noble lord's weights: Everyone who needs to weigh

something comes and takes the weights from the Jew's house and afterwards returns them to the Jew, paying him a fee." See note 32. On the *arendarz's* responsibility for ensuring "fair" (i.e., uniform) weights see AR XIX, 5: 222–27, no. 12.

152. See Mielczarski, *Rynek zbożowy*, 72. In the largest towns on the Radziwiłł estates, like Słuck, where the townspeople retained greater rights than in smaller ones, responsibility for the scales remained with the municipal council. See AR XXIX, 9, n.p., 13/6/1760. In Kopyś, it was the *wójt* who held this responsibility: AR XXV, 1789: 8.

153. Despite this, manipulation of the weights was frowned upon. In places where the Jewish community leased the town *arenda* in order to let it on a sublease and so make a profit, responsibility for the scales remained with the *kahal*. See *Zikhronot Dov Ber*, 68. The 1761 regulations of the Lithuanian Jewish Council rule, "The Rabbi of each community must put the matter of weights and measures in order. All the shops and alcohol vendors must have uniform measures; inspectors should be appointed to [check] this." *Pinkas Medinat Lita*, no. 964. See also *Pinkas Tiktin*, no. 185, paragraphs 23–24.

154. See, for example, the complaint against Joshua ben Michael, the previous general *arendarz* of Świerżeń, in AR V, 15467, n.p., 18/12/1746. The psychological influence that the *arendarz* had on the non-Jewish townspeople (especially in their dealings with Jews) should not be underestimated, since he was clearly acting as Radziwiłł's representative in the urban market.

155. See Rosman, *The Lords' Jews*, 109.

156. Ibid. See also the petitions on this issue in AR XXIII, 149.

157. NARBM, 694, opis 2, teka 2281: 97; AR XXIII, 93, "Propinacja miejska": 40–42; AR XXIII, 149, n.p., which is a 1762 report of the committee established to check the state of the Radziwiłł estates following the death of Michał Kazimierz Radziwiłł. Among other things it revealed that the general *arendarze* from Kopyś were dragging out payment of a debt of 23,000 tynf.

158. The only *arendarz* whom Michał Kazimierz Radziwiłł seems to have threatened directly was Joshua ben Michael, the Świerżeń *arendarz*: AR XXIX, 7: 882 and 890.

159. AR XXIX, 5: 427.

160. AR XXIX, 8: 84b. In another case Radziwiłł ordered the local *kahal* to sell all the property belonging to the son and the son-in-law of a general *arendarz* who had fled and to use the money to cover his debts: AR XXIX, 7: 647.

161. AR XXIX, 7: 86–87 and 710; and AR V, 3407: 51–54.

162. AR XXIX, 8: 91a–b; and AR V, 12424, n.p., letters from 4/3/1752 and 11/3/1752.

163. AR XXIX, 7: 836–37. See also Goldberg, *Ha-ḥevrah ha-yehudit*, 159–70.

164. See AR XXIX, 9, n.p., 29/12/1756; and *Solomon Maimon: An Autobiography*, 40. In the general *arenda* contract from Ołyka in Volhynia, the general *arendarze* had a special clause inserted giving themselves the exclusive right to collect debts from secondary *arendarze*: AR XXIX, 9, n.p., 27/1/1757.

165. Goldberg, *Ha-ḥevrah ha-yehudit*, 241–50.

166. AR XXIX, 7: 492–97, and AR XIX, 9, n.p., 20/11/1758.

167. In particular, Rosman, *The Lords' Jews*.

168. Mahler, *Toledot ha-yehudim*, 168–75.

169. See Chapter Three.

170. AR IV kopie, 6: 573b; AR IV kop. 253, letter 308; and AR IV kop. 252, letter 269. See the Introduction, note 32. The Radziwiłł archives contain documentation of a case involving the noble Marcin Matuszewicz, who was accused of attacking a Jewish woman *arendarka* and stealing a quantity of ox wool from her. He was eventually forced to recompense her: AR XXIX, 5: 245 and AR V, 7170: 62. This incident is not mentioned in Matuszewicz's autobiography.

171. AR XXIX, 9, n.p., 12/8/1756; AR V, 7170: 98–101.

172. This is especially true in the case of the secondary *arendarze* who did not enjoy Radziwiłł's protection and so found it much harder to defend themselves from the attacks of a hostile nobility. See AR XXIII, 137: 113; AR XXIX, 5: 245; and *Solomon Maimon: An Autobiography*, 8–10.

173. There does not seem to have been a difference between Orthodox and Catholic priests in this regard. On its own estates the Roman Catholic Church was prepared to lease the right of *propinacja* to Jewish *arendarze*.

174. AR XXIX, 9, n.p., 7/1/1756 and 14/11/1760. In one case, the priest in the small town of Wizuń (presumably to be identified as Wiżuny [Vyžuonos, Lithuania]) persuaded a member of the estate administration to support him, even though his activity had caused a drop in *arenda* income: AR IV kopie, 6: 573b.

175. AR IV kopie, 6: 428a, 573b.

176. *Regesty i nadpisy*, no. 1765; AR V, 15782: 68–69.

177. AR V, 7132: 5–7.

178. Ibid.

179. *Solomon Maimon: An Autobiography*, 14–17. In any discussion of relations between the *arendarze* and the priests, as between any groups on the estates, we must bear in mind that the sources pay greater attention to conflict than cooperation.

180. See Kaźmierczyk, "The Problem of Christian Servants," 23–40. In addition to everyday help, Christian servants could be very useful as partners for the sale of *hametz* at Passover. See Shmuel bar Elkana, *Sefer makom Shmuel*, "Orah haim," no. 17, 31–32.

181. There is a great deal of documentation from Słuck on this issue. See especially the complaints in AR XXIII, 137, passim. See also NARBM, 694, opis 4, teka 1163: 13a–14a. On the canon law basis for this argument see Chazan, *Church, State, and Jew*, 27–35; and Weinryb, *The Jews of Poland*, 130–31. On the use of this argument as part of the struggle of the Lithuanian towns against Jewish trade, see Schiper, *Dzieje handlu*, 205–10.

182. See Michal Kazimierz Radziwiłł's warning to the townspeople of Łachwa not to impede the *arendarze* in the town: AR XXIII, 149, n.p., 24/1/1729.

183. The medieval system of handing over an inn to a peasant in perpetuity in exchange for a fixed annual sum had not entirely disappeared however. See AR XXIX, 6: 128 and 344–45; and AR XXIX, 7: 149–50. In these cases the peasant received a

ruined tavern and in return promised to rebuild it. The annual payment was not made directly to Radziwiłł but to the general *arendarz*. There were also some very rare cases when monopoly rights were leased to a non-Jew: AR XXIX, 5: 575–83; AR XXIX, 8: 42b; and AR XXIII, 146: 124.

184. He was not always a complete outsider. On occasion even intimate relations could develop, as the manager of one *folwark* reported: "The scribe Szawelkiewicz has returned . . . and reported that a young Jew living with the *arendarz* of Laplówka has got the Christian maid working there pregnant." AR XXIII, 146: 9.

185. These feelings are clearly expressed in one of the petitions that the peasants of Kopyś sent to their lord: "we would add 1,000 złoty so that no Jew would rule over a Christian." AR XXIII, 33, n.p., n.d. See also AR XVII, 123: 42.

186. See note 135.

187. See the discussion of the 1740 peasant rebellion in Krzyczew in Chapter Four.

188. See, for example, AR XXIX:, 8: 20b–21a; and AR XXIII, 4: 282. Such clauses were not unique to the Radziwiłł estates: Inglot, "Organizacja folwarku," 115–16.

189. AR XXIII, 149, passim.

190. AR XVII, 123: 5–12, no. 5.

191. A large collection of peasant complaints and petitions may be found in AR XXIII, 33. Only a very few of them mention Jews. For another collection see AR XVII, 123. The letters there deal mostly with the activities of the Ickowicz brothers, who acted as Jewish *dzierżawcy*. Their economic policy was quite exceptional and unlike that of the noble leaseholders. See Chapter Four.

192. AR XXIII, 149, n.p., n.d., a petition sent by the general *arendarz* of Korelicze.

193. Of course the general *arendarze* continued to pay taxes to the Commonwealth's central authorities.

194. "We, the undersigned leaders of the community pledge [together] with the leaders of the *arendarze* . . . " National Library of Israel, Jerusalem, Manuscript Department Heb 4° 103, 473. See also Alexandrov, "Derzhavtses," 121–24.

195. See the surety for the *arendarze* of Biała signed by the local community in AR XXIII, 9, plik 1, n.p., 14/8/1755. See also *Pinkas Kahal Tiktin*, no. 139.

196. AR XXIX, 9, n.p., 29/6/1760. On the dismissal of such a bookkeeper by an *arendarz*, see AR V, 3407: 104–6.

197. Weinryb, "Kavim le-toledot ha-kalkalah," 90–113.

198. In his study of the Jews of Opatów, *The Jews in a Polish Private Town*, 96–97, Hundert notes that income from the *kropka* disappeared from the communal budget in the second half of the eighteenth century. It may be that there too the *kropka* was included in the general *arenda*. This whole issue needs further study.

199. See the complaint of the Biała community on this issue: AR XXIII, 146: 117a.

200. The National Library of Israel, Jerusalem, Manuscript Department Heb 4° 103, 473. This was an issue on estates other than the Radziwiłłs'. See Goldberg, "Tlutan ve'atzmautan," 141–46.

201. AR XXIX, 7: 271. See also Shmuel bar Elkana, *Sefer makom Shmuel*, no. 105, 112–14. Arguments about the communities' jurisdiction over neighboring towns and villages were nothing new in the eighteenth century. See Dubnow, "Va'ad 'arba' aratzot," 250–61; Halperin, *Yehudim va-yahadut*, 139–51; and Nadav, "Aspekty," 75–80.

202. "We . . . leaders of the community . . . with the leaders of the *arendarze* . . . have drawn up a register of the settlements [under our jurisdiction] from the poll-tax [records] . . . and we have given it to the above *arendarze*. The *arendarze* have received authority from the kahal only for collecting the above register. The *arendarze* have permission to use all the exactions, punishments, and collection methods until they have received the whole sum [owed them]." See note 200. A similar arrangement was also in force in the Tykocin community: *Pinkas Tiktin*, no. 64.

203. AR XXIX, 9, n.p., 10/9/1757 and 29/9/1758. See also Goldberg, "Tlutan ve'atzmautan," 141–46.

204. In the Horki community in Belarus the *arendarze* demanded official representation on the community council. See National Library of Israel, Jerusalem, Manuscript Department Heb 4° 920, 29. In another case the *arendarz* of the Kamieniec Litweski *starostwo* offered to pay 70 czerwony złoty (about 1,260 złoty) to acquire the post of rabbi for the candidate he supported: AR V, 7170: 91.

205. See Chapter Three.

206. In the contracts the general *arenda* is given the name of the estate to which the rights pertained: for example, the Mir general *arenda* or the Biała general *arenda*.

CHAPTER SIX

1. See Chapter Five.

2. In her research on an estate in Małopolska, Leskiewiczowa noted that approximately a quarter of its grain production was sold directly on the market (another quarter was used for *propinacja* and a half was used for food by the farm population and so not sold). See Leskiewiczowa, *Próba analizy*, 56. On some occasions *folwark* produce was used in place of money to pay salaries.

3. See Guldon, *Związki handlowe*.

4. According to the inventories in AR XXV, labor levels did not exceed two or three days a week in the mid-eighteenth century.

5. On the economy of eastern Belarus, see Topolska, "Peculiarities," 37–49.

6. See Czapliński and Długosz, *Życie codzienne*, 105–28.

7. For data on Michał Kazimierz Radziwiłł's purchases for himself, his court, and his latifundium, see AR XXIX, 5–11, passim.

8. The tendency to restrict estate merchants from attending external fairs generated a lively internal trade on the latifundium. Especially important were the ties between eastern Belarus and the markets in Mir and Nowy Świerżeń. See NABRM 694, opis 4, 1159: 337–38; AR V, 15467, n.p., 18.12.1746; and AR XIX, U II, 9: 2. See also AR IV kopie, 6, plik 9: 608–9, and Kamieńska, *Manufaktura szklana*, 192.

9. AR XXIX, 5: 622–28; AR XXIX, 9, n.p., 22/4/1757. The volume of such trade

on the Radziwiłł estate was limited. On the cattle trade in general see Baszanowski, *Z dziejów handlu.*

10. Some merchants, particularly from eastern Belarus, sent goods down the Dwina River to sell in Rīga. See AR XX, 80: 1–35; AR XX, 81; and AR V, 12424 (II), n.p., 24.2.1762.

11. A corollary of this policy was the family's encouragement of the fairs held by the towns on the estate. See Grochulska, "Jarmarki," 799. There were major fairs in the following towns on the Radziwiłł family estates in western Belarus: Słuck, Nieśwież, Nowy Świerżeń, Mir, Dawidgródek, and Łachwa. A fairly broad selection of goods was available in Nowy Świerżeń, the main port for the river trade with Königsberg, and in Słuck, where Hieronim Florian Radziwiłł had his principal residence. See NABRM 694, opis 3, 4487: 23–24; AR XXIX, 9, n.p., 6.2.1759; and AR XXIX, 10, n.p., 12.12.1762.

12. AR XXV, 678: 46–47. In addition the Radziwiłłs did not hesitate to intervene and restrict what merchants sold if they believed that it was detrimental to their interests or to public order and safety. For example, in 1751, Michał Kazimierz Radziwiłł issued a proclamation to the communities of Nieśwież and Mir, forbidding stall owners to trade in poisons: AR XXIX, 6: 414–15. The document has been published in Kaźmierczyk, *Żydzi polscy*, 66–67. See also AR V, 12424 (II). For other cases of interference in local trade by the Radziwiłłs see AR XXIX, 7: 518–19; and AR XIX, U II, 9: 2.

13. AR XXIX, 7: 83. The owner of Klewań issued a parallel ruling regarding those of his estate residents who traded at the fair at Ołyka. See Rosman, *The Lords' Jews*, 80.

14. This was possible because the family itself provided most of the flotilla of rafts on which the goods were shipped. The money was collected in the form of freight payments.

15. The history of Jewish trade in Poland-Lithuania has been the subject of intensive research. Among the studies most important for the present discussion are: Schiper, *Dzieje handlu*; Wischnitzer, "Die Stellung," 113–23; Wyrobisz, "Materiały," 703–16; Leszczyński, *Żydzi*, 143–66; Hundert, "The Role of the Jews," 245–75; Mahler, *Toledot ha-yehudim*, 98–108 and 258–74; Goldberg, "Ha-mishar ha-kimona'i," 11–64; Hundert, "Kivunei hitpathut," 225–36; Kalik, "Ha-yahas," 43–57; and Kazusek, *Żydzi*. On Jewish commerce on the magnate estates see Rosman, *The Lords' Jews*, 75–105, and Hundert, *The Jews in a Polish Private Town*, 46–68.

16. AR XXIX, 5: 519; NABRM 694, opis 7, 457: 4; and Goldberg, *Jewish Privileges*, I: 301. This phenomenon was not unique to Radziwiłł-owned towns: Kaźmierczyk, *Żydzi*, 91–131.

17. AR XXIII, 146: 116; AR XXIX, 5: 493–94; AR XXIX, 7: 866; and AR XXIX, 11: n.p., 2/6/1764. Other estate owners, such as the Czartoryskis, followed a similar policy. See the letters from August Czartoryski to the Radziwiłł family about his Jewish merchants: AR V, 2578 (II): 22, 29–30, and 56. See also Rosman, *The Lords' Jews*, 77–85.

18. Gierszewski "Magnaci i szlachta," 1–13; Tazbir, *Kultura*, 34–36. Both Tazbir

and Gierszewski point out that some of the poorer members of the nobles did engage in trade, particularly that in agricultural produce. This did not, however, affect the nobility's negative attitude towards commerce in general.

19. In general, nobles wanted to sell the agricultural produce of their estates at high prices and purchase other commodities, mainly luxuries, at low prices. By contrast, the townspeople, organized in commercial and other guilds, held mercantile monopolies that allowed them to set low prices for the agricultural produce they purchased and high prices for the goods they sold.

20. Various economic writers of the seventeenth and eighteenth centuries emphasized this in their texts. See, for example: Gostomski, *Gospodarstwo*, 100–105; Górski, *Poglądy*, 144–45, 161–67, and 198–202.

21. A manuscript by Hieronim Florian Radziwiłł, most likely written when he was a young man, includes his thoughts on various economic and social issues. For example: "Townspeople should not be allowed to study outside their town, or even to leave it, on pain of losing their home, because [education outside the town] provides a young man with skills that base fellows never exploit to advantage, but only apply to harm and cheat their lord. It would be better for those knaves to learn a trade, so the guilds will stay full and the towns flourish from the trade they do, thus making a profit for their lord." See Biblioteka Czartoryska, rkps. 1721. The text is published in Radziwiłł, *Diariusze*, 196. Radziwiłł was nothing out of the ordinary in the importance he ascribed to towns as a source of revenue. See Bergerówna, *Księżna pani*, 270, and Rosman, *The Lords' Jews*, 79. On the nobility's attitude towards towns: Wyrobisz, "Power and Towns," 611–30.

22. "The noble lord starosta must provide protection to merchants, to stall owners, and to families that engage in trade and see to it that they conduct as few lawsuits among themselves as possible, because that damages their trade." AR XXIX, 5: 612. See also AR XXIX, 5: 523; AR XXIX, 7: 518–19; and AR XXV, 236: 27; and Kalik, "The Attitude," 55–56.

23. AR XXIII, 149, n.p., n.d., the response to a petition by the merchants of Pińsk-Karlin (Pinsk-Karalin, Belarus) to Anna Radziwiłł, asking her to protect their business dealings.

24. See Chapter Two; Goldberg, "Ha-mishar ha-kimona'i," 11–13; and Schiper, *Dzieje handlu*, 269–70.

25. Hundert, "Jewish Urban Residence," 25–34; Hundert, "The Role of the Jews," 259.

26. This led the non-Jewish townspeople to switch from commerce to agriculture.

27. AR XXIX, 6: 148.

28. Surviving data do not allow us to measure the volume of trade conducted in each stall. The descriptive sources state clearly that most local trade was in Jewish hands. See Mahler, *Toledot ha-yehudim*, 258–74.

29. Goldberg, "Ha-mishar ha-kimona'i," 12–13.

30. In 1730, Anna Radziwiłł sent an architect to Mir to plan the construction of stalls there. AR XXIII, 91, n.p., 9.3.1730. See also Topolska, "Szkłów," 15–17.

31. See Frick, *Kith, Kin, and Neighbors*, 432, note 21. Frick finds in the sources from Vilnius that the "stalls" there were defined simply as places where retail trade was done and they could, actually, be found inside houses. As Goldberg has pointed out (note 15), there was no uniformity of usage.

32. See Rosman, *The Lords' Jews*, 75–105.

33. This drop in Jewish stall ownership paralleled the overall decrease in the number of stalls in the town, owing to the town's general decline and the rapid growth of nearby Szkłów (Shkloŭ, Belarus) as the major trading center in the region. On the rise of Szkłów, see Topolska, "Szkłów," and Gritskevich, *Chastnovladel'cheskiye goroda*, 141.

34. See Chapter One and Chapter Four.

35. AR XXV, 3834.

36. AR XXV, 3837 and AR XXV, 3838. For comparison, in Opatów in Małopolska, 80 percent of the merchants were Jews in 1788: Hundert, *The Jews in a Polish Private Town*, 50. In Szkłów in eastern Belarus, "only" half of the merchants were Jews: Topolska, "Szkłów," 17. See also Gelber, *Toledot yehudei Brody*, 31.

37. Nadav, "Kehillat Pinsk," 153–96.

38. Birkenthal, *Zikhronot R. Dov Ber*, 85. On the development of Brody in this period see Kuzmany, *Die Stadt Brody*, 47–54.

39. Matuszewicz, *Diariusz*, I: 85 and 395. Rosman, *The Lords' Jews*, 80. See also Goldberg, *Jewish Privileges*, I: 103–5.

40. See, for example, the record of a debt of 1,853 złoty and 6 groszy owed to Michał Kazimierz Radziwiłł by the merchant and *arendarz* Joshua of Nowy Świerżeń. This was not a one-time loan, but a debt that had accrued over a period of 15 years. In the end Joshua settled it by purchasing goods for Radziwiłł in Königsberg: AR VIII, 376: 33–34.

41. AR XXIII, 93, plik 1, n.p., n.d.

42. AR V, 15467, n.p., 19.7.1750. See also Schiper, *Dzieje handlu*, 219–20.

43. In *The Jews in a Polish Private Town*, 98, Hundert found very little evidence of the community giving mercantile loans in Opatów either.

44. Schiper, *Dzieje handlu*, 211–20; and Mahler, *Toledot ha-yehudim*, 324–27.

45. Kalik, "Patterns of Contact," 102–22. See also *Pinkas ha-ksherim*, no. 2023.

46. Hundert, "Kivunei hitpathut," 225–36. As early as the second half of the seventeenth century, the electors (*ksherim*) of the Poznań community tried to get the *kahal* to stop making loans because of the difficulties in collecting them. *Pinkas ha-ksherim*, no. 1514.

47. AR XXIII, 150, n.p., n.d. "Foreign" here means "from outside the estate."

48. AR XXIX, 5: 519, 611, 619. In this case Radziwiłł merchants seem to have been giving foreign merchants credit. The credit market was clearly not a one-way street.

49. Mahler, *Toledot ha-yehudim*, 107–8, and Breger, *Zur Handelsgeschichte*, 45–46.

50. AR XXIII, 149, n.p., document dated 1713.

51. AR XXV, 2622: 231–32; AR IV kopie, 6, plik 9: 608v–609v; AR XXIII, 146: 116; AR XXIII, 149, n.p., no. 10.

52. AR X, "Ickowicz": 5.

53. See note 45.

54. AR V, 2578 (II): 29–30; AR V, 3407: 29. See NABRM 694, opis 2, 2281: 93–96.

55. On this: Kula, *An Economic Theory*, 28–36; and Burzyński, "Struktura dochodów," 31.

56. See Ḥaim Kohen, *Responsa*, Ḥoshen Mishpat, no. 19. See also Homecki, *Produkcja i handel*, 35–40.

57. They tended to buy grain from peasants on their way to the towns. By doing deals outside the towns the Jewish merchants evaded the monopoly conditions that the Christian merchants had laid down for the urban markets. This caused no little resentment from as early as the sixteenth century. Such complaints about "unfair" Jewish competition were not unknown on the Radziwiłł latifundium in Lithuania in the eighteenth century. See, for example, AR XXIII, 137: 130.

58. AR V, 7170: 142; AR XXIX, 6: 303. See also AR XXIII, 146: 116. In his study of grain production and trade in Małoposka (*Produkcja i handel*, 33 and 37), Homecki found that urban merchants (chiefly Jews) played a key role in the local market in grain, but that this market flourished only when exports to Gdańsk were blocked by war or other troubles. See also Rosman, *The Lords' Jews*, 88–89.

59. AR XXIX, 7: 335, 666, and 789–90; and AR XXIX, 8: 13.

60. Unger, "Trade through the Sound," 206–21.

61. AR IV kopie, 6: 195 and 361; and AR XX, 34.

62. AR IV kopie, 6: 338.

63. NABRM 694, opis 2, 4187: 26–27. For a 1736 contract with two Jews who received 400 złoty from the estate manager to purchase flax: NABRM 694, opis 2, 4185: 501.

64. On Jews who purchased flax and hemp for their own business: AR XX, 19, passim; AR IV, 132: 12–15; and AR XXIX, 11, n.p., 18.8.1763.

65. AR V, 12424 (II), n.p., 6.4.1764.

66. AR V, 12424 (II), n.p., 24.2.1764. The situation was different in southern Poland, where flax was given to estate owners as feudal dues only after it had been processed into linen. The linen was then sold to Jews, who distributed it to markets near and far: Bieniarzówna, "The Role of the Jews," 104.

67. Kula, "Początki," 60–61, and Goldberg, "Ośrodki przemysłowe," 78–79.

68. Kula, *Szkice*, 65–66. Very little attention has been devoted to the Jews' role in these early attempts at industrialization in Poland and Lithuania. See Goldberg, *Ha-ḥevrah ha-yehudit*, 252–63.

69. A special fond of the Radziwiłł archives, AR XIX, contains all the documentation on the manufactories.

70. Kamieńska, *Manufaktura szklana*, 42.

71. Kula, *Szkice*, 44.

72. AR XXIX, 7: 187. Some of the peasants were paid small amounts of cash, though these amounted to negligible sums.

73. AR XIX, U VI 2: 15; Kamieńska, "Fachowcy," 519–35.

74. For the case of a Jew who was involved in the management of the Czartoryski sword factory in Staszów: Rosman, *The Lords' Jews*, 258.

75. On the essential difference between these two forms of involvement: Goldberg, *Ha-ḥevrah ha-yehudit*, 258. On the periodization of manufactory development in eighteenth-century Poland-Lithuania: Kula, *Szkice*, 14–15, and 30.

76. Goldberg, *Ha-ḥevrah ha-yehudit*, 253–54; Ringelblum, *Projekty i próby*, 32–57.

77. See, for example, AR XIX, NSZ VII 6: 1–3. On Jews as laborers in textile mills: Ringelblum, *Projekty i próby*, 32–57.

78. AR XIX, U VII 1.

79. AR XIX, NSZ V 2: 7–32. See also AR XXIX, 9, n.p., 26.10.1759. Of course Jewish merchants were not the only suppliers of raw materials to the factories.

80. AR XIX, U V 2: 56. Kamieńska (*Manufaktura szklana*, 169–74) notes the problem of excessive consumption of alcohol by factory workers and the contradiction between the family's desire to increase its revenue from *propinacja* and its need to run an efficient and profitable factory. The fact that the Urzecz manufactory suffered from a continuing problem of alcoholism among its workforce is probably evidence that the administration attached greater importance to the *arenda* revenue than to profits from the factory.

81. At least some of the liquidity problems may have been due to corrupt managers who embezzled the available funds: Kula, *Szkice*, 48–50.

82. This is another example of the lessees' key role in the operation of the estate economy: ibid., 47–48 and 214–15; and Kamieńska, *Manufaktura szklana*, 173.

83. Kula, *Szkice*, 60. The rest of the stock remained in the factory's warehouse.

84. AR XIX, U V 2: 40; and AR XIX, U VII 3: 11–12. He was also responsible for coordinating factory supply.

85. Smoleńska, "Materiały," 84.

86. AR XIX, NSZ II 1: 234–316.

87. Ibid., passim.

88. In such cases it is hard to tell whether the Jewish buyer was the mercantile agent (*faktor* in Polish) of a nobleman, an independent merchant who had received an order from a nobleman, or simply a merchant passing himself off as a noble agent in order to enjoy various tax exemptions.

89. See the complaint by the factory manager in 1737, "Because of the terrible road, few people visit the factory," AR XIX, U VI 1: 4. On the issue of factory location in the eighteenth century: Goldberg, *Ha-ḥevrah ha-yehudit*, 251–54.

90. AR XIX, U V 2: 40; Smoleńska, "Materiały," 84.

91. Some of the stock was exported to the courts in St. Petersburg and Berlin, though this does not seem to have been a common practice. Ibid., 85–86.

92. AR XIX, U VII 3: 11–12; Smoleńska, "Materiały," 84.

93. AR XXIX, 6: 359–361.

94. AR XXIX, 7: 518–19; AR XIX, U II 9: 2. According to this last document, the protectionist policy failed to prevent trade in competing products. See also Kula, *Szkice*, 60–61.

95. Kula, *An Economic Theory*, 135–37.

96. On the Jews' role in commerce in eighteenth century Königsberg, see Glinski, *Die Königsberger Kaufmannschaft*, 168–98, and Storm, "Culture and Exchange," 115–44.

97. The purchases included amber, pepper, cinnamon, turmeric, rice, Italian noodles, Venetian lacquer, soup, olives, lemons, sugar, and paper. For a list of the luxury items that Hieronim Florian Radziwiłł purchased in Königsberg in 1742 see AR XX, 41: 8–9.

98. NABRM 694, opis 7, 712: 10; and AR XXIX, 11, n.p., 11.5.1763.

99. AR XX, 62: 11. These twelve slaves cost 2,000 thaler, while the shipping costs were a little under 500 thaler. This means that the price of an African slave in Lithuania in the eighteenth century was around 225 thaler, or 1,800 Polish złoty.

100. In Königsberg, 1 łaszt was the equivalent of approximately 3,500 liters.

101. In Polish, *sztab*.

102. AR XX, 76: 20; AR XX, 49: 18–20; and AR XX, 50: 41.

103. AR XX, 62: 1–9.

104. Ibid., 11.

105. AR XX, 75: 14–19. It is not clear just how frequently rafts sailed from the Radziwiłł family's southern estates to Gdańsk: Guldon, *Związki handlowe*, 70.

106. Ibid., 114–15.

107. Ibid., 62–74.

108. Burszta, "Handel," 210. Topolska estimates flax sales by the Czartoryski family in Rīga at the end of the seventeenth century as averaging about 50,000 złoty a year, but gives no details of their purchases: Topolska, "Związki handlowe," 22 and 25.

109. Homecki, *Produkcja i handel*, 55–56 and 110. According to Burszta, rye sold for 266 złoty a łaszt in Gdańsk in 1719. As a rough approximation then, the Lubomirski family's average income must have been 37,000 złoty.

110. Guldon, *Związki handlowe*, 112–27. Though these figures do not indicate much about what was bought with all this money at Gdańsk, details of the Sieniawski-Czartoryski trade there indicate that the family's purchases were meant for court and estate supply: Rosman, "Ha-yehudim be-saḥar ha-neharot," 70–83.

111. They played an important role in financing it however. On this see below.

112. Mączak, "Money and Society," 69–104; Guldon, *Związki handlowe*, 75–111; Burszta, "Handel," 174–235.

113. Most of his business correspondence with the Radziwiłłs can be found scattered throughout AR XX and AR XXIX: 5–11. His more personal correspondence with the family is in AR V: 16339.

114. On the roles of this Jewish agent see AR XX, 18, passim; AR XX, 13: 16; AR XX, 58: 20; AR XXIX, 5: 769–72; XXIX, 6: 279; and AR XX, 7: 257. One Jew, Hirsh ben Joseph, managed four rafts in Hieronim Florian Radziwiłł's flotilla in 1759: AR XX, 41: 128–29, and AR XX, 50: 33–40. No other details about his life and career have survived.

115. They helped the family find goods and even extended it credit from time to

time. The correspondence between the brothers and the Radziwiłł family can be found in AR V, 13955. The brothers' ties with the Radziwiłł family continued into the 1770s, when Friedrich served as a counselor to the king of Prussia. See Bersohn, *Dyplomataryusz*, 194, no. 334. See also Gause, *Saturgus*.

116. AR XXIII, 4, 68; AR XXIII, 9, n.p., 11.3.1757. On Michał Kazimierz Radziwiłł's diverse dealings with the wealthy Rabinowicz family of Brody see Teller, "Radziwill," 246–76.

117. AR XXIX, 5: 134. The debt was never paid. Nearly fifteen years later, Abraham's heirs sued Radziwiłł for payment of the principal, 44,180 złoty and 26 groszy. AR XXIX, 9, n.p., 22.7.1760. See also AR V, 2578 (II): 37.

118. AR XXIX, 5: 518–19; AR XXIX, 6: 248–49; and AR XXIX, 11, n.p., 11.1.1763.

119. The family also patronized a merchant (a baptized Jew) from Smolensk who helped them acquire goods from Russia. AR IV, 139: 19–20; AR V, 972: 5–7, 15.

120. AR XXIX, 5, 499; AR XXIX, 6: 115 and 225.

121. Małka, Mirka, Nehamka, Bejla, Chajka, Dawidówka, Zelmanowa, Feyga, Meierowa, Joskowa, Berkowa, Gdalowa, Rochel, Rejza. The documentation on all the merchants who supplied the Radziwiłłs and their court is found chiefly in AR XXIX, 6–9, passim.

122. On Jewish domination of the cloth trade in Poland and Lithuania in those years, see Wyrobisz, "Materiały," 703–16.

123. The most common fabrics included wool, linen, cotton, silk, velvet, and satin. Fabrics in diverse colors and sometimes with floral and other patterns were both local and imported from France, England, and Venice. In addition to fabrics, large quantities of both plain and ornamental ribbons in gold and silver were sold.

124. AR XXIX, 7: 789–90. Michał Kazimierz Radziwiłł's wife had a Jewish agent in Nieśwież named Małka who helped her acquire supplies for the family kitchen, among other things: AR XXIX, 6: 146 and 431–32.

125. Since it is likely that there were other accounts that have not survived, this is presumably only a partial record.

126. AR XXIX, 8: 13.

127. AR XXIX, 7: 603.

128. AR XXIX, 7: 391–93.

129. AR XXIX, 7: 637.

130. AR XXIX, 8: 83, 88, and 92; and AR XXIX, 9, n.p., 11.2.1756.

131. AR XXIX, 9, n.p., 10.6.1758.

132. To this should be added accounts submitted by Nechama for 1751 and 1752 amounting to another 2,500 złoty. These were not included in the reckoning for 1753 (presumably they had been paid on time): AR XXIX, 6: 431–32.

133. Nowak, "Feyga Lejbowiczowa," 211–36.

134. Teller, "Ha-pe'ilut ha-kalkalit," 209–24.

135. Jordan, "Jews on Top," 39–56, and Jordan, "Women and Credit," 33–62.

136. Luria, *She'elot u-teshuvot*, no. 99. See also the privilege granted to the community of Zwoleń in Małopolska, which refers to Jewish women merchants (and

bakers) in the town in 1661: Goldberg, *Jewish Privileges*, I: 386, To judge by a 1620 regulation from the community *pinkas* (record book) of Żółkiew, the Jewish women merchants held their own in commercial competition and evidently gave the community leaders cause to fear harsh reactions from non-Jews: "Women who sit in the market place must not get into arguments with any non-Jew, subject to a fine . . ." See Buber, *Kiryah nisgavah*, 83.

137. This seems to have been a general phenomenon: Salmon-Mack, *Tan-du*, 135–61. On the similar situation in the early modern German lands see Kaplan, "Women and Worth," 93–113.

138. Rosman, "Lihiyot 'isha," 426–31.

139. On this: Salmon-Mack, *Tan-du*, 163–214.

140. See, for example, a case from Kraków in 1646, in which a woman named Idel asked the rabbinic court to release her from her husband's creditors. Her argument was that because he had not earned enough to support her as Jewish law demands of a husband, her profits should not be confiscated to cover his debts. She then demanded total economic independence from her husband. The court granted her petition. Wettstein, "Mi-pinkasei ha-kahal," 74–75.

141. Hundert, "Approaches," 22, based on the records for the municipal scales of Lublin, argued that very few Jewish women were involved in commerce there. Only relatively large transactions had to be recorded at these scales, however, so the lists say nothing about small retailers active in the town.

142. Bogucka, "Rodzina," 500–501; Bogucka, "Women," 185–94; Karpiński, *Kobieta*, 69–84; and Karpiński, "The Woman on the Marketplace," 283–92.

143. Hundert, "Approaches," 22.

144. "That from this day forth, no woman will go out with merchandise of any sort to the houses of non-Jews or to any priest or official, nor shall two or three go together, by any means whatsoever. . . . No woman shall work as a peddler, what is called a *tendlerke*." *Pinkas Medinat Lita*, no. 547. Apparently these women were acting as agents for their husbands or shopkeepers, who gave them merchandise to sell from door to door among non-Jews. Woman peddlers were known among the non-Jewish residents of the towns of Poland and Germany (where they were called *Täntlerin*), and they, too, roused the opposition of the urban authorities: Wiesner, *Working Women*, 134–42; Karpiński, "The Woman on the Marketplace," 289.

145. *Pinkas Medinat Lita*, no. 547. See also the criticism by the kabbalist Peretz ben Moshe of Brody: "For this reason it is a warning to women more than men, because profanation of the Sabbath is more common among them." With regard to female peddlers he notes that "in the summer they go about in the markets and streets without proper dress, wearing only a white shift that has no hem and their flesh peeks through." Perez ben Moshe, *Beit Peretz*, 26.

146. See, for example, the details given in Wyrobisz, "Materiały," 708–9, about a Jewish woman merchant from Tarłów. Hundert's figures on women who used the municipal scales in Lublin suggest that at least one or two did engage in large-scale

commerce: see our note 141. See also Nowak, "Feyga Lejbowiczowa." On well-to-do female merchants in Polish society, see Karpiński, *Kobieta*, 69–71.

147. AR XXIX, 5: 639–41.

148. AR XXIX, 7: 111–15; and AR XXIII, 150, n.p., 10.6.1755.

149. AR XXIX, 7: 769; AR XXIX, 8: 24, 29, 42, 62; and AR XXIX, 9, n.p., 1.8.1758 and 20.3.1760.

150. Because it is impossible to identify the husbands of most of these female merchants, we can only wonder whether they were supporting husbands who were full-time Torah scholars. Hundert, drawing on economic and other sources, maintains, probably correctly, that this arrangement was unknown in Poland and Lithuania before the nineteenth century. Hundert, "Approaches," 17–28.

151. AR XXIX, 6: 148; and AR XXIX, 8: 24, 30, and 42.

152. AR VI, 80a–II: 980.

153. Another sign of this may be seen in the fact that some of these women received appointments as official agents to Michał Kazimierz Radziwiłł and his wife. One such, who lived outside the estate (in the town of Brześć), was even given permission to hang the Radziwiłł crest outside her store. AR XXIX, 6: 146 and 248–49.

154. AR V, 12424, letters dated April 11, April 15, and July 9, 1752. This blood libel accusation against the *arendarze* may be connected with the one recounted by Solomon Maimon in his memoirs, which targeted his grandfather who lived nearby: *Solomon Maimon: An Autobiography*, 14–17.

155. AR XXIX, 6: 148; and AR XXIX, 8: 24, 30, and 42.

156. AR XX, 62: 1–9.

157. In 1742, Hieronim Florian Radziwiłł bought fabric worth 2,176 thalers (approximately 4,500 złoty); in 1759 he acquired twenty-two bundles of cloth for his private army. AR XX, 41: 8–9; AR XX, 50: 41. This was a commodity that the Radziwiłłs only rarely purchased in Königsberg, possibly due to the overall decline of the textile market there: Unger, "Trade through the Sound," 211.

158. For these data see Chapter Two, and earlier in this chapter. For further examples from other parts of the Commonwealth: Hundert, *Jews in Poland-Lithuania*, 33–34.

159. *Regesty i nadpisy* II, no. 1730. See also Schiper, *Dzieje handlu*, 269–70.

160. Zawadzki, *Polska*, 388, 407, and 479.

161. Coxe, *Travels into Poland*, 201.

162. See Bogucka, "Kupcy żydowscy," 797–98.

163. Though they seem to have been less dominant in this field and certainly less well represented among the richest merchants: Hundert, "The Role of the Jews," 274.

164. AR XXIX, 5: 72 and 622–28; AR XXIX, 7: 233, 527, and 531; AR XXIX, 9, n.p., 22.4.1757; AR V, 2190: 27 and 37; AR XXIII, 146: 81 and 83; and NABRM 694, opis 7, 712: 108.

165. AR XXIII, 146: 76; NABRM 694, opis 7, 712: 115; and AR XXIX, 11, n.p., 2.6.1764.

166. One traveler can even be identified in estate records, Solomon of Biała. In his diary entry for June 17, 1737, the manager of the Biała *folwark* wrote as follows: "The Jew Zalman [Solomon] wrote from Leipzig that he will return here this week." AR XXIII, 146: 69. On Solomon's registration at the Leipzig fair in that year: Freudenthal, *Leipziger Messegäste*, 45. The Leipzig list for 1737 includes the names of five other merchants from the Lithuanian estates, four from Biała and one from Słuck.

167. A number of such contracts can be found in NABRM 694, opis 4, 2201.

168. AR XXIII, 137: 119. Jewish merchants were not the only, nor even the wealthiest, wholesalers in Słuck, so it would not be correct to claim that the Jews controlled this sector.

169. This refers to *prawo składku*, which required nonresident traders, mainly wholesalers who visited town, to store their wares in the municipal warehouse on arrival and sell them only to local merchants. The law was intended to strengthen local traders against major merchants from out of town, by allowing the locals to set lower prices for the imports and so increase their profit margins from retail sales. See Rutkowski, *Historia gospodarcza*, 86–91 and 157–63.

170. Bardach, *O dawnej i niedawnej Litwie*, 72–119.

171. *Pinkas Medinat Lita*, no. 302.

172. AR XXIII, 137: 130. The document is undated, so the dating proposed here is based on the palaeography.

173. One might assume that they dared to do this because they knew that they the owner of the town would give them his support. If this so, then this is a case in which the noble estate owner and the Jewish merchants were working together against both the townspeople and the Jewish institutions.

174. For example, "When they buy food and grain, the Jews cause great damage when they crowd by the gate and purchase in the street. Nor do they limit their purchases to certain hours." AR XXIII, 137: 130, no. 2 and no. 8.

175. AR XXIII, 137: 130, no. 3; and AR XXIII, 137: 72.

176. This situation was not unique to the Radziwiłł estates. For example, in Lublin in 1736 the Jews did not even bother to appear before a municipal committee convened to consider their situation. When it ruled that they should be expelled from town they simply appealed to the king, who canceled the decree: Balaban, *Die Judenstadt*, 6.

177. See Sosis, "Tsu der sotsyaler geshikhte," 6.

178. AR XXIII, 33, plik 6, n.p.

179. This seems to be the meaning of transferring his residence from one side of the city to the other, as mentioned in the document, though it is not entirely clear. According to the inventory of Żagory, no Jews lived in the town in 1742 owing to an expulsion order issued in 1738 (see Chapter One): AR XXV, 4169.

180. The text mentions the wide variety of goods that Ber ben Meir sold on his stall.

181. AR XXV, 4636.

182. This argument was made most famously by Werner Sombart in *The Jews*

and Modern Capitalism. For a discussion of Sombart's reception and influence, see Muller, *Capitalism and the Jews*, 51–60.

183. This is emphasized in Goldberg, "Ha-mishar ha-kimonaʻi, 11–64.

184. On the importance of the *arendarze* in supplying village society, see Chapter Five.

185. Matuszewicz, *Diariusz.*

186. For a list of some of these Turkish goods see Goldberg, "Ha-mishar ha-kimonaʻi," 33, no. 4.

187. This presumably means that the taxes on the fair were not collected directly by the family but by the *arendarz* as part of his contract.

188. Matuszewicz, *Diariusz*, I: 395.

189. Little scholarly attention has been devoted to the Niemen river trade between Belarus and Königsberg in the eighteenth century. See: Guldon and Wijaczka, "Handel," 39–46; Gierszewski, "Port w Królewcu," 53–59; Derdeko, "Handel zbożem," 282–83. It is also mentioned in Mieleszko, "Handel," 693–96. The Jews' role in this river trade has not been studied at all.

190. It was called *fracht* in Radziwiłł family documents, and *frocht* or *frokt* in documents of the San and Vistula flotillas from southeastern Poland to Gdańsk. The word is derived from the German *Fracht* (freight). In the discussion below shipments of private goods are referred to as "freight shipments."

191. Burszta, "Handel," 174–235; Rosman, *The Lords' Jews*, 89–105; and Rosman, "Ha-yehudim be-sahar ha-neharot," 70–83.

192. Mieleszko, "Handel," 693–96; Topolska, "Związku handlowe," 25–27.

193. AR XX, 76: 1–40.

194. He shipped potash and hemp fiber worth more than 120 Lithuanian kop (250 złoty). AR XX, 1: 1–2; AR XX, 2, passim.

195. AR XX, 5: 1–9. According to Mączak, who computed the total revenues for the years 1626–1629, 1631, and 1634, the income from freight shipments accounted for 32 percent of the total revenue for those years: Mączak, "Money and Society," 69–104.

196. See, for example, AR XX, 6: 3 and 57–60.

197. Trade with Rīga does not seem to have achieved the same volume as with the other two ports: Mieleszko, "Handel."

198. Burszta, "Handel," 193. The importance of this was, of course, that it left more space on the rafts for private shipments.

199. Ibid., 219, and Guldon, *Związki handlowe*, 84.

200. The regular accounts for freight shipments began in 1727–1728: AR XX, 53. A few merchants paid for freight shipments to Königsberg in 1725: AR XX, 58: 1–40. The 1722 flotilla did not carry any freight at all: AR XX, 11: 1–4. The river trade may have revived because Friedrich Wilhelm of Prussia abolished the restrictions on the salt trade in Königsberg in 1727, encouraging Lithuanian merchants to frequent the markets there. See Kirby, *Northern Europe*, 368.

201. AR XXIX, 9, n.p., 26.5.1760.

202. The data on trade in Gdańsk is in Rosman, "Ha-yehudim be-saḥar ha-neharot," 79.

203. There was certainly trade in other goods as well, since some shippers paid a global sum for "miscellaneous items" not otherwise identified in the list.

204. See Burszta, "Handel," 202–4; Rosman, "Ha-yehudim be-saḥar ha-neharot," 80–82.

205. The existence of salt mines in southern Poland, Gdańsk's major Polish hinterland, made such imports unnecessary.

206. Unger, "Trade through the Sound," 211, notes a general decline in the cloth trade in Königsberg.

207. A similar picture for a later period is found in Żytkowicz, "Kilka uwag," 87–101. According to the list there, textiles accounted for 9 percent of all Lithuania's foreign trade. Unger, "Trade through the Sound," 207–9, locates the origins of these goods.

208. See, for example, AR XXIX, 6: 108–9. Things were done in much the same way in the river trade to Gdańsk: Burszta, "Handel," 194.

209. For references to the river trade see *Solomon Maimon: An Autobiography*, 20–21 and 38–39; and Teller, "Zikhronot," 6–10.

210. There were smaller ports in the towns of Mosty, Słobodka, Jeremicze, and Delaticze. There was also a small port in the village of Żukowy Borek where Solomon Maimon grew up. See Teller, "Zikhronot," 2–6.

211. AR V. 15467, n.p., 18.12.1756; and NABRM 694, opis 4, 2201, passim. Merchants from Russia joined the flotilla in 1752 and 1760. Given that they sent mainly flour, they do not seem to have been making transshipments but were engaged in local commerce. See AR XX, 52: 74–75 and 90–104.

212. The clerics included local priests and representatives of monasteries, such as Bernardines and Jesuits (presumably both from Nieśwież). The monasteries often maintained ties with Königsberg by giving Radziwiłł a shopping list to be filled for them there. It is not clear who paid the bill. See, for example, AR XXIX, 5: 7–20, 475, and 530–38; and AR XX, 41: 122–25.

213. These were referred to simply as *pan* (mister), so could have belonged to the lower nobility or the wealthier burghers.

214. One of the noble shippers traded on a scale that suggests he might have made his living buying and selling. This is the "distinguished lord Jakub Wołkowicz" (Imci Pan Jakub Wołkowicz), a minor nobleman on the estates. In 1738, Wołkowicz paid 4,555 złoty and 23 groszy freight charges and 3,095 złoty and 13 groszy to ship goods back upriver. It seems unlikely that such large quantities of goods were intended for the private consumption of a minor nobleman, so he may well have been a professional merchant. On the phenomenon of noblemen who pursued trade as a business, see note 18.

215. For a discussion of the magnate's protection of freight shippers on the San-Vistula route, see Rosman, *The Lords' Jews*, 81–85.

216. AR XXIX, 9, n.p., 26.5.1760.

217. For cases of money loans see AR XX, 43: 9; AR XXIX, 7: 886; and AR XX, 120, n.p., This last is an application for credit by Moses ben Zelig Ginzburg, dated 1771, which seems to have been granted, because appended to it is the following text (in Hebrew): "My signature attests, with the force of a hundred valid witnesses, that I am obliged to pay the lord commissioner [i.e., the flotilla manager] the sum of 400 crowns [Prussian thalers] as per the document in my hand, as well as 50 Polish złoty, that I received in cash to cover expenses. Today, Friday, the eve of the Sabbath, 21 [should be 22] Kislev 5532 [i.e., November 29, 1771], here. Signed, Moses Israel the son of Azriel Zelig Ginzburg."

218. See, for example, the accounts with the well-to-do merchant Baruch ben Getz, *arendarz* of Słuck, and other Jewish businessmen: AR XX, 52: 114–16 and 118–21.

219. On him see Chapter Five.

220. AR XXIX, 7: 890; and AR XXIX, 9: n.p., 23.4.1756.

221. In 1738 he paid some 8,000 złoty, in 1746 3,200 złoty, and in 1760 more than 9,000 złoty.

222. AR VIII, 376: 33–34; AR XX, 52: 107; AR XXIX, 6: 256, 352, and 376; and AR XXIX, 7: 95, 476, 643, and 682.

223. AR XX, 15, kop. 20, n.p., 22.6.1761.

224. The leaseholder's name was Aryeh ben Yedidyah.

225. AR XXIX, 9, n.p., 26.5.1760.

226. AR XXIX, 5: 156–66; AR XXIX, 6: 279; AR XXIX, 7: 107, 418, and 866; and AR V, 972: 14 and passim.

227. AR XXIX, 6: 109. See also AR XX, 76: 73.

228. See his correspondence: AR V, 16339.

229. As evidenced by the fact that he was the subject of a number of complaints for unfair dealing made by Jews from Nowy Świerżeń: AR V, 15467.

230. Joshua's original complaint is in AR XX, 13: 16. The documents of the investigation and trial can be found in AR XX, 18, passim.

231. Topolewski's letter dated January 26, 1754, begging Radziwiłł for mercy can be found in AR V, 16339. Starting in 1755, the noble Jerzy Paszkowski ran the flotilla for Michał Kazimierz Radziwiłł: AR XXIX, 7: 825 ff.

232. *Solomon Maimon: An Autobiography*, 38–39. According to Maimon, his father won his case but was unable to get his money back. See also the complaints by Jewish merchants from Nowy Świerżeń who were harassed by various noblemen: AR V, 15467, passim.

233. On the tension between the hostility of the local nobility towards Jews and the magnate's desire to protect them: Teller, "In the Land of Their Enemies," 431–46.

234. This phenomenon was by no means limited to the Radziwiłł latifundium but could be seen across all the estates and private towns of the Commonwealth.

CONCLUSION

1. Greif, *Institutions*, 58–90.

2. Of course, it was not always the case that Christian society looked down on

mercantile activity. Greif (*Institutions*, 398) examines in detail the case of the highly developed institutions of the Genoese merchants in the High Middle Ages that he sees as possibly having "cultivated the seeds of the Rise of the West." Medieval and early modern East Central Europe, however, did not see comparable developments. For a broader discussion of all the issues raised here, see Mokyr, "The Economics," 195–206.

3. On this see Becker, *Human Capital*.

4. Botticini and Eckstein, *The Chosen Few*, 264–73. My presentation here puts to one side Sombart's thesis in *The Jews and Modern Capitalism*. Though its thrust is similar, its argumentation is crude and at times racist.

5. For a full discussion of the very complex legal system that Jews on the magnate estates had to use, see Kaźmierczyk, *Żydzi*.

6. Muller, *Capitalism and the Jews*, 5. As distinguished a figure as Simon Kuznets viewed what he termed the "constraints imposed by the minority's historical heritage and distinctive equipment in the way of training and experience" as one of only five factors determining the economic development of American Jewry. Kuznets, "Economic Structure of U.S. Jewry," 112–14. For a critique of the historiography on this point, see Lederhendler, "American Jews, American Capitalism," 504–46.

7. There is a huge literature on entrepreneurship but still no fully agreed definition of the term. I rely here on Sobel's encyclopedia entry, "Entrepreneurship." See also Mole, "Introduction," 1–10. Two classic discussions remain valuable: Schumpeter, "Economic Theory," 253–71, and Kirzner, *Competition and Entrepreneurship*, 30–87.

8. Light and Gold, *Ethnic Economies*, 3–26, the quotation is on page 25.

9. Teller, "Telling the Difference," 109–41. In addition, since they were marginal to the sociocultural configuration of Christian urban society, Jews could ignore the constraints of its propriety and custom more easily than Christian merchants. This allowed them greater flexibility in pursuit of profitable business.

10. As defined here, an economic niche, unlike an ethnically dominated economy, has a clearly defined role within the wider economic system. It is the niche's importance for the economy as a whole that determines the power and influence of those working in it. For bibliographical references, see the Introduction, note 8.

11. Dillon and Godley, "The Evolution," 35–61; Stern, *Court Jew*; Israel, "The Sephardi Contribution," 365–98; and Toch, "Between Impotence and Power," Chapter XXI, 221–43.

12. For a discussion of the heterogeneous nature of an early modern Sephardic trade network based in Livorno, see Trivellato, *The Familiarity of Strangers*, 194–223.

13. In fact, there is a good case for arguing that the development of the Jews' ethnic niche in the Polish-Lithuanian Commonwealth is the best example of this phenomenon.

14. The only group on the latifundium that rarely had harsh things to say about the Jews was the Radziwiłł family itself. Only the somewhat sadistic and perhaps even psycopathic Hieronim Florian Radziwiłł expressed strong anti-Jewish sentiments.

15. This support was particularly evident at the time of the peasant uprising against the Ickowicz brothers (see Chapter Four). Not only did Hieronim Florian Radziwiłł suppress the uprising with great brutality, he also directed that help be given to the Jews to rebuild their lives and resume their economic activities as soon as possible.

16. A graphic description of the sufferings of an arendarz and his family on the Radziwiłł estates during a period when the lord's protection was missing can be found in *Solomon Maimon: An Autobiography*, 6–18.

17. See note 9.

18. Hundert, "Ha-kehillah be-Polin," 43–52.

19. See the discussion in Chapter Five.

20. This was not a new phenomenon in the eighteenth century, but seems to have spread much more widely at that time: Teller, "Tradition and Crisis?" 1–39.

21. On this see Shahar, *Bikoret ha-ḥevrah*.

22. Anusik and Strojnowski, "Radziwiłłowie," 29–57; Zielińska, "Mechanizm sejmikowy," 397–419.

23. Anusik and Strojnowski, "Problemy majątkowe," 79–112.

24. Rosman, *The Lords' Jews*. For the situation of the Jews on other estates: Hundert, *The Jews in a Polish Private Town*, 134–58; Bergerówna, *Księżna pani*, 310–19; Goldberg, *Ha-ḥevrah ha-yehudit*, 144–70, 232–50.

25. There was a downside to this development. The Jews were so closely identified with the magnate economic system that when it began to break down under the weight of its internal contradictions (it was creating wealth on the basis of squeezing existing resources rather than creating new ones), they had nowhere to turn. As a new political, social, and economic order struggled to develop during the nineteenth century, the rule of the magnates was held responsible for the country's problems. The Jews, who had been so important to the old regime, took much of the blame and found it difficult to find a place in the new order. The nineteenth century saw them socially and economically marginalized, and eventually reduced to great poverty. On the fate of Jews who leased taverns at that time: Dynner, *Yankel's Tavern*.

Glossary

arenda   A lease taken on an estate or a source of income from an estate.

arendarz   The holder of an *arenda*.

czynsz   A property tax paid to the estate owner.

Council of the Four Lands   The supra-regional Jewish council, a kind of parliamentary body, representing all the Jews of Poland, with particular responsibility for the assessment and collection of the Jewish poll-tax.

Council of the Lithuanian Land   The regional Jewish council representing all the Jews of Lithuania.

Court Jew   A wealthy Jewish financier, granted a special and elevated legal status to serve one of the absolutist rulers of the Holy Roman Empire.

dzierżawa   A lease taken on an estate. In this sense it seems to be little different from an *arenda*.

dzierżawca   The holder of a *dzierżawa*.

ekonom   A senior administrator, usually a nobleman, in the Radziwiłł administration responsible for managing all the agricultural activity in a single, complete estate. The title could have slightly different meanings in estates owned by other noblemen.

ekonomja   A type of royal estate. There were nine such estates in Crown Poland and a further seven in the Grand Duchy of Lithuania. Their special purpose was to provide income to cover the expenses of the royal court. The king generally gave them on leasehold to members of magnate families.

folwark   A seigneurial farm belonging to the owner of the estate. Most of the peasants' dues to their feudal lord were due in the form of corvée labor on the local *folwark*.

fracht   A payment made to the estate administration to rent space on the Radziwiłł rafts carrying produce along the Niemen River to Königsberg. In this period, *fracht* (sometimes called *frocht*) was collected by other magnate families, such as the Sieniawskis and Czartoryskis, whose rafts were floated down the Vistula River to Gdańsk.

grosz   A Polish coin, called "gadol" by the Jews. There were thirty grosze to one złoty.

gubernator   A regional governor, usually a nobleman of high standing, appointed by the Radziwiłłs themselves. The *gubernators* on the Radziwiłł estates were by no means the powerful figures they would become in tsarist Russia during the nineteenth century.

jurydyka   An area or enclave within a town owned by a nobleman. Under Polish law this area was excluded from municipal jurisdiction and was run solely by its owner. Such enclaves proved very attractive to Jews and others who wanted to evade the restrictions imposed upon them by the municipal council without having to leave the town.

kropka   An indirect tax imposed by Jewish communities from about the middle of the seventeenth century. The tax was initially collected from the sale of kosher meat, but was later expanded to cover all transactions made by Jews in the local market. It was a major source of income for the community, which would sometimes lease out the right to collect it to a wealthy member.

latifundium (plural, latifundia)   An extremely large estate—or, most often in the Polish-Lithuanian Commonwealth, a huge complex of noncontiguous estates with a single owner.

łaszt   A measure of volume used in trade between the Radziwiłł estates and Königsberg. In the period under discussion, one *łaszt* equaled about 3,500 liters.

magnate   A member of one of the top noble families. Such families were fabulously wealthy, owned huge latifundia, and held the highest offices of state, which entitled them to seats in the Senate, the upper house of the Sejm. In the eighteenth century the magnates made up a small, socially closed group of about twenty families.

miednica   A measure of liquid, which on the Radziwiłł estates contained about 34 liters.

propinacja   The right to manufacture and sell alcoholic beverages. This right was a monopoly held by each estate owner. In the period studied here, the right—in practice, the right to collect the revenues from all alcohol sales—was given on lease to Jewish businessmen living on the estate. The contracts for these leases were often the cause of bidding wars between various businessmen interested in taking them.

Sejm   The parliament of the Polish-Lithuanian Commonwealth (and of Poland in its various incarnations up to the present). In the period of this study the right to elect or be elected to the Sejm was the sole prerogative of the nobility. The Sejm had two chambers, the House of Representatives and the Senate. Voting in the Sejm followed the principle of unanimity. In the period of this study the "free veto" (*liberum veto*) was in place, which meant that one dissenting voice would not only halt a proposed piece of legislation but also force the dissolution of the Sejm and require new elections.

sejmik   A gathering of local nobility charged with choosing candidates to represent the locality in the Sejm and giving them instructions on how to vote. The *sejmik* had two other roles: first, receiving reports of the previous Sejm's discussions and implementing in the region any legislation it might have passed, and second, acting as a local authority with legislative and administrative powers.

starosta   A governor in one of the royal towns. Once appointed he received a royal estate and all its incomes for the time of his tenure. Various areas in and around the town fell under his jurisdiction rather than that of the municipal council. The *starosta* ran the important castle court (*sąd grodzki*) held in his place of residence.

starostwo   The areas of land under the *starosta*'s jurisdiction.

szlachta   The Polish nobility. A single nobleman was called a *szlachcic*.

thaler   A coin worth eight złoty in the period studied here. The word "thaler" is the root of "dollar."

tynf   A coin, originally minted at the end of the seventeenth century, that took its name from the German who minted it—Andreas Tümpe or Tymf. In the period studied here, each tynf was worth one Polish złoty and eight grosze.

widerkaff   A long-term or standing loan bearing a low rate of simple interest, usually 7 percent annually. It was generally secured by a piece of real estate.

wojewoda   A royally appointed regional governor. During the Middle Ages this post lost its authority, eventually becoming a sinecure granted to members of magnate families. One of the *wojewoda*'s most important functions in the Polish-Lithuanian Commonwealth was assuming responsibility for the Jewish population through the special "Jews' court" that he officially ran. In reality the court was usually run by the *wojewoda*'s deputy together with a special "Jews' Judge"—a Christian who sat in judgment on cases involving Jews and Christians.

województwo   One of the administrative regions of the Polish-Lithuanian Commonwealth. Each *województwo* was headed by a *wojewoda*.

wójt   The senior judge in a village or town. The magnate would usually appoint each *wójt* himself.

złoty   A Polish coin called "zahuv" or "gulden" by the Jews. There were two kinds of złoty—a regular Polish złoty and a so-called red złoty (*czerwony złoty*). The latter had a higher gold content so its value fluctuated relative to the Polish złoty. For most of the period studied here, each red złoty was worth eighteen Polish ones.

Bibliography

MANUSCRIPT SOURCES

AR: Archiwum Główne Akt Dawnych w Warszawie (AGAD; Central Archives of Historical Records in Warsaw)

Archiwum Radziwiłłów

IV, 20, 44, 45, 128, 131, 132, 470

IV kopie, 6, 7

V, 972, 1334, 2473, 2578, 3407, 3689, 4041, 4273, 5596, 5597, 5598, 6943, 7132, 7170, 8470, 10725, 12424, 13817, 13955, 15467, 15476, 15782, 15984, 16039, 16339, 18655

VI, 79–II, 80–II, 81–II

VII, 707

VIII, 376

X, "Czartoryski", "Ickowicz", "Sanguszko"

XI, 122, 140, 145, 222

XV, 5, 18, 20, 24

XVII, 121, 123

XIX, NSZ II 1; NSZ V 2; NSZ VII 2, 6; U II 9; U III 1; U V 2; U VI 1, 2; U VII 1, 3

XX, 1, 2, 6, 8, 11, 13, 15, 18, 19, 20, 34, 41, 43, 48, 49, 50, 51, 52, 58, 62, 75, 76, 80, 81, 85, 86, 87, 88, 94, 95, 120

XXIII, 3, 4, 9, 33, 54, 91, 93, 94, 122, 131, 132, 137, 146, 149, 150, 154, 155, 158

XXV, 1, 6, 123, 124, 125, 127, 137, 235, 236, 240, 243, 677, 678, 679, 680, 681, 698, 702, 923, 925, 1044, 1045, 1046, 1047, 1076, 1617, 1620, 1624, 1706, 1709, 1727, 1730, 1774, 1775, 1777, 1779, 1782/1, 1788, 1789, 1790, 1791, 1797, 1811, 1921, 1928, 1929, 1932, 1935, 1936, 2029, 2071, 2168, 2170, 2172, 2444, 2447, 2448, 2451/1, 2457/1, 2458, 2619, 2614, 2617, 2619, 2622, 2624, 2626, 2670/1, 2675, 2693, 3506, 3511, 3537, 3538, 3543, 3552, 3557, 3672, 3686, 3693, 3831, 3833, 3834/1, 3835, 3836, 3837, 3838, 3839, 4167, 4168, 4169, 4172, 4301/1, 4636.

XXIX, 5, 6, 7, 8, 9, 10, 11

Archiwum Roskie

Komisja Spraw Wewnętrznych
3159E

Metryka Koronna
Sigillata 25

Archiwum Państwowe w Krakowie (AP Kraków: State Archive in Kraków)
Teki Schneidra
II–81

Biblioteka Książąt Czartoryskich, Kraków (Museum of the Princes Czartoryski, Kraków)
Rkps. 1721, 5835

Ossolineum, Wrocław (Zakład Narodowy im. Ossolińskich; National Ossoliński Institute, Wrocław)
Rkps. 2540

L'vivs'ka Natsional'na Naukova Biblioteka Ukraïny imeni V. Stefanika
(L'viv V. Stefanik National Scientific Library of Ukraine)
Fond 103
Opis 1, teka 6801

Natsional'niï Arkhiv Respubliki Belarus', Minsk (NABRM; National Archive of the Republic of Belarus, Minsk)
Fond 694
Opis 2, 1700, 1701, 2281, 4185, 4187, 7421
Opis 3, 35, 38, 4487
Opis 4, 905, 1154, 1159, 1163, 1593, 2201
Opis 7, 457, 712
Opis 14, 278

Lietuvos TSR Centrinis Valstybęs Istorijos Archyvas, Vilnius (Lithuanian State Historical Archive, Vilnius)
SA b. 3739

National Library of Israel (NLI, Jerusalem)
Manuscript Division
Heb 4° 103
Heb 4° 920
Heb 4° 927

PUBLISHED SOURCES

Akty izdavaemye vilenskoĭ komissieĭ dlia razbora drevnykh aktov [Documents Published by the Vilna Commission for the Collection of Old Documents]. Vol. XXIX. Vilnius: Russkiy Pochin', 1902.

Assaf, Sh. "Mi-pinkas Zabludova" [From the Zabłudów Pinkas]. *Kiryat Sefer* 1 (1924/25): 307–17.

Baranowski, Bohdan, Julian Bartyś, and Antonina Keckowa, eds. *Instrukcje gospodarcze dla dóbr magnackich i szlacheckich z XVII–XIX wieku* [Economic Instructions for Magnate and Noble Estates from the 17th–19th Centuries]. 2 vols. Wrocław: Zakład Narodowy im. Ossolińskich, 1963.

Bersohn, Mathias. *Dyplomataryusz dotyczący Żydów w dawnej Polsce na zródłach archiwalnych osnuty (1388–1782)* [Documents on the Jews in Old Poland Based on Archival Sources (1388–1782)]. Warsaw: Edward Nicz i Spółka, 1910.

Birkenthal, Dov Ber. *Zikhronot R. Dov Ber mi-Boleḥov (1723–1805)*. Edited with an introduction by Mark Vishnitzer. Berlin: Klal, 1922.

Buber, Salomon. *Kiryah nisgavah*. Kraków: Ha-Eshkol, 1903.

Coxe, William. *Travels into Poland, Russia, Sweden, and Denmark. Interspersed with Historical Relations and Political Enquiries*, I. Dublin: Price, Moncrieffe, Colles, Walker, Jenkin, Wilson, White, Burton, Cash, and Byrne, 1784.

Emden, Ya'akov. *Va-yakem 'edut be-Ya'akov* [He Established a Testimonial for the Jews]. No place; no publisher, 1756.

Goldberg, Jacob. *Jewish Privileges in the Polish Commonwealth: Charters of Rights Granted to Jewish Communities in Poland-Lithuania in the Sixteenth to Eighteenth Centuries*. 3 vols. Jerusalem: Israel Academy of Sciences and Humanities, 1985–2002.

Gostomski, Anzelm. *Gospodarstwo* [The Farm]. Edited by S. Inglot. Wrocław: Zakład Narodowy im. Ossolińskich, 1951.

Halperin, Yisrael. *Tosafot u-milu'im le-pinkas ha-medinah* [Additional Materials for the Lithuanian Council Record Book]. Jerusalem: Salomon, 1937.

Hanover, Nathan Note ben Moshe. *Yavein Metsulah*. Venice: Be-komisariah Vendramina, 1653.

Icones familiae ducalis Radivillianae [The Portraits of the Ducal Radziwiłł Family]. Nesvisium (Nieśwież): in Typ. Privilegiata Ducali Radiviliana Collegii Societatis Jesu, 1758.

Katzenellenbogen, Pinhas. *Sefer yesh manḥilin*. Jerusalem: Makhon Ḥatam Sofer, 1986.

Kaźmierczyk, Adam, ed. *Żydzi Polscy 1648–1772: Źródła* [Polish Jews, 1648–1772: Sources]. Kraków: Uniwersytet Jagielloński, Katedra Judaistyki, 2001.

Kitowicz, Jędrzej. *Opis obyczajów za panowania Augusta III* [A Description of the Way of Life under the Rule of August III]. Edited by R. Pollack. Wrocław: Zakład Narodowy im. Ossolińskich, 1951.

Koidanover, Zvi Hirsh. *Sefer kav ha-yashar*. Frankfurt am Main: Johann Wauscht, 17.

Litwin, A. "Mi-pinkasei Nesvizh mi-shnat 511" [From the Nieśwież Pinkassim from 1751]. *Reshumot* (n.s.) 1 (1946): 161–62.

Luria, Shlomo ben Yeḥi'el. *Sefer she'elot u-teshuvot ha-Maharshal*. L'viv (Lemberg): David Zvi Schrenzel, 1859.

Maimon, Solomon. *Solomon Maimon: An Autobiography*. Translated by J. Clark Murray. Urbana: University of Illinois Press, 2001.

Matuszewicz, Marcin. *Diariusz życia mego* [The Diary of My Life]. Edited by B. Krolokowski. 2 vols. Warsaw: Państwowy Instytut Wydawniczy, 1986.

Peretz ben Moshe. *Beit Peretz*. Zholkva (Żółkiew): Gershon ben Ḥaim, David Segal, David ben Menaḥem Man, Ḥaim David ben Aharon Segal, 1759.

Pinkas ha-ksherim shel Kehillat Pozna (1621–1835) [The Electors' Record Book of the Poznań Community (1621–1835)]. Edited by Dov Avron. Jerusalem: Mekitzei Nirdamim, 1967.

Pinkas Kahal Tiktin, 1621–1806 [The Tykocin Community Record Book, 1621–1806]. Edited by M. Nadav. 2 vols. Jerusalem: The Israel Academy of Sciences, 1997–2000.

Pinkas Medinat Lita [The Record Book of the Lithuanian Council]. Edited by Simon Dubnow. Berlin: Ajanoth, 1925.

Pinkas Va'ad Arba Ha'aratzot [*PVDA*; The Record Book of the Council of Four Lands]. Edited by I. Halperin. Jerusalem: Mossad Bialik, 1945.

Puḥovitser, Yehuda Leib. *Sefer kevod ḥakhamim.*Venice: A. Bragadin, 1700.

Radziwiłł, Hieronim Florian. *Hieronima Floriana Radziwiłła diariusze i pisma różne* [Hieronim Florian Radziwiłł's Diaries and Various Writings]. Edited by Maria Strycharska-Brzezina. Warsaw: Wydawnictwo Energeia, 1998.

Radziwiłł, Mikołaj Krzysztof Sierotka. *Podróż do Ziemi Świętej, Syrii i Egiptu (1582–1584)* [A Journey to the Holy Land, Syria, and Egypt (1582–1584)]. Edited by Leszek Kukulski. Warsaw: Państwowy Instytut Wydawniczy, 1962.

Rapoport, Ḥaim Kohen. *She'elot ve-tshuvot rabeinu Ḥaim Kohen*. L'viv: S. Beck and A.J. Menkes, 1861.

Regesty i nadpisy: Svod materialov dlia istorii Yevreyev v Rossii [Summaries and Notes: A Collection of Materials for the History of the Jews in Russia]. 3 vols. St. Petersburg: Ts. Krajz i Ko., 1899–1913.

Sefer Shivḥei Ha-Besht. Edited by A. Rubinstein. Jerusalem: Reuven Mass, 1991.

Shmuel bar Elkana. *Sefer makom Shmuel*. Altona: Aharon ben Eli Katz, 1738.

Sirkes, Yo'el. *She'elot ve-tshuvot ha-baḥ ha-yeshanot*. Frankfurt am Main: Johann Wauscht, 1697.

Slomka, Jan. *From Serfdom to Self-Government: Memoirs of a Polish Village Mayor, 1842–1927*. Translated by William John Rose. London: Minerva, 1941.

Teki Gabryela Junoszy Podoskiego [The Gabryel Junosz Podoski Files]. Vol. 4. Edited by K. Jarochowski. Poznań: N. Kamieński, 1851.

Weinryb, Bernard D., ed. *Texts and Studies in the Communal History of Polish Jewry*. New York: The American Academy of Jewish Research, 1950.

Wettstein, Feivish. "Mi-pinkasei ha-kahal be-Kraka'—Le-korot Yisra'el ve-ḥakhamav, rabanav, u-manhigav ba-Polin bi-khlal u-be-Kraka' bi-frat" [From the Krakow Community Record Books: On the History of the Jews, Their Sages, Their Rabbis, and Their Leaders in Poland in General and in Kraków in Particular]. In M. Brann and F. Rosenthal, eds., *Gedenkbuch zur Erinnerung an David Kaufmann*. Wrocław (Breslau): Schlesische Verlags-Anstalt, 1900.

Wilensky, Mordekhai. *Ḥasidim u-mitnagdim: Le-toledot ha-pulmus beineihem ba-shanim 1772–1815* [Hasidim and Mitnagdim: A Study of the Controversy between Them in the Years 1772–1815]. 2 vols. Jerusalem: Mossad Bialik, 1970.

Yehoshua Heshel ben Yosef. *She'elot ve-tshuvot Pnei Yehoshua*. Vol. II. L'viv (Lemberg): Zalman Leib Flekir, 1860.

Zawadzki, Wacław, ed. *Polska Stanisławowska w oczach cudzoziemców* [The Poland of Stanisław August through the Eyes of Foreigners]. 2 vols. Warsaw: Państwowy Instytut Wydawniczy, 1963.

STUDIES

Alexandrov, Hillel. "Derzhavtses un kahal" [The Leaseholders and the Kahal]. *Tsaytshrift Minsk* 4 (1930): 121–24.

———. "Di Yidishe bafelkerung in Vaysrusland in der tsayt fun di tseteylungen fun Poyln" [The Jewish Population of Belarus during the Partitions of Poland]. *Tsaytshrift Minsk* 4 (1930): 31–83.

Alexandrowicz, Stanisław. "Miasteczka Białorusi i Litwy jako ośrodki handlu w XVI i w połowie XVII wieku" [Small Towns in Belarus and Lithuania as Trade Centers in the Sixteenth and the First Half of the Seventeenth Centuries]. *Rocznik Białostocki* 1 (1961): 63–130.

———. *Rozwój kartografii Wielkiego Księstwa Litweskiego od XV do połowy XVIII wieku* [The Development of the Cartography of the Grand Duchy of Lithuania from the Fifteenth to the Second Half of the Eighteenth Centuries]. 2 vols. Poznań: Uniwersytet im. Adama Mickiewicza w Poznaniu, 1989.

———. "Zaludnienie miasteczek Litwy i Białorusi w XVI i pierwszej połowie XVII wieku" [The Population of the Small Towns in Lithuania and Belarus in the Sixteenth and Early Seventeenth Centuries]. *Roczniki Dziejów Społecznych i Gospodarczych* 27 (1966): 35–67.

Anusik, Zbigniew, and Andrzej Strojnowski. "Problemy majątkowe Radziwiłłów w XVIII w." [The Problematics of the Radziwiłł Estates in the Eighteenth Century]. *Roczniki Dziejów Społecznych i Gospodarczych* 48 (1987): 79–112.

———. "Radziwiłłowie w epoce saskiej: Zarys dziejów politicznych i majątkowych" [The Radziwiłłs in the Saxon Era: An Outline of Their Political History and the Development of Their Estates]. *Acta Universitatis Lodziensis. Folia Historica* 33 (1989): 29–58.

Aust, Cornelia. "Commercial Cosmopolitans: Networks of Jewish Merchants between Warsaw and Amsterdam, 1750–1820." PhD diss., University of Pennsylvania, 2010.

Bałaban, Majer. "Ha-'otonomiyah ha-yehudit" [Jewish Autonomy]. In I. Halperin, ed., *Beit Yisrael be-Polin*, 1: 44–65. Jerusalem, 1948.

———. *Historja Żydów w Krakowie i na Kazimierzu, 1304–1868* [History of the Jews in Kraków and Kazimierz, 1304–1868]. 2 vols. Kraków: Nadzieja, 1931–1936.

———. *Joseph Jonas Theomin-Fränkel, Rabbiner in Krakau (1742–1745) und seine Zeit: archivalische Studie* [Joseph Jonah Theomim Fränkel, Rabbi in Kraków (1742–1745) and His Time: Archival Study]. Wrocław (Breslau): A. Favorke, 1917.

———. *Die Judenstadt von Lublin* [The Jewish Town in Lublin]. Berlin: Jüdischer Verlag, 1919.

———. *Le-toledot ha-tenu'ah ha-Frankit* [On the History of the Frankist Movement]. 2 vols. Tel Aviv: Dvir, 1934.

———. "Zalmen der rosh-hokohel fun Drohobitsh" [Zalman, Head of the Community in Drohobycz]. In Balaban, *Yidn in Poyln*, 67–87. Vilnius (Vilne): B. Kletzkin, 1930.

Bańkowski, P. "Polskie archiwa magnackie w Centralnym Państwowym Archiwum Historycznym w Kijowie" [Polish Magnate Archives in the Central State Historical Archive in Kyiv]. *Archeion* 40 (1964): 161–76.

Baranowski, Bohdan. *Polska karczma, restauracja, kawiarnia* [The Polish Tavern: Restaurant-Cafe]. Wrocław: Zakład Narodowy im. Ossolińskich, 1979.

———. *Życie codzienne małego miasteczka w XVII i XVIII wieku* [The Daily Life of Small Towns in the Seventeenth and Eighteenth Centuries]. Warsaw: Instytut Wydawniczy, 1975.

Bardach, Juliusz. *Historia państwa i prawa polskiego* [The History of the Polish State and Its Laws]. Vol I. Warsaw: Państwowe Wydawnictwo Naukowe, 1964.

———. *O dawnej i niedawnej Litwie* [On Lithuania, Ancient and Recent]. Poznań: Wydawnictwo Naukowe UAM, 1988.

———. "Żydzi w Birżach radziwiłłowskich w XVII–XVIII wieku" [The Jews in the Radziwiłłs' Birże in the 16th–17th Centuries]. *Przegląd Historyczny* 81, nos. 1–2 (1990): 199–220.

Baron, Salo W. *A Social and Religious History of the Jews.* Vol. 16. New York-London-Philadelphia: Jewish Publication Society, 1976.

Barzilay, Isaac. *Yoseph Shlomo Delmedigo, Yashar of Candia: His Life, Works and Times.* Leiden: Brill, 1974.

Baszanowski, Jan. *Z dziejów handlu polskiego w XVI–XVIII wieku: handel wołami* [From the History of Polish Trade in the 16th–18th Centuries: The Trade in Oxen]. Gdańsk: Zakład Narodowy im. Ossolińskich, 1977.

Ben Sasson, H. H. "Takkanot issurei-shabbat shel Polin u-mashmautan ha-ḥevratit ve-ha-kalkalit" [The Regulations Concerning Sabbath Keeping in Poland and Their Socio-Economic Significance]. *Tziyon* 21 (1956): 183–206.

Bergerówna, J. *Księżna pani na Kocku i Semiatyczach* [Princess of Kock and Semiatycze]. Lwów: Towarzystwo naukowe we Lwowie, 1936.

Bershadskiĭ, S. *Litovskie Yevrei* [The Lithuanian Jews]. St. Petersburg: M. M. Stasiulevicha, 1883.

Bieniarzowna, Janina. "The Role of the Jews in Polish Foreign Trade, 1648–1764."

In Andrzej K. Paluch, ed., *The Jews in Poland*, I: 101–9. Kraków: Jagiellonian University, Research Center on Jewish History and Culture in Poland, 1992.

Blom, Ida. "The History of Widowhood: A Bibliographic Overview." *Journal of Family History* 16, no. 2 (1991): 191–210.

Bobrzyński, Michał. "Prawo propinacji w dawnej Polsce" [The Right of Propinacja in Old Poland]. In Bobrzyński, *Szkice i studja historyczne*, II: 232–97. Kraków: Krakowska Spółka Wydawnicza, 1922.

Bogucka, Maria. "Kupcy żydowscy w Gdańsku w pierwszej połowie XVII wieku" [Jewish Merchants in Gdańsk in the First Half of the Seventeenth Century]. *Przegląd Historyczny* 80, no. 4 (1989): 791–99.

———. "Rodzina w polskim mieście XVI–XVII wieku: Wprowadzenie w problematykę" [The Family in the Polish Town in the Sixteenth-Seventeenth Centuries: An Introduction to the Problematic]. *Przegląd Historyczny* 74, no. 3 (1983): 495–507.

———. "Women and Economic Life in the Polish Cities during the 16th–17th Centuries." In S. Cavaciocchi, ed., *La donna nell'economia secc. XIII–XVIII*, 185–94. Prato: Istituto internazionale di storia economica "F. Datini," 1990.

Bogucka, Maria, and Henryk Samsonowicz. *Dzieje miast i mieszczaństwa w Polsce przedrozbiorowej* [A History of Towns and Townspeople in Pre-Partition Poland]. Wrocław: Zakład Narodowy im. Ossolińskich, 1986.

Boldizzoni, Francesco. *The Poverty of Clio: Resurrecting Economic History*. Princeton: Princeton University Press, 2011.

Bonacich, Edna. "A Theory of Middleman Minorities." *American Sociological Review* 38, no. 5 (October 1973): 583–94.

Borawski, Piotr. "Tatarzy—ziemianie w dobrach Radziwiłłów (XVI–XVIII w.)" [Tatars—Landowners on the Radziwiłł Estates (16th–18th Centuries)]. *Przegląd Historyczny* 82, no. 1 (1981): 33–49.

———. "Tatarzy w miastach i jurydykach Radziwiłłów" [Tatars in the Radziwiłł Towns and Enclaves]. *Przegląd Historyczny* 83, no. 1 (1992): 65–81.

Breger, Marcus. *Zur Handelsgeschichte der Juden in Polen während des 17. Jahrhundert* [On the Mercantile History of the Jews in Poland during the 17th Century]. Berlin: Buchhandlung R. Mass, 1932.

Burszta, Józef. "Handel magnacki i kupiecki między Sieniawą nad Sanem a Gdańskiem od końca XVII do połowy XVIII wieku" [Magnate and Merchant Trade between Sieniawa on the San and Gdańsk from the End of the Seventeenth to the Mid-Eighteenth Century]. *Roczniki Dziejów Społecznych i Gospodarczych* 16 (1954): 174–223.

———. *Wieś i karczma: rola karczmy w życiu wsi pańszczyźnianej* [Village and Tavern: The Role of the Tavern in Village Life under Serfdom]. Warsaw: Ludowa Spółdzielnia Wydawnicza, 1950.

Burzyński, Andrzej. *Struktura dochodów wielkiej własności ziemskiej XVI–XVIII wieku (Próba analizy na przykładzie dóbr królewskich województwa sandomierskiego)* [The Structure of the Incomes from Great Landed Property in the Sixteenth and

Seventeenth Centuries (An Attempted Analysis on the Example of the Royal Estates in the Sandomierz Region)]. Poznań: Poznańskie Towarzystwo Przyjaciół Nauk, 1973.

Chazan, Robert, ed. *Church, State, and Jew in the Middle Ages.* New York: Behrman House, 1980.

Cieśla, Maria. "Żydzi w Wielkim Księstwie Litewskim, 1632–1764: Sytuacja prawna, demografia, działalność gospodarcza" [The Jews in the Grand Duchy of Lithuania: Legal Status, Demography, Economic Activity]. PhD diss., Institute of History, Polish Academy of Sciences, 2010.

Cipolla, Carlo M. *Between History and Economics: An Introduction to Economic History.* Oxford: Blackwell, 1991.

Coase, Ronald. "The New Institutional Economics." *The American Economic Review* 88, no. 2 (May 1998): 72–74.

Codello, Aleksander. "Zbiegostwo mieszczan rzeszowskich w pierwszej połowie XVIII w." [Fugitive Townspeople from Rzeszów in the First Half of the Eighteenth Century]. *Małopolskie Studia Historyczne* 1, no. 1 (1958): 17–28.

———. "Rywalizacja Paców i Radziwiłłów w latach 1666–1669" [The Rivalry between the Paces and the Radziwiłłs, 1666–1669]. *Kwartalnik Historyczny* 71, no. 4 (1964): 913–30.

Coser, Lewis A. "The Alien as Servant of Power: Court Jews and Christian Renegades." *American Sociological Review* 37, no. 5 (October 1972): 574–81.

Czapliński, Władysław. "Rządy oligarchii w Polsce nowożytnej" [The Oligarchic Regime in Modern Poland]. *Przegląd Historyczny* 52, no 3 (1961): 445–65. Reprinted in Czapliński, *O Polsce siedemnastowiecznej: problemy i sprawy.* Warsaw: Państwowy Instytut Wydawniczy, 1966.

———, and Józef Długosz. *Życie codzienne magnaterii polskiej w XVII wieku* [The Daily Life of the Polish Magnates in the 17th Century]. Warsaw: Państwowy Instytut Wydawniczy, 1976.

Dąbkowski, Przemysław. *Prawo prywatne polskie* [Polish Private Law]. 2 vols. L'viv (Lwów): Towarzystwo dla Popierania Nauki Polskiej, 1910.

Degiel, Rafał. *Protestanci i prawosławni: Patronat wyznaniowy Radziwiłłów birżańskich nad Cerkwią prawosławną w księstwie słuckim w XVII w.* [Protestants and Orthodox: The Religious Patronage of the Birże Radziwiłłs over the Orthodox Church in the Słuck Principality in the Seventeenth Century]. Warsaw: Neriton, 2000.

Dembitzer, Ḥaim Natan. *Kelilat Yofi* [Perfect in Beauty]. 2 vols. Krakow: Yosef Fischer, 1888–93.

Dillon, Phyllis, and Andrew Godley. "The Evolution of the Jewish Garment Industry, 1840–1940." In Rebecca Kobrin, ed., *Chosen Capital: The Jewish Encounter with American Capitalism.* New Brunswick, NJ: Rutgers University Press, 2012.

Dinur, Ben Zion. "Reshitah shel ha-ḥasidut ve-yesodoteha ha-sotzialiyim ve-ha-meshiḥiyim" [The Beginnings of Hasidism and Its Social and Messianic Foundations]. In Dinur, *Be-mifneh ha-dorot*, 83–227. Jerusalem: Mossad Bialik 1955.

Dubnow, Simon. "Va'ad 'arba' aratzot be-Polin ve-yahaso el' ha-kehilot" [The Council of Four Lands in Poland and Its Attitude Towards the Communities]. In *Sefer ha-yovel li-khvod Naḥum Sokolov*, 250–61. Warsaw: Shuldberg ve-shutafo, 1903.

Dynner, Glenn. *Yankel's Tavern: Jews, Liquor, and Life in the Kingdom of Poland.* New York: Oxford University Press, 2015.

Edelmann, Zevi Hirsch. *Gedulat Shaul* [Saul's Greatness]. London: no publisher, 1854.

Eggertsson, Thráinn. *Economic Behavior and Institutions.* Cambridge: Cambridge University Press, 1990.

Eichhorn, Karl Friedrich. *Stosunek książęcego domu Radziwiłłów do domów książęcych Niemczech uważany ze stanowiska historyczne* [The Relations of the Princely Radziwiłł Dynasty with the Princely German Dynasties Viewed from a Historical Standpoint]. Warsaw: A. E. Glücksberg, 1843.

Ettinger, Shmuel. "Ḥelkam shel ha-yehudim ba-kolonizatziah shel Ukraina (1569–1648)" [The Role of the Jews in the Colonization of Ukraine (1569–1648)]. *Tziyon* 21 (1956): 107–42.

Falniowska-Gradowska, Alicja. *Królewszczyzny i starostwie w dawnej Rzeczypospolitej* [Royal Estates and Starostwos in the Old Republic]. Wrocław and Kraków: Zakład Narodowy im. Ossolińskich, 1984.

Fram, Edward. *Ideals Face Reality: Jewish Law and Life in Poland, 1550–1655.* Cincinnati: Hebrew Union College Press, 1997.

Freudenthal, Max. *Leipziger Messgäste: Die jüdischen Besucher der Leipziger Messen in den Jahren 1675 bis 1764.* Frankfurt am Main: J. Kauffmann, 1928.

Frick, David A. *Kith, Kin, and Neighbors: Communities and Confessions in Seventeenth-Century Wilno.* Ithaca: Cornell University Press, 2013.

Frost, Robert I. *The Northern Wars, 1558–1721.* Harlow: Longman, 2000.

Fünn, Samuel Josef. *Kiryah ne'emanah* [Faithful Town]. Vilnius: Reuven Yosef Rom, 1860.

Galant, Il'ya. "Zadolzhennost' yevreĭskikh obshchin v XVII veke" [The Indebtedness of the Jewish Communities in the 17th Century]. *Yevreĭskaia Starina* 6 (1913): 129–32.

Gause, F. *Der Grundbesitz der Familie Saturgus in Königsberg* [The Saturgus Family's Real Estate in Königsberg]. http://www.kant.uni-mainz.de/ikonographie/Ikont .PDF/T110.pdf (retrieved 02/04/2016). Originally published in 1956.

Gelber, Natan Michael. *Toledot yehudei Brody* [A History of the Jews of Brody]. Jerusalem: Mossad Ha-Rav Kook, 1956.

Gelman, Aryeh Leib. *Ha-Noda' Bi-Yehudah u-mishnato* [The Noda Bi-yehudah and His Teaching]. Jerusalem: Mossad Ha-Rav Kook, 1962.

Gessen, Yulii. "Lipman, Levi." *Yevreĭskaya Ėntsiklopediia.* Vol. 10. St. Petersburg, 1908–1913.

Gierowski, Józef. *Między saskim absolutyzmem a złotą wolnością: Z dziejów wewnętrznych Rzeczypospolitej w latach 1712–1715* [Between Saxon Absolutism

and the Golden Freedom: The Internal History of the Republic 1712–1715].
Wrocław: Zakład im. Ossolińskich Wydawnictwo Polskiej Akademii Nauk, 1953.

———. *The Polish-Lithuanian Commonwealth in the XVIIIth Century: From Anarchy to Well-Organised State.* Kraków: Nakładem Polskiej Akademii Umiejętności, 1996.

Gierszewski, Stanisław. "Magnaci i szlachta jako zawodowi kupcy-przewoźnicy w XVI–XVIII wieku" [Magnates and Noblemen as Professional Merchants and Carriers in the Sixteenth–Eighteenth Centuries]. *Roczniki Dziejów Społecznych i Gospodarczych* 47 (1987): 1–13.

———. "Port w Królewcu—z dziejów jego zaplecza w XVI–XVIII wieku" [The Port in Königsberg—From the History of Its Hinterland in the Sixteenth–Eighteenth Centuries]. *Komunikaty Mazursko-Warmińskie* 1 (1993): 53–60.

Gladstein-Kastenberg, Ruth. "Ḥezkat-ha-yishuv, ḥerem ha-yishuv ve-ha-metzi'ut shel yemei-ha-beinayim" [Ḥezkat-Ha-yishuv, Ḥerem Ha-yishuv and Medieval Reality]. *Tarbitz* 47 (1978): 216–29.

Glinski, Gerhard von. *Die Königsberger Kaufmannschaft des 17. und 18. Jahrhunderts* [The Königsberg Merchants in the 17th and 18th Centuries]. Marburg (Lahn): Johann Gottfried Herder-Institut, 1964.

Goldberg, Jacob. "Bein ḥofesh le-netinut: Sugei ha-tlut ha-fe'udalit shel ha-Yehudim ba-Polin" [Between Freedom and Subject-hood: Types of Jewish Feudal Dependency in Poland]. *Divrei ha-kongress ha'olami ha-ḥamishi le-mada'ei ha-yahadut* 2 (1972): 107–13.

———. "The Changes in Attitude of Polish Society toward the Jews in the 18th Century." *Polin* 1 (1986): 35–48.

———. *Ha-ḥevrah ha-yehudit ba-mamlekhet Polin-Lita* [Jewish Society in the Polish-Lithuanian Commonwealth]. Jerusalem: Merkaz Zalman Shazar le-Toledot Yisrael, 1999.

———. "Ha-mishar ha-kimona'i ha-yehudi be-Polin ba-me'ah ha-18: Takanot la-ḥenvanim be-Zaslav u-ve-Brody ve-she'elat ha-mekorot ha-ivri'm-ha-polani'im le-toledot ha-mishar ve-ha-ḥevrah ha-yehudi'im" [The Jewish Retail Trade in Eighteenth Century Poland: Shopkeepers' Regulations in Zasław and Brody and the Question of Hebrew-Polish Sources for the History of Jewish Society and Trade]. In Ezra Mendelsohn and Chone Shmeruk, eds., *Kovetz meḥkarim 'al yehudei Polin: Sefer lezikhro shel Paul Glikson*, 11–64. Jerusalem: Ha-Merkaz le-Ḥeker Toledot Yehudei Polin ve-Tarbutam, The Hebrew University, 1987.

———. "O budownictwie żydowskim w Polsce w XVII–XVIII wieku" [On Jewish Building in Sixteenth- and Seventeenth-Century Poland]. In Goldberg, *Żydzi w społeczeństwie, gospodarce i kulturze Rzeczypospolitej szlacheckiej*, 107–21. Kraków: Polska Akademia Umiejętności, 2012.

———. "Ośrodki przemysłowe we wschodniej Wielkopolsce w XVIII w." [Industrial Centers in Eastern Wielkopolska in the Eighteenth Century]. *Roczniki Dziejów Społecznych i Gospodarczych* 29 (1968): 55–85.

———. "Rolnictwo wśród Żydów w ziemi wieluńskiej w drugiej połowie XVIII wieku" [Agriculture among the Jews of the Wieluń District in the Second Half of the 18th Century]. *Biuletyn Żydowskiego Instytutu Historycznego* 27 (1958): 62–89.

———. "Tlutan ve'atzma'utan shel kehilot yehudiyot ba-mamlekhet Polin-Lita" [The Dependence and Independence of Jewish Communities in the Polish-Lithuanian Commonwealth]. *Divrei ha-kongres ha-'olami ha-tshiyi la-mada'ei ha-yahadut* 2–1 (1986): 141–86.

Gomer, Abba. *Beiträge zur Kultur- und Sozialgeschichte des litauischen Judentums im 17. u. 18. Jahrhundert* [Contributions to the Cultural and Social History of Lithuanian Jewry in the 17th and 18th Centuries]. Bochum: F.W. Fretlöh, 1930.

Górski, Janusz. *Poglądy merkantylistyczne w polskiej myśli ekonomicznej XVI i XVII wieku* [Mercantilistic Views in the Polish Economic Thought of the Sixteenth and Seventeenth Centuries]. Wrocław: Zakład Narodowy im. Ossolińskich Wydawnictwo Polskiej Akademii Nauk, 1958.

Grochulska, Barbara. "Jarmarki w handlu polskim w drugiej połowie XVIII w." [Fairs in Polish Trade in the Second Half of the Eighteenth Century]. *Przegląd Historyczny* 64, no. 4 (1973): 793–821.

Greenbaum, Alfred Abraham. *Jewish Scholarship and Scholarly Institutions in Soviet Russia, 1918–1953*. Jerusalem: Hebrew University of Jerusalem, Centre for Research and Documentation of East European Jewry, 1978.

Greenbaum, Masha. *The Jews of Lithuania: A History of Remarkable Community, 1316–1945*. Jerusalem: Gefen, 1995.

Greif, Avner. *Institutions and the Path to the Modern Economy: Lessons from Medieval Trade*. Cambridge: Cambridge University Press, 2006.

Gritskevich, Anatolii Petrovich. *Chastnovladel'cheskiye goroda Belorussii v XVI–XVII vv.* [The Private Towns of Belarus in the Sixteenth–Eighteenth Centuries]. Minsk: Nauka i Tekhnika, 1975.

———. [Hryckiewicz, Anatol]. "Milicje miast magnackich na Białorusi i Litwie w XVI–XVIII w." [Militias in the Magnate Towns in Belarus and Lithuania in the Sixteenth–Eighteenth Centuries]. *Kwartalnik Historyczny* 77, no. 1 (1970): 47–62.

———. *Sotsiyal'naia borba gorozhan Belorussii: XVI–XVII vv.* [The Social Struggle of the Belarussian Townspeople: Sixteenth–Eighteenth Centuries]. Minsk: Nauka i Tekhnika, 1979.

Guldon, Zenon. "Źródła i metody szacunków liczebności żydowskiej w końca XVIII wieku" [Sources and Methods for Calculating the Number of Jews at the End of the 18th Century]. *Kwartalnik Historii Kultury Materialnej* 2 (1986): 249–63.

———. *Związki handlowe dóbr magnackich na prawobrzeżnej Ukrainie z Gdańskiem w XVIII wieku* [The Mercantile Connections between the Magnate Estates in Right Bank Ukraine and Gdańsk in the 18th Century]. Toruń: Wydawnictwo Uniwersytetu Mikołaja Kopernika, 1966.

Guldon, Zenon, and Mikola Krikun. "Przyczynek do krytyki spisów ludności żydowskiej w końca XVIII wieku" [A Contribution to the Critical Reading of Jewish Censuses from the End of the 18th Century]. *Studia Źródłoznawcze, Commentationes* 23 (1978): 153–57.

Guldon, Zenon, and Jacek Wijaczka. *Procesy o mordy rytualne w Polsce w XVI–XVIII wieku* [Ritual Murder Trials in Sixteenth-Eighteenth Century Poland]. Kielce: DCF, 1995.

Halamshtok, L. "Der yiddisher lebenshteiger in akhtsen yh." *Zeitshrift Minsk* 4 (1930): 86–98.

Halperin, Israel, ed. *Bet Yisrael be-Polin: Mi-yamim rish'onim ve-'ad li-yemot ha-ḥurban* [The Jews in Poland: From the Earliest Days until the Holocaust]. 2 vols. Jerusalem: Ha-Maḥlakah le-'Inyenei ha-No'ar shel ha-Histadrut ha-Tsiyonit, 1948–1954.

———. *Yehudim ve-yahadut ba-mizraḥ 'eiropa* [Jews and Judaism in Eastern Europe]. Jerusalem: Magnes Press, 1969.

Handrack, Udo. *Der Handel der Stadt Riga im 18. Jahrhundert* [Rīga's Trade in the 18th Century]. Libau: Meyer, 1932.

Hedemann, Otton. *Dzisna i Druje, magdeburskie miasta* [Dzisna and Druje, Towns of Magdeburg Law]. Vilnius (Wilno): Towarzystwo Przyjaciół Nauk, 1934.

Hendel, Michael. "Ha-yehudim be-Biala" [The Jews in Biała]. In M. Feigenboim, ed., *Sefer Biala Podlaska*, 9–29. Tel-Aviv: Kupat Gmilut Hesed 'al shem Kehillat Biala Podlaska, 1961.

Homecki, Adam. *Produkcja i handel zbożowy w latyfundium Lubomirskich w drugiej połowie XVII i pierwszej XVIII wieku* [Production and Trade in Grain on the Lubomirski Latifundium in the Second Half of the Seventeenth and the First Half of the Eighteenth Century]. Wrocław: Zakład Narodowy im. Ossolińskich Wydawnictwo PAN, 1970.

Horn, Maurycy. "The Chronology and Distribution of Jewish Craft Guilds in Old Poland." In Antony Polonsky et al., eds., *The Jews in Old Poland, 1000–1795*, 249–66. London: I. B. Tauris, 1993.

Hoszowski, Stanisław. "The Polish Baltic Trade in the 15th–18th Centuries." In *Poland at the XIth International Congress of Historical Sciences in Stockholm*, 117–54. Warsaw: The Institute of History, Polish Academy of Sciences, 1960.

Hundert, Gershon David. "Approaches to the History of the Jewish Family in Early Modern Poland-Lithuania." In Steven M. Cohen and Paula E. Hyman, eds., *The Jewish Family: Myths and Reality*, 17–28. New York: Holmes & Meier, 1986.

———. "Ha-kehillah be-Polin: 'Aspektim shonim" [The Community in Poland: Various Aspects]. In I. Bartal, ed., *Kahal yisra'el: Ha-shilton ha-yehudi le-dorotav*, vol. 3: 43–52. Jerusalem: Merkaz Zalman Shazar le-Toledot Yisrael, 2004.

———. "Kahal i samorząd miejski w miastach prywatnych w XVII i XVIII w." [The Kahal and Municipal Autonomy in Private Towns in the Seventeenth and Eighteenth Centuries]. In Andrzej Link-Lenczowski and Tomasz Polański, eds., *Żydzi w dawnej Rzeczypospolitej*, 66–74. Wrocław: Zakład Narodowy im. Ossolińskich, 1991.

―――. "Kivunei hitpatḥut shel ha-misḥar ha-sitona'i ha-yehudi be-Polin ba-me'ot ha-17–18" [Developmental Trends in the Jews' Wholesale Trade in Poland in the 17th–18th Centuries]. In N. Gross, ed., *Yehudim ba-kalkalah*, 225–36. Jerusalem: Merkaz Zalman Shazar le-Toledot Yisrael, 1985.

―――. "Jewish Urban Residence in the Polish Commonwealth in the Early Modern Period." *Jewish Journal of Sociology* 26 (1984): 25–34.

―――. *The Jews in a Polish Private Town: The Case of Opatów in the Eighteenth Century.* Baltimore: Johns Hopkins University Press, 1992.

―――. *Jews in Poland-Lithuania in the Eighteenth Century: A Genealogy of Modernity.* Berkeley: University of California Press, 2004.

―――. "On the Jewish Community of Poland during the Seventeenth Century: Some Comparative Perspectives." *Revue des Etudes Juives* 142, no. 3 (1983): 349–72.

―――. "The Role of the Jews in Commerce in Early Modern Poland-Lithuania." *Journal of European Economic History* 16, no. 2 (1987): 245–75.

―――. "Shkiy' at yira't kavod be-kehillot beit Yisrael be-Polin-Lita'" [The Decline of Deference in the Jewish Communities of Poland-Lithuania]. *Bar-Ilan* 24–25 (1989): 41–50.

―――. "Was There an East European Analogue to Court Jews?" In Andrzej K. Paluch, ed., *The Jews in Poland*, 67–75. Kraków: Jagellionian University, 1992.

Hyczko, Gustawa. "Straty i zniszczenia wojenne we wsiach lubelskich oraz ich skutki w latach trzeciej wojny polnocnej" [War Losses and Destruction in the Villages of the Lublin District During the Third Northern War]. *Roczniki Dziejów Społecznych i Gospodarczych* 29 (1968): 33–54.

Inglot, Stefan. "Organizacja folwarku na Białorusi na przełomie XVIII i XIX wieku [The Organization of the Folwark in Belarus at the Turn of the 18th and 19th Centuries]." *Ekonomista* 31 (1931).

―――, ed. *Historia chłopów polskich* [A History of Polish Peasants]. Warsaw: Ludowa Spółdzielnia Wydawnicza, 1970.

Israel, Jonathan. "Central European Jewry During the Thirty Years War, 1618–1648." *Central European History* 16 (1983): 3–30.

―――. "The Sephardi Contribution to Economic Life and Colonization in Europe and the New World (16th–18th Centuries)." In Ḥaim Beinart, ed., *Moreshet Sepharad: The Sephardi Legacy*, II: 365–98. Jerusalem: Magnes Press, Hebrew University, 1992.

Jordan, William Chester. "Jews on Top: Women and the Availability of Consumption Loans in Northern France in the Mid-Thirteenth Century." *Journal of Jewish Studies* 29 (Spring 1978): 45–56.

―――. "Women and Credit in the Middle Ages: Problems and Directions." *The Journal of European Economic History* 17, no. 1 (Spring 1988): 33–61.

Kaczmarczyk, Zdzisław, and Bogusław Leśnodorski. *Historia państwa i prawa Polski* [A History of Poland and Polish Law]. 2 vols. Warsaw: Państwowe Wydawnictwo Naukowe, 1966.

Kalik, Judith (Julia). "Ha-yaḥas shel ha-shlakhta la-misḥar ha-yehudi ba-me'ot ha-17–18" [The Attitude of the Szlachta to Jewish Trade in the Seventeenth and Eighteenth Centuries]. *Gal-Ed* 13 (1993): 43–57.

———. "Hafkadah ve-viderkaf be-fe'ilutam ha-kalkalit shel yehudei mamlekhet Polin-Lita" [Mortgages and Standing Loans in the Economic Activity of the Jews in the Polish-Lithuanian Commonwealth]. In Ran Aharonson and Shaul Stampfer, eds., *Yazamut yehudit ba'et ha-ḥadashah: Mizraḥ 'Eiropah ve-'Eretz Yisra'el*, 25–47. Jerusalem: Magnes Press, 2001.

———. "Patterns of Contact between the Catholic Church and the Jews in the Polish-Lithuanian Commonwealth during the 17–18th Centuries: Jewish Debts." In Adam Teller, ed., *Studies in the History of the Jews in Old Poland: In Honor of Jacob Goldberg. Scripta Hierosolomitana 38*, 102–22. Jerusalem: Magnes Press; The Hebrew University, Center for Research on the History and Culture of Polish Jews, 1998.

———. "Szlachta Attitudes towards Jewish Arenda in the Seventeenth and Eighteenth Centuries." *Gal-Ed* 14 (1995): 15–25.

———. *Scepter of Judah: The Jewish Autonomy in the Eighteenth-Century Crown Poland*. Leiden and Boston: Brill, 2009.

Kalinowski, Wojciech. "Zabudowa i struktura przestrzenna miast polskich od połowy XVII do schyłku XVIII wieku" [The Building and Spatial Structure of Polish Towns from the Mid-Seventeenth to the End of the Eighteenth Century]. In M. Gajewska et al., *Dom i mieszkanie w Polsce (druga połowa XVII–XIX w.)*. Wrocław: Zakład im. Ossolińskich Wydawnictwo Polskiej Akademii Nauk, 1975.

Kamenetskiĭ, A. "Yevreĭskiĭ dokument o bitve pod Slonimom v 1764 g." [A Hebrew Document about the Battle near Slonim in 1764]. *Perezhitoye: Sbornik, posviashchennyĭ obshchsetvennoĭ i kul'turnoĭ istorii yevreyev v Rossii* 4 (1913).

Kamieńska, Zofia. "Fachowcy cudzoziemscy w manufakturach magnackich XVIII wieku. (Manufaktura urzecka Radziwiłłów)" [Foreign Experts in the Magnate Manufactories in the Eighteenth Century (The Radziwiłł's Urzecz Manufactory)]. *Przegląd Historyczny* 43, nos. 3–4 (1952): 518–35, 633–35.

———. *Manufaktura szklana w Urzeczu 1737–1846* [The Glass Manufactory in Urzecz 1737–1846]. Warsaw: Państwowe Wydawnictwo Naukowe, 1946.

Kaplan, Debra. "Women and Worth: Female Access to Property in Early Modern Urban Jewish Communities." *Leo Baeck Institute Year Book* 55 (2010): 93–113.

Karkucińska, Wanda. *Anna z Sanguszków Radziwiłłowa (1676–1746): Działalność gospodarcza i mecenat* [Anna Radziwiłł née Sanguszko (1646–1746): Economic Activity and Patronage]. Warsaw: Wydawnictwo Naukowe Semper, 2000.

———. "Działalność gospodarcza i kulturalna Anny z Sanguszków Radziwiłłowej w Białej" [The Economic and Cultural Activity of Anna Radziwiłłowa in Biała]. In Tadeusz Wasilewski and Tadeusz Krawczuk, eds., *Z nieznanej przeszłości Białej i Podlasia* [From the Unknown History of Biała and Podlasia]. Biała Podlaska: PTSK, 1990.

Karp, Jonathan. "Economic History and Jewish Modernity—Ideological Versus Structural Change." *Jahrbuch des Simon-Dubnow-Instituts* 6 (2007): 249–66.

Karpiński, Andrzej. *Kobieta w mieście polskim w drugiej połowie XVI i w XVII wieku* [The Woman in the Polish Town in the Second Half of the Sixteenth and in the Seventeenth Century]. Warsaw: Instytut Historii PAN, 1995.

———. "The Woman on the Marketplace: The Scale of Feminization of Retail Trade in Polish Towns in the Second Half of the 16th and in the 17th Century." In Simona Cavaciocchi, ed., *La donna nell'economia secc. XIII–XVIII*, 283–92. Florence: Prato, 1990.

Katz, Jacob. *Goy shel Shabbat: Ha-reka' ha-kalkali-ḥevrati ve-ha-yesod ha-halakhi le-ha'asakat nokhri be-shabatot u-be-ḥagei Yisra'el* [The Sabbath Gentile: The Socio-Economic Background and Halakhic Basis for Employing a Non-Jew on Sabbaths and Jewish Festivals]. Jerusalem: Merkaz Zalman Shazar le-Toledot Yisrael, 1984.

———. *Tradition and Crisis: Jewish Society at the End of the Middle Ages.* Translated by Bernard Dov Cooperman. New York: New York University Press, 1993.

Kazusek, Szymon. *Żydzi w handlu Krakowa w połowie XVII wieku* [The Jews in Kraków's Trade in the Second Half of the Seventeenth Century]. Kraków: Wydawnictwo Towarzystwa Naukowego Societas Vistulana, 2005.

Kaźmierczyk, Adam. "Jakub Becal: King Jan III Sobieski's Jewish Factor." *Polin* 15 (2002): 249–66.

———. "The Problem of Christian Servants as Reflected in the Legal Codes of the Polish-Lithuanian Commonwealth during the Second Half of the Seventeenth Century and in the Saxon Period." *Gal-Ed* 15–16 (1997): 23–40.

———. *Żydzi w dobrach prywatnych w świetle sądowniczej i administracyjnej praktyki dóbr magnackich w wiekach XVI–XVIII.* Kraków: Uniwersytet Jagielloński. Katedra Judaistyki: Księgarnia Akademicka, 2002.

Kersten, Adam. "Problem władzy w Rzeczpospolitej czasu Wazów" [The Problem of Power in the Commonwealth during the Time of the Wazas]. In Józef Gierowski et al., eds., *O naprawę Rzeczpospolitej: XVII–XVIII: Prace ofiarowane Władysławowi Czaplińskiemu w 60 rocznicę urodzin*, 23–36. Warsaw: Państwowe Wydawnictwo Naukowe, 1965.

Kirby, David. *Northern Europe in the Early Modern Period: The Baltic World, 1492–1772.* London and New York: Longman, 1990.

Kirzner, Israel M. *Competition and Entrepreneurship.* Chicago: University of Chicago Press, 1973.

Kizik, Edmund. "Mieszczaństwo gdańskie wobec Żydów w XVII–XVIII wieku" [Gdansk Burghers against the Jews in the Seventeenth-Eighteeenth Centuries]. *Kwartalnik Historii Żydów* 207 (2003): 435–43.

Kloizner, Yisra'el. "Yehudah safra' ve-dayna' (Ha-Yesod): Le-dmutam shel ha-yeḥasim ve-ha-nimusim ha-tziburiim be-Vilna ba-me'ah ha-18" [Yehudah, Scribe and Judge: Towards a Portrait of Social Relations in Eighteenth-Century Vilna]. *Tsiyon* 2 (1937): 137–52.

————. "Toledot ha-yehudim be-Lita" [History of the Jews in Lithuania]. In *Yahadut Lita*. Tel-Aviv: 'Am Ha-Sefer, 1960.

————. *Toledot ha-kehillah- ha-'ivrit be-Vilna* [History of the Hebrew Community in Vilnius]. Vilnius (Wilno): Ha-Kehillah ha-'Ivrit be-Vilna, 1935.

Kobrin, Rebecca, ed. *Chosen Capital: The Jewish Encounter with American Capitalism*. New Brunswick, NJ: Rutgers University Press, 2012.

————, and Adam Teller. "Purchasing Power: The Economics of Modern Jewish History." In Kobrin and Teller, eds., *Purchasing Power: The Economics of Modern Jewish History*, 1–24. Philadelphia: University of Pennsylvania Press, 2015.

Korobkov, Kh. G. "Perepis' yevreĭskogo naseleniia vitebskoĭ gubernii v 1772 g." [The Census of the Jewish Population of Vitebsk Region in 1772]. *Yevreĭskaia Starina* 5 (1912): 164–77.

————. "Statistika yevreĭskogo naseleniia Pol'shi i Litvy vo vtoroĭ polovine XVIII veka" [The Statistics of the Jewish Population in Poland and Lithuania in the Second Half of the 18th Century]. *Yevreĭskaia Starina* 4 (1911): 541–62.

Kościałkowski, Stanisław. *Antoni Tyzenhauz: Podskarbi nadworny litewski* [*Antoni Tyzenhauz, Crown Treasurer of the Grand Duchy of Lithuania*]. 2 vols. London: Wydawnictwo Społeczności Akademickiej Uniwersytetu Stefana Batorego w Londynie, 1970–1971.

Kosman, Marceli. *Historia Białorusi* [History of Belarus]. Wrocław: Zakład Narodowy im. Ossolińskich, 1979.

————. "Pomiara włoczna na Polesiu pinskim" [Land Remeasurement in the Pinsk Region of Polesie]. *Roczniki Dziejów Społecznych i Gospodarczych* 31 (1970): 103–41.

Kossoy, Edward, and Abraham Ohry. *The Felshers: Medical, Sociological and Historical Aspects of Practitioners of Medicine with below University Level Education*. Jerusalem: Magnes Press, 1992.

Kotłubaj, Edward. *Galerja nieświeżka portretów radziwiłłowskich* [The Nieśwież Gallery of Radziwiłł Portraits]. Vilnius (Wilno): no publisher, 1857.

Kozłowskij, P. G. "Struktura własności ziemskiej i faktycznego posiadania ziemi w zachodniej i środkowej Białorusi w drugiej połowic XVIII w." [Estate Structure and Actual Landholding in Western and Central Belarus in the Second Half of the Eighteenth Century]. *Roczniki Dziejów Społecznych i Gospodarczych* 23 (1972): 61–88.

Kramerówna, Perła. "Żydowskie cechy rzemieślnicze w dawnej Polsce" [Jewish Craft Guilds in Old Poland]. *Miesięcznik Żydowski* 2 (1932): 259–98.

Kremer, Moshe. "Der anteil fun Yidishe balei-mloches in di kristlikhe tzechn in amolikn Poyln" [The Participation of Jewish Craftsmen in Christian Guilds in Old Poland]. *Bleter far geshichte* 2 (1938): 3–32.

————. "Le-ḥeker ha-mela'chah ve-ḥevrot ba'alei mela'chah 'etzel Yehudei Polin ba-me'ot ha-17–ha-18" [On the Study of Crafts and Guilds among Polish Jews in the 17th and 18th Centuries]. *Tsiyon* 2 (1937): 294–325.

Krupa, Jacek. *Żydzi w Rzeczypospolitej w czasach Augusta II (1697–1733)* [The Jews in

the Polish-Lithuanian Commonwealth in the Reign of August II (1697–1733)].
Kraków: Księgarnia Akademicka, 2009.

Kuchowicz, Zbigniew. *Człowiek polskiego baroku* [Polish Baroque Man]. Łódź:
Wydawnictwo Łódzkie, 1992.

Kula, Witold. *An Economic Theory of the Feudal System: Towards a Model of the
Polish Economy 1500–1800.* Translated by Lawrence Garner. London and New
York: Verso, 1987.

———. *Measures and Men.* Translated by R. Szreter. Princeton, NJ: Princeton University Press, 1986.

———. "Początki układu kapitalistycznego w Polsce XVIII wieku" [The Beginnings of Capitalism in Eighteenth-Century Poland]. *Przegląd Historyczny* 42
(1951): 36–81, 478>->81.

———. *Problemy i metody historii gospodarczej* [Problems and Methods in Economic History]. Warsaw: Państwowe Wydawnictswo Naukowe, 1963.

———. *Szkice o manufakturach w Polsce XVIII wieku* [Sketches of the Manufactories in Eighteenth Century Poland]. 3 vols. Warsaw: Państwowe Wydawnictwo
Naukowe, 1956.

Kulejewska-Topolska, Zofia. *Nowe lokacje miejskie w Wielkopolsce od XVI do końca
XVIII wieku: Studium historyczno-prawne* [New Foundations of Towns in Great
Poland from the Sixteenth to the End of the Eighteenth Century: A Historical-
Legal Study]. Poznań: Uniwersytet im. Adama Mickiewicza, 1964.

Kutrzeba, Stanisław. *Historia ustroju Polski w zarysie I: Korona* [An Outline History
of the Polish Constitution: The Crown]. Lwów-Warsaw: Księgarnia Polska Bernarda Połonieckiego and E. Wende, 1912.

———. *Historia ustroju Polski w zarysie II: Litwa* [An Outline History of the Polish Constitution II: Lithuania]. Lwów and Warsaw: Ksicgarnia Polska Bernarda
Połonieckiego, 1921.

Kuzmany, Börries. "Die Stadt Brody im langen 19. Jahrhundert—Eine Misserfolgsgeschichte" [The Town of Brody in the Long Nineteenth Century: A History of Failure]. PhD diss., Universität Wien, 2008.

Kuznets, Simon. "Economic Structure of U.S. Jewry: Recent Trends." In Kuznets,
Jewish Economies: Development and Migration in America and Beyond. Edited
by Stephanie Lo and E. Glen Weyl. 2 vols. New Brunswick, NJ: Transaction
Publishers, 2011.

Landsberger, Franz. "The Jewish Artist before the Time of the Emancipation." *Hebrew Union College Annual* 16 (1941): 321–414.

Lech, Marian J. "Milicje Radziwiłłów jako oręż feudałów w walce z ruchami
chłopskimi na Białorusi i Litwie" [The Radziwiłł Militias as a Weapon of the
Feudal Lords in the Battle Against Peasant Movements in Belarus and Lithuania].
Rocznik Białostocki 3 (1962): 33–60.

———. "Powstanie chłopów białoruskich w starostwie krzyczewskim (1740r.)"
[The Belarusian Peasant Uprising on the Krzyczew Starostwo (1740)]. *Przegląd
Historyczny* 51 (1960): 314–30.

Lederhendler, Eli. "American Jews, American Capitalism, and the Politics of History." In Eli Lederhendler and Jack Wertheimer, eds., *Text and Contex: Essays in Modern Jewish History in Honor of Ismar Schorsch.* New York: The Jewish Theological Seminary, 2005.

———. "The Decline of the Polish-Lithuanian Kahal." *Polin* 2 (1987): 150–60.

———. *Jewish Immigrants and American Capitalism, 1880–1920: From Caste to Class.* Cambridge and New York: Cambridge University Press, 2009.

Lesiński, Jerzy. "Spory o dobra neuburskie" [Disputes over the Neuburg Estates]. *Miscellanea Historico-Archivistica* 6 (1996): 95–132.

Leskiewiczowa, Janina. "Inwentarze dóbr ziemskich jako źródło do historii chłopów w Polsce" [Inventories of Landed Property as a Source for the History of Peasants in Poland]. *Kwartalnik Historyczny* 60 (1953): 363–78.

———. *Próba analizy gospodarki dóbr magnackich w Polsce: Dobra wilanowskie na przełomie XVIII/XIX wieku* [An Attempt at an Analysis of the Economy of Magnate Estates in Poland: The Wilanów Estates at the Turn of the Eighteenth and Nineteenth Centuries]. Warsaw: Państwowe Wydawnictwo Naukowe, 1964.

Leszczyński, Anatol. *Żydzi ziemi Bielskiej od połowy XVII w. do 1795 r.* [The Jews of the Biała Region from the Second Half of the Seventeenth Century to 1795]. Wrocław: Zakład Narodowy im. Ossolińskich, 1980.

Levine, Hillel. "Gentry, Jews, and Serfs: The Rise of Polish Vodka." *Review* 4, no. 2 (Fall 1980): 223–50.

Lewin, Izak. *Klątwa żydowska na Litwie w XVII i XVIII wieku* [The Herem in 17th- and 18th-Century Lithuania]. *Pamiętnik Historyczno-Prawny,* vol. 10, no. 4. Lwów, 1932.

Light, Ivan H., and Steven J. Gold. *Ethnic Economies.* San Diego, CA, and London: Academic, 2000.

Litwin, Henryk. *Napływ szlachty polskiej na Ukrainę 1569–1648.* Warsaw: Semper, 2000.

———. "The Polish Magnates, 1454–1648: The Shaping of an Estate." *Acta Poloniae Historica* 53 (1986): 63–92.

Lipman, David Matityahu. *Le-Toledot ha-Yehudim ba-Kovna ve-Slobodka* [On the History of the Jews in Kovna and Slobodka]. Kėdainiai: Movshovitch and Cohen, 1931.

Łukasik, Ryszard. *Rachunkowość rolna w dawnej Polsce* [Agricultural Accounting in Old Poland]. Warsaw: Państwowe Wydawnictwo Ekonomiczne, 1963.

Lukowski, Jerzy. *Disorderly Liberty: The Political Culture of the Polish-Lithuanian Commonwealth in the Eighteenth Century.* London and New York: Bloomsbury Academic, 2010.

———. *Liberty's Folly: The Polish-Lithuanian Commonwealth in the Eighteenth Century 1697–1795.* London: Routledge, 1991.

Maggid, David. *Sefer toledot mishpaḥot Gintzburg* [A History of the Ginsburg Families]. St. Petersburg: L. Rabinovitch and Sh. Sokolovsky, 1899.

Maggid-Steinschneider, Hillel Noah. *'Ir Vilna* [The City of Vilna]. Vilnius (Vilna): Widow & Brothers Rom, 1900.

Mahler, Raphael. "Shmoteihem shel mekomot yehudiim be-Polin ha-yeshanah" [Jewish Place-Names in Old Poland]. *Reshumot* 5 (1953): 146–61.

———. *Toledot ha-yehudim be-Polin* [History of the Jews in Poland]. Merḥavia, Israel: Sifriyat Poʻaliym, 1946.

———. *Yidn in amolikn Poyln in likht fun tsifern* [A Quantitative History of the Jews in Old Poland]. Warsaw: Yidish Bukh, 1958.

Maroszek, Józef. "Żydzi wiejscy na Podlasiu w XVII i XVIII wieku w świetle przemian struktury rynku wewnętrznego" [Village Jews in Podlasie in the Seventeenth and Eighteenth Centuries in Light of Changes in the Structure of the Internal Market]. *Studia Podlaskie* 2 (1989): 56–70.

Mączak, Antoni. "Money and Society in Poland and Lithuania in the 16th and 17th Centuries." *Journal of European Economic History* 5, no. 1 (1976): 69–104.

Meisl, Josef. *Geschichte der Juden in Polen und Russland* [A History of the Jews in Poland and Russia]. 2 vols. Berlin: C. A. Schwetschke & Sohn, 1922.

Mevorah, Barukh. "Maʻasei ha-hishtadlut be'Eiropah le-meniyʻat gerusham shel yehudei Bohemia u-Moraviah, 1744–1755" [The Acts of Intercession in Europe to Prevent the Expulsion of the Jews from Bohemia and Moravia, 1744–1755]. *Tsiyon* 28 (1963): 125–64.

Michałowska-Mycielska, Anna. *Sejm Żydów Litewskich (1623–1764)* [The Lithuanian Jewish Parliament (1623–1764)]. Warsaw: Wydawnictwo Akademickie Dialog, 2014.

———. "Władza dominialna a konflikt w gminie: Wybory władz gminnych i rabina w Słucku 1709–1711" [Seigneurial Authority and a Communal Conflict: The Community and Rabbinic Elections in Słuck, 1709–1711]. In Marcin Wodziński and Anna Michałowska-Mycielska, eds., *Małżeństwo z rozsądku? Żydzi w społeczeństwie dawnej Rzeczypospolitej*. Wrocław: Wydawnictwo Uniwersytetu Wrocławskiego, 2007.

Mielczarski, Stanisław. *Rynek zbożowy na ziemiach polskich w drugiej połowie XVI i pierwszej połowie XVII wieku* [The Grain Market on Polish Lands in the Second Half of the Sixteenth and the First Half of the Seventeenth Centuries]. Gdańsk: Gdańskie Towarzystwo Naukowe, 1962.

Mieleszko, Wasyl. L. "Formy i struktura feudalnej własności ziemskiej we wschodniej Białorusi w drugiej połowie XVII i w XVIII wieku" [Forms and Structure of Feudal Landholding in Eastern Belarus in the Second Half of the Seventeenth and in the Eighteenth Centuries]. *Roczniki Dziejów Społecznych i Gospodarczych* 23 (1972): 33–59.

———. "Handel i stosunki handlowe Białorusi wschodniej z miastami nadbałtyckimi w końcu XVII i w XVIII w." [Trade and Trading Relations of Eastern Belarus with the Baltic Towns at the End of the Seventeenth and in the Eighteenth Centuries]. *Zapiski Historyczne* 33 (1968): 53–91.

Miluński, Marek. "Zarząd dóbr Bogusława Radziwiłła w latach 1636–1669" [The Administration of Bogusław Radziwiłł's Estates from 1636–1669]. In Urszula Augustyniak, ed., *Administracja i życie codzienne w dobrach Radziwiłłów XVI–XVIII wieku*. Warsaw: Wydawnictwo DiG, 2009.

Mokyr, Joel. "The Economics of Being Jewish." *Critical Review: A Journal of Politics and Society* 23, nos. 1–2 (2011): 195–206.

Mole, Kevin. "Introduction." In Kevin Mole and Monder Ram, eds., *Perspectives in Entrepreneurship: A Critical Approach.* Basingstoke, Hamps.: Palgrave Macmillan Ltd., 2012.

Morales, Maria Cristina. "Ethnic Niches, Pathway to Economic Incorporation or Exploitation? Labor Market Experiences of Latina/os." PhD diss., Texas A&M University, 2004.

Morgensztern Janina. "Zadłużenie gmin żydowskich w Ordynacji Zamoyskiej w II połowie XVII w" [The Indebtedness of the Jewish Communities on the Zamoyski Entail in the Second Half of the 17th Century]. *Biuletyn Żydowskiego Instytutu Historycznego* 73 (1970): 47–65.

Muller, Jerry Z. *Capitalism and the Jews.* Princeton, NJ: Princeton University Press 2011.

Nadav, Mordekhai. "Aspekty regionalnej autonomii żydów polskich na podstawie Pinkasu Tykocińskiego z lat 1660–1795" [Aspects of the Polish Jews' Autonomy on the Basis of the Tykocin Community Record Book, 1660–1795]. In Andrzej Link-Lenczowski and T. Polański, eds., *Żydzi w dawnej Rzeczypospolitej: materiały z konferencji "Autonomia Żydów w Rzeczypospolitej Szlacheckiej" Międzywydziałowy Zakład Historii i Kultury Żydów w Polsce Uniwersytet Jagielloński 22–26 IX 1986.* Wrocław: Zakład Narodowy im. Ossolińskich, 1987.

———. "'Iyun be-hitraḥashuyot be-shalosh kehilot ba-Polin-Lita bi-yemei milḥemet ha-tzafon ve-aḥareyha (ba-shlish ha-rishon shel ha-me'ah ha-18)" [An Examination of Events in Three Polish-Lithuanian Communities during and after the Northern War (In the First Third of the Eighteenth Century)]. In *Divrei ha-kongress ha-'olami ha-shemini le-mada'ei ha-yahadut*, Section II, vol. 2, 89–96. Jerusalem: *Ha-kongress ha-'Olami le-Mada'ei ha-Yahadut*, 1982.

———. *The Jews of Pinsk, 1506–1880.* Stanford: Stanford University Press, 2008.

———. "Kehillat Pinsk ba-tekufah she-mi-gzeirot taḥ-tat 'ad shalom Andrushov (1648–1667)" [The Pinsk Community in the Period from the Chmielnicki Uprising to the Peace of Andruszów (1648–1667)]. *Tziyon* 31 (1966): 153–96.

———. "Le-toledot ha-hityashvut ha-yehudit be-kfarei Mazovia ba-sof ha-me'ah ha-17 u-va-meah ha-18" [On the History of Jewish Settlement in the Villages of Mazovia at the End of the 17th and in the 18th Centuries]. In R. Bonfil, M. Ben-Sasson, and Y. Hacker, eds., *Tarbut va-ḥevrah be-toledot Yisrael bi-ymei-ha-beinayim*, 717–24. Jerusalem: Merkaz Zalman Shazar le-Toledot Yisra'el, 1989.

———. "Ma'asei 'alimut hadadit bein yehudim le-lo-yehudim ba-Lita lifnei 1648" [Acts of Mutual Violence between Jews and non-Jews in Lithuania before 1648]. *Gal-Ed* 7–8 (1985): 41–56.

North, Douglass C. *Structure and Change in Economic History.* New York: W. W. Norton & Company 1981.

———. *Understanding the Process of Economic Change.* Princeton, NJ: Princeton University Press, 2005.

Nowak, Janusz. "Feyga Lejbowiczowa: Arendarka w Końskowoli Sieniawskich; Z dziejów gospodarczej aktywności kobiet żydowskich w początkach XVIII wieku" [Feyga Leybowiczowa, Female Leaseholder in the Sieniawskis' Konskowola: From the History of Jewish Women's Economic Activity at the Beginning of the Eighteenth Century]. *Rocznik Biblioteki Naukowej PAU i PAN w Krakowie* 48 (2003): 211–36.

Ochmański, Jerzy. *Historia Litwy* [The History of Lithuania]. Wrocław, Warsaw, Kraków: Zakład Narodowy im. Ossolińskich, 1990.

———. "Reforma włoczna na Litwie i Białorusie w XVI wieku." [Land Reform in Lithuania and Belarus in the Sixteenth Century]. In Ochmański, *Dawna Litwa: Studia historyczne*, 158–74. Olsztyn: Pojezierze, 1986.

———. "Reforma włoczna w dobrach magnackich i kościelnych w Wielkim Księstwie Litewskim w drugiej połowie XVI wieku." [Land Reform on the Magnate and Church Estates in the Grand Duchy of Lithuania in the Second Half of the Sixteenth Century]. In Ochmański, *Dawna Litwa: Studia historyczne*, 175–97. Olsztyn: Pojezierze, 1986.

———. "W kwestii agrarnego charakteru miast Wielkiego Księstwa Litewskiego w XVI wieku" [On the Question of the Agrarian Nature of Towns in the Grand Duchy of Lithuania in the 16th Century]. In Aleksander Gieysztor et al., eds., *Studia historica: W 35-lecie pracy naukowej Henryka Łowmiańskiego*. Warsaw: Państwowe Wydawnictwo Naukowe, 1958.

Opalski, Magdalena. *The Jewish Tavern-Keeper and His Tavern in Nineteenth-Century Polish Literature*. Jerusalem: Zalman Shazar Center for the Furtherance of the Study of Jewish History, 1986.

Opas, Tomasz. "Miasta prywatne a Rzeczpospolita" [Private Towns and the Republic]. *Kwartalnik Historyczny* 78 (1971): 28–48.

———. "Sytuacja ludności żydowskiej w miastach szlacheckich województwa lubelskiego w drugiej połowie XVII i w XVIII wieku" [The Situation of the Jewish Population in the Noble Towns of the Lublin District in the Second Half of the Seventeenth and in the Eighteenth Centuries]. *Biuletyn Żydowskiego Instytutu Historycznego* 67 (1968): 3–37.

———. "Wolność osobista mieszczan miast szlacheckich województwa lubelskiego w drugiej połowie XVII i w XVIII wieku" [The Personal Freedom of Townspeople in the Private Towns of the Lublin Region in the Second Half of the Seventeenth and in the Eighteenth Centuries]. *Przegląd Historyczny* 61 (1970): 609–29.

Pasztor, Maria. "Milicje magnackie Radziwiłłów: Michała Kazimierza 'Rybeńki' i Karola Stanisława 'Panie Kochanku': Skład, organizacja, funkcje" [The Radziwiłł Magnate Militias: Michał Kazimierz Radziwiłł "Rybeńko" and Karol Stanisław "Pani Kochanku"—Composition, Organization, Functions]. In Łukasz Kądziel et al., eds., *Trudne stulecia: Studia z dziejów XVII i XVIII wieku*. Warsaw: Semper, 1994.

Pęckowski, Jan. *Dzieje miasta Rzeszowa do końca XVIII wieku* [The History of

Rzeszów to the End of the Eighteenth Century]. Rzeszów: Nakład Gminy Miasta Rzeszowa, 1913.

Pendzich, Barbara M. "The Burghers of the Grand Duchy of Lithuania during the War of 1654–1667: Resiliency and Cohesion in the Face of Muscovite Annexation." PhD diss., Georgetown University, 1998.

———. "The Jewish Community of Sluck after the Polish-Muscovite War of 1654–1667." *Proceedings of the Eleventh World Congress of Jewish Studies.* Jerusalem, 1994, Section B: I, 173–80.

Podraza, Antoni. "Żydzi i wieś w dawnej Rzeczypospolitej." In Andrzej Link-Lenczowski and Tomasz Polański, eds., *Żydzi w dawnej Rzeczypospolitej: materiały z konferencji "Autonomia Żydów w Rzeczypospolitej Szlacheckiej" Międzywydziałowy Zakład Historii i Kultury Żydów w Polsce, Uniwersytet Jagielloński 22–26 IX 1986.* Wroclaw: Zakład Narodowy im. Ossolińskich, 1991.

Popielarz, Pamela A., and Zachary P. Neal. "The Niche as a Theoretical Tool." *Annual Review of Sociology* 33 (2007): 65–84.

Pośpiech, Andrzej, and Wojciech Tygielski. "The Social Role of the Magnates' Courts in Poland (From the End of the 16th up to the 18th Century)." *Acta Poloniae Historica* 43 (1981): 75–100.

Raba, Joel. *Between Remembrance and Denial: The Fate of the Jews in the Wars of the Polish Commonwealth during the Mid-Seventeenth Century as Shown in Contemporary Writings and Historical Research.* Boulder: East European Monographs, 1995.

Rabinowicz, Louis I. *Herem Hayyishub: A Contribution to the Medieval Economic History of the Jews.* London: E. Goldston, 1945.

Rachuba, Andrzej. "Biała pod rządami Radziwiłłów w latach 1568–1813" [Biała under Radziwiłł Administration in 1568–1813]. In Tadeusz Wasilewski and Tadeusz Krawczuk, eds., *Z nieznanej przeszłości Białej i Podlasia*, 37–67. Biała Podlaska: PTSK, 1990.

Reynolds, Susan. *Fiefs and Vassals: The Medieval Evidence Reinterpreted.* New York and Oxford: Oxford University Press, 1994.

Ringelblum, Emanuel. "Projekty i próby przewarstwowienia Żydów w epoce stanisławowskiej" [Projects and Attempts to Restructure the Jews in the Period of King Stanislaw August]. Offprint from *Sprawy Narodowościowe* 8 (1934): 1–30 and 181–224.

———. "Shmuel Zbytkover: 'Askan tsiburi-kalkali be-Polin bi-ymei halukatah" [Shmuel Zbytkower: A Jewish Leader in Public and Economic Affairs in Poland during the Period of the Partitions]. *Tsiyon* 3 (1938): 246–66 and 337–55.

———. "Yidishe feldshers in amolikn Poyln." In Ringelblum, *Kapitlen geshikhte fun amolikn yidishn lebn in Polyn*, 351–60. Edited by Jacob Shatzky. Buenos Aires: Tsentral-farband fun Polyishe Yidn in Argentine, 1953.

Rosman, Murray Jay (Moshe). "An Exploitative Regime and the Opposition to It in Miedzyboz, ca. 1730." In Shmuel Almog et al., eds., *Transition and Change in Modern Jewish History: Essays Presented in Honor of Shmuel Ettinger*, xi–xxx.

Jerusalem: Historical Society of Israel and the Zalman Shazar Center for Jewish History, 1987.

———. "Ha-yahas bein ha-hokher ha-yehudi la-ba'al ha-'ahuza ha-polani: Ha-tzad ha-sheni" [Relations between the Jewish Leaseholder and the Polish Estate Owner: The Other Side]. In Nahum Gross, ed., *Ha-yehudim Ba-kalkala*, 237–43. Jerusalem: Merkaz Zalman Shazar le-Toledot Yisra'el, 1985.

———. "Ha-yehudim be-sahar ha-neharot mi-drom-mizrah Polin le-Gdansk (1695–1726) shel mishpahat magnatim a'hat" [The Jews in the River Trade of One Magnate Family from South-East Poland to Gdańsk (1695–1726)]. *Gal-Ed* 7–8 (1985): 70–83.

———. "The Indebtedness of the Lublin Kahal in the 18th Century." In Adam Teller, ed., *Studies in the History of the Jews in Old Poland in Honor of Jacob Goldberg. Scripta Hierosolymitana* 38 (1998): 166–83.

———. "Lihiyot 'isha yehudiyah ba-Polin-Lita be-reishit ha-'et ha-hadashah" [To be a Jewish Woman in Early Modern Poland-Lithuania]. In Israel Bartal and Israel Gutman, eds., *Kiyum va-shever: Yehudei Polin le-doroteihem*, 2: 415–34. Jerusalem: Merkaz Zalman Shazar le-Toledot Yisra'el, 2001.

———. *The Lords' Jews: Magnate-Jewish Relations in the Polish-Lithuanian Commonwealth during the 18th Century*. Cambridge: Harvard University Press, 1990.

Rostworowski, Emanuel, ed. *Polski Słownik Biograficzny* [The Polish Biographical Dictionary]. Vol. 30. Wrocław-Warsawa-Kraków-Gdańsk-Łódź: Zakład Narodowy im. Ossolińskich and Polska Akademia Nauk, 1987.

Rusiński, Władysław. "O rynku wewnętrznym w Polsce drugiej połowy XVIII w." [On the Internal Market in Poland in the Second Half of the Seventeenth Century]. *Roczniki Dziejów Społecznych i Gospodarczych* 16 (1954): 113–47.

Rutkowski, Jan. *Badania nad podziałem dochodów w Polsce w czasach nowożytnych* [Studies on the Division of Revenues in Modern Poland]. Reprinted in Rutkowski, *Wokół teorii ustroju feudalnego: Prace historyczne*, 255–353. Edited by Jerzy Topolski. Warsaw: Państwowy Instytut Wydawniczy, 1982.

———. *Historia gospodarcza Polski: Czasy przedrozbiorowe* [The Economic History of Poland: The Pre-Partition Period]. Poznań: Księgarnia Akademicka, 1947.

Rybarski, Roman. *Handel i polityka handlowa Polski w XVI stuleciu* [Poland's Trade and Mercantile Politics in the Sixteenth Century]. Poznań: Towarzystwo Miłośników Miasta Poznania, 1928.

Rychlikowa, Irena. *Klucz wielkoporębski Wodzickich w drugiej połowie XVIII wieku* [The Wielkoporęba Estate of the Wodzickis in the Second Half of the Eighteenth Century]. Wrocław: Zakład Narodowy im. Ossolińskich Wydawnictwo PAN, 1960.

———. *Produkcja zbożowa wielkiej własnosci w Małopolsce w latach 1764–1805* [Grain Production on the Great Estates of Lesser Poland from 1764–1805]. Warsaw and Poznań: Państwowe Wydawnictwo Naukowe, 1967.

Sajkowski, Alojzy. *Od Sierotki do Rybeńki: W kręgu radziwiłłowskiego mecenatu* [From Sierotka to Rybeńko: In the Circle of Radziwiłł Patronage]. Poznań: Wydawnictwo Poznańskie, 1965.

Salmon-Mack, Tamar. *Tan-du: 'Al nisu'in u-mashbereihem be-yahadut Poli-Lita, 1650–1800* [On Marriage and Its Crises among Polish Jewry, 1650–1800]. Jerusalem-Benei Brak: Hakibbutz Ha-Me'uḥad, 2012.

Schiper, Ignacy. *Dzieje handlu Żydowskiego na ziemiach polskich* [A History of Jewish Trade on Polish Lands]. Warsaw: Centrala Związku Kupców, 1937.

———. "Żydzi w Tarnowie do końca XVIII w." [The Jews in Tarnów until the End of the 18th Century]. *Kwartalnik Historyczny* 19 (1905): 228–39.

Schnee, Heinrich. *Der Hoffinanz und der moderne Staat* [Court Finance and the Modern State]. Berlin: Duncker und Humblot. 1953.

Schorr, Mojżesz. *Żydzi w Przemyślu do końca XVIII wieku* [The Jews in Przemyśl until the End of the Eighteenth Century]. L'viv (Lwów): Fundusz konkursowy, 1903.

Schumpeter, Joseph A. "Economic Theory and Entrepreneurial History." In Schumpeter, *Essays on Entrepreneurs, Innovations, Business Cycles, and the Evolution of Capitalism*, 253–71. Edited by Richard V. Clemence. New Brunswick-London: Transaction Publishers, 1997.

Serczyk, Władysław A. *Gospodarstwo magnackie w województwie podolskim w drugiej połowie XVIII wieku* [The Magnate Economy in the Podolia Region in the Second Half of the Eighteenth Century]. Wrocław: Zakład Narodowy im. Ossolińskich Wydawnictwo PAN, 1965.

Shahar, Isaiah. *Bikoret ha-ḥevrah ve-hanhagat ha-tsibur be-sifrut ha-musar u-ba-drush be-Polin ba-me'ah ha-shmonah-'esreh* [Social Criticism and Social Leadership in the Ethical and Homiletic Literature in Eighteenth Century Poland]. Jerusalem: Merkaz Dinur, 1992.

Shmeruk, Chone. "Ha-ḥasidut ve-'iskei ha-ḥakhirot" [Hasidism and the Arenda Business]. *Tziyon* 35 (1970): 182–92.

Siekierski, Maciej. "Landed Wealth in the Grand Duchy of Lithuania: The Economic Affairs of Prince Nicholas Christopher Radziwill (1549–1616)." PhD diss., University of California, Berkeley, 1984.

Siemiaticki, Mordekhai. "Ḥezkat-ha-yishuv be-Polin" [Ḥezkat-Ha-yishuv in Poland]. *Ha-mishpat ha-'ivri* 5 (1936–1937): 199–253.

Skibiński, Mieczysław. *Europa a Polska w dobie wojny o sukcesję austryacką w latach 1740–1745* [Europe and Poland during the War of the Austrian Succession, 1740–1745]. Kraków: Akademia Umiejętnośći, nakladem Funduszu Nestora Bucewicza, 1912–1913.

Smolcńska, Barbara. "Materiały do dziejów huty szklanej w Nalibokach z XVIII wieku" [Materials for the History of the Naliboki Glass Works from the Eighteenth Century]. *Teki Archiwalne* 1 (1953): 79–147.

Sobczak, Jacek. "Zadłużenie kahałów żydowskich w końcu XVIII wieku w świetle obliczeń sądu ziemiańskiego w Kaliszu" [The Indebtedness of the Jewish Communities in Light of the Assessment of the Kalisz Regional Court]. *Rocznik Kaliski* 11 (1978): 107–23.

Sobel, Russell S. "Entrepreneurship." In David R. Henderson, ed., *The Concise En-*

cyclopedia of Economics. Indianapolis: Liberty Fund, 2008. http://www.econlib
.org/library/Enc/Entrepreneurship.html; accessed Oct. 13, 2014.

Soloveichik, Ḥaim. *Halakhah, kalkalah, ve-dimui 'atzmi: Ha-mishkona'ut bi-yemei ha-beinayim* [Jewish Law, Economics, and Self-Image: Pawnbroking in the Middle Ages]. Jerusalem: Magnes Press, 1985.

Sombart, Werner. *The Jews and Modern Capitalism*. New Brunswick: Trasaction Books, 1982.

Sosis, Y. (Israel). "Tsu der sotsyaler geshikhte fun yidn in Lite un Vaysrusland." *Tzaytshrift* (Minsk) 1 (1926): 1–24.

———. "Yidishe balmelokhes un zeyere arbeter in Lite, Vaysrusland un Ukraine in 18-tn yarhundert" [Jewish Craftsmen and Their Workers in 18th-Century Lithuania, Belarus, and Ukraine]. *Tzaytshrift* (Minsk) 4 (1930): 1–29.

Stampfer, Shaul. "The 1764 Census of Lithuanian Jewry and What It Can Teach Us." In Sergio DellaPergola and Judith Even, eds., *Papers in Jewish Demography 1993*. Jerusalem: World Union of Jewish Studies; Association for Jewish Demography and Statistics, 1997.

Stańczak, Edward. *Kamera saska za czasów Augusta III* [The Saxon Treasury in the Time of August III]. Warsaw: Państwowe Wydawnictwo Naukowe, 1973.

Stashevskiĭ, Yevgeniĭ D. *Istoriia dokapitalisticheskoĭ renty na Pravoberezhnoĭ Ukraine v XVIII– pervoĭ polovine XIX v.* [A History of Pre-Capitalist Rents in Right-Bank Ukraine in the 18th and the First Half of the 19th Centuries]. Moscow: Nauka, 1968.

Stern, Selma. *The Court Jew: A Contribution to the History of the Period of Absolutism in Central Europe*. Translated by Ralph Weiman. Philadelphia: Jewish Publication Society of America, 1950.

Storm, Jill. "Culture and Exchange: The Jews of Königsberg, 1700–1820." PhD diss., Washington University, 2010.

Stow, Kenneth R. *Alienated Minority: The Jews of Medieval Latin Europe*. Cambridge: Harvard University Press, 1992.

Szkurłatowski, Zygmunt. "Organizacja administracji i pracy w dobrach wielkiej własności feudalnej w Polsce w XVII i XVIII wieku w świetle instruktarzy ekonomicznyzch" [The Organization of the Administration and of Work on the Great Feudal Estates of Poland in the 17th and 18th Centuries in Light of Economic Instructions]. In *Zeszyty Naukowe Uniwersytetu Wrocławskiego*, Ser. A., No. 8, Wrocław, 1957.

Taurogiński (Tuhan-Taurogiński), Bolesław. *Z dziejów Nieświeża* [From the History of Nieśwież]. Warsaw: Archiwum Ordynacji Nieświeskiej, 1937.

———. "Geneza powstania Archiwum Radziwiłłów oraz wartość zbiorów dla nauki polskiej" [The Genesis of the Radziwiłł Archive and the Value of the Collections for Polish Academic Research]. Warsaw, 1955. Typescript no. 9067, Polish National Library, Warsaw.

Tazbir, Janusz. *Kultura szlachecka w Polsce* [Noble Culture in Poland]. Warsaw: Wiedza Powszechna, 1979.

Teller, Adam. "'Ha-'aspaklaryah shel malkhut Polin' me'et Sebastian Michinski: He'arot makdimot" ['The Mirror to the Polish Crown': Introductory Remarks]. In Elchanan Reiner, ed., *Kroke-Kazimierz-Krakow: Meḥkarim be-toledot yehudei Krakow*, 329–37. Tel Aviv: Universitat Tel Aviv, 2001.

———. "Ha-pe'ilut ha-kalkalit shel ha-yehudim ba-Polin ba-maḥatzit ha-sheniyah shel ha-me'ah ha-17 u-ba-me'ah ha-18" [The Economic Activity of the Jews in Poland in the Second Half of the Seventeenth and in the Eighteenth Centuries]. In Israel Bartal and Israel Gutman, eds., *Kiyum va-shever: Yehudei Polin le-doroteihem*, I: 209–24. Jerusalem: Merkaz Zalman Shazar le-Toledot Yisrael, 1997.

———. "In the Land of Their Enemies? On the Duality of Jewish Existence in 18th Century Poland." *Polin* 19 (2007): 431–46.

———. "Masoret Slutzk 'al re'shit darkho shel ha-Besht" [The Tradition from Slutzk about the Besht's Early Days]. In David Assaf, Yosef Dan, and Immanuel Etkes, eds., *Meḥkarei Ḥasidut (Meḥkarei Yerushalayim ba-Maḥshevet Yisrael 15)*, 15–38. Jerusalem: The Hebrew University of Jerusalem, Institute of Jewish Studies, 1999.

———. "Radziwill, Rabinowicz, and the Rabbi of Swierz: The Magnates' Attitude Towards Jewish Regional Autonomy in 18th-Century Poland-Lithuania." In Adam Teller, ed., *Studies in the History of the Jews in Old Poland: In Honor of Jacob Goldberg. Scripta Hierosolomitana 38*, 248–78. Jerusalem: Magnes Press; The Hebrew University, Center for Research on the History and Culture of Polish Jews, 1998.

———. "Radziwiłłowie a Żydzi w czasach saskich" [The Radziwiłłs and the Jews in the Saxon Period]. In Andrzej Link-Lenczowski and Mariusz Markiewicz, eds., *Rzeczpospolita wielu narodów i jej tradycje*, 149–61. Kraków: Historia Iagellonica, 1999.

———. "Tarbut ha-diyur shel yehudei Polin ba-me'ah ha-17: Yehudim, Polanim ve-ha-rova' ha-yehudi" [The Residential Culture of Polish Jews in the Seventeenth Century: Jews, Poles, and the Jewish Quarter]. In Ben-Zion Kedar, ed., *Ha-tarbut ha-'amamit*, 197–208. Jerusalem: Merkaz Zalman Shazar le-Toledot Yisrael, 1996.

———. "Telling the Difference: Some Comparative Perspectives on the Jews' Legal Status in Poland and the Holy Roman Empire." *Polin* 22 (2010): 109–41.

———. "Tradition and Crisis? Eighteenth Century Critiques of the Polish-Lithuanian Rabbinate." *Jewish Social Studies* 17, no. 3 (2011): 1–39.

———. "Zikhronot Shlomo Maimon: Beḥinat meheimanut" [The Memoirs of Solomon Maimon: Assessing Their Reliability]. *Gal-Ed* 14 (1995): 1–10.

Tisdell, Clem, and Irmi Seidl. "Niches and Economic Competition: Implications for Economic Efficiency, Growth and Diversity." *Structural Change and Economic Dynamics* 15, no. 2 (June 2004): 119–35.

Toch, Michael. "Between Impotence and Power: The Jews in the Economy and Polity of Medieval Europe." In Toch, *Peasants and Jews in Medieval Germany:*

Studies in Cultural, Social, and Economic History. Aldershot, Hamps., and Burlington, VT: Ashgate, 2003.

Topolska, Maria Barbara. "Peculiarities of the Economic Structure of Eastern White Russia in the Sixteenth–Eighteenth Centuries." *Studia Historiae Oeconomicae* 6 (1971): 34–49.

———. *Dobra szkłowskie na Białorusi wschodniej w XVII i XVIII wieku* [The Szkłów Estates in Eastern Belarus in the 17th and 18th Centuries]. Warsaw: PWN, Oddział w Poznaniu, 1969.

———. "Szkłów i jego rola w gospodarce Białorusi Wschodniej w XVII i XVIII wieku" [Szklów and Its Role in the Economy of Eastern Belarus in the Seventeenth and Eighteenth Centuries]. *Roczniki Dziejów Społecznych i Gospodarczych* 30 (1969): 1–32.

———. "Związku handlowe Białorusi Wschodniej z Rygą w końcu XVII i na początku XVIII wieku" [Trading Connections between Eastern Belarus and Riga in the Late Seventeenth and Early Eightcenth Centuries]. *Roczniki Dziejów Społecznych i Gospodarczych* 29 (1968): 9–31.

Topolski, Jerzy. *Gospodarska polska a europejska w XVI–XVIII wieku* [The Polish and European Economies in the Sixteenth–Eighteenth Centuries]. Poznań: Wydawnictwo Poznańskie, 1977.

Trivellato, Francesca. *The Familiarity of Strangers: The Sephardic Diaspora, Livorno, and Cross-Cultural Trade in the Early Modern Period.* New Haven: Yale University Press, 2009.

Unger, W. S. "Trade through the Sound in the Seventeenth and Eighteenth Centuries." *Economic History Review* 12, no. 2 (1959): 206–21.

Waliszewski, Kazimierz. *Potoccy i Czartoryscy: Walka stronnictw i programów politzcynzch przed upadkiem Rzeczypospolitej, 1734–1763* [The Potockis and the Czartoryskis: Factional Struggle and Political Programs before the Fall of the Commonwealth, 1734–1763]. Kraków: no publisher, 1887.

Wasilewski, Tadeusz, and Tadeusz Krawczuk. *Z nieznanej przeszłości Białej i Podlasia* [From the Unknown History of Biała and Podlasia]. Biała Podlaska: PTSK, 1990.

Weinryb, Bernard D. "Beiträge zur Finanzgeschichte der jüdischen Gemeinden in Polen" [Contributions to the Economic History of the Jewish Communities in Poland]. I, *Monatsschrift für Geschichte und Wissenschaft des Judentums* 82, no. 4 (1938): 248–63; II, *Hebrew Union College Annual* 16 (1941): 187–214.

———. *The Jews of Poland: A Social and Economic History of the Jewish Community in Poland from 1100 to 1800.* Philadelphia: Jewish Publication Society of America, 1982.

———. "Kavim le-toledot ha-kalkalah ve-ha-finansim shel ha-yehudim ba'arei Polin ve-Lita ba-me'ot ha-17–ha18" [A Contribution to the History of the Jews' Economy and Finances in the Towns of Poland and Lithuania in the 17th and 18th Centuries]. In *Meḥkarim u-mekorot le-toledot Yisrael ba'et ha-hadashah,* 68–113. Jerusalem: Hotza'at Makor, 1976.

Widacka, Hanna. "Działalność Hirsza Leybowicza i innych rytowników na dworze nieświeskim Michała Kazimierza Radziwiłła 'Rybeńki' w świetle badań archiwalnych" [The Activity of Hirsz Leybowicz and Other Engravers at the Nieśwież Court of Michał Kazimierz Radziwiłł "Rybeńko" in Light of Archival Research]. *Biuletyn Historii Sztuki* 39, no. 1 (1977): 62–72.

Wieczorek, Władysław. *Z dziejów ustroju rolnego Wielkiego Księstwa Litewskiego w XVIII w.* [From the History of the Agrarian Regime in the Grand Duchy of Lithuanua in the 18th Century]. Poznań: Poznańskie Towarzystwo Przyjaciół Nauk, 1929.

Wiesner, Merry E. *Working Women in Renaissance Germany*. New Brunswick, NJ: Rutgers University Press, 1986.

Wijaczka, Jacek, and Zenon Guldon. "Handel ekonomii litewskich z Królewcem w latach 1765–1768" [The Trade of the Lithuanian Ekonomias with Königsberg, 1765–1768]. *Zapiski Historyczne* 60, nos. 2–3 (1995): 39–47.

Williamson, Oliver E. "The New Institutional Economics: Taking Stock, Looking Ahead." *Journal of Economic Literature* 38, no. 3 (2000): 595–613.

Wischnitzer, Mark. *A History of Jewish Crafts and Guilds*. New York: Jonathan David Publishers, 1965.

———. "Die Stellung der Brodyer Juden im internationalen Handel in der Zweiten Hälfte des XVIII Jahrhunderts" [The Position of Brody Jewry in International Trade in the Second Half of the Eighteenth Century]. In Ismar Elbogen, Josef Meisl, and Mark Wischnitzer, eds., *Festschrift zu Simon Dubnows siebzigstem Geburtstag*. Berlin: Jüdischer Verlag, 1930.

———. "Di struktur fun yidishe tzechn in Poyln, Lite un Vaysrusland inem 17-tn un 18-tn yarhundert" [The Structure of Jewish Guilds in Poland, Lithuania, and Belarus in the 17th and 18th Centuries]. *Tzaytshrift* (Minsk) 2–3 (1928): 73–88.

Wunderbar, Reuben Joseph. *Geschichte der Juden in der Provinzen Liv- und Kurland, seit ihrer frühesten Niederlassung daselbst bis auf die gegenwärtige Zeit* [The History of the Jews in the Provinces of Livonia and Courland, from the Earliest Settlement to the Present Time]. Jelgava (Mitau): J. H. Hoffmann und A. Johannsohn, 1853.

Wyczański, Andrzej. *Polska Rzeczą Pospolitą szlachecką* [Poland, the Noble Republic]. Warsaw: Państwowe Wydawnictwo Naukowe, 1991.

———. *Studia nad gospodarką starostwa korczyńskiego 1500–1600* [Studies on the Economy of the Korczyn Starostwo, 1500–1600]. Warsaw: Państwowe Wydawnictwo Naukowe, 1964.

Wyrobisz, Andrzej. "Materiały do dziejów handlu w miasteczkach polskich na początku XVIII wieku" [Materials on the History of Trade in Polish Small Towns at the Beginning of the Eighteenth Century]. *Przegląd Historyczny* 62, no. 4 (1971): 703–16.

———. "Polityka Firlejów wobec miast w XVI wieku i założenie Janowca nad Wisłą" [The Firleys' Policy Towards Towns in the Sixteenth Century and the Foundation of Janowiec nad Wisłą]. *Przegląd Historyczny* 61 (1970): 577–606.

———. "Power and Towns in the Polish-Gentry Commonwealth: The Polish-

Lithuanian State in the Sixteenth and Seventeenth Centuries." *Theory and Society* 18, no. 5 (1989): 611–30.

———. "Typy funkcjonalne miast polskich w XVI–XVIII wieku" [A Functional Typology of Polish Towns in the 16th-18th Centuries]. *Przegląd Historyczny* 72 (1981): 25–49.

Yalen, Deborah Hope. "Red Kasrilevke: Ethnographies of Economic Transformation in the Soviet Shtetl." PhD diss., University of California, Berkeley, 2007.

Yerushalmi, Yosef Ḥaim. *Zakhor: Jewish History and Jewish Memory*. Seattle: University of Washington Press, 1982.

Żabko-Potopowicz, Antoni. *Praca najemna i najemnik w rolnictwie w Wielkiem Księstwie Litewskiem w wieku osiemnastym* [Hired Labor and the Laborer in the Agriculture of the Grand Duchy of Lithuania during the Eighteenth Century]. Warsaw: no publisher, 1929.

Zaremska, Hanna. *Żydzi w średniowiecznej Polsce: Gmina Krakowa*. Warsaw: Instytut Historii Nauki PAN, 2011.

Zenner, Walter P. *Minorities in the Middle: A Cross-Cultural Analysis*. Albany: State University of New York Press, 1991.

Zielińska, Teresa. "Archiwa Radziwiłłów i ich twórcy" [The Radziwiłł Archives and Their Creators]. *Archeion* 66 (1978): 105–29 and 364–65.

———. "Kariera i upadek żydowskiego potentata w dobrach radziwiłłowskich XVIII wieku" [The Career and Fall of a Jewish Potentate on the Radziwiłł Estates of the Eighteenth Century]. *Kwartalnik Historyczny* 98, no. 3 (1991): 33 –49.

———. *Magnateria polska epoki saskiej: Funkcje urzędów i królewszczyzn w procesie przeobrażeń warstwy społecznej* [The Polish Magnates of the Saxon Era: The Functions of Offices and Royal Estates in the Process of the Transformation of a Social Stratum]. Wrocław: Zakład Narodowy im. Ossolińskich, 1977.

———. "Mechanizm sejmikowy i klientela radziwiłłowska za Sasów" [The Sejmik Mechanism and the Radziwiłł Clients in the Saxon Age]. *Przegląd Historzcyny* 93 (1986): 397–417.

———. "Ordinacje w dawnej Polsce" [Entailed Estates in Old Poland]. *Przegląd Historyczny* 68 (1977): 17–30.

———. "Przyczynek do kwestii konfliktu pokoleń na tle majątkowym w osiemnastowiecznym środowisku magnackim" [A Contribution to the Question of Generational Conflict on Estate Issues in the Eighteenth-Century Magnate Setting]. In Łukasz Kadziela et al., eds., *Trudne Stulecia: Studia z dziejów XVII i XVIII wieku*. Warsaw: Wydawnictwo Naukowe Semper, 1994.

———. "Więź rodowa domu radziwiłłowskiego w świetle diariusza Michała Kazimierza Radziwiłła 'Rybeńka'" [The Family Ties of the Radziwiłł Dynasty in Light of the Diary of Michał Kazimierz Radziwiłł "Rybeńko"]. *Miscellanea Historico-Archivistica* 3 (1989): 175–90.

———, ed. *Archiwum Główne Akt Dawnych w Warszawie: Informator o zasobie* [The Central Archive for Old Documents in Warsaw: Guide to Resources]. Warsaw: Naczelna Dyrekcja Archiwów Państwowych, 1992.

Zielińska, Zofia. *Walka "familii" o reformę Rzeczypospolitej 1734–1752* [The Struggle of the "Family" to Reform the Republic, 1734–1752]. Warsaw: Państwowe Wydawnictwo Naukowe, 1983.

Zienkowska, Krystyna. "Spór o Nową Jerozolimę" [The Dispute over Nowa Jerozolimska]. *Kwartalnik Historyczny* 93 (1986): 351–76.

Żytkowicz, Leonid. "Kilka uwag o handle zewnętrznym Wielkiego Księstwa Litewskiego w ostatnich latach Rzeczypospolitaj" [A Few Comments on Internal Trade in the Grand Duchy of Lithuania During the Commonwealth's Last Years]. *Zapiski Historyczne* 41 (1976): 87–101.

Index

Note: Page numbers followed by "*m*" or "*t*" refer to the map or the tables, respectively.